WONDER AND THE MARVELLOUS FROM HOMER

Wonder and wonders constituted a central theme in ancient Greek culture. In this book, Jessica Lightfoot provides the first full-length examination of its significance from Homer to the Hellenistic period. She demonstrates that wonder was an important term of aesthetic response and occupied a central position in concepts of what philosophy and literature are and do. She also argues that it became a means of expressing the manner in which the realms of the human and the divine interrelate with one another; and that it was central to the articulation of the ways in which the relationships between self and other, near and far, and familiar and unfamiliar were conceived. The book provides a much-needed starting point for reassessments of the impact of wonder as a literary critical and cultural concept both in antiquity and in later periods.

JESSICA LIGHTFOOT is Junior Research Fellow in Classics at Trinity College, Cambridge and Lecturer in Ancient Greek Literature at the University of Birmingham.

CAMBRIDGE CLASSICAL STUDIES

General editors
J. P. T. CLACKSON, W. M. BEARD, G. BETEGH, R. L. HUNTER,
M. J. MILLETT,
S. P. OAKLEY, R. G. OSBORNE, T. J. G. WHITMARSH

WONDER AND THE MARVELLOUS FROM HOMER TO THE HELLENISTIC WORLD

JESSICA LIGHTFOOT
University of Birmingham

CAMBRIDGE
UNIVERSITY PRESS

University Printing House, Cambridge CB2 8BS, United Kingdom

One Liberty Plaza, 20th Floor, New York, NY 10006, USA

477 Williamstown Road, Port Melbourne, VIC 3207, Australia

314–321, 3rd Floor, Plot 3, Splendor Forum, Jasola District Centre,
New Delhi – 110025, India

103 Penang Road, #05-06/07, Visioncrest Commercial, Singapore 238467

Cambridge University Press is part of the University of Cambridge.

It furthers the University's mission by disseminating knowledge in the pursuit of education, learning, and research at the highest international levels of excellence.

www.cambridge.org
Information on this title: www.cambridge.org/9781316518830
DOI: 10.1017/9781009003551

© Faculty of Classics, University of Cambridge 2021

This work is in copyright. It is subject to statutory exceptions and to the provisions of relevant licensing agreements; with the exception of the Creative Commons version the link for which is provided below, no reproduction of any part of this work may take place without the written permission of Cambridge University Press.

An online version of this work is published at doi.org/10.1017/9781009003551 under a Creative Commons Open Access license CC-BY-NC-ND 4.0 which permits re-use, distribution and reproduction in any medium for non-commercial purposes providing appropriate credit to the original work is given. You may not distribute derivative works without permission. To view a copy of this license, visit https://creativecommons.org/licenses/by-nc-nd/4.0

All versions of this work may contain content reproduced under license from third parties.

Permission to reproduce this third-party content must be obtained from these third-parties directly.

When citing this work, please include a reference to the DOI 10.1017/9781009003551

First published 2021

A catalogue record for this publication is available from the British Library.

Library of Congress Cataloging-in-Publication Data
NAMES: Lightfoot, Jessica, 1991– author.
TITLE: Wonder and the marvellous from Homer to the Hellenistic world / Jessica Lightfoot.
OTHER TITLES: Cambridge classical studies.
DESCRIPTION: New York : Cambridge University Press, 2021. | Series: Cambridge classical studies | Includes bibliographical references and index.
IDENTIFIERS: LCCN 2021008438 (print) | LCCN 2021008439 (ebook) | ISBN 9781316518830 (hardback) | ISBN 9781009003551 (ebook)
SUBJECTS: LCSH: Greek literature – History and criticism. | Marvelous, The, in literature. | Homer – Criticism and interpretation. | BISAC: HISTORY / Ancient / General | HISTORY / Ancient / General
CLASSIFICATION: LCC PA3015.M37 L54 2021 (print) | LCC PA3015.M37 (ebook) | DDC 880.9/38–dc23
LC record available at https://lccn.loc.gov/2021008438
LC ebook record available at https://lccn.loc.gov/2021008439

ISBN 978-1-316-51883-0 Hardback
ISBN 978-1-009-00914-0 Paperback

Cambridge University Press has no responsibility for the persistence or accuracy of URLs for external or third-party internet websites referred to in this publication and does not guarantee that any content on such websites is, or will remain, accurate or appropriate.

CONTENTS

Acknowledgements *page* vii
List of Abbreviations ix

1 Beginning with *Thauma* 1

2 The Art of *Thauma*: Nature, Artifice and
  the Marvellous 17
  2.1 Wondrous Visions: Charmides as *Agalma* 19
  2.2 Plato's Marvellous Young Men: Theaetetus and
      Charmides as *Thaumata* 23
  2.3 Critias the Poet, Charmides the Actor 26
  2.4 *Thauma Idesthai*: Wonder, Divine Artworks and
      the Ekphrastic Tradition 31

3 Reading *Thauma*: Paradoxography and the
  Textual Collection of Marvels 42
  3.1 Collecting *Thaumata*: The Emergence of the
      Paradoxographical Collection 46
  3.2 Taming Zoological *Thaumata*: Archelaus the Egyptian's
      Peculiar Forms and the Ptolemaic Court 52
  3.3 *Thaumata* and the Ethnographic Tradition: Herodotus
      and the Edges of the Earth 58
  3.4 Reactivating *Thauma*: Paradoxography and the Aristotelian
      Tradition 68
  3.5 Textual *Thaumata*: Paradoxography and the Poetics
      of Hellenistic Literature 78

4 The Sound of *Thauma*: Music and the Marvellous 80
  4.1 Homer the Proto-Paradoxographer: Poetry, Music
      and Science in Antigonus' *Collection of Marvellous
      Investigations* 83
  4.2 Giving Voice to the Dead: *Thauma* and the Lyre
      in the *Homeric Hymn to Hermes* 88
  4.3 Hermes' Signs and Songs: *Thaumata* and *Semata* 92
  4.4 Collapsing Boundaries: Epiphanic *Thauma*,
      Choreia and Song 98

Contents

5 **The Experience of *Thauma*: Cognition, Recognition, Wonder and Disbelief** — 107
   5.1 Recognition, Realisation and *Thauma*: The Meeting of Priam and Achilles — 112
   5.2 Marvels at the Margins: Geographical and Mythic Innovation in Euripides' *Iphigenia among the Taurians* — 119
   5.3 Wonders beyond *Mythoi*: Recognition and *Thauma* in Euripides' *Iphigenia among the Taurians* — 127
   5.4 Marvels at the Centre: Delphi, Athens and *Thauma* in Euripides' *Ion* — 132

6 **Near and Distant Marvels: Defamiliarising and Refamiliarising *Thauma*** — 138
   6.1 The Wonder of Nephelococcygia: Aristophanes' *Birds* and the Edges of the Earth — 142
   6.2 Familiar *Thaumata*: The Bird-Chorus' Wondrous Travels — 149
   6.3 The Wonder of Athens: Thucydides and *Thauma* — 158

7 **Making Marvels: *Thaumatopoiia* and *Thaumatourgia*** — 174
   7.1 The Meaning of Marvel-Making: Theatrical *Thaumatopoiia* — 176
   7.2 Sympotic *Thaumatopoiia*: Wonder-Working in Xenophon's *Symposium* — 181
   7.3 *Thaumatopoiia* and Perspective in Plato's *Republic* and *Sophist* — 187
   7.4 Socratic Marvel-Making: *Thaumatopoiia* in the Cave — 192

8 **Epilogue: *Thaumata Polla*** — 199
   8.1 *Thauma* as the Beginning of Philosophy – or *Nil Admirari*? — 200
   8.2 Mediating between Gods and Men, Nature and Artifice: Automata and *Thauma* in Hero of Alexandria's Mechanical Treatises — 208
   8.3 *Mera Miracula*: *Thauma*, Textuality and the Marvels of Aulus Gellius' *Noctes Atticae* — 215

Bibliography — 228
Subject Index — 250
Index Locorum — 253

ACKNOWLEDGEMENTS

This book is a revised version of my doctoral thesis, submitted in Oxford in the summer of 2018. It is a pleasure to acknowledge and thank the many people and institutions who have helped me along the way at every stage. I am very grateful to the Arts and Humanities Research Council for funding my doctoral work and to St John's College, Oxford for further financial support over the course of my graduate studies. My election to a Junior Research Fellowship at Trinity College, Cambridge in 2018 made the transformation from thesis to book possible. I am grateful to both the College and the Faculty of Classics at Cambridge for providing me with such an enjoyable and stimulating intellectual environment over the last few years. I am also grateful to the Department of Classics, Ancient History and Archaeology at the University of Birmingham for allowing me to take leave to complete the final stages of this book. I thank all of these institutions for their generous and sustained support.

I was extremely lucky to benefit from the insight of two wonderful supervisors and many other marvellous interlocutors over the course of my time in Oxford. Chris Pelling went above and beyond the call of duty while helping me to navigate the difficult early stages of this project and has always been on hand with kind and wise guidance. Felix Budelmann has been a constant source of encouragement and has been ever generous with his time and sage advice. I am very thankful to both for their continued support. I would also particularly like to thank Gregory Hutchinson and Richard Rutherford for offering kind and useful feedback over the course of the early stages of the thesis; Oliver Thomas for sharing his then unpublished work on the *Homeric Hymn to Hermes* with me; and my examiners, Tim Whitmarsh and Tim Rood, for their thoughtful advice.

Acknowledgements

Over the last few years I have been incredibly fortunate in having the opportunity to teach so many wonderful students, many of whom allowed me to first try out and discuss – perhaps without quite realising it at the time – so many of the ideas in this book. My time as a Lecturer at Magdalen College, Oxford in 2015–17 during my doctoral studies was particularly formative. I thank all those students who patiently put up with my thaumatic thoughts in this period, and after.

I owe an especial debt of thanks to Richard Hunter, who first encouraged me while I was completing my MPhil in Cambridge in 2014 and has been a tremendous source of support ever since. A better mentor is impossible to imagine. As well as helping me sharpen my thoughts on many points, Rebbeca Lämmle has done much to keep my chin up with an incredible mixture of both humour and erudition over the last few years. During this same period I have also been extremely fortunate to benefit from Renaud Gagné's wise discussions and advice. At a crucial stage on this book's route to publication, Armand D'Angour was incredibly generous with his time and – most crucially – encouragement. I will be forever grateful for James Clackson's advice and kindness. I thank them all.

I would also like to thank Michael Sharp and his team at Cambridge University Press, and the two anonymous readers, whose comments very much improved the final product.

Last, but not least, I am very grateful to my family and Peter Agócs for their unfailing love and support.

ABBREVIATIONS

Abbreviations of ancient authors and titles follow the conventions of the *Oxford Classical Dictionary* (4th edition).

AB	Austin, C. and Bastianini, G. (2002) *Posidippi Pellaei quae supersunt omnia*. Milan.
CVA Australia I	Cambitoglou, A. and Turner, M. (eds.) (2008) *Corpus Vasorum Antiquorum: Australia [Fasc. 1]. The Nicholson Museum, The University of Sydney: The Red Figure Pottery of Apulia*. Sydney.
CVA British Museum 2	Smith, A. H. and Pryce, F. N. (eds.) (1926) *Corpus Vasorum Antiquorum: Great Britain. British Museum 2*. London.
CVA Naples III	Rocco, A. (1954) *Corpus Vasorum Antiquorum. Italia 24. Napoli, Museo Nazionale 3*. Rome.
DK	Diels, H. and Kranz, W. (1951–2) *Die Fragmente der Vorsokratiker* (6th ed.). 3 vols. Berlin.
FGE	Page, D. L. (1981) *Further Greek Epigrams*. Cambridge.
LCS I	Trendall, A. D. (1967) *The Red-Figured Vases of Lucania, Campania and Sicily, Vol. 1*. Oxford.
LCS II	Trendall, A. D. (1967) *The Red-Figured Vases of Lucania, Campania and Sicily, Vol. 2*. Oxford.

List of Abbreviations

LM	Laks, A. and Most, G. W. (eds.) (2016) *Early Greek Philosophy.* 9 vols. Cambridge, MA.
Pf.	Pfeiffer, R. (1949) *Callimachus, Vol. I: Fragmenta.* Oxford.
PGR	Giannini, A. (1966) *Paradoxographorum Graecorum reliquiae.* Milan.
PhV²	Trendall A. D. (1967) *Phlyax Vases* (2nd ed.). London.
P. Oxy.	Grenfell, B. P. and Hunt, A. S. (1898–) *The Oxyrhynchus Papyri.* London.
PPSupp.	Trendall A. D. (1952) 'Paestan Pottery: A Revision and a Supplement'. *PBSR* 10: 1–53.
RVP	Trendall, A. D. (1987) *The Red-Figured Vases of Paestum.* London.
Sb.	Sbardella, L. (2000) *Filita: Testimonianze e frammenti poetici.* Rome.
SH	Lloyd-Jones, H. and Parsons, P. (eds.) (1983) *Supplementum Hellenisticum.* Berlin.
TrGF Kannicht	Kannicht, R. (2004) *Tragicorum Graecorum Fragmenta, Vol. 5.1: Euripides.* Göttingen.
TrGF Radt	Radt, S. (1999) *Tragicorum Graecorum Fragmenta, Vol. 4: Sophocles.* Göttingen.

1

BEGINNING WITH *THAUMA*

ἦ θαύματα πολλά
Yes, truly, marvels are many…
Pindar, *Olympian* 1.28

μάλα γὰρ φιλοσόφου τοῦτο τὸ πάθος, τὸ θαυμάζειν· οὐ γὰρ ἄλλη ἀρχὴ φιλοσοφίας ἢ αὕτη.
This experience – wondering – is very much characteristic of the philosopher. There's no other beginning to philosophy than this.
Plato, *Theaetetus* 155d

διὰ γὰρ τὸ θαυμάζειν οἱ ἄνθρωποι καὶ νῦν καὶ τὸ πρῶτον ἤρξαντο φιλοσοφεῖν, ἐξ ἀρχῆς μὲν τὰ πρόχειρα τῶν ἀτόπων θαυμάσαντες, εἶτα κατὰ μικρὸν οὕτω προϊόντες καὶ περὶ τῶν μειζόνων διαπορήσαντες.

Through wonder men now begin, and once first began, to philosophise: from the beginning they have wondered at strange things which were near at hand, and then progressed forward step-by-step in this way, raising questions about greater matters.[1]
Aristotle, *Metaphysics* 982b12–15

For both Plato and Aristotle, the value and place of wonder (*thauma*) is clear. *Thauma* comes first: without wonder, philosophical inquiry would not even begin to get off the ground. As the crucial spark that first stokes and then continually provokes intellectual curiosity, the importance of *thauma* in both philosophers' conception of what philosophy is and does should not be underestimated. But it was not in the realm of philosophy alone that wonder occupied a significant conceptual place by the time Plato and Aristotle were writing. As Pindar's famous, gnomic observation about the inherent multiplicity of marvels cited above suggests, conceptions of and responses to wonder and wonders in antiquity were both multiform and multivalent. In the same spirit,

---
[1] Throughout this book all translations are my own.

1

this book does not seek to impose singular, monolithic definitions of what wonder is and what it does in Greek literature and culture but instead endeavours to begin to open up the subject of ancient wonder as a more comprehensive and coherent field of inquiry in the modern world for the first time. Its main aim is twofold: to put *thauma* on the critical map and to demonstrate that wonder and the marvellous are concepts which we can – and should – take much fuller account of when considering Greek culture more broadly.

The Greeks are already engaged with the marvellous from the very beginning of their literary tradition. Homer presents a world full of visual marvels linked to the divine, from the Shield of Achilles to epiphanic appearances of the gods themselves before mortals. Already in the Homeric poems, the marvellous is linked to transgression of the boundaries that separate the human and divine realms, and also the natural and the artificial. Over time, certain continuities, complexities and differences in the treatment of and responses to wonder and the marvellous in the Greek world begin to emerge. For example, *thauma* becomes a paradigmatic response to visual art, music and poetry in the Greek world. It expresses the manner in which the realms of the human and divine interrelate with one another. It begins to occupy a central position in concepts of what philosophy and literature are and what they do. It evolves into a central concept in the articulation of relationships between self and other, near and far, familiar and unfamiliar. In the subsequent chapters of this book, these issues and many more will be explored. In the process, texts from a range of literary genres, such as early Greek hexameter poetry, tragedy, comedy, historiography, epigrams, philosophy and Hellenistic paradoxographical collections, will be examined, interrogated and juxtaposed to demonstrate that far from being a tangential concern of the Greek literary tradition, wonder and wonders constitute a constant and central theme in Greek culture.

Beginning with the terms the Greeks themselves most often used to describe and refer to the experience of wonder is one obvious starting point for any investigation seeking to build a firmer view of what wonder is and what it does in ancient Greek culture. By far the most important textual signpost pointing towards the Greek experience of wonder is the use of some form of either the noun *thauma* or the verb *thaumazein*, or one of their various cognates. One of the chief difficulties in studying Greek concepts of wonder springs from the inherent slipperiness of the noun *thauma*, which can refer both to objects which cause wonder and astonishment (cf. the use of 'a wonder' or 'a marvel' in English), as well as to a more general and often abstract feeling of wonder, surprise or astonishment.[2] A few examples picked at random make this particular distinction clear: in the *Iliad*, Achilles describes his old armour, an object which Hector has now stripped from Patroclus' dead body, as 'a marvel to see' (θαῦμα ἰδέσθαι, *Il.* 18.83), while later in book 18 his famous new shield, an even more impressive object, is made into 'a marvel' (*thauma*) when Hephaestus' wondrous artistic power makes the glittering depiction of a field upon its surface realistically appear as though it has been freshly ploughed.[3] In contrast to these uses of *thauma* as a concrete noun, the *Odyssey* provides us with a good example of its potentially more abstract use as a noun denoting a general feeling of astonishment or wonder. In book 10, Circe is 'held by *thauma*' when she notices that Odysseus is completely and unexpectedly impervious to her powerful drugs – a surprising and unprecedented incident which has never occurred before.[4] As these examples suggest, one of the most striking aspects of objects which are labelled as 'marvels' (*thaumata*), or of phenomena which inspire a more general sense of wonder, at least in Archaic poetry, is their visual appearance. This is unsurprising as it is highly likely that the word *thauma* and its cognates are derived from the verb *theasthai* – 'to see, gaze at, behold'.[5]

The appearance of *thauma* in reference to this kind of feeling is paralleled by the use of another term which is often applied to the

---

[2] Greenblatt (1991) 22 designates the double aspect of wonder as both a thing and a feeling as an integral part of its effect; cf. Neer (2010) 67 on the doubleness of *thauma*: 'in Greek as in English, one wonders at wonders. The word itself shuttles between "here" and "there"'; see also Neer and Kurke (2019) 60–1.

[3] *Il.* 18.548–9: ἡ δὲ μελαίνετ' ὄπισθεν, ἀρηρομένη δὲ ἐῴκει, | χρυσείη περ ἐοῦσα· τὸ δὴ περὶ θαῦμα τέτυκτο.

[4] *Od.* 10.326: θαῦμά μ' ἔχει ὡς οὔ τι πιὼν τάδε φάρμακ' ἐθέλχθης.

[5] See Prior (1989) 82. Beekes (2010) 535 is more tentative and suggests that it is possible, though not certain, that *thauma* is a sort of verbal noun related to *theasthai*. In antiquity itself *thauma* was already etymologically derived from *th-* root words denoting vision, seeing and sight: see *Etym. Magn.* 443.37–48.

effect of the marvellous: the noun *ekplexis* and its associated verbal form, *ekplessein*. Words from this root usually refer to a more extreme sense of wonder than *thauma* – something which Aristotle picks up on in his *Topica* when he explicitly defines *ekplexis* as an 'excess' of *thauma*.[6] This intensification of *thauma* can often spill over into a feeling of astonishment so strong that it causes both a cognitive and a somatic reaction. Rather than provoking curiosity, thought and inquiry, this type of wonder potentially leads to a stultifying mental and physical stasis – something that is hinted at by some of the more literal meanings of the verb *ekplessein*: 'to strike out, drive away, expel from [i.e. the senses]'. Once again, a few examples help to make these specific nuances of *ekplexis* clearer. In Euripides' *Helen*, for instance, the stultifying physical and mental effect of ekplektic wonder becomes apparent when Menelaus – who has been misled by a phantom of his wife Helen and has not yet realised that his real wife was in Egypt all along – finally recognises the authentic Helen and exclaims: 'you have rendered me speechless with astonishment!' (ἔκπληξιν ἡμῖν ἀφασίαν τε προστίθης, 549). Dumbstruck silence is also the response which the famous Sicilian sophist and rhetorician Gorgias associates with this type of wonder, as we see in one of his speeches when he notes that '*ekplexis* leads to being at a loss for speech by necessity' (διὰ δὲ τὴν ἔκπληξιν ἀπορεῖν ἀνάγκη τῷ λόγῳ, *Palamedes* 4).[7] The potential of excessive ekplektic wonder to cause a sort of cognitive and somatic stasis which renders thought and speech impossible is something Plato emphasises as well in his *Euthydemus*, a work which strongly and repeatedly associates the potentially stultifying effects of too much *thauma* with Socrates' two main interlocutors in the dialogue, the sophistic brothers Euthydemus and Dionysodorus. The astonishing and stultifying effect of the two sophists' frequent and often absurd

---

[6] Arist. *Top.* 126b17–24: δοκεῖ γὰρ ἡ ἔκπληξις θαυμασιότης εἶναι ὑπερβάλλουσα ... ἡ ἔκπληξις ὑπερβολή ἐστι θαυμασιότητος.
[7] On Gorgias and *ekplexis*, see O'Sullivan (1992) 21. *Ekplexis* is one of the chief responses with which Gorgias' own complex and beguiling rhetoric is associated in later testimonia relating to the impact of his speeches on their audiences: see, e.g., the report of Diodorus Siculus (12.53.3) that Gorgias 'astonished the Athenians with the strangeness of his language' (τῷ ξενίζοντι τῆς λέξεως ἐξέπληξε τοὺς Ἀθηναίους ὄντας εὐφυεῖς καὶ φιλολόγους) on a visit to Athens in 427 BCE.

Beginning with *Thauma*

eristic arguments is succinctly summed up by the divergent responses of their habitual followers and those, like Socrates and his friends, who have not yet witnessed the brothers' wondrous sophistic performances. When treated to a particularly stunning argumentative display, the former group, who were already very familiar with the brothers' linguistic tricks, 'laughed long and hard and cheered, admiring (ἀγασθέντες) the wisdom of the pair', while Socrates and his friends 'were astonished and stayed silent' (ἡμεῖς ἐκπεπληγμένοι ἐσιωπῶμεν, *Euthydemus* 276d). The contrast between the raucous laughter of the sophists' friends, who are filled with a reverential and admiring sense of wonder at the brothers' cleverness (denoted by the use of a form of the verb *agasthai* – 'to wonder at, admire'), and the dumbstruck astonishment of those unfamiliar with the spectacle before them points to the potential danger of falling prey to an ekplektic sense of wonder while engaging in philosophy, since in this case no further argument or inquiry is possible in the aftermath of the astonishing sophistic display. Unlike *thauma*, which has the potential to provoke curiosity, inquiry and dialogue, *ekplexis* thus has the potential to cause a debilitating mental, emotional and physical stasis.

Of course, *thauma* and *ekplexis* are not the only lexical terms which may explicitly signpost us towards wonder. Others, such as *thambos* and *agasthai*, will appear frequently in this study – though *thauma* in particular does seem to be the most powerful and frequent indicator of wondrous experiences. Nor is it the case that any of these terms absolutely needs to be present to denote the presence of wondrous experience in Greek literature. But as a starting point for inquiry it is useful (and necessary) to examine the presence and meanings of *thauma* as a means of initially mapping out the varied range and spectrum of responses to wonder and the marvellous which occur over time in Greek culture and to help avoid the risk of imposing anachronistic modern definitions and assumptions about the range and meaning of the marvellous onto the ancient material. This lexical approach is, however, only a starting point. This study does not depend on the appearance of particular words in any single case, though it has often proven useful and productive to begin with an examination of the use of certain terms across a given work, in order to establish how the construction of thought and theme works in those texts as a whole. The approach taken here also builds upon the limited amount of work on *thauma* in Greek culture which has appeared to date.[8] Among recent studies, Richard Neer's work on the place of *thauma* as an important aesthetic term in relation to Classical sculpture provides a particularly important model for my own study.[9] For the first time, Neer examines the significance of the creation and evocation of wonder in relation to the visual arts and concludes that as a term relating to aesthetic response in the Greek world 'the importance of wonder can hardly be overstated' and that '[*t*]*hauma* is, in fact, a basic and hugely neglected element of Greek thinking about depiction'.[10] In his introduction, Neer even writes that his own conclusions about the importance of *thauma* suggest that '[w]e need to make the Classical strange again, uncanny; we need to restore its wonder'.[11] This invocation to 'restore the wonder' of the Classical period is something my own study wholeheartedly attempts to achieve, especially since Neer's work on the place of *thauma* in Greek thinking of depiction needs to be extended to Greek ideas about all sorts of literary, visual and cultural representation.

This study also builds upon work outside of the field of Classics, where the concept of wonder has assumed an increasingly

[8] The few studies on wonder in Greek literature which do exist tend to focus on particular authors, works or genres: see, e.g., Nenci (1957/8), Prier (1989), Hunzinger (1993) and (2018), and Fisher (1995) on wonder in Homer and early Greek hexameter poetry; Jouanna (1992) 223–36, Kazantzidis (2019) 1–40 and Lightfoot (2019a) 163–82 on *thauma* in Greek medical writings; Barth (1968), Hunzinger (1995) and Munson (2001) 232–65 on Herodotus; Kurke (2013) 123–70 on Plato; Pajón Leyra (2011) on Greek paradoxographical collections. Two exceptions to the general tendency to focus on single authors or genres are Mette (1960), a brief study of the use of *thauma*-words from Homer to the Classical period, and Hunzinger (2015), an excellent study which begins to outline the importance of *thauma* in aesthetic terms. Three recent edited volumes, Bianchi and Thévenaz (2004), Hardie (2009) and Gerolemou (2018), have also contributed a range of papers which touch on wonder in antiquity to varying degrees: the first examines *mirabilia* in various texts, genres and periods; the second concentrates on paradox and the marvellous in Augustan literature and culture; the third examines miracles in various texts in antiquity and beyond. For an overview of the importance of marvels and the 'wonder-culture' of the Roman empire in the Imperial period, see ní Mheallaigh (2014) 261–77.
[9] Neer (2010), especially the introduction and chapters 1 and 2.
[10] Neer (2010) 57.
[11] Neer (2010) 2.

significant place in critical theory and cultural history over the last few decades.[12] In recent years New Historicist critics have shown a special interest in the nature and function of wonder and the marvellous in relation to literature and culture. In particular, Stephen Greenblatt, the founder of New Historicism, has picked up on the potential of wonder as a useful theoretical concept which is able to mediate between inside and outside, subjects and objects, and texts and contexts in the practice of cultural poetics.[13] In his 1990 article, 'Resonance and Wonder', Greenblatt places wonder at the very heart of his own critical approach, stating that rather than necessarily seeking to approach works of art 'in a spirit of veneration' (as he perceives some Formalist critics to do), he seeks rather to approach them 'in a spirit that is best described as wonder'.[14] The importance of approaching texts with a marvelling eye is reinforced when Greenblatt ends his article by affirming the place of wonder in the practice of New Historicism as a whole, declaring that 'it is the function of new historicism continually to renew the marvelous at the heart of the resonant'.[15] Greenblatt's theoretical approach to wonder is of great importance to my own study, not only because it provides a new way of thinking about the interactions between wonder and the effect of literature, but also because his work on wonder as

---

[12] For this study the following works have been particularly influential: Greenblatt (1991), Daston and Park (1998), Campbell (1999), and the collected papers in Evans and Marr (2006) on wonder from the Early Modern period onwards; Bishop (1996) and Platt (1997) on wonder in Shakespeare; Kareem (2014) on eighteenth-century fiction and wonder; Kenny (1998), (2004) and (2006) on the concept of curiosity in the Early Modern period. Todorov (1970), which includes a theoretical discussion of the nature, form and definition of the marvellous in relation to the fantastic as a broader genre, has also influenced my thinking, particularly in the way he examines the notion of the marvellous in relation to the uncanny (*Unheimlich*), a concept which itself inherently places the relationship between the familiar and the unfamiliar under the spotlight.

[13] Greenblatt (1991) 16: 'Someone witnesses something amazing, but what most matters takes place not "out there" or along the receptive surfaces of the body where the self encounters the world, but deep within, at the vital, emotional center of the witness'. Cf. Greenblatt (1991) 22: 'For the early voyagers, wonder not only marked the new but mediated between outside and inside'. Cf. Neer (2010) 68 on *thauma*: 'to wonder, in Greek is to be poised between two possible modes of existence, to shimmer between what we might be tempted to call subject and object', cf. Neer and Kurke (2019) 60; see also Hunzinger (2018) 263–4 on *thauma* as an 'in-between' state.

[14] Greenblatt (1990) 19.

[15] Greenblatt (1990) 34. On the importance of wonder to the aims and practice of New Historicism and on how shifting the objects which we think of as marvels provokes radically different interpretations, see Gallagher and Greenblatt (2000) 9, 12.

a theoretical concept bears a complicated relation to the concept of wonder in antiquity which has not thoroughly been probed before. The year after the publication of 'Resonance and Wonder', Greenblatt returned to the place of wonder in both New Historicism and Western culture in his 1991 monograph *Marvelous Possessions: The Wonder of the New World*. In this work, he focuses on the integral place of the marvellous in European responses to the New World, exploring how and why '[w]onder is ... the decisive emotional and intellectual experience in the presence of radical difference'.[16] The influence of textual accounts of marvels from antiquity over later European responses to people and cultures perceived as radically other is drawn out at several points in Greenblatt's study.[17] In particular, Herodotus' *Histories* is named as the key text which 'had instituted certain key discursive principles that the many subsequent attacks on his veracity and the ensuing oblivion did not displace'.[18] Greenblatt sketches out the importance of Herodotus as the figurehead of a long tradition of historiographical responses to the marvellous by drawing heavily on the work of François Hartog, in particular his 1980 monograph *Le miroir d'Hérodote*.[19] As the editor of the University of California Press series *The New Historicism: Studies in Cultural Poetics*, in which the English translation of *Le miroir d'Hérodote* first appeared, Greenblatt was well aware of Hartog's pioneering approach to the concept of wonder in Herodotus' *Histories* even as he conducted his own study of Renaissance attitudes towards wonder, and he is correct when he adduces that 'Herodotus is at once a decisive shaping force and a very marginal figure' in *Marvelous Possessions*.[20] But Herodotus is not the only pivotal figure in the development of a discourse of the Greek

---

[16] Greenblatt (1991) 14.
[17] Ancient discussions of the properties of the earth's edges were particularly influential, as Greenblatt (1991) 22 notes: 'The discovery of the New World at once discredits the Ancients who did not know of these lands and, by raising the possibility that what had seemed gross exaggerations and lies were in fact sober accounts of radical otherness, gives classical accounts of prodigies a new life.'
[18] Greenblatt (1991) 123.
[19] Hartog (1980). On the importance of Herodotus as the shaping force of later responses to wonder, see Greenblatt (1991) 123–8.
[20] Greenblatt (1991) 122. Hartog's *Le miroir d'Hérodote* first appeared in English in 1988 as *The Mirror of Herodotus: The Representation of the Other in the Writing of History*. Cf. Pelling (1997) 64–5, where the potential for the productive application of Greenblatt's ideas in *Marvelous Possessions* to Herodotus is noted.

Beginning with *Thauma*

marvellous in antiquity, and the historiographer's own attitude to marvels is itself shaped by a complex tradition relating to wonder which must be examined in more detail. It is one of the aims of this book to fill in some of the gaps left in this vision of the influence of ancient discourses of wonder on later approaches to wonder and the marvellous.[21]

It is therefore because of the special place which wonder holds in recent historicising approaches to literature, and because of the influence which responses to the marvellous in antiquity go on to have on later responses to marvels and the marvellous, that a thorough examination of the place of *thauma* in the Greek world from the Archaic to the Hellenistic period is long overdue. My own double-edged interest in both the cultural poetics of Greek wonder and Greek wonder's place in the practice not only of cultural poetics but in subsequent discourses of the marvellous more generally, will hopefully be clear throughout. But this is not my only focus; one of the most attractive aspects of working on the relationship between the marvellous and texts in antiquity is the fact that wonder is a concept that mediates between formalist and historicist approaches to literature.[22] One particular idea which I return to and re-examine through the lens of Greek wonder is Viktor Shklovsky's concept of 'defamiliarisation', first outlined in his influential 1916 essay 'Art as Technique'. Shklovsky's claim, in its broadest terms, is that '[t]he technique of art is to make objects unfamiliar', due to the fact that over time our day-to-day perception becomes habitual and automatic, rendering objects overfamiliar and unremarkable.[23] In other words, the strangeness and wonder of objects is deadened over time, and it becomes the

---

[21] In this respect, I hope this book will appeal beyond the field of Classics, especially since ancient Greek conceptions of wonder are currently attracting interest elsewhere: Harb (2020), a very recent study of the importance of wonder in the poetics of Classical Arabic literature, demonstrates how important the reception, adaptation and reformulation of Aristotle's views on *thauma* and *ekplexis* in the *Poetics* and *Rhetoric* were in Classical Arabic literary theory (see especially pp. 75–134) and points the way towards some potential fruitful avenues for future study.

[22] As Greenblatt himself notes (1990) 19: 'Wonder has not been alien to literary criticism, but it has been associated (if only implicitly) with formalism rather than historicism. I wish to extend this wonder beyond the formal boundaries of works of art, just as I wish to intensify resonance within those boundaries.'

[23] Shklovsky (1916), translated in Lemon and Reis (1965) 12.

task of the artist to 'reactivate' these feelings in the reader, listener or viewer. It is this artistic phenomenon of 'making the familiar seem strange again' that Shklovsky calls 'defamiliarisation'. He turns to Aristotle as a significant antecedent to his own ideas about the defamiliarisation effects which occur on a lexical level in poetry when he notes that '[i]n studying poetic speech ... we find material obviously created to remove the automatism of perception ... According to Aristotle, poetic language must appear strange and wonderful.'[24] Shklovsky is referring here to Aristotle's comments at *Rhetoric* 1404b8–14 on the necessity of 'making language strange' (δεῖ ποιεῖν ξένην τὴν διάλεκτον) because such language provokes wonder, and 'the wondrous is pleasurable' (ἡδὺ δὲ τὸ θαυμαστόν). In this book, I probe the significant connection between defamiliarisation and wonder which Shklovsky hints at here, demonstrating that in antiquity there was a firm interest not only in the creation of defamiliarisation effects but in what I have termed 'refamiliarisation' effects as well: that is, making what is unfamiliar and wondrous actually seem extremely familiar.[25]

This book is therefore an attempt both to outline the significance of *thauma* in Greek culture from the Archaic period onwards and to provide a history of early conceptualisations of the connection between wonder and literature which may be useful when considering the impact of wonder as a literary-critical and cultural concept in later periods and contexts. The study focuses predominantly on Greek literary texts from the early Greek hexameter tradition to the early Hellenistic period. Since it is impossible to begin to make sense of subsequent attitudes towards *thauma* without examining the associations carried by the marvellous from the early Greek hexameter tradition onwards, the Homeric poems are the earliest texts which are examined here with *thauma* in mind. The chronological end point of the study lies in the early Hellenistic period, with the emergence of a new and very different type of text: the paradoxographical collection. These texts are

---

[24] Shklovsky (1916), in Lemon and Reis (1965) 21–2.
[25] For an example of the application of the concept of 'refamiliarisation', see Pelling (2016), which considers the creation of effects of 'refamiliarisation' as well as defamiliarisation in his study of Herodotus' Persian stories.

Beginning with *Thauma*

marvel-collections which attempt to astonish the reader through the juxtaposition of canonical literary texts of the past with contemporary scientific writing: they represent the first purely textual collections of Greek marvels which seemingly exist for no other purpose than causing the reader to wonder. Rather than following a strictly chronological arrangement, I instead take my cue in this book from the Greek paradoxographers by working thematically, deliberately juxtaposing texts from different contexts and genres and placing them in dialogue with one another to explore evolving continuities and ruptures in the discursive use and resonance of the marvellous over time. In this sense, the book enacts, in the form and arrangement of its chapters and themes, one of its own central discoveries concerning the aesthetic and emotional resonance of *thauma* as a concept in ancient literature and culture. It is an experiment in reading and writing 'thaumatically' through the juxtaposition of texts from previously disparate genres and periods in order to create unexpected connections, startling discontinuities and radical new perspectives.

The book falls into two main parts (Chapters 2 to 4, and Chapters 5 to 7). Chapters 2 to 4 concentrate on the varied ways in which a poetics of wonder is created and articulated in Greek literature, and explore the sustained development of *thauma* as a model for aesthetic response from the Archaic to the early Hellenistic period. *Thauma* is shown to be a paradigmatic response to visual art, music and poetry in Greek culture which is particularly associated with moments when the boundaries between humans and gods, inside and outside, and familiar and unfamiliar collapse. While *thauma* begins as a response to overwhelming visual stimuli, it rapidly comes to serve as a model for all manner of aesthetic responses, whether to the size of an impressive building, the movement of a tragic chorus, a mythical or geographical narrative, or a particularly beautiful performance of music or poetry.

In Chapter 2 ('The Art of *Thauma*: Nature, Artifice and the Marvellous') the complicated relationship between visual, verbal and textual wonder and wonders is explored. The chapter begins with a case study of Plato's *Charmides*, a dialogue which demonstrates the complicated uses of *thauma* as a term of aesthetic response by the beginning of the fourth century BCE. In this dialogue the boundaries between the inanimate and animate are blurred as the beautiful Charmides is compared to a wonder-inspiring statue. The marvellous effect of Charmides' beauty is emphasised in a way which allows Plato to draw out the potentially dangerous results of falling under the influence of visual spectacles which leave the observer open to the potentially stultifying and misleading effects of *thauma*. The power of *thauma* in the phenomenal realm is one of Plato's prime concerns regarding wonder, and one which will be discussed in more detail in Chapter 7. Here, however, Plato's concerns about *thauma* provide a means of thinking about the strong connection between *thauma* and the visual, a connection which is particularly significant when the place of *thauma* in the tradition of poetic ekphrasis is considered. By their very nature, passages of ekphrastic description highlight tensions between the verbal and the visual and are often replete with the language of wonder. By concentrating on the relationship between ekphrasis and *thauma* from Homer onwards, it is also possible to see more clearly the transition from the conception of a marvel as a purely visual object or as an oral report to the sense of a marvel as something which is written down.

Chapter 3 ('Reading *Thauma*: Paradoxography and the Textual Collection of Marvels') turns to examine the way in which *thauma* gradually becomes an aesthetic response to purely literary form by re-examining the purpose and poetics of Hellenistic paradoxographical collections. The range, scope, generic roots and cultural context of paradoxographical collections are thoroughly reassessed to demonstrate that the production of such texts can be seen as a textual manifestation of a new and increasingly influential interest of Hellenistic monarchs in the collection of objects which inspire *thauma*. The relationships between paradoxography, previous traditions of Greek ethnographic writing and contemporary Peripatetic scientific writing are outlined. Herodotus' treatment in the *Histories* of the marvels associated with the distant edges of the earth is examined as a case study to demonstrate that Greek ethnographic writing exerted particular influence over the precise form Hellenistic paradoxographical collections came to take. The influence of Peripatetic writing on early Hellenistic paradoxography is also examined, as are the extensive and hitherto underappreciated links between this mode of writing and various contemporary Hellenistic poetic genres.

Chapter 4 ('The Sound of *Thauma*: Music and the Marvellous') begins by examining certain aspects of Hellenistic paradoxography's engagement with the poetry and music of the past, before turning to the significance of *thauma* in ancient conceptions of music, choral song and dance more generally. The *Homeric Hymn to Hermes* is examined as a case study in which the rich relationship between music, *semata* (signs) and *thauma* in the Greek imagination is particularly evident. The essential role of *thauma* in ancient religious thought as an effect which often accompanies epiphanic encounters between gods and humans is examined, as is the association of *thauma* with the collapse of strict boundaries between the realms of mortal and immortal, something that in the Archaic oral culture takes place especially within the ritual space created by song-performance, as the effects of music, dance and song allow the ritual space of performance to become for mortals, temporarily at least, equivalent to the kind of marvellous utopian existence available to the gods at all times on Olympus. This chapter outlines how Greek texts explore these effects of *thauma* from the *Odyssey* onwards and concludes with two further case studies, one on the thaumatic impact of the *choreia* of the Delian Maidens in the *Homeric Hymn to Apollo* and one on the Apollonian epiphany of Arion in Herodotus' *Histories*.

In Chapters 5 to 7, I build on the understanding of *thauma* as a category of experience outlined in the first three chapters by narrowing my focus and examining the significance of wonder and the marvellous in texts of the late Classical period to demonstrate that by the late fifth century BCE *thauma* was a vital concept in the articulation of encounters between the Greek and wider, non-Greek worlds, between the human and the divine, and between the natural and the artificial. These chapters also explore how ideas about the causes and effects of wonder began to shift along with various other boundaries of contemporary intellectual discourse. As a result, in various literary genres over the course of the fifth and fourth centuries BCE in Classical Athens, a distinctive rhetoric of wonder and the marvellous developed which established *thauma* not only as an instinctive reaction to difference but also as something which can be found closer to home. As *thauma* increasingly becomes a means of defamiliarising experience, of making the familiar strange again and worthy of renewed attention, we find, over the course of the Classical period, the development of a new and deeply ambivalent attitude towards wonder and its effects.

Chapter 5 ('The Experience of *Thauma*: Cognition, Recognition, Wonder and Disbelief') begins to map out the increasingly complicated status of *thauma* in the intellectual discourse of late fifth-century Athens by focusing on connections between *thauma* and concepts of cognition, recognition, belief and disbelief in that quintessentially Athenian genre: tragedy. After considering the relationship between *thauma* and recognition in Homer as a means of contextualising the interpretation of *thauma* and *ekplexis* as emotional and cognitive responses to scenes of *anagnorisis* in Athenian tragedy – a connection which Aristotle outlines in the *Poetics* – the chapter turns to Athenian tragedy itself and to the plays of Euripides in particular. The nature of *thauma* and its effects in Euripides' *Iphigenia among the Taurians* and *Ion* are examined to explore and illustrate the playwright's interest in the potential of the tragic recognition scene to raise questions concerning the nature of *thauma* and (dis)belief in relation to broader questions of the contemporary relevance of the mythic tradition itself.

In these case studies of *Iphigenia among the Taurians* and *Ion*, another significant aspect of the way in which *thauma* is configured as a category of experience in this period is brought to the fore: wonder is something which is able to render the unfamiliar familiar and the familiar unfamiliar, in ways which destabilise boundaries and cultural oppositions that were previously clearly drawn. In Chapter 6 ('Near and Distant Marvels: Defamiliarising and Refamiliarising *Thauma*') the significance of this dynamic and its effects in texts from the late fifth and early fourth centuries BCE is outlined in greater detail. In texts which comment upon Athens' increasing imperial power during this period, it is notable that one way of expressing and implicitly interrogating Athenian dominance is by representing Athenian customs, practices, objects and people as somehow wondrous, and suggesting that the city of

Beginning with *Thauma*

Athens herself may now be the greatest 'marvel' of all. The ambivalent attitudes which this new concept of specifically Athenian *thauma* provoked are explored further by concentrating on the place of marvels and the marvellous in Aristophanes' *Birds* and Thucydides' *History*.

In the *Birds*, Aristophanes approaches his contemporary society with the estranging eye of an ethnographer in order to defamiliarise the everyday world of Athens and potentially nudge the audience towards a reassessment of their place in the world. In doing so he picks up on the importance of the theme of distant wonders and untold riches at the edges of the earth in Athenian public discourse, hinting particularly at their capacity to incite a dangerous and over-daring sense of desire (*eros*) for imperial conquest – an issue which was in the air at the moment of the play's first production in 414 BCE in relation to Athens' campaign against Sicily. In his account of the Sicilian expedition Thucydides subjects the same idea – the place of *thauma* within the discourse of imperial Athens – to an even more brutal and disillusioned scrutiny. Whereas Aristophanes' *Birds* hints at the potentially dangerous and deceptive power of marvels and the marvellous, Thucydides' *History* emphasises this aspect of *thauma* much more strongly, explicitly showing the results of wonder's ability to skew strategic perspectives and perceptions. As this chapter demonstrates, this potentially misleading aspect of *thauma* is, as the late fifth century turns into the fourth, attributed above all else to the power of language over its hearers. In both of these works, it is perhaps that most Athenian of all man-made products, rhetoric, which is now able to wield the greatest thaumatic power.

The idea that linguistic and artistic *thauma* may be double-edged, potentially deceptive or dangerous is explored further in Chapter 7 ('Making Marvels: *Thaumatopoiia* and *Thaumatourgia*'). This chapter returns to the important and often ambivalent place of *thauma* in Plato's dialogues and assesses the significance of conceptions of wonder as an affective and cognitive effect on individuals and collective audiences, especially in relation to mimetic artistic representations. The famous Cave Allegory in Plato's *Republic* illustrates particular anxieties surrounding the manipulation of wonder: it is the very displays of shadowy marvels (*thaumata*) made by men who are described as being like *thaumatopoioi* (marvel-makers) that are said to captivate and mislead the bound prisoners. This chapter offers a new reading of this famous philosophical passage through the lens of *thauma* in an effort to open up new perspectives on both the *Republic* and Plato's broader conception of what philosophy is and what it does. Moreover, a comprehensive overview of the evidence for *thaumatopoiia/thaumatourgia* (marvel-making/wonder-working), a specific form of Greek performance tradition, is presented here for the first time, as well as an examination of the power of *thauma* and *thaumatopoiia* in a philosophical text which offers an alternative yet complementary viewpoint on conceptions of the power of *thauma* and its relation to the formation of philosophy as a discourse in this period: Xenophon's *Symposium*. The book then ends with a concluding epilogue consisting of three diverse case studies which both sum up many of the main continuities and differences in the treatment of *thauma* in Greek literature and culture from Homer to the early Hellenistic period and simultaneously point towards some further directions for the study of wonder in antiquity and beyond.

As this summary suggests, texts from many different genres are purposefully brought into dialogue with one another throughout this book. As the practice of the paradoxographers makes clear, the wondrous ability of texts to relate to each other and to talk with each other both backwards and forwards is one of the key ways in which the creation of a sense of wonder is itself created, as marvels became textualised and transformed into a sort of written *Wunderkammer*. It is in this respect that this book most truly embodies one of the key discursive practices connected with *thauma* in the period with which this study concerns itself: it is difficult to talk about *thauma* without slipping to some extent into the poetics of Greek wonder.

2

THE ART OF *THAUMA*: NATURE, ARTIFICE AND THE MARVELLOUS

καὶ ἅμα ταῦτ' αὐτοῦ λέγοντος ὁ Χαρμίδης εἰσέρχεται. ἐμοὶ μὲν οὖν, ὦ ἑταῖρε, οὐδὲν σταθμητόν· ἀτεχνῶς γὰρ λευκὴ στάθμη εἰμὶ πρὸς τοὺς καλούς – σχεδὸν γάρ τί μοι πάντες οἱ ἐν τῇ ἡλικίᾳ καλοὶ φαίνονται· ἀτὰρ οὖν δὴ καὶ τότε ἐκεῖνος ἐμοὶ θαυμαστὸς ἐφάνη τό τε μέγεθος καὶ τὸ κάλλος, οἱ δὲ δὴ ἄλλοι πάντες ἐρᾶν ἔμοιγε ἐδόκουν αὐτοῦ – οὕτως ἐκπεπληγμένοι τε καὶ τεθορυβημένοι ἦσαν, ἡνίκ' εἰσῄει – πολλοὶ δὲ δὴ ἄλλοι ἐρασταὶ καὶ ἐν τοῖς ὄπισθεν εἵποντο. καὶ τὸ μὲν ἡμέτερον τὸ τῶν ἀνδρῶν ἧττον θαυμαστὸν ἦν· ἀλλ' ἐγὼ καὶ τοῖς παισὶ προσέσχον τὸν νοῦν, ὡς οὐδεὶς ἄλλοσ' ἔβλεπεν αὐτῶν, οὐδ' ὅστις σμικρότατος ἦν, ἀλλὰ πάντες ὥσπερ ἄγαλμα ἐθεῶντο αὐτόν. καὶ ὁ Χαιρεφῶν καλέσας με, Τί σοι φαίνεται ὁ νεανίσκος, ἔφη, ὦ Σώκρατες; οὐκ εὐπρόσωπος; Ὑπερφυῶς, ἦν δ' ἐγώ.

Plato, *Charmides* 154b–d

And as he was saying this, in comes Charmides. Now I, my friend, am no judge. I am simply a 'white line' when it comes to beautiful people.[1] For almost all lads at that time of life seem beautiful to me. But right at that moment that boy seemed to me to be a marvel both in terms of his size and his beauty, and everyone else seemed to be in love with him, since they were so astonished and bewildered when he entered. And many other lovers trailed in his wake. Now our behaviour – that's to say that of the older men – is no wonder. But I was paying attention to the boys as well, and none of them looked elsewhere, not even the smallest, but everyone gazed at him as if he were a statue (*agalma*). And Chaerephon called me over and said: 'How do you like the young man, Socrates? Is he not good looking on the outside?' 'Preternaturally so,' I said.

The importance of *thauma* as a term of aesthetic response to the visual arts in the Classical period has recently been explored in Richard Neer's study of the effects of Archaic and Classical sculpture, which suggests that the pursuit of *thauma* increasingly drives artistic innovation over the course of the Classical and into

---

[1] A common proverb which seems to mean something like 'I am unable to judge correctly', 'I am indiscriminate'. As explained at Σ ad. *Chrm.* 154b, the imagery is from the realm of building and architecture: a white chalk line used as a straight rule is not distinguishable if the stone or marble being cut is itself white.

17

The Art of *Thauma*

the Hellenistic period.² But *thauma* is not only a key term in relation to visual art. It is also a response which eventually comes to be associated with the effects of written texts on their readers. Over the course of the Classical period and into the Hellenistic age, the written text itself becomes the most powerful example of what a *thauma* is and does. In this chapter, I will begin to examine certain aspects of the relationship between the visual, the verbal and the textual which are explicitly shown to elicit wonder from very early on in the Greek literary tradition, particularly in passages of ekphrasis, before moving on to explore the relationship between text and *thauma* more fully in the next chapter, taking Hellenistic paradoxographical collections as my primary examples. But before exploring these issues fully, it is first worth turning to the image of the beautiful young Charmides as a wondrous *agalma* at the opening of the Platonic dialogue which bears his name to introduce some of the main themes of the forthcoming discussion.

In many of Plato's works, the framing scenes or opening details of the narrative foreshadow the eventual philosophical outcome of the dialogue.³ *Charmides* is no exception to this tendency: the sense of wonder which surrounds the young man on his entrance into the palaestra of Taureas will go on to colour our response as the dialogue draws on. Charmides' wondrous effect on the assembled company in this scene is explicitly caused by his beautiful appearance. The astonishment this beauty causes in his viewers is in fact so great that it is akin to the kind of aesthetic response provoked by artworks. There is something uncanny about Charmides in Socrates' description here – he is a moving, living man compared to a perfectly formed, static, inanimate statue: an *agalma*. This explicit comparison of a human being to an *agalma* from the point of view of the assembled company is somewhat

---

[2] See especially Neer (2010) 20–103; cf. also Neer and Kurke (2019) 59–61 on *thauma* and artworks.

[3] For example, in relation to this dialogue, Reece (1998) shows how the erotic motifs in the opening of the *Charmides* are worked out in the text's later discussion of *sophrosyne*. Many other recent works have demonstrated the significance of the opening scenes of Platonic dialogues in relation to the later main philosophical discussion: cf. e.g. Clay (1992), Tschemplik (1993), Johnson (1998), Rudebusch (2002), Gonzalez (2003), Segvic (2006), Trivigno (2011), Kaklamanou and Pavlou (2016), De Sanctis (2016).

2.1 Wondrous Visions: Charmides as *Agalma*

unusual.[4] But the inversion of this comparison, the idea that an inanimate statue or artwork is actually in some sense 'alive', has a long history in Greek culture.[5] In fact, the ability of an artwork or object of craft to move itself in some sense is an archetypal *thauma* from Homer onwards. What does Plato mean then by inverting this idea, comparing a young man to a marvellous artwork, and what is the significance of this gesture in the broader context of the *Charmides*? And what does Plato's use of the connection between visual artworks and wonder here tell us about the place of *thauma* in Greek literature and culture in this period?

2.1 Wondrous Visions: Charmides as *Agalma*

As the passage quoted above in the epigraph demonstrates, the immediate response of the assembled company to Charmides' entrance into the palaestra is one of sheer astonishment. Even the young boys who are present are physically transfixed with amazement at the sight, while their minds too are 'astonished and bewildered' (ἐκπεπληγμένοι τε καὶ τεθορυβημένοι) by Charmides' wondrous beauty upon his sudden, almost epiphanic arrival before them. The immediate, imposed fixity of the stunned audience, physically paralysed by *eros*, contrasts with Charmides' onrushing entrance – we might have expected the spectators to be described as statuesque, rather than Charmides himself. The way in which the beautiful young man's arrival suffuses the whole setting with wonder is emphasised even further by Socrates' pun on *thauma*

---

[4] There is another prominent example of a living human being compared to an *agalma* while focalised through the eyes of another in Euripides' *Hecuba* when Talthybius describes how Polyxena bares her breasts and appears beautifully 'like an *agalma*' (ὡς ἀγάλματος, 560) moments before she is slain. This comparison to an *agalma* also has a distinctly erotic tinge, just as it does at the beginning of the *Charmides*: on this pre-sacrificial erotic aestheticisation, see Scodel (1996) 111–28; cf. Thalmann (1993) 143–8 and Steiner (2001) 197, 207 on the connection between *eros* and *agalma* in the *Hecuba*. Another striking aspect of this comparison is the fact that Polyxena is on the verge of death at this moment and is about to change from an animate to an inanimate being. The antithesis between animate/inanimate and living/dead is crucial to the perceived power of the *agalma* as an artwork: the simile is therefore especially apt at this point in the *Hecuba* since it reflects Polyxena's transitional state as she approaches her inevitable end.

[5] See Spivey (1997) 442–59, Steiner (2001), Hersey (2009) and Neer (2010) on the ancient idea of animated statues; see also Faraone (1987) 18–21 on Hephaestus as the animator of statues, and Morris (1992) 215–37 on Daedalus as the creator of animated statues.

when he describes the older spectators' astonishment at the sight of the young man's beauty as being a matter of 'no wonder' (ἧττον θαυμαστὸν ἦν). On the one hand, this is a vaguely humorous repetition of *thauma*-language which picks up on the description of Charmides' marvellous physical qualities to make a joke at the expense of the older males in the dialogue, who are portrayed as predictably and unsurprisingly reacting to the erotic charms of a younger man – nothing to wonder at in that type of response, Socrates knowingly assures us. But at the same time, this pun keeps what is and is not a cause of wonder foremost in our minds as we reach the unexpected climax of the whole description: the comparison of the young man's form to that of a statue. Most surprisingly, this description suddenly collapses the boundaries between the animate and the inanimate: are the viewers here simply lusting after a young man, or a work of art?

The choice of the word *agalma* here increases the sense that the visual effect of Charmides' entrance is truly marvellous. In fact, there might even be a further boundary being blurred here – that between mortal and god. The word *agalma* suggests that the statue in question is a depiction of a god rather than that of a man and hints that the representation is a special cause of delight.[6] The wondrous effect of his appearance can even be seen as a sort of pseudo-divine epiphany.[7] The very boundaries between gods and men, and inanimate and animate objects, are seemingly challenged by the young man's marvellous beauty.[8] Indeed, Socrates picks up

---

[6] Other words for statues, such as ἀνδριάς, are much more common for depictions of mortals (especially real-life mortals rather than mythical figures). Platt (2011) 90 sums up the wondrous effect which the connection of *agalmata* to the divine sphere tends to produce: 'the *agalma* projected a glorious radiance that pertained to the immortal sphere, but was also closely bound to the material significance of precious objects, simultaneously encompassing the notion of things mysteriously alive and the splendid, "thaumastic" effects of superior craftsmanship'.

[7] Steiner (2001) 130: 'the youth's advent and appearance have all the qualities of a divine epiphany'. Cf. Platt (2011) 56: 'In the vocabulary of archaic Greek experience, an epiphany functions as the ultimate form of *thauma*.'

[8] The use of the word *agalma* in instances involving overwhelming beauty and/or overwhelming *eros* which blurs the boundaries between mortal and divine is found elsewhere in Plato's work, most notably at *Phdr.* 252d, where a lover is said to treat his beautiful beloved 'as if he were his god, he crafts him and adorns him, like an *agalma*' (ὡς θεὸν αὐτὸν ἐκεῖνον ὄντα ἑαυτῷ οἷον ἄγαλμα τεκταίνεταί τε καὶ κατακοσμεῖ). In the *Symposium* Alcibiades plays with similar imagery three times in his speech in praise of Socrates, first when he compares the older man to a statue of Silenus containing

2.1 Wondrous Visions: Charmides as *Agalma*

on this sense that Charmides' physique somehow goes 'beyond the bounds' of what is natural in his response to Chaerephon when he affirms that the young man is indeed 'exceedingly' (ὑπερφυῶς) beautiful. The adverb takes on the sense of 'preternaturally' here in conjunction with the use of *agalma*; the idea is that this is not a normal, human sort of beauty.[9] There is, however, a certain ambivalence inherent in this description. The use of *agalma* hints that Charmides' looks are worthy of the gods themselves. In the Classical period, the surface appearance of a sculpture becomes particularly important in creating a dazzling thaumatic effect, and Charmides is certainly able to do that.[10] But, on the other hand, a potential superficiality and hollowness are also being hinted at here. Is Charmides all surface dazzle and hollow within, just as a statue is? Or is he beautiful on the inside as well as on the surface?

We know that the possible content of the interior spaces of statues fascinated the Greeks.[11] The issue of what is inside the *agalma*-like Charmides soon becomes a similar object of fascination to Socrates and his friend Chaerephon. Immediately after the young man's entrance, Chaerephon tells Socrates (154d) that Charmides' current clothed form pales in comparison with his

---

'*agalmata* of the gods within it' (ἔνδοθεν ἀγάλματα ἔχοντες θεῶν, 215b), second when he claims that 'the *agalmata* inside ... are godlike and golden and utterly beautiful and wondrous' (τὰ ἐντὸς ἀγάλματα ... θεῖα καὶ χρυσᾶ εἶναι καὶ πάγκαλα καὶ θαυμαστά, 216e–17a), and finally when he claims that once Socrates' arguments have been opened up the '*agalmata* of virtue' (ἀγάλματ' ἀρετῆς, 222a) they contain can be seen by everyone. As well as containing and producing wondrous *agalmata* Socrates is also said to elicit wonder in his listeners through his speech several times in Alcibiades' speech: see *Symp.* 215b (θαυμασιώτερος); 215d (ἐκπεπληγμένοι); 216c (θαυμασίαν). On the repeated use of *agalmata* in the *Symposium*, see Reeve (2006) 124–46.

[9] On the significance of the deliberate use of ὑπερφυῶς here to mean 'preternaturally', see McAvoy (1996) 73. Cf. Reece (1998) 66 on Charmides' seemingly beyond-human beauty and Power (2011) 85 on the 'praeternatural valency' of Charmides as a superhumanly beautiful *thauma* which occupies 'an ontologically intermediate position between divine and human'.

[10] See especially Neer (2010) 142 ff. Cf. Stewart (1990) 40 on this point: 'A perfect finish attracts a customer or delights a god: the work becomes a "wonder" (*thauma*), one of the most powerful terms of commendation in the Greek language.'

[11] See Steiner (2001) 79–134; cf. Neer (2010) 124: 'Classical drapery insists that *there is something beneath the carved surface*'; see also 142 ff. on the importance of drapery for the creation of the suggestion that statues have some sort of interior life; cf. Neer and Kurke (2019) 60 on *thauma* and lifelike effects in artworks.

21

naked body: his beautiful face would be an object of no interest whatsoever if only he would strip his clothes off and reveal his astonishing physique. But Socrates wants to strip Charmides down even further. He is not so much concerned with what lies beneath Charmides' drapery, but with what lies within the young man himself: is his soul 'well-formed' (εὖ πεφυκώς, 154e)? Chaerephon promises that Charmides is indeed just as well-made on the inside as he is on the outside, since he is 'beautiful and good' (καλὸς καὶ ἀγαθός, 154e) in these respects too – but this remains to be tested. As a result, Socrates declares that he will now duly 'strip this (inside) part of him and have a look at it before looking at his external appearance' (ἀπεδύσαμεν αὐτοῦ αὐτὸ τοῦτο καὶ ἐθεασάμεθα πρότερον τοῦ εἴδους, 154e). But this immediate impetus to probe into the matter of Charmides' soul is almost entirely derailed when the young man approaches and Socrates discovers that he is even more beautiful than he had realised (155c–d). The play with inside and outside continues as Socrates accidentally catches a glimpse of what lies beneath Charmides' cloak when he sits next to him: totally overwhelming and paralysing *eros* is the result of this snatched sight of Charmides' wondrously beautiful naked body.[12]

There is an obvious playfulness to Socrates' reaction to Charmides throughout the opening of this dialogue. But, as so often with Platonic openings, the finer details of the *Charmides*' initial framing scenes do much to establish many of the main concerns of the subsequent discussion. In this case, the reaction of Socrates and his fellow spectators to Charmides' wondrous looks and *agalma*-like appearance is crucial in setting up the antithesis between surface appearance and inner morality and intellectual capacity which goes on to play an important role throughout the dialogue, as well as raising questions about the nature of the dialogue's central philosophical concept, *sophrosyne* (self-control), and its relation to wondrous and erotic sights. In addition to these specific themes, the *thauma* surrounding the quasi-epiphanic entrance of Charmides at the opening of this dialogue hints at the paradoxical double role which *thauma* more

---

[12] *Chrm* 155d: εἶδόν τε τὰ ἐντὸς τοῦ ἱματίου καὶ ἐφλεγόμην καὶ οὐκέτ' ἐν ἐμαυτοῦ ἦν (I saw what was inside his cloak and I was inflamed and no longer in possession of myself). See McCabe (2007) 12–14 on the play with the idea of Charmides' inside and outside at the moment when Socrates catches sight of what lies beneath his cloak.

2.2 Plato's Marvellous Young Men

generally plays in Plato's dialogues as both a possible spur to philosophical inquiry and a potentially dangerous (though often alluring) distraction.

2.2 Plato's Marvellous Young Men: Theaetetus and Charmides as *Thaumata*

It is helpful at this point to pause and think briefly about another Platonic young man who is also strongly associated with thaumatic effects of a very different sort. As he is presented in his eponymous dialogue, Theaetetus is in many respects the polar opposite of Charmides. Clever, brave and undoubtedly ugly, the young mathematician is explicitly figured as a youthful double of Socrates from the very opening scenes of the dialogue in terms of both his marvellous military bravery and obvious intellectual abilities. While the first image we get of Charmides is of stunning youth and beauty, in the *Theaetetus* the opening image of Socrates' interlocutor is Euclides' description to Terpsion of a youthful warrior cut off in his prime, 'grievously injured by his wounds and scarcely clinging on to life' (ζῶντι καὶ μάλα μόλις· χαλεπῶς μὲν γὰρ ἔχει καὶ ὑπὸ τραυμάτων τινῶν, 142b). Terpsion replies that it is not at all strange that Theaetetus has been praised by others for his bravery in battle at Corinth; the only strange and potentially 'much more marvellous' (πολὺ θαυμαστότερον, 142b) outcome would have been if Theaetetus had not fought so bravely in battle, since he is the sort of man who habitually wins praise for his actions.

This opening description of Theaetetus' marvellous bravery is not without a purpose, for this is the first described aspect of his behaviour which recalls that of Socrates himself, whose own brave martial exploits were well-known.[13] These are mentioned at several points in Plato's dialogues, not least in the reference to Socrates' return to Athens (in May 429 BCE) after fighting at Potidaea in the opening words of the *Charmides*.[14] Socrates' ability to withstand the rigours of campaign and fight bravely at

---

[13] For an excellent overview of Socrates' military career and its depiction in Plato's dialogues, see Nails (2002) 264–5.
[14] *Chrm.* 153a: ἥκομεν τῇ προτεραίᾳ ἑσπέρας ἐκ Ποτειδαίας ἀπὸ τοῦ στρατοπέδου (We arrived yesterday evening from the camp at Potidaea).

23

The Art of *Thauma*

Potidaea also figures prominently in Alcibiades' repeated mentions of the 'marvellous' aspects of his behaviour in the *Symposium*.[15] His bravery in the retreat from Delium (424 BCE) is also mentioned both in that dialogue (221a–c) and in the *Laches* (181b), where Socrates' own brave conduct provides a starting point for the wider discussion of *andreia* (bravery) itself.

Theaetetus' military exploits will one day turn out to be equally impressive. But on Socrates' first meeting with the young man it is his intellectual qualities alone that elicit wonder. This becomes apparent before Socrates even meets Theaetetus in the flesh, when Theodorus praises the young man at length (143e–44b):

καὶ μήν, ὦ Σώκρατες, ἐμοί τε εἰπεῖν καὶ σοὶ ἀκοῦσαι πάνυ ἄξιον, οἵῳ ὑμῖν τῶν πολιτῶν μειρακίῳ ἐντετύχηκα. καὶ εἰ μὲν ἦν καλός, ἐφοβούμην ἂν σφόδρα λέγειν, μὴ καί τῳ δόξω ἐν ἐπιθυμίᾳ αὐτοῦ εἶναι· νῦν δέ – καὶ μή μοι ἄχθου – οὐκ ἔστι καλός, προσέοικε δὲ σοὶ τήν τε σιμότητα καὶ τὸ ἔξω τῶν ὀμμάτων· ἧττον δὲ ἢ σὺ ταῦτ' ἔχει. ἀδεῶς δὴ λέγω. εὖ γὰρ ἴσθι ὅτι ὧν δὴ πώποτε ἐνέτυχον – καὶ πάνυ πολλοῖς πεπλησίακα – οὐδένα πω ᾐσθόμην οὕτω θαυμαστῶς εὖ πεφυκότα. τὸ γὰρ εὐμαθῆ ὄντα, ὡς ἄλλῳ χαλεπόν, πρᾷον αὖ εἶναι διαφερόντως, καὶ ἐπὶ τούτοις ἀνδρεῖον παρ' ὁντινοῦν, ἐγὼ μὲν οὔτ' ἂν ᾠόμην γενέσθαι οὔτε ὁρῶ γιγνόμενον· ἀλλ' οἵ τε ὀξεῖς ὥσπερ οὗτος καὶ ἀγχίνοι καὶ μνήμονες ὡς τὰ πολλὰ καὶ πρὸς τὰς ὀργὰς ὀξύρροποί εἰσι, καὶ ᾄττοντες φέρονται ὥσπερ τὰ ἀνερμάτιστα πλοῖα, καὶ μανικώτεροι ἢ ἀνδρειότεροι φύονται, οἵ τε αὖ ἐμβριθέστεροι νωθροί πως ἀπαντῶσι πρὸς τὰς μαθήσεις καὶ λήθης γέμοντες. ὁ δὲ οὕτω λείως τε καὶ ἀπταίστως καὶ ἀνυσίμως ἔρχεται ἐπὶ τὰς μαθήσεις τε καὶ ζητήσεις μετὰ πολλῆς πρᾳότητος, οἷον ἐλαίου ῥεῦμα ἀψοφητὶ ῥέοντος, ὥστε θαυμάσαι τὸ τηλικοῦτον ὄντα οὕτως ταῦτα διαπράττεσθαι.

Well, Socrates, I think it's very worthy of me telling, and well worthy of you hearing, about a young man I have met with, one of your fellow citizens. And if he were beautiful, I would be very much afraid of speaking, in case I might seem to desire him. But as it is – and don't be aggrieved with me – he isn't beautiful, in fact he resembles you with his snub nose and protruding eyes (though these features are less pronounced in him than in you). Indeed, I speak fearlessly. Be assured that of all of those I have ever met – and I have associated with very many – I have never yet seen anyone so marvellously gifted by nature. He is quick to learn, beyond the capacity of other people, and unusually gentle, and on top of

---

[15] E.g. at *Symp.* 220a–b, where Socrates' ability to withstand the cold while on campaign at Potidaea is one example of the many 'wondrous deeds he was undertaking' (θαυμάσια εἰργάζετο); Socrates' ability to stand in one spot considering a philosophical problem for an entire day while on campaign was yet another *thauma*-inducing feat which caused some Ionian soldiers to wonder at him (θαυμάζοντες, 220c).

2.2 Plato's Marvellous Young Men

all this he is brave compared to any other. I would not have thought such a combination could exist, nor do I see it coming into existence. Instead, those who are sharp and shrewd and with good memories like him are usually quick to anger too, and darting off they are swept away just like ships without ballast, and they are more frenzied than courageous, and those who are steadier are somewhat dull in approaching their studies and are weighed down with forgetfulness. But this young man approaches his studies and inquiries with great gentleness, smoothly, without stumbling, and effectively, like a stream of oil flowing soundlessly, with the result that it is a marvel how he accomplishes these things at such an age as his.

According to Theodorus' high praise here, even the words of Theaetetus are as surprising and worthy of listening to as any marvel. Moreover, his uncanny physical resemblance to Socrates more than reiterates the point: this young man is a wonderful interlocutor in an intellectual sense, clearly cast as a sort of potential youthful double of Socrates himself.

The contrast with Charmides could not be starker. Theaetetus is certainly not an object of aesthetic *thauma* in the way that Charmides is, though wonder nevertheless plays a very important part in his characterisation. Out of all of Socrates' interlocutors, Theaetetus is the one who wonders most intently at the type of problems which occupy Socrates himself, as we see at *Theaetetus* 154c:

σμικρὸν λαβὲ παράδειγμα, καὶ πάντα εἴσῃ ἃ βούλομαι. ἀστραγάλους γάρ που ἕξ, ἂν μὲν τέτταρας αὐτοῖς προσενέγκῃς, πλείους φαμὲν εἶναι τῶν τεττάρων καὶ ἡμιολίους, ἐὰν δὲ δώδεκα, ἐλάττους καὶ ἡμίσεις, καὶ οὐδὲ ἀνεκτὸν ἄλλως λέγειν· ἢ σὺ ἀνέξῃ;

Take a small example, and you will know everything that I mean. There are, let's suppose, six knuckle-bones. If you place four beside them, we say that the six knuckle-bones are more than four – half as many more. But if you place twelve beside the six knuckle-bones, we say the six knuckle-bones are fewer – half as many fewer. And surely it's not acceptable to say this? Or will you accept it?

Theaetetus' immediate response to this mathematical problem reveals how intense his engagement with such problems is when he exclaims: 'By the gods, Socrates, I'm wondering excessively at the meaning of this: sometimes when I'm looking into these things I feel truly dizzy' (καὶ νὴ τοὺς θεούς γε, ὦ Σώκρατες, ὑπερφυῶς ὡς θαυμάζω τί ποτ' ἐστὶ ταῦτα, καὶ ἐνίοτε ὡς ἀληθῶς βλέπων εἰς αὐτὰ

25

σκοτοδινιῶ, 155c). Mathematics is the marvel here, not a beautiful body or a sophistic display or a work of art, things which are the causes of a very different type of marvelling in Platonic dialogues.[16] In fact, as Socrates himself goes on to tell Theaetetus, it is precisely the type of wonder he is feeling now that constitutes the 'beginning of philosophy' (ἀρχὴ φιλοσοφίας, 155d) itself.[17]

For Charmides, in contrast, wonder as it exists for Socrates and Theaetetus – the wonder that leads to curiosity and cognitive advancement – is completely alien. In Plato's view, the amazement caused by real-world objects is a potentially dangerous, deceptive and cognitively paralysing state which must be avoided if possible, or handled carefully if not. Charmides *himself* presents a particular risk: he is a desirable object of wonder who physically embodies the distracting and stunning potential of marvelling at the objects of the phenomenal realm. The point of the emphasis placed on Charmides' appearance at the beginning of the dialogue thus becomes obvious enough as the work draws on: the young man is wondrously beautiful on the outside – but not much lies beneath.

2.3 Critias the Poet, Charmides the Actor

As it turns out, over the course of the *Charmides* it emerges that there is little intellectual material at all inside the dialogue's eponymous beautiful young man: like a bronze statue, his exterior causes him to become a delightful object of wonder, though he remains somehow hollow at the core. Once Socrates begins his customary elenctic questioning it does not take long for the suspicion that this might be the case to arise. Soon after the young man's grand entrance, Socrates embarks on a conversation with Charmides about the nature of *sophrosyne*. But Socrates' questions are not directed directly at Charmides alone for very long. His cousin and guardian Critias soon has to step in and take over the answerer's role once Charmides' initial ideas – that *sophrosyne*

---

[16] This latter form of Platonic marvelling will be more fully explored in Chapter 7.
[17] On the significance of this saying in ancient philosophical thought, see also Llewelyn (1988) 173–91.

2.3 Critias the Poet, Charmides the Actor

consists of 'doing everything in an orderly and calm fashion' (σωφροσύνη εἶναι τὸ κοσμίως πάντα πράττειν καὶ ἡσυχῇ, 159b), or that *'sophrosyne* makes a man feel shame and modest, and that having a sense of shame is *sophrosyne*' (αἰσχύνεσθαι ποιεῖν ἡ σωφροσύνη καὶ αἰσχυντηλὸν τὸν ἄνθρωπον, καὶ εἶναι ὅπερ αἰδὼς ἡ σωφροσύνη, 160e) – both founder.

In fact, it soon turns out that Charmides' third definition of *sophrosyne* – that it is 'minding one's own business' (σωφροσύνη ἂν εἴη τὸ τὰ ἑαυτοῦ πράττειν, 161b) – merely parrots ideas which really belong to his cousin Critias. Socrates immediately suspects that this is the case, and after struggling to defend the proposition at any length Charmides, glancing significantly at Critias, confirms his suspicion. He excuses his own difficulties by claiming that the original author of the idea he has been advancing probably did not actually know what it meant either.[18] Critias' response to Charmides' move is telling (162c–d):

καὶ ὁ Κριτίας δῆλος μὲν ἦν καὶ πάλαι ἀγωνιῶν καὶ φιλοτίμως πρός τε τὸν Χαρμίδην καὶ πρὸς τοὺς παρόντας ἔχων, μόγις δ' ἑαυτὸν ἐν τῷ πρόσθεν κατέχων τότε οὐχ οἷός τε ἐγένετο· δοκεῖ γάρ μοι παντὸς μᾶλλον ἀληθὲς εἶναι, ὃ ἐγὼ ὑπέλαβον, τοῦ Κριτίου ἀκηκοέναι τὸν Χαρμίδην ταύτην τὴν ἀπόκρισιν περὶ τῆς σωφροσύνης. ὁ μὲν οὖν Χαρμίδης βουλόμενος μὴ αὐτὸς ὑπέχειν λόγον ἀλλ' ἐκεῖνον τῆς ἀποκρίσεως, ὑπεκίνει αὐτὸν ἐκεῖνον, καὶ ἐνεδείκνυτο ὡς ἐξεληλεγμένος εἴη· ὁ δ' οὐκ ἠνέσχετο, ἀλλά μοι ἔδοξεν ὀργισθῆναι αὐτῷ ὥσπερ ποιητὴς ὑποκριτῇ κακῶς διατιθέντι τὰ ἑαυτοῦ ποιήματα.

And it was clear that Critias had been distressed for a while and was eager for distinction in the eyes of Charmides and those present, and having scarcely restrained himself before, he was no longer then able at all. For it seems to me that what I had suspected before was completely true, that Charmides had heard his answer about *sophrosyne* from Critias. And so Charmides, since he did not want to play the answerer himself, began to nudge Critias towards it, and pointed out that he had been refuted. But Critias could not bear this, and seemed to me to be angry with him just as a poet is angry at an actor who recites his works badly.

Here a second simile is added to the earlier idea of Charmides as a wonder-inducing *agalma*. Charmides is now an actor, and Critias has become a poet. There is of course a joke here as well: Critias

---

[18] *Chrm.* 162b: ἀλλ' ἴσως οὐδὲν κωλύει μηδὲ τὸν λέγοντα μηδὲν εἰδέναι ὅ τι ἐνόει. καὶ ἅμα ταῦτα λέγων ὑπεγέλα τε καὶ εἰς τὸν Κριτίαν ἀπέβλεπεν ('But perhaps the one who said this did not know what he meant'. And at the same time as he said this he began to giggle and looked intently at Critias).

27

was an extremely prolific writer and poet, known to have written hexameter and elegiac poems, tragedies and a satyr play, as well as numerous prose works of various sorts.[19] What is most important here, however, is the sense that Critias has been providing Charmides with an intellectual 'script' by providing pre-prepared answers for the discussion with Socrates about the nature of *sophrosyne*. At this point in the dialogue, then, we have been introduced to two similes which indelibly colour our view of Charmides as a Socratic interlocutor. He is beautiful and provokes a paralysing sort of wonder, like an aesthetically beautiful *agalma*, and his intellectual performance has been compared to that of an actor performing someone else's text – at least up until the point here when he mischievously performs in a way which his director/the author of the text he is performing (i.e. Critias) fails to anticipate.

How are these two images linked, and how do they relate to the wonder Charmides inspires in his viewers? One answer suggests itself by thinking about other instances in Plato where Socrates' implicit and humorous criticism of Charmides' reliance on Critias' ideas is echoed. One such place is the discussion of the advantages and disadvantages of using written texts at the end of the *Phaedrus* (274b–8e). Just as writing cannot spontaneously adapt itself in the moment to the (oral) questioner at hand since, being fixed, it 'always says one and the same thing' (ἕν τι σημαίνει μόνον ταὐτὸν ἀεί, 275d) when someone questions it, leading to it always 'needing its father [i.e. the author] to come to its aid since it is unable to defend or help itself' (τοῦ πατρὸς ἀεὶ δεῖται βοηθοῦ· αὐτὸς γὰρ οὔτ' ἀμύνασθαι οὔτε βοηθῆσαι δυνατὸς αὑτῷ, 275e), so too Charmides is incapable of standing up to the rigours of Socratic questioning when advancing a Critian line. Just like a text, he soon needs his (literal) guardian to step in and take over. For Plato, the problem with both writing and with relying on the intellectual ideas of another without examining them for oneself is thus essentially the same: in both cases, the ideas being voiced belong to someone else.

---

[19] For an overview of Critias' literary career, see Nails (2002) 110–11. Solon was famously Critias' ancestor (see *Chrm.* 155a; *Tim.* 20e), and it is possible that he saw himself as a similar sort of statesman-poet: see Wilson (2003) 187 on Critias' mimicry of Solon.

2.3 Critias the Poet, Charmides the Actor

In other philosophical and rhetorical works of the fourth century BCE the same sorts of problems are shown to occur even if the text happens to be one's own. Certain wonderful pre-planned rhetorical effects may be reliably wielded by a speaker, but the written text can never *adapt* effectively to new and unexpected arguments that are put to it in the cut and thrust of living debate. This is one of the reasons why Socrates had equated written texts with painted figures earlier on in the *Phaedrus*: figures in a painting may give the appearance of life, but they, like written texts, are unable to speak to the precise question put to them, remaining silent instead.[20] As we shall see in the next section, this quality of *seeming* to be alive – the animation of inanimate material – is one of the qualities most strongly associated with the arousal of *thauma*. We see this problem outlined even more clearly in the thoughts of one of Plato's contemporaries, the rhetorician Alcidamas. In his treatise *On Sophists*, Alcidamas argues for the superiority of creating extemporised speeches rather than relying on pre-prepared written speeches, in terms which recall some of Socrates' arguments in the *Phaedrus*.[21] Alcidamas argues (*On Sophists* 27) that speeches written down beforehand are the 'images and outlines and imitations of speeches' (εἴδωλα καὶ σχήματα καὶ μιμήματα λόγων) made up on the spot, and we can think about them in the same way as we think about 'bronze statues and stone monuments and pictures of living things' (χαλκῶν ἀνδριάντων καὶ λιθίνων ἀγαλμάτων καὶ γεγραμμένων ζῴων) because these works of art are similar imitations of 'real bodies' (ἀληθινῶν σωμάτων) which might 'provide pleasure when looking at them' (τέρψιν μὲν ἐπὶ τῆς θεωρίας ἔχει), but ultimately offer 'nothing of use' (χρῆσιν δ' οὐδεμίαν) beyond that.[22] He goes on to weigh up one of the advantages of

---

[20] *Phdr.* 275d: δεινὸν γάρ που, ὦ Φαῖδρε, τοῦτ' ἔχει γραφή, καὶ ὡς ἀληθῶς ὅμοιον ζωγραφίᾳ. καὶ γὰρ τὰ ἐκείνης ἔκγονα ἕστηκε μὲν ὡς ζῶντα, ἐὰν δ' ἀνέρῃ τι, σεμνῶς πάνυ σιγᾷ. (For writing, Phaedrus, possesses this strange quality, and is truly like painting. For the figures of that art stand as if they are alive, but if you ask them anything, they remain solemnly maintaining complete silence). Plato is obviously drawing on and complicating an already well-established parallel between performed speech and artistic object here: cf. e.g. the opening of Pindar's *Nemean* 5 for the comparison of statue and song.
[21] On parallels between ideas in Plato's *Phaedrus* and those in Alcidamas' work, see O'Sullivan (1992) 100–2.
[22] On Alcidamas' use of this comparison between written speeches and the plastic arts in *On Sophists*, see Ford (2002) 233–5.

The Art of Thauma

using a written speech – the ability to deploy astonishing effects – with the concomitant disadvantages of this approach (28):

τὸν αὐτὸν τρόπον ὁ γεγραμμένος λόγος, ἑνὶ σχήματι καὶ τάξει κεχρημένος, ἐκ βιβλίου <μὲν> θεωρούμενος ἔχει τινὰς ἐκπλήξεις, ἐπὶ δὲ τῶν καιρῶν ἀκίνητος ὢν οὐδεμίαν ὠφέλειαν τοῖς κεκτημένοις παραδίδωσιν. ἀλλ' ὥσπερ ἀνδριάντων καλῶν ἀληθινὰ σώματα πολὺ χείρους τὰς εὐμορφίας ἔχοντα πολλαπλασίους ἐπὶ τῶν ἔργων τὰς ὠφελείας παραδίδωσιν, οὕτω καὶ λόγος ὁ μὲν ἀπ' αὐτῆς τῆς διανοίας ἐν τῷ παραυτίκα λεγόμενος ἔμψυχός ἐστι καὶ ζῇ καὶ τοῖς πράγμασιν ἕπεται καὶ τοῖς ἀληθέσιν ἀφωμοίωται σώμασιν, ὁ δὲ γεγραμμένος εἰκόνι λόγου τὴν φύσιν ὁμοίαν ἔχων ἁπάσης ἐνεργείας ἄμοιρος καθέστηκεν.

In the same way a written speech, which has one form and arrangement, has certain astonishing features when consulted from a book, but being incapable of movement at critical times, it provides no benefit to the user. And just as real bodies are much less well-formed than beautiful statues, but they provide very many benefits in getting things done, so is the speech which is spoken from the mind on the spur of the moment ensouled and living, and it keeps up with events and is like those real bodies. But the written speech has a nature which is like a mere image of a real speech and is devoid of all active force.

Premeditation and planning supposedly lead to guaranteed *ekplexis* here, but at the expense of the ability of one's argument to move around of its own accord and adapt to the current situation: precisely what Socrates describes in the *Phaedrus*. There is a deeper dichotomy implied by Alcidamas' words here – that between style and content. Ekplektic devices (τινὰς ἐκπλήξεις) can be pre-prepared with a particular stunning effect in mind, he seems to be saying, but the sacrifice this entails is the loss of the ability to move around within an argument.[23] Here again pre-written/pre-prepared speeches have become only imitations of 'real bodies' and are not themselves truly alive – though the implication is that such speeches might give such a marvellous and thrilling approximation of being alive that it becomes almost impossible, at least for the audience, to tell the difference.[24]

In Plato's view either becoming a producer of or falling prey to the *thauma* created by these astonishing pre-planned performances is a risky business. The comparisons of Charmides to an *agalma* and

---

[23] See O'Sullivan (1992) 74–5 on the place of *ekplexis* in Alcidamas' work.
[24] Cf. McCoy (2009) 49–51 and Muir (2001) 62 on the contrast between living, moving speeches and inanimate text here.

2.4 *Thauma Idesthai*: Wonder and the Ekphrastic Tradition

an actor are both parallel to and equally prescient of the eventual aporetic outcome of the dialogue, and even the eventual disastrous outcome of Charmides' life. Socrates' failure to have any real effect on the young man is particularly poignant given his continued association with Critias and their eventual violent ends. Both men lost their lives after involvement with the tumultuous regime of the Thirty: Critias as the notoriously violent leader and figurehead of the group and Charmides as a member of the Piraeus Ten.[25] Within the setting of the dialogue, the young man's status as a wondrous object of *eros* and his inability to make much headway with his attempts to engage in philosophic thinking really matter: by the end of the dialogue, the failure of Socratic philosophy and the inability to resist certain types of *thaumata* are shown to have a terrible price.

2.4 *Thauma Idesthai*: Wonder, Divine Artworks and the Ekphrastic Tradition

In the *Charmides*, *Theaetetus* and numerous other dialogues Plato plays with the distinctly visual aspects of *thaumata* and compares and contrasts these objects of the phenomenal world with the *thaumata* of philosophical reasoning, which are not visible at all. Why does Plato return to the lure of this type of wonder so frequently in his dialogues? And why does he hit upon *thauma* as one of the most powerful (and potentially disturbing) effects of verbal and visual artworks alike?

To begin to answer this question, it is necessary to examine the connection between wonder and vision in Greek culture from the archaic period onwards.[26] This connection is extremely strong. In

---

[25] See Nails (2002) 90–4, 108–13 on the involvement of Critias and Charmides with the actions of the Thirty. For recent discussions of the relevance of the later political careers of Charmides and Critias in relation to Plato's dialogue, see Danzig (2013) 486–519 and (2014) 507–24 and Flores (2018) 162–88.

[26] Prior (1989) provides the best overview of the strong connections between *thauma* and vision in his phenomenological account of sight and appearance in Archaic Greek poetry; see also Hunzinger (1993), (2015) and (2018) on *thauma* and the visual from Homer onwards; cf. D'Angour (2011) 134, 148–50 on the connections between the concept of novelty and *thauma*, dazzling light, vision and responses to visual artworks in ancient Greek culture.

The Art of *Thauma*

early Greek hexameter poetry, sight is the sense most clearly linked to the marvellous.[27] In Homer and Hesiod the formulaic phrase *thauma idesthai* ('a wonder to see') points to this, and it is primarily their impressive visual aspects that make phenomena explicitly labelled as *thaumata* induce wonder in their viewers in early hexameter poetry. For example, impressive weaponry or armour is often said to inspire wonder in its beholder, especially in the *Iliad*: such objects described in that poem as 'wonders to see' include the chariot with special gold, silver and bronze wheels prepared by Hera and Athene to aid the Achaeans (5.724–5), Rhesus' golden armour (10.439–40), and Achilles' original armour, once given by the gods to his father Peleus (18.82–4). Beautiful houses or palaces and their contents are described as similarly visually striking in both of the Homeric poems: Hephaestus' workshop, for example, dazzles Thetis with its marvellous self-propelled tripods at *Iliad* 18.372–7, while Telemachus and his companions wonder at Menelaus' magnificent palace at *Odyssey* 4.43–4.

Other, more elaborate objects of craft elicit even greater wonder from their viewers. In longer passages of epic ekphrasis the

---

[27] There are a few exceptions in early Greek hexameter poetry which designate sound or speech as a *thauma*, though in general the question of the relation of *thauma* to what is heard is explored much more intensely later in the Greek tradition. The exceptions which we do find in Archaic poetry include Telemachus' ever more daring speeches in the *Odyssey*, which increasingly astonish Penelope and the suitors as the narrative proceeds (see *Od.* 1.381–2: repeated at 18.410–11 and 20.268–9). But it is not primarily the sound of Telemachus' speech or even the speech itself which causes the *thauma* in these cases, but the overall impression created by the rapid change in his behaviour. More ambiguous perhaps is the suitors' wondering response at *Od.* 4.638–9 to the report that Telemachus has dared to go to Pylos without their prior knowledge. In this case it is not only Telemachus' unexpected behaviour but the surprising nature of the report which has caused this awestruck response. This second example is very much the exception to the general rule that Homeric *thauma*, in terms of its sensory basis, is grounded primarily in the visual. An even more interesting example is Hes. *Theog.* 834, where the many voices and sounds which Typhon utters are said to be 'marvels to hear' (θαύματ' ἀκοῦσαι). Pindar picks up on this unusual Hesiodic passage in his own description of the wonder of Aetna (whose eruptions are actually caused by Typhon, who is imprisoned beneath the mountain) near the beginning of *Pythian* 1, where he puts his own twist on what 'hearing' a marvel is by claiming that even hearing a *report* of Typhon's angry outbursts, rather than seeing him, or hearing the noises he makes, is enough to constitute a *thauma* (*Pyth.* 1.26): θαυμάσιον προσιδέσθαι θαῦμα δὲ καὶ παρεόντων ἀκοῦσαι (a wonder to see, and a wonder even to hear of from those present). On the sense of 'ecphrastic wonderment' created at this moment in Pindar's ode, see Fearn (2017) 187–8; on the connection between Hes. *Theog.* 834 and Pind. *Pyth.* 1.26, see Passmore (2018) 733–49.

2.4 *Thauma Idesthai*: Wonder and the Ekphrastic Tradition

designation of a beautiful object of (often divine) material craft as a *thauma idesthai* becomes a *topos* of ekphrastic form from Homer onwards.[28] The shield of Achilles in *Iliad* 18 is the most important and obvious example. In fact, the creation of *thauma* is revealed to be one purpose of the construction of Achilles' new shield even before Hephaestus sets to work making it. The god tells Thetis that his aim is to ensure that future viewers will wonder at the object which he crafts, and this ability to cause future *thauma* is explicitly modelled as a consolation for the fact that he is unable to protect Achilles from his inevitable death (18.462–7):

> τὴν δ' ἠμείβετ' ἔπειτα περικλυτὸς ἀμφιγυήεις·
> θάρσει· μή τοι ταῦτα μετὰ φρεσὶ σῇσι μελόντων.
> αἲ γάρ μιν θανάτοιο δυσηχέος ὧδε δυναίμην
> νόσφιν ἀποκρύψαι, ὅτε μιν μόρος αἰνὸς ἱκάνοι,
> ὥς οἱ τεύχεα καλὰ παρέσσεται, οἷά τις αὖτε
> ἀνθρώπων πολέων θαυμάσσεται, ὅς κεν ἴδηται.

Then the famous lame god replied to her: 'Take heart, and do not let these things trouble your mind. If only I could hide him away far from screeching death, when dreadful fate reaches him, as surely as beautiful armour will be his, such that anyone among the multitude of men will marvel at it, whoever sees it.'

Achilles' possession of the ultimate object of divine craft comes to symbolise his liminal position between gods and men, a position which attracts a wondering response from others. Furthermore, the potential *thauma* which the shield will inspire in the future is parallel to the workings of *kleos* itself as a compensation for Achilles' mortality. As such, we here find the first hint that the ekphrastic passage to follow, and the *thauma* it both describes and causes, is in some sense analogous to the sense of wonder the listener putatively feels at hearing the accounts of heroic *kleos*

---

[28] The best discussion of the importance of *thauma* as a reaction to ekphrasis and as a means for poets to make claims for the power of their own art remains that of Cunningham (2007) 65–6, who argues that *thauma* is '[t]he prophetic word of the ekphrastic' and that the 'thaumaturgical force' surrounding the ekphrastic object is something that 'writing and writers want to share, and are in fact claiming by proxy, by analogy, by such intermedial intrusions into the text'. For other good recent discussions of the importance of *thauma* in ekphrasis, see e.g. Gutzwiller (2002) 96–7, Becker (1992) 12–13, 18–19 and (1995) 29–37, 110, 129, Race (1988) 56–67 and Squire (2013) 159–63.

enshrined within the *Iliad* itself.[29] The scenes on the shield reinforce this idea. One of the main reasons for the guarantee of this future *thauma* is presumably the combination of movement and voice on Achilles' shield, which renders it a special wonder to look upon. In fact, the shield's depiction of the reaction of the young women who stand and marvel at the sight of men whirling about and dancing to the sound of flutes and lyres potentially models the ideal wondering response to the visual and verbal impact of both the described object and the ekphrasis itself (18.494–6):

> κοῦροι δ' ὀρχηστῆρες ἐδίνεον, ἐν δ' ἄρα τοῖσιν
> αὐλοὶ φόρμιγγές τε βοὴν ἔχον· αἱ δὲ γυναῖκες
> ἱστάμεναι θαύμαζον ἐπὶ προθύροισιν ἑκάστη.

And the young dancing men were whirling around, and with them the flutes and the lyres blared, and each woman stood at her doorway and marvelled.

The later description of the shield even suggests that the depiction is so realistic and wondrous that the figures upon it seem almost to be alive, as the depiction of two forces clashing and fighting with figures who are like 'living mortals' makes clear (ὥς τε ζωοὶ βροτοί, 18.539). The fact that the shield, a work of plastic art, somehow manages to involve movement and sound as well is one of the primary aspects of the wonder it inspires; it creates the impression that in some sense the work itself is a living and breathing object. The play between the animate and the inanimate, the static and the illusionistic impression of realism that this creates, is of the utmost importance, as the 'great marvel' of Hephaestus' depiction of a ploughed field emphasises (18.548–9): 'And the earth behind was black and looked like it had been ploughed, even though it was made of gold: in this way the outstanding marvel was crafted' (ἡ δὲ μελαίνετ' ὄπισθεν,

---

[29] For the view in antiquity that ekphrastic objects in some sense reflect the poet's own verbal craft cf. Σ ad. *Il.* 3.126–7 on Helen's tapestry, which depicts the battles of Trojans and Achaeans: ἀξιόχρεων ἀρχέτυπον ἀνέπλασεν ὁ ποιητὴς τῆς ἰδίας ποιήσεως (the poet has fashioned a worthy model of his own craft). See Becker (1995) 55 on this comment. However, cf. also the note of caution regarding reading the Shield of Achilles as a direct analogue of the poet's art at Ford (1992) 168–9 and (2002) 115–16.

2.4 Thauma Idesthai: Wonder and the Ekphrastic Tradition

ἀρηρομένη δὲ ἐῴκει, | χρυσείη περ ἐοῦσα· τὸ δὴ περὶ θαῦμα τέτυκτο).

The verbal depiction of movement and sound in a description of a seemingly static and voiceless work of visual art becomes the most crucial ingredient of the ekphrastic *thauma* of Achilles' shield. It also becomes an essential *topos* of the later ekphrastic tradition. The description of the shield of Heracles in the Hesiodic *Scutum* bears witness to the importance of such thaumatic elements in the later ekphrastic tradition. The shield described in the Hesiodic poem is explicitly designated a *thauma idesthai* (140), with various specific details of its depiction singled out as especially worthy of wonder, such as fearsome burning snakes, which are labelled 'wondrous works' (θαυματὰ ἔργα, 165), and the figure of Perseus floating off the ground, which becomes a 'great wonder to consider' (θαῦμα μέγα φράσσασθ', 218). Once again, sight, sound, movement and an uncanny lifelikeness are often combined on the shield: a depiction of deadly Fate 'glares terribly and bellows with clanging sounds' (δεινὸν δερκομένη καναχῇσί τε βεβρυχυῖα, 160); when the Gorgons rush after Perseus 'the shield was crying out sharply and shrilly with a great din' (ἰάχεσκε σάκος μεγάλῳ ὀρυμαγδῷ | ὀξέα καὶ λιγέως, 232–3); figures of women crying out and rending their cheeks 'resemble living women' (ζωῇσιν ἴκελαι, 244). Certain other details present an especially hyperbolic rendering of the thaumatic features of the Iliadic shield (314–20):

> ἀμφὶ δ' ἴτυν ῥέεν Ὠκεανὸς πλήθοντι ἐοικώς,
> πᾶν δὲ συνεῖχε σάκος πολυδαίδαλον· οἱ δὲ κατ'αὐτὸν
> κύκνοι ἀερσιπόται μεγάλ' ἤπυον, οἵ ῥά τε πολλοὶ
> νῆχον ἐπ' ἄκρον ὕδωρ· παρὰ δ' ἰχθύες ἐκλονέοντο·
> θαῦμα ἰδεῖν καὶ Ζηνὶ βαρυκτύπῳ, οὗ διὰ βουλὰς
> Ἥφαιστος ποίησε σάκος μέγα τε στιβαρόν τε,
> ἀρσάμενος παλάμῃσι.

And around the rim Ocean was flowing as if in full flood, and it was surrounding the highly-wrought shield on all sides. And upon it were high-soaring swans calling loudly, and many were swimming on the water's surface. And beside them the fishes were being driven in confusion. It was a wonder to see even for deep-thundering Zeus, through whose designs Hephaestus made the great and sturdy shield, joining it together with his hands.

The Art of *Thauma*

While Achilles' shield will inspire wonder in any mortal who sees it (θαυμάσσεται, ὅς κεν ἴδηται, 18.467), Heracles' shield goes one better: even Zeus, most powerful of all the gods, marvels at Hephaestus' wondrous craft in this instance.[30] The Hesiodic *Scutum* is thus the first major example we have of a work which plays with the thaumatic *topoi* of ekphrasis initiated in the extant tradition by the description of Achilles' Iliadic shield.

Thauma remains an important element of ekphrastic descriptions of artworks and objects of craft in the ancient literary tradition. By the time we reach the Hellenistic period, the power of *thauma* within ekphrastic description is explored in increasingly sophisticated ways. The sense that the distinctions between the living products of nature and the products of human craft which imitate those natural beings are collapsing is particularly prevalent. A new emphasis on the capability of the artwork to speak and move as if it were alive is yoked to a parallel amplification of the sense that the *thauma* of the work of visual art being described also applies to the poet's verbal art. Furthermore, the invented object of the poetic description often points, even more emphatically than Homer's shield, to the poem itself.

This is certainly the case in the ekphrasis of the goatherd's cup in Theocritus' first *Idyll*, where we find a much more explicit connection between the parallel processes of visual, verbal and textual artmaking. *Thauma* is referred to most directly when Theocritus, in his most forceful gesture of this kind in the poem, directs our response towards the cup-as-poetry at the end of the ekphrasis, when the acanthus curling round the cup is described as 'a wonder of the world of the goatherd: a marvel to astonish your heart' (αἰπολικὸν θάημα· τέρας κέ τυ θυμὸν ἀτύξαι, 1.56). The cup itself is offered in exchange for song within the narrative of the *Idyll*: Thyrsis' song – and by extension, Theocritus' own bucolic song – is therefore held up as inspiring a similar sense of *thauma* as the cup. Moreover, *thauma* has already been hinted at in the beginning of the ekphrasis, through the choice of the *Homeric*

---

[30] For a discussion of other passages in the *Scutum* which make similarly hyperbolic use of references to sound, spectacular sights, colour and movement in comparison to the concomitant descriptions of similar elements on the Iliadic shield, see Martin (2005) 158–60.

2.4 Thauma Idesthai: Wonder and the Ekphrastic Tradition

Hymn to Dionysus as the model for the description of the ivy tendrils that surround the cup (1.29–31):

τῶ ποτὶ μὲν χείλη μαρύεται ὑψόθι κισσός,
κισσὸς ἑλιχρύσῳ κεκονιμένος· ἁ δὲ κατ' αὐτόν
καρπῷ ἕλιξ εἰλεῖται ἀγαλλομένα κροκόεντι.

High up on the lip winds ivy, ivy sprinkled with helichryse, and along it curls round the ivy tendril exulting in its yellow fruit.

Gutzwiller has correctly pointed out that the description of the ivy which entwines itself around the mast of the ship in the following passage of the *Homeric Hymn* (38–41) forms the background to Theocritus' version here:

αὐτίκα δ' ἀκρότατον παρὰ ἱστίον ἐξετανύσθη
ἄμπελος ἔνθα καὶ ἔνθα, κατεκρημνῶντο δὲ πολλοί
βότρυες· ἀμφ' ἱστὸν δὲ μέλας εἱλίσσετο κισσός
ἄνθεσι τηλεθάων, χαρίεις δ' ἐπὶ καρπὸς ὀρώρει.

Now along the topmost part of the sail a vine spread out this side and that, and many clusters of grapes hung from it. Ivy was circling around the dark mast, blooming with flowers, and lovely fruit grew on it.

The rapid and spontaneous appearance of ivy winding its way over the ship is one of a series of 'wondrous deeds' (θαυματὰ ἔργα, 34) through which Dionysus manifests himself to the pirates on board the ship in the *Hymn*: the point of this echo is to imbue the Theocritean cup with the same sort of wondrous feeling as the description of Dionysus' series of epiphanic *thaumata* in that poem. Gutzwiller describes this perfectly: '[w]hat Theocritus has done here is to recast a miracle, which was acceptable under the terms of archaic religious thought, into a description of an object of art, marvelous in that its motion suggests either supreme artistic workmanship or the naïve imagination of the goatherd'.[31] Moreover, Theocritus' own careful use of language in this description demonstrates the way in which striving for mimetically realistic effects in order to produce *thauma* is an aim of his own art as well. For example, the complex word order in these lines reflects

---

[31] Gutzwiller (1986) 254. See also Hunter (1999) 78 on the way in which 'one Dionysiac miracle prompting amazement (*h. Dion.* 37) is used to describe another' in this passage.

37

the intertwined nature of the plants described, with the mimetic potential of the text on the page activating yet another source of *thauma* for the reader as Theocritus creates a visual representation of the artefact he is describing through words.[32] This kind of play with the look of the written text on the page reminds us of other Hellenistic innovations which perhaps aim at a similar sort of *thauma*: the so-called 'pattern-poems' (*technopaignia*), and the increasing use of acrostics in verse of the period.[33]

The Milan Papyrus epigrams of Posidippus provide further examples of the significant role *thauma* comes to play in the increasingly complex relationship between verbal, visual and written artworks in the Hellenistic period. The language of *thauma* takes on a programmatic significance in the descriptions of wondrous engraved stones which open the collection. In this section, labelled *Lithika*, the precious stones which are described become objects of amazement through their combination of wondrous natural properties and skilful applications of human craft. Moreover, Posidippus' ability to transform conventionally prosaic or technical material on stones into aesthetically pleasing epigrammatic texts becomes a *thauma* in itself.[34] But unlike contemporary prose technical treatises on stones, such as those of Theophrastus, the ekphrastic descriptions of gems in Posidippus' epigrams do not aim at elucidating the causes or context of these naturally occurring *thaumata*. Instead the aim of these epigrams, as Krevans astutely points out, is to provoke 'not the satisfied "aha!" of understanding, but the round-eyed "oh!" of wonder'.[35] This 'aesthetic of wonder' is created primarily by the speaker's focus on the combination of the naturally wondrous properties of stones and the marvellous human skill (*techne*) involved in

---

[32] See Hunter (1999) 78 on the mimetic qualities of the word order reflecting the movement of the plants in this passage.

[33] See Luz (2010) for an overview of the use of *technopaignia* and acrostics in this period.

[34] On the strong links between the contents of the Milan Papyrus and contemporary prose treatises, see Krevans (2005) 88. See also M. Smith (2004) 109 for the idea that in the *Lithika* Posidippus reworks the scientific prose of Theophrastus' writings on stones in the same way as a real-life craftsman works up gems into beautiful aesthetic objects.

[35] See Krevans (2005) 91; cf. Krevans (2011) 126: 'In paradoxography, science is converted into ecphrasis: stop, look, and wonder'. See Bing (2005) 134 and Krevans (2005) 89–92 on the similarities in thematic content between Posidippus' *Lithika* and contemporary paradoxographical collections. See M. Smith (2004) 105 and Elsner (2014) 159–62 for a more general discussion of the repeated use of the language of *thauma* in the *Lithika*.

2.4 Thauma Idesthai: Wonder and the Ekphrastic Tradition

gem carving. Three closely connected epigrams (13, 15 and 17 AB) make the focus on this particular combination of natural and manmade *thauma* very explicit:

κ[ερδα]λέη λίθος ἥδε· λιπα[ινομένη]ς γε μὲν αὐτῆς,
[φέγγο]ς ὅλους ὄγκους, θαῦ[μ' ἀπάτη]ς, περιθεῖ·
ὄ[γκων] δ' ἀσκελέων, ὠκὺ γ[λυπτὸς λ]ὶς ὁ Πέρσης
[τε]ίνων ἀστράπτει πρὸς καλὸν ἠέλιον.

This is a crafty stone. When oiled a light runs around its entire mass, a wonder of deception. But when the mass is dry, straightaway the carved Persian lion flashes forth, extending himself towards the beautiful sun.

⌊οὐ ποταμ⌋ὸς κελάδων ἐπὶ χείλεσιν, ἀλλὰ δράκοντος
εἶχέ ποτ' εὐπώγων τόνδε λίθον κεφαλή
πυκνὰ φαληριόωντα· τὸ δὲ γλυφὲν ἅρμα κατ' αὐτ⌊ο⌋ῦ
τοῦθ' ὑπὸ Λυγκείου βλέμματος ἐγλύφετο
ψεύδεϊ χειρὸς ὅμοιον· ἀποπλασθὲν γὰρ ὁρᾶται
ἅρμα, κατὰ πλάτεος δ' οὐκ ἂν ἴδοις προβόλους·
ἧι καὶ θαῦμα πέλει μόχθου μέγα, πῶς ὁ λιθουργὸς
⌊τὰς⌋ ἀτενιζούσας οὐκ ἐμόγησε κόρας.

Not a river sounding upon its banks, but the well-bearded head of a snake once held this stone, thickly crested with foam. The carved chariot upon it, like a white mark on a fingernail,[36] was carved by the eyesight of Lynceus. For a chariot is seen to be formed there, but on the surface you cannot see anything that projects out. This is the great wonder of his toil, how the stone-cutter did not damage his eyes while looking intently.

σκέψαι ὁ Μύσιος οἷον ἀνερρίζωσεν Ὄλυμπος
τόνδε λίθον διπλῆι θαυμάσιον δυνάμει·
τῆιδε μὲν ἕλκει ῥεῖα τὸν ἀντήεντα σίδηρον
μάγνης οἷα λίθος, τῆιδε δ' ἄπωθεν ἐλᾶι,
πλευρῆι ἐναντιοεργός· ὃ καὶ τέρας ἐξ ἑνὸς αὐτοῦ,
πῶς δύο μιμεῖται χερμάδας εἰς προβολάς.

Look hard at what Mysian Olympus has uprooted: this stone marvellous because of its double power. On the one side it attracts the iron pitted against it easily, like a magnet. But on the other side it thrusts away causing the opposite effect. And the marvel is how one stone on its own imitates two stones with its impulses.[37]

---

[36] The meaning and interpretation of the phrase ψεύδεϊ χειρὸς ὅμοιον has long puzzled scholars: see Gow (1954) 198 and Gow and Page (1965) 500–1 for the suggestion that this phrase refers to white marks on fingernails.
[37] The meaning of εἰς προβολάς is ambiguous: see Pajón Leyra and Sánchez Muñoz (2015) 32–3 on possible interpretations of this phrase.

In the first epigram (13) the combination of human and natural *thauma* is emphasised – the stone has a naturally astonishing lustre when oiled, though its effect is made all the more marvellous when the Persian lion added by the human engraver is spotted when the stone is dry. The special abilities of either man or nature to make stones something to wonder at are then examined in turn. In epigram 15, the stone itself is not said to have any particular exceptional qualities, but it soon becomes something to marvel at due to the craftsman Lynceus' labour. In epigram 17, the magnetic stone described needs no human helping hand to become doubly wondrous because of its already inherently paradoxical qualities. In each case, Posidippus' ability to transform the dry scholarly material of the Peripatetic school on the subject of stones into a series of intricate and interconnected textual 'gems' is surely intended to provoke a concomitant sense of double wonder at his own skill as a writer. What makes the Milan Papyrus particularly interesting is the fact that here a new element has been introduced into the already conventional ekphrastic contest between the verbal and the visual: there is no longer a simple implied contest between verbal and plastic skill, but a new entanglement between the visual, verbal and textual works of human artists. Posidippus' achievement in creating an artwork out of the seemingly intractable material provided by previous technical and scientific prose literature turns the text itself into the ultimate object of aesthetic craft, something which naturally causes *thauma* in the reader. We are beginning to get a sense that in the world of the book, the sculpting of radically different texts and genres out of the raw material of the literary tradition has now become one of the most wondrous crafts of all. It is this process which lies at the heart of the aesthetics of the Hellenistic paradoxographer, as the next chapter will demonstrate.

When viewed from this angle it becomes easier to understand why a writer working in an excerpting and miscellanistic mode can, contrary to modern value judgements about the aesthetic quality of such texts, come to be seen as an extremely accomplished and wonder-inducing artist in their own right. In the Hellenistic period it is the paradoxographer who takes this search for artistic *thauma* to its logical extreme and produces marvels of

2.4 *Thauma Idesthai*: Wonder and the Ekphrastic Tradition

his own through the deft and surprising manipulation of pre-existing writings to form the textual marvel-collection. The emergence of paradoxographical collections therefore need not be viewed as a strange, unmotivated and pointless aberration, but as a cultural manifestation of the tendency to strive towards the production of artistic works which aim at arousing *thauma* first and foremost. It is this production of such textual *thaumata* that the next chapter examines.

3

READING *THAUMA*: PARADOXOGRAPHY AND THE TEXTUAL COLLECTION OF MARVELS

ἴδιον δὲ καὶ τοῦτο, νεκρῶν τινων τοῦ μυελοῦ σαπέντος ἐκ τῆς ῥάχεως ὀφίδια γίνεσθαι, ἐὰν πρὸ τοῦ τελευτᾶν ὄφεως τεθνηκότος ἑλκύσωσι τὴν ὀσμήν. καί τινι καὶ ἐπιγραμματίῳ περιπεπτώκαμεν Ἀρχελάου, οὗ καὶ πρότερον ἐμνήσθημεν, ὃς περὶ τῶν θαυμασίων καὶ τοῦτο καταγράφει, καί φησι·

> πάντα δι' ἀλλήλων ὁ πολὺς σφραγίζεται αἰών·
> ἀνδρὸς γὰρ κοίλης ἐκ μυελοῦ ῥάχεως
> δεινὸς γίνετ' ὄφις, νέκυος δειλοῖο σαπέντος,
> ὃς νέον ἐκ τούτου πνεῦμα λάβῃ τέραος,
> τεθνεότος ζωὴν ἕλκων φύσιν· εἰ δὲ τόδ' ἐστίν,
> οὐ θαῦμα βλαστεῖν τὸν διφυῆ Κέκροπα.

And this is also strange: little snakes are born out of the rotten spinal marrow of dead men if they breathe in the stench of a dead snake before death. And I have encountered an epigram on this theme by Archelaus, whom I mentioned before, who writes on marvels and says this:

> Long life puts its own stamp on each thing, marking one by another,
>   for from the marrow of the hollow spine of a man
> a terrible snake is born, from a wretched corpse that has rotted away,
>   a snake which draws new breath from this prodigy,
> dragging a living nature from a dead man: and if this is the case,
>   it is no wonder that the bi-formed Cecrops blossomed forth.

Antigonus of Carystus, *Collection of Marvellous Investigations* 89

By the time we reach this graphic poetic account of spontaneous generation by Archelaus the Egyptian, cited in a Hellenistic paradoxographical collection attributed to Antigonus of Carystus (fl. c. 240 BCE) called the *Collection of Marvellous Investigations* (Ἱστοριῶν παραδόξων συναγωγή), the reader has already encountered eighty-eight tantalisingly brief accounts of equally enigmatic *thaumata*.[1]

---

[1] This paradoxographical collection survives in a single ms. copy (*Cod. Pal. graec.* 398), now in Heidelberg. See *PGR* 32–115 for the remaining fragments. The name 'Antigonus' is inscribed at the collection's opening and most probably refers to Antigonus of Carystus, a

Reading *Thauma*

Without any explanation or reasoning, we have been repeatedly asked to marvel at many brief and bizarre accounts of zoological wonders. The customary extreme brevity and unexpected lack of contextual detail included in each marvel becomes clearer from a few examples. For instance, we are told that 'near the regions of Carystia and Andria there is an island called Gyaros: the mice gnaw through iron there' (τῆς δὲ Καρυστίας καὶ τῆς Ἀνδρίας χώρας ἐστὶν πλησίον νῆσος, ἡ καλουμένη Γύαρος· ἐνταῦθα οἱ μύες διατρώγουσιν τὸν σίδηρον, 18). Later we are informed that 'as soon as the sun starts to go down, nanny goats turn around to face it and lie down' (ὅταν τάχιστα ὁ ἥλιος τραπῇ, ἀντιβλέπουσαι αὐτῷ αἱ αἶγες κατάκεινται, 60). Later still it is revealed that 'in Phrygia there are oxen which wiggle their horns' (ἐν Φρυγίᾳ δὲ βοῦς εἶναι, οἳ κινοῦσι τὰ κέρατα, 75).

Compared to the usual brief entries in Antigonus' collection, the epigram cited above, by the author Antigonus has earlier referred to as 'Archelaus the Egyptian' (Ἀρχέλαος Αἰγύπτιος, 19), is certainly a longer and more obviously artful treatment of paradoxical themes than most other entries in this marvel-collection.[2] Read in isolation, Archelaus' epigram appears to represent a typically Hellenistic poetic production, a skilful transformation of a bizarre scientific theory concerning spontaneous generation into a more refined poetic form comparable with Posidippus' transformation of Peripatetic scientific prose into artful epigrams in his *Lithika*, or Aratus' recasting of Eudoxus of Cnidus' scientific astronomical prose treatise into hexameters

---

third-century BCE author associated with the court at Pergamon, who wrote a work entitled *Lives of Philosophers* and probably also produced treatises on sculpture, art history and diction. Musso (1976) 1–10, (1977) 15–17 and (1985) 9 argues against Antigonus' authorship of the *Collection of Marvellous Investigations* and suggests that it is the product of later Byzantine scholarship, but the dating of at least the core of the collection to the third century BCE seems secure, as all of the authors cited date from either the time before Antigonus of Carystus was active or are roughly contemporaneous with him. Dorandi (1999) xi–xxxii and (2005) 121–4, believes that the attribution to Antigonus of Carystus is uncertain and suggests that another unknown Antigonus may be the author. Although it is not possible to attribute the collection to Antigonus of Carystus with certainty, the arguments for Antigonan authorship put forth by Wilamowitz (1881) 16–26 remain compelling (cf. Schepens and Delcroix (1996) 401 n. 89): as a result, I refer to the author of this paradoxographical collection as Antigonus of Carystus here, though none of my arguments depend on this attribution.

[2] Archelaus the Egyptian is also known as Archelaus of Chersonesus (see e.g. Athenaeus *Deipnosophistae* 409c: Ἀρχελάῳ τῷ Χερρονησίτῃ). This Chersonesus is presumably Chersonesus Mikra, an Egyptian settlement very close to Alexandria (see e.g. Strabo *Geography* 17.1.14).

in his didactic *Phaenomena*.[3] For the modern reader, it is perhaps tempting to excerpt this excerpted epigram of Archelaus from its broader context, ignoring the surrounding paradoxographical prose and the relation of that text to the more polished lines of verse which follow. This temptation becomes stronger if we examine the entries which come before and after Archelaus' epigram. The preceding prose entry clearly anticipates the theme of spontaneous generation which the epigram explores by presenting us with an instance of a living body expelling another living biological form of a completely different species. This marvel, however, is presented very differently from Archelaus' polished verse (*Collection* 88):

ἐν δὲ τῷ σώματι τῶν ἀνθρώπων γίνεσθαι οἷον ἰόνθους μικρούς· τούτους δὲ ἐάν τις κεντήσῃ, ἐξέρχεσθαι φθεῖρας, καὶ ἐὰν ὑγράσῃ τις, νόσημα τοῦτο ἐμπίπτειν ὥσπερ Ἀλκμᾶνι τῷ λυρικῷ καὶ Φερεκύδει τῷ Συρίῳ.

Small boils appear on men's bodies. And if someone pricks these, lice come out. And if someone has a moist nature, this illness befalls them, just as happened to Alcman the lyric poet and Pherecydes of Syros.

This prose marvel ultimately derives from a longer passage in Aristotle's *Historia animalium* (556b28–557a3), which Antigonus has here abbreviated and adapted before turning to Archelaus' much more stylistically polished epigram on a similar theme concerning the generation of one biological form from another. In fact, it is to Aristotle's *Historia animalium* (557b6–8) that Antigonus turns once again as a source for the ninetieth entry in his marvel collection after the citation of Archelaus' epigram. This entry consists of a single sentence, and once more puts the wondrous process of spontaneous generation under the spotlight: 'Aristotle says that an animal is born in wax, which seems to be the smallest animal and is called *akari* [i.e. a type of mite]' (ὁ δὲ Ἀριστοτέλης [λέγειν] ἐν κηρῷ φησιν γίνεσθαι ζῷον, ὃ δὴ δοκεῖν ἐλάχιστον εἶναι καὶ καλεῖσθαι ἀκαρί, *Collection* 90).

These three consecutive marvels are typical of Antigonus' method throughout his *Collection of Marvellous Investigations*.

---

[3] On the use of verse in prose paradoxographical collections, and the effect of prosimetrum which sometimes ensues, see Schepens and Delcroix (1996) 399 and Bartoňková (1999) 63–7.

Reading *Thauma*

They encapsulate some of the issues which modern readers have faced when presented with Antigonus' work. Why does the paradoxographer choose to cite and adapt these texts where and when he does? Is there any point and purpose in his choices and his method of ordering his material? Is there anything really wondrous about the material he chooses to focus on at all?

These questions have proved difficult to answer. Like many later miscellanistic texts, Antigonus' *Collection* has primarily been seen as a random assemblage of knowledge with no overriding literary purpose: a mess of texts fit only to be mined and plundered for the occasional useful snippet of geographical or prosopographical information, or an intriguing textual variant, or a few precious lines of poetry. This approach has led to many misunderstandings about the nature of these texts. These have been compounded by the perceived failure of paradoxographical collections to fit in with preconceived generic norms of ancient historiography or scientific prose literature, two modes of writing with which paradoxographical collections have been seen to share certain similarities, in terms of both thematic focus and style. Furthermore, the perceived difficulty of discerning any immediately explicit aesthetic principles behind the composition of these texts has only exacerbated matters further. As the entries from paradoxographical collections cited throughout this chapter demonstrate, the reasons behind the paradoxographer's presentation and arrangement of material are not immediately obvious to the reader. As a result of all of these factors, it would be an understatement to say that Hellenistic paradoxographical collections have not enjoyed high critical esteem in recent centuries.

But to berate these texts for their failure to conform to supposed standards of ancient historiography or scientific and technical treatises is to miss the point entirely. The paradoxographical collection aims first and foremost to make the reader marvel, and the very form of these texts is inextricably tied up with this aim. In this chapter it is precisely the nature, purpose and poetics of these paradoxographical collections which will be re-examined, in order to demonstrate that as texts which, as products of excerption and radical abbreviation, are very self-consciously created out of other texts, these purely textual *thaumata* ask us to wonder at the new possibilities provided by the world of the Hellenistic library, as much as at the oddities of the natural world. The paradoxographer's principles of arrangement may seem opaque at first glance, but a closer look will reveal that there is more to these texts than first meets the eye.

In the first section of this chapter, the range and scope of the material included in extant paradoxographical collections will be assessed and previous approaches to paradoxography in modern criticism briefly outlined. In the second section, the renewed interest in literary collections of natural *thaumata* in the early Hellenistic court of the Ptolemies will be examined in relation to a concomitant increase in the production, collation and collection of textual *thaumata* which took place in Alexandria during this same period. Sections three and four then turn to the relationship between the Hellenistic paradoxographical collection and its two most influential generic antecedents, ethnography and the Peripatetic writings of Aristotle's followers. The chapter concludes with a brief assessment of the relation of the paradoxographical collection to other general trends exhibited in Hellenistic texts of other literary genres.

3.1 Collecting *Thaumata*: The Emergence of the Paradoxographical Collection

Paradoxographical collections, which are essentially catalogues of marvels presented to the reader with little contextual information and seldom any authorial comment, begin to appear in the early Hellenistic period. The term 'paradoxographer' was not used in the Hellenistic period and is not found until the Byzantine age, where it first appears in the work of the twelfth-century scholar John Tzetzes (ὁ παραδοξογράφος, *Chiliades* 2.35.154).[4] Nonetheless, the corpus of these texts, when viewed together, reveals certain formal rhetorical properties and features which show that we are dealing with a well-defined mode of writing. The titles of these collections, which often include terms such as 'collection of marvels'

---

[4] It was Westermann's edition (1839) which introduced the term paradoxography to the modern world. Cf. Wenskus (2000) 309–12 on the history of paradoxography. Giannini's edition (1966) similarly groups collections of marvels under the term 'paradoxography'. On the notion of paradoxography as a distinct literary genre in antiquity see, Pajón Leyra (2011).

3.1 The Emergence of the Paradoxographical Collection

(θαυμάτων/θαυμασίων συναγωγή), 'collection of things contrary to expectation' (παραδόξων συναγωγή), 'concerning marvels' (περὶ θαυμασίων) or 'concerning things contrary to expectation' (περὶ παραδόξων), are preserved in ancient testimonia and suggest that the capacity of the entries contained within to provoke wonder is the primary focus of this mode of writing.[5] In their earliest form, these marvel-catalogues consist predominantly of strange zoological or geological observations which are starkly juxtaposed to one another.[6] These observations are cited from the works of previous (usually named) prose or verse authors, and are almost always completely devoid of any explanatory context. It is this lack of context which often renders the entries surprising and seemingly inexplicable. The paradoxographer does not claim to have undertaken autoptic research to confirm the truth of these *thaumata*, and the evidence behind each wondrous observation reported is almost always entirely neglected. Instead, the name of the original textual authority in which the *thauma* has been found is often included as an authorising gesture which implicitly guarantees the marvel's veracity.[7]

The first paradoxographical collection of which we have knowledge was produced by Callimachus in Alexandria: it is possible that he invented this mode of writing. The marvels in Callimachus' collection seem to have focused mainly on rivers and geological oddities and were arranged geographically. This is reflected in the collection's title, *Collection of Marvels from Every Land Arranged According to Places* (Θαυμάτων τῶν εἰς ἅπασαν τὴν γῆν κατὰ τόπους ὄντων συναγωγή).[8] We do not possess Callimachus'

---

[5] See Schepens and Delcroix (1996) 380 on the emergence of marvel-collections with titles along these lines in the Hellenistic period. See each author entry in *PGR* for testimonia of the titles of the respective paradoxographical collections. The titles of later Roman marvel-collections seem to have followed a similar pattern: the title of Cicero's *Admiranda* is preserved in Pliny's *HN* (31.12; 31.51), and Varro's *Gallus de admirandis* in Macrobius (*Sat.* 3.15.8). For a detailed overview of the lexicon of the marvellous used within paradoxographical collections, see Pajón Leyra (2011) 41–50.
[6] Peculiar ethnographic *thaumata* are very occasionally included, though this is extremely uncommon in the earliest collections. The move towards the inclusion of ethnographic entries in paradoxographical collections does, however, become more common as time goes on.
[7] See Schepens and Delcroix (1996) 382–9 on the inclusion of source 'citations' as a means of emphasising the credibility of the marvels reported in paradoxographical collections.
[8] This title is listed in the *Suda* s.v. Καλλίμαχος; see also the mention of Callimachus' collection of marvels (ἐκλογὴν τῶν παραδόξων) at Antigonus *Collection* 129. On

Reading *Thauma*

marvel-collection in its entirety, but a sizable chunk of it is excerpted and used in Antigonus' *Collection of Marvellous Investigations* (entries 129–73).[9] Antigonus introduces the Callimachean material in entry 129 of his own collection as follows:

129. πεποίηται δέ τινα καὶ ὁ Κυρηναῖος Καλλίμαχος ἐκλογὴν τῶν παραδόξων, ἧς ἀναγράφομεν ὅσα ποτὲ ἡμῖν ἐφαίνετο εἶναι ἀκοῆς ἄξια. φησὶν Εὔδοξον ἱστορεῖν, ὅτι ἐν τῇ κατὰ Ἱερὸν ὄρος θαλάττῃ τῆς Θρᾴκης ἐπιπολάζει κατά τινας χρόνους ἄσφαλτος. ἡ δὲ κατὰ Χελιδονίας ὅτι ἐπὶ πολὺν τόπον ἔχει γλυκείας πηγάς.

And Callimachus the Cyrenaean has also made a collection of marvels, from which I have recorded all which were seeming to me to be worthy of hearing. He [Callimachus] says that Eudoxus reports that bitumen comes to the surface at certain times in the sea in the region of the Sacred Mountain in Thrace. But the sea below the Chelidoniai [Islands] has sweet-tasting springs over a large space.

The following entries (164–6) are typical of the Callimachean geographical and geological marvels which Antigonus goes on to transmit at greater length:

164. ἐν δὲ Λυγκήσταις Θεόπομπον φάσκειν τι εἶναι ὕδωρ ὀξύ· τοὺς δὲ ἐκ τούτου πίνοντας ὥσπερ ἀπὸ τῶν οἴνων ἀλλοιοῦσθαι. καὶ τοῦθ' ὑπὸ πλειόνων μαρτυρεῖται.

He [i.e. Callimachus] says that Theopompus says that there is a type of bitter water among the Lyncestae. And those drinking from it become confused in their minds, just as they do from wine. And this is attested by several people.

165. τὸ δ' ἐκ τῆς πέτρας Ἀρμενίων ἐκπίπτον Κτησίαν ἱστορεῖν, ὅτι συμβάλλει ἰχθῦς μέλανας, ὧν τὸν ἀπογευσάμενον τελευτᾶν.

He [i.e Callimachus] says that Ctesias reports that the water flowing out from the rock in Armenia spits out black fish which kill whoever tastes them.

Callimachus' prose work and the strong interest in both paradoxography and aetiology which it exhibits, see Krevans (2004) 173–6 and (2011) 124–6.

[9] For the remaining fragments and testimonia of Callimachus' paradoxographical collection, see frs. 407–11 Pf. and *PGR* 15–19.

3.1 The Emergence of the Paradoxographical Collection

166. περὶ δὲ πυρὸς Κτησίαν φησὶν ἱστορεῖν, ὅτι περὶ τὴν τῶν Φασηλιτῶν χώραν ἐπὶ τοῦ τῆς Χιμαίρας ὄρους ἔστιν τὸ καλούμενον ἀθάνατον πῦρ· τοῦτο δέ, ἐὰν μέν τις ὕδωρ ἐμβάλῃ, καίεσθαι βελτίον, ἐὰν δὲ φορυτὸν ἐπιβαλὼν πήξῃ τις, σβέννυσθαι.

And concerning fire he [i.e. Callimachus] says that Ctesias reports that there is a so-called 'immortal fire' near the land of the Phaselitai on Mount Chimaera. And this fire, if someone casts water on it, burns more intensely, but if someone throws flammable material straight into it, is extinguished.

This strong interest in marvels involving water, fires and similar geological phenomena seems to have been a staple of the genre from Callimachus onwards, and is found in most of the other extant collections.[10]

Other paradoxographical collections dating from the Hellenistic period include *On Marvellous Things Heard* (Περὶ θαυμασίων ἀκουσμάτων), attributed to Aristotle in antiquity and transmitted to us within the Corpus Aristotelicum, but now almost universally attributed to an unknown writer of the Peripatetic school.[11] A collection entitled *Marvellous Investigations* (Ἱστορίαι θαυμάσιαι) by an author known as Apollonius Paradoxographus, dated to the second century BCE, also mostly consists of accounts of geographical and zoological marvels of the natural world.[12] There is some evidence that local historians of the third century BCE specialised in paradoxographical collections focusing on local marvels. The Lesbian Myrsilus of Methymna was said to have produced a work entitled *Investigations into Things Contrary to Expectation* (Ἱστορικὰ παράδοξα), while Nymphodorus supposedly composed

---

[10] For good overviews of the contents of the extant paradoxographical collections, see Ziegler (1949) 1137–66, Wenskus (2000) 309–12, Giannini (1963) and (1964), Schepens and Delcroix (1996), Hansen (1996) 2–16 and Pajón Leyra (2011).

[11] The pseudo-Aristotelian *On Marvellous Things Heard* consists of a 'core' of third-century BCE Peripatetic material which was expanded over time. On the place of the *On Marvellous Things Heard* within the third-century BCE paradoxographical tradition, see Flashar (1972) 50–5 and Vanotti (2007) 46–53.

[12] On Apollonius Paradoxographus, see also Pajón Leyra (2014) 304–5, which notes that there is an as yet unpublished Oxyrhynchus papyrus dating from the second century CE which preserves his *Marvellous Investigations* 49.1.1–6.

49

a geographically-circumscribed collection called *Concerning the Marvels of Sicily* (Περὶ τῶν ἐν Σικελίᾳ θαυμαζομένων). Forms of verse paradoxography also developed: as well as the aforementioned epigrams of Archelaus the Egyptian, whose work I will return to in more detail in the next section, we possess paradoxographical epigrams by Philostephanus of Cyrene, a pupil of Callimachus who seems to have built on his teacher's paradoxographical interests in a work entitled *On Marvellous Rivers* (Περὶ παραδόξων ποταμῶν).

As we move into the second century BCE the production of marvel-collections continues unabated. Athenaeus claims that Polemon of Ilium, a prominent periegetic writer, wrote an *On Marvels* (Περὶ θαυμασίων), while the historian and geographer Agatharchides of Cnidus is said to have produced a *Collection of Marvellous Winds* (Συναγωγὴ θαυμασίων ἀνέμων).[13] There are also three extant anonymous Greek paradoxographical collections from the Roman period. The *Paradoxographus Florentinus* concentrates entirely on marvels connected with water, while the *Paradoxographus Vaticanus* (second century CE) and *Paradoxographus Palatinus* (third century CE) exhibit the customary mixture of natural marvels.[14] Another collection from the second century CE survives: the *On Marvels* (Περὶ θαυμασίων) by Phlegon of Tralleis, a Greek freedman of the emperor Hadrian. In terms of focus, this collection differs from its antecedents, mostly concentrating on bizarre transformations and prodigies relating to human rather than animal bodies.[15] This shift towards material which focuses on marvels relating to the human rather than the animal realm is also seen in a fragmentary Oxyrhynchus papyrus (*P. Oxy.* II 218), which dates to the third century CE. It seems to preserve the remains of a paradoxographical collection by an unknown author with

---

[13] On Polemon's interest in marvels, see Angelucci (2014) 9–25.
[14] For an overview, translation and commentary of the *Paradoxographus Vaticanus*, see Stern (2008) 437–66.
[15] On the unusual focus of Phlegon's collection, see Hansen (1996) 11; on Phlegon's sources, see Shannon-Henderson (2020) 159–78.

3.1 The Emergence of the Paradoxographical Collection

descriptions of strange customs and other ethnographic details.[16] Modern critical assessments concerning the reasons for the emergence of paradoxographical collections in the third century BCE have tended to focus on three essential causes: decadence, decay and distraction.[17] The assumption that paradoxographical collections aim at a serious historiographical or scientific purpose which they manifestly fail to fulfil is the cause of much of the critical disappointment which this material has attracted. This disappointment is summed up by Schmid-Stählin's evaluation of paradoxography as '*ein Parasitengewächs am Baum der historischen und naturwissenschaftlichen Literatur*' (a parasitical growth on the tree of historical and scientific literature) – a peculiarly botanical image which would no doubt have appealed to the natural scientific interests of the paradoxographers themselves.[18] The consensus remains that the paradoxographical collection 'is to be regarded as a perverted, or misdirected product of Aristotelean research'.[19] Fraser's monumental study of Alexandria under the Ptolemies goes further in explaining the apparent degeneration of a once 'pure' (i.e. properly Greek) Aristotelian scientific spirit, by linking the alleged new interest in this material to a supposed native Egyptian (i.e. eastern and decadent) love of marvellous stories.[20] In addition to the irresistible lurch into the realm of the marvellous which the Egyptian land and people supposedly caused, Fraser proposes that Greeks in Alexandria were inevitably led towards an interest in paradoxography, and a concomitant and

---

[16] *P. Oxy.* II 218 was originally published in Grenfell and Hunt (1899) 35–9; for a new edition of and commentary on this papyrus, see now Pajón Leyra (2014) 304–30.

[17] For the rhetoric of 'decay' and 'decadence' which surrounds paradoxographical collections, see e.g. Giannini (1963) 248 on paradoxography as a degenerate and late development of original interest in the unknown. Cf. Wenskus (2000) 309–12: '19th- and 20th-cent. philologists regard the interest in *mirabilia* mostly as a phenomenon of decadence', and Schepens and Delcroix (1996) 378: 'time and again, paradoxography is depicted as a symptom of decay, as a degeneration of the original, healthy spirit of curiosity and inquiry that was the hallmark of Ionian culture from Homer onwards to Herodotos'.

[18] Schmid–Stählin (1920–4) 237, cited at Schepens and Delcroix (1996) 378.

[19] Fraser (1972a) 774. On the relationship between Aristotelian research and paradoxography, see Giannini (1963) 261–2, Romm (1992) 92, Stramaglia (2006) 303, Stern (2008) 442, Vanotti (2007) 25–6 and Pajón Leyra (2011) 241–63.

[20] On the supposed prominence of marvels in Egyptian stories, see Fraser (1972a) 675, 685.

unavoidable intellectual decline, through the presence of too much written material in the Alexandrian library: on this model, the presence of too many books in Egypt was catastrophic for the scientific and historiographical abilities of the ethnic Greeks, as it 'distracted their minds from speculation and historical reflection and turned them towards the collection and explanation of obscure events and phenomena'.[21] The groundless charge that the collection of *thaumata* represented an inexorable intellectual decline or deviation from reason prompted by contact with the Other, or a comforting escape from serious engagement with the increasing cultural complexities of the real world, is also present in more recent examinations of paradoxographical collections.[22] These assumptions about the supposed lack of intellectual interest or value in this material have also led to the allegation that these collections must have been aimed at a popular audience, which is also supposedly an automatically credulous audience.[23]

These views, however, do not take sufficient account of the status and meaning of wonder within the Greek literary, philosophical and scientific traditions by the time that the first Hellenistic marvel-collections began to appear. In short, they do not take sufficient account of *thauma* itself: it is only by thinking about the place of wonder within Greek culture that the point and purpose of these texts becomes clearer. In the following three sections the reasons for the strong focus on specific types of *thaumata* in these texts and the complicated relationships between paradoxography and related contemporary literary discourses will be examined.

3.2 Taming Zoological *Thaumata*: Archelaus the Egyptian's *Peculiar Forms* and the Ptolemaic Court

Over the course of the early third century BCE, the production of textual collections of marvels took off apace in line with an increasing general emphasis on the processes of ordering knowledge which took shape together with the development of great

---

[21] Fraser (1972a) 551.
[22] See Gabba (1981) 53 on the 'escapist' nature of paradoxography.
[23] See Giannini (1963) 248, Gabba (1981) 53, Jacob (1983) 122 and Hansen (1996) 9.

3.2 Archelaus the Egyptian's *Peculiar Forms*

libraries in various centres of power and learning.[24] The zoological and geological focus of most extant paradoxographical collections is significant when the wider ideological import of the taming and collection of actual natural *thaumata* under the rule of the early Hellenistic monarchs is considered. The textual collation of geological and zoological *thaumata* in Hellenistic paradoxographical collections represents a sort of symbolic control over the earth's most wondrous natural resources. Ptolemaic interest in natural *thaumata* certainly seems to have extended to the zoological as well as the geological realm. Many sources attest that the acquisition and subsequent display of exotic animals was a particular fascination of Ptolemy II Philadelphus.[25] According to the second-century BCE historian Agatharchides of Cnidus (see fr. 1 Burstein), whose *On the Erythraean Sea* focuses on Ptolemaic exploration of areas around the Red Sea, Philadelphus was the first Ptolemy to pursue elephant hunting and similar exotic zoological endeavours with the aim of bringing together in one location animals which nature had separated – in other words, Philadephus was a collector of zoological *thaumata*.

The most famous report of Philadelphus' zoological obsessions is found in a lengthy account in Diodorus Siculus, probably derived from Agatharchides' work. Diodorus describes the king's love of hunting, collecting and displaying unusual animals in Alexandria (3.36–7), and claims that Ptolemy not only delighted in hunting and capturing elephants for the very practical purpose of waging war but even valued the acquisition of unknown beasts for the sake of widening the knowledge of 'unseen and unusually formed' (ἀθεωρήτους καὶ παραδόξους φύσεις) creatures among his fellow Greeks.[26] A group of opportunistic hunters soon realised

---

[24] For recent appraisals of the relationship between the acquisition and collection of texts and imperial political and cultural power in ancient Greece and Rome, see e.g. Jacob (2013a) 57–81, Woolf (2013) 6–9, Johnstone (2014) 347–93. Cf. König and Whitmarsh (2007) 8–10 on the Hellenistic antecedents for the textualisation and ordering of knowledge in the Roman Imperial period. On the library of Alexandria and Ptolemaic power, see e.g. Erskine (1995) 38–48 and Gutzwiller (2007) 19–23.

[25] See Hubbell (1935) 68–7, Rice (1983) 86–7 and Burstein (1989) 4–10 on Ptolemy Philadelphus' particular interest in collecting unusual and exotic zoological specimens.

[26] Cf. also Diod. Sic. 3.18.4 and Strabo *Geography* 16.4.5–7 and 17.1.5 on Ptolemaic elephant hunting. See Casson (1993) 247–60 on Ptolemy II's particular interest in the acquisition of elephants; see also Scullard (1974) 120–45 and Alonso Troncoso (2013)

that great rewards were at stake for capturing rare animals, and embarked on the dangerous, and eventually successful, pursuit of a gigantic, 'thirty cubit long snake' (ἕνα τῶν ὄφεων τριάκοντα πηχῶν).[27] The animal was captured and tamed, Ptolemy was mightily pleased, and the snake was immediately put on display, where it soon became the 'greatest and most incredible sight for the tourists who enter his kingdom' (τοῖς εἰς τὴν βασιλείαν παραβάλλουσι ξένοις μέγιστον παρεχόμενον καὶ παραδοξότατον θέαμα). According to the account of Hellenistic writer Callixeinus of Rhodes (c. second century BCE), which is preserved in excerpted form in Athenaeus' *Deipnosophistae* (197c–203b), astonishing and unusual animals from far-off lands subject to Ptolemaic influence were among the impressive creatures displayed by Philadephus in the 270s BCE during his famous Dionysian procession through Alexandria, including 'one hundred and thirty Ethiopian sheep, three hundred sheep from Arabia and twenty from Euboia, twenty six Indian and eight Ethiopian cows, one white bear, fourteen leopards, sixteen panthers, four caracals, three panther cubs, one giraffe and one Ethiopian rhinoceros' (πρόβατα Αἰθιοπικὰ ἑκατὸν τριάκοντα, Ἀράβια τριακόσια, Εὐβοϊκὰ εἴκοσι, ὁλόλευκοι βόες Ἰνδικοὶ εἴκοσι ἕξ, Αἰθιοπικοὶ ὀκτώ, ἄρκτος λευκὴ μεγάλη μία, παρδάλεις ιδ', πάνθηροι ις', λυγκία δ', ἄρκηλοι γ', καμηλοπάρδαλις μία, ῥινόκερως Αἰθιοπικὸς α', 201b–c).[28]

It is now worth returning to the entry from Antigonus' *Collection of Marvellous Investigations* cited at the beginning of this chapter – Archelaus the Egyptian's epigram about the spontaneous generation of vipers from rotting human spinal marrow –

254–70 on the significance of the possession of elephants in the self-fashioning of Ptolemaic kingship in the Hellenistic period.

[27] Cf. Ael. *NA* 16.39, where the story of two huge Ethiopian snakes brought to Alexandria for Ptolemy Philadelphus is recounted; three large snakes were also presented to his successor Ptolemy Euergetes. There is also evidence preserved in the Zenon archive that the presentation of unusual animals to Ptolemy could play a useful political role in this period: see *P. Cair. Zen.* I 59075, a letter dated to 257 BCE which describes the presentation to Ptolemy of several rare wild animals and crossbreeds by a local ruler (see Edgar (1925) for the text and Hauben (1984–6) 89–93 for discussion of how the animals presented in this letter relate to Ptolemy's zoological interests).

[28] On the significance of this part of Ptolemy's procession and its use of Dionysus' triumphal return from India as an opportunity to display exotic animals, see Rice (1983) 82–99.

3.2 Archelaus the Egyptian's *Peculiar Forms*

with the wider ideological import of the taming and collection of actual natural *thaumata* under the rule of the early Ptolemies in mind. Two fragments of similar epigrams belonging to Archelaus are cited earlier in the *Collection*, along with a contextual note from Antigonus which reveals that the Egyptian epigrammatist was probably attached to the Alexandrian court of either Ptolemy II Philadelphus (309–246 BCE) or Ptolemy III Euergetes (c. 284–222).[29] Archelaus' court context becomes clear when Antigonus introduces his poems by explicitly stating that the main purpose of the poet's production of epigrammatic *thaumata* was to elucidate paradoxical zoological matters for the reigning Ptolemy (*Collection* 19):

καί τις Ἀρχέλαος Αἰγύπτιος τῶν ἐν ἐπιγράμμασιν ἐξηγουμένων τὰ παράδοξα τῷ Πτολεμαίῳ περὶ μὲν τῶν σκορπίων οὕτως εἴρηκεν·

    εἰς ὑμᾶς κροκόδειλον ἀποφθίμενον διαλύει,
    σκορπίοι, ἡ πάντα ζῳοθετοῦσα φύσις.

περὶ δὲ τῶν σφηκῶν·

    ἐκ νέκυος ταύτην ἵππου γράψασθε γενέθλην,
    σφῆκας· ἴδ' ἐξ οἵων οἷα τίθησι φύσις.

And a certain Archelaus the Egyptian, the one who explained astonishing matters to Ptolemy with his epigrams, spoke in this way concerning scorpions:

Into you Nature dissolves a putrefied crocodile,
    O scorpions, Nature who makes everything alive.

And like this concerning wasps:

Make a note of this birth from the corpse of a horse: wasps!
    Look! What Nature makes from such material!

The epigram about the spontaneous generation of snakes with which this chapter began, along with these poetic fragments about the generation of scorpions from dead crocodiles and wasps from dead horses, are most likely derived from an epigram

---

[29] At *FGE* 21 Page suggests that Archelaus' patron was either Ptolemy II or III; Berrey (2017) 61 thinks Ptolemy III is most probable, as does Fraser (1972a) 779; Voutiras (2000) 388–9, however, suggests that Ptolemy IV Philopator may have been the monarch in question.

collection by Archelaus entitled *Peculiar Forms* (Ἰδιοφυῆ), of which we have other testimonia and fragments relating similar sorts of zoological marvels.[30] In fact, a few other marvels described in these surviving fragments also focus specifically on examples of wondrous spontaneous generation, just as those in Antigonus' paradoxographical collection do.[31]

The fragments of Archelaus' epigrams preserved in Antigonus' *Collection* thus provide us with a tantalising window onto what seems to have been a flourishing tradition of Ptolemaic verse paradoxography. These epigrams for Ptolemy reflect the wider ideological import of the acquiring and taming of actual natural *thaumata* in third-century BCE Alexandria. The presentation of such poems to the king himself (whichever Ptolemy he may have been) seems even more apt in such a context. In fact, Archelaus' verse paradoxography can be seen as a symbolic textual manifestation of a broader desire for the

[30] See *FGE* 20–4 and *SH* 125–9 for the longer extant epigrams; cf. *PGR* 24–8 for a comprehensive overview of all the remaining fragments. On the evidence for Archelaus' life and poetry, see *FGE* 20–4, Fraser (1972a) 778–9 and Berrey (2017) 61–2. The title *Peculiar Forms*, the work which Archelaus seems to have been best known for, is specified at Athenaeus *Deipnosophistae* 409c, Diog. Laert. 2.17 and Σ ad. Nic. *Ther.* 823. On the basis of the title Fraser (1972a) 778 asserts that the *Peculiar Forms* 'was probably in prose', but this was before the discovery of the Posidippus Milan Papyrus, when the use of such 'technical' titles in connection with epigrams was thought to be almost impossible. Berrey (2017) 61 also states that Archelaus produced prose works, but there is no proof of this: all of the extant fragments of Archelaus' work are in verse. In addition to the explicit mention of epigrams in connection with Archelaus at Antigonus *Collection* 19, we are also told by Varro (*Rust.* 3.16.4) that Archelaus wrote 'in epigrams' (*Archelaus in epigrammate ait* ...). It is possible that more than one collection of poems with this title was produced under the early Ptolemies. In fact, a Ptolemaic king may himself have written a poetic work entitled *Peculiar Forms*, though the evidence for this is debated: see *FGE* 84–5, *SH* 712, Maass (1892) 79, Fraser (1972a) 592 (alongside Fraser (1972b) 841 n. 305), (1972a) 780 and (1972b) 1090, Martin (1974) 10, Voutiras (2000) 392–3 and Berrey (2017) 31, 62.

[31] See also Varro, *Rust.* 3.16.4 for other verses from Archelaus on the generation of bees from dead cows, wasps from dead horses and bees from dead calves. Other zoological *thaumata* which later ancient writers claim Archelaus wrote about include: moray eels, which have teeth similar to vipers and come up onto the land to mate with them (see Σ ad. Nic. *Ther.* 823); a 'katablepas' (lit. 'downward-looking' animal), which seems to have been a bull/antelope-like creature capable of turning living beings into stone like a Gorgon (see Athenaeus *Deipnosophistae* 409c and cf. 221b; cf. also Plin. *HN* 8.77 and Ael. *NH* 7.5); a basilisk snake (see Ael. *NH* 2.7); female partridges which conceive when they hear the voices of male partridges (see Varro, *Rust.* 3.2.4); goats which breathe through the ears instead of through the nostrils (see Varro, *Rust.* 2.3.5); and hares whose age can be determined from the number of their orifices (see Varro, *Rust.* 3.12.4–5 and Plin. *HN* 8.218).

3.2 Archelaus the Egyptian's *Peculiar Forms*

possession, subjection and classification of natural *thaumata* in the Ptolemaic period.[32] Although the strange biological processes which form the content of Archelaus' epigrams may seem uncontrollable and unruly, the epigrammatist's smooth and sophisticated poetic handling of these natural wonders is anything but disorderly. In fact, the epigram form, with its relative tautness of expression and general insistence on controlled and pointed diction, provides an ideal medium in which to articulate this symbolic taming of natural wonders. But the ability to arouse *thauma* is not confined to verse alone. As we shall see, the clipped form of the prose entries in paradoxographical collections has many similarities to the epigram form in terms of the creation of wonder through the curtailment of wider contextual framing, and both the prose and verse resources of the Hellenistic library were utilised to yield new *thaumata* as writers worked to reorganise and re-form knowledge itself in an effort to create impressive new bodies of purely textual marvels.[33]

But before turning to consider the way in which this reorganisation of knowledge was accomplished at the level of the individual paradoxographical collection, the emergence of these texts in this period must be examined in relation to two of their most influential generic antecedents: the treatment of the marvels of nature in the ethnographic writing of the past, and then the place of *thauma* and *thaumata* within the philosophical and scientific framework created by Aristotle and his Peripatetic followers.

---

[32] Cf. Schepens and Delcroix (1996) 406, who suggest that the activities of paradoxographers can be seen as a 'literary counterpart to the activities of explorers and hunters'. See also Bing (2005) 135 on Posidippus' *Lithika* as an expression of Ptolemaic interest in expanding cultural and scientific knowledge in conjunction with their desire for territorial expansion and control over material wealth and, more generally, Romm (1992) 84 on Greek travel narratives and ethnographic accounts of eastern lands written in the wake of Alexander's conquest as texts 'with imperial ambitions of their own, paralleling at a cognitive level the sallies of the great generals of the age'. Cf. Woolf (2011) 80–8 on the connection between wonder and Roman imperialism in Latin ethnographic writing.

[33] On the paradoxographers' dependence on the world of the library, see Schepens and Delcroix (1996) 388–9.

3.3 *Thaumata* and the Ethnographic Tradition: Herodotus and the Edges of the Earth

As noted earlier, modern scholars have often berated the writers of paradoxographical collections for their lack of adherence to a proper sense of historiographical or scientific purpose. But to expect that a paradoxographer was attempting to produce historiography or Aristotelian science in the first place is to misunderstand the fact that this type of text has its own unique aesthetic and form. This is not, however, to say that traditions of Greek historical and scientific writing did not play influential parts in the paradoxographer's conception of his own art. In this respect the work of Herodotus in particular looms large in the background. The first half of the *Histories* shows the expectation that ethnographic discussions should include mention of any particular *thaumata* (or rather *thomata*, in the Ionian dialect of Herodotus' work).[34] Like the marvels of the epic tradition, actual physical entities which are designated as Herodotean *thomata* are often visually impressive objects of astonishing magnitude or beauty.[35] But it is not visual objects alone which constitute Herodotean *thomata*: unusual customs and traditions discovered in the course of the historian's inquiry are equally likely to be held up as marvels which simultaneously foster curiosity about other cultures while testing the boundaries of belief and credulity.[36] Paradoxographical collections, which put forth a series of *thaumata* culled from the works of other authorities, similarly present the reader with reports which invite questions about the believability of previous traditions, although, unlike Herodotus' *Histories*, there is little evidence of the paradoxographer's own weighing-up of the evidence for each report, as every marvel is presented as an indisputable fact. As already noted, the focus of Hellenistic marvel-collections also remains firmly fixed on the *thaumata* of nature rather than

---

[34] See Jacoby (1913) 331–2, Hartog (1988) 230–1, Hunzinger (1995) 48 n. 6 and Munson (2001) 234–42 on the inclusion of a region's *thaumata* as a conventional element of ethnographic descriptions.

[35] On the strongly (though not exclusively) visual emphasis of Herodotean wonder, see Hartog (1988) 230–7, Hunzinger (1995) 50–1 and Priestley (2014) 58.

[36] Wonder and inquiry are strongly linked in the *Histories*: see Munson (2001) 233–4, 259 and Priestley (2014) 70.

3.3 *Thaumata* and the Ethnographic Tradition

those of human culture, whereas Herodotus does not make such firm distinctions.[37] However, in terms of the form in which accounts of *thaumata* relating to distant lands and peoples are narrated in the *Histories* there are some very significant similarities to the way *thaumata* are presented in later paradoxographical collections.

For example, it has been noted that Herodotean *thomata* tend to provide a temporary excursion from the primary narrative of historical events in the *Histories*, and that multiple marvels often cluster together within the first four books of Herodotus' work.[38] Rather than offering up one marvel about distant lands at a time, Herodotus presents us with multiple descriptions of increasingly bizarre *thomata* in a dense, almost catalogic form which perhaps reflects the supposed abundance of such strange and wondrous phenomena in exotic locations.[39] This tendency is nowhere more apparent than in Herodotus' discussion of the inhabited lands at the edges of the earth (the *eschatiai*), in which the creation of a more extreme sense of wonder in the reader is emphasised as the narrative moves further and further out into descriptions of the world's extremities.[40]

It is in book 3 of the *Histories* that we are introduced to a prolonged discussion of the inherently wondrous nature of the world's most extreme peripheries. Herodotus begins his description with the basic contention that 'the furthest edges of the known world possess the finest goods' (αἱ δ' ἐσχατιαί κως τῆς οἰκεομένης τὰ κάλλιστα ἔλαχον, 3.106) simply by dint of being located near the edges of the earth. It is thus clear from the start that the geographical extremes of the known world are to be linked with

---

[37] See Clarke (2018) 136–52 on natural and man-made marvels in Herodotus.
[38] On the connection between Herodotean *thoma* and narrative excursuses in the *Histories*, see Hartog (1988) 234, Gould (1989) 58 and Hunzinger (1995) 62–3.
[39] See Romm (1992) 91–3 on the tendency in the ethnographic tradition towards the creation of a catalogic effect in descriptions of marvels at the earth's edges, and the effect this has on Herodotus' presentation of *thomata* in the *Histories*.
[40] See Karttunen (2002) 457–74 on the connection between *thomata* and the earth's edges in the *Histories*; cf. also Rood (2006) 297–8 and Clarke (2018) 146–9. On the increasing prevalence of encounters with the marvellous the further one travels towards the peripheries, away from the Greek 'centre' of the world, see Redfield (1985) 110 and Gould (1989) 94. Cf. also Hartog (1988) 232–3, Hunzinger (1995) 62 n. 60 and Priestley (2014) 58 on the increasing 'escalation' of wonder in the *Histories*' narrative of the *eschatiai*.

Reading *Thauma*

extremities of description and content. Herodotus then becomes more specific and first mentions 'the region near the eastern edge of the known world, India' (τοῦτο μὲν γὰρ πρὸς τὴν ἠῶ ἐσχάτη τῶν οἰκεομένων ἡ Ἰνδική ἐστι, 3.106). He has already described this land of strange geological and zoological *thomata* in detail in the immediately preceding sections (3.98–105). For example, earlier in that description we were treated to the fabulous report of the extraction of gold in India involving 'ants smaller than dogs and bigger than foxes' (μύρμηκες μεγάθεα ἔχοντες κυνῶν μὲν ἐλάσσω, ἀλωπέκων δὲ μέζω, 3.102). The reader has thus already been primed by the earlier descriptions of marvels for the parallel and comparably wondrous collection of fine objects said to be found in the land Herodotus turns to next, 'the region near the southern edge of the regions of the known world, Arabia' (πρὸς δ' αὖ μεσαμβρίης ἐσχάτη Ἀραβίη τῶν οἰκεομένων χωρέων ἐστί, 3.107).

In the dense description of the marvels of Arabia which follows, Herodotus adopts a mode of description which later paradoxographical collections come to echo: a compact list of increasingly marvellous objects and customs is quickly built up to reinforce the impression that this distant land is teeming with *thomata* as yet unfamiliar to the Greek world.[41] Herodotus first lays out Arabia's special claim to possession of the most beautiful and wondrous objects by beginning with a description of the region's abundance in rare spices, noting that 'out of all lands this one alone produces frankincense, myrrh, cassia, cinnamon and gum mastic' (ἐν δὲ ταύτῃ λιβανωτός τέ ἐστι μούνῃ χωρέων πασέων φυόμενος καὶ σμύρνη καὶ κασίη καὶ κινάμωμον καὶ λήδανον, 3.107). He then goes on to treat the collection of each of these spices in turn, with the exception of myrrh, which he claims is the only one that is easy to obtain. It becomes apparent that rather than simply listing successive fabulous stories of the collection of each spice, Herodotus is linking the transitions between each section of his excursus in a skilful and purposeful way, connecting further

[41] Cf. Romm (1992) 84–93 on the similar emphasis placed on abundance and diversity in Greek descriptions of the *thaumata* of India: this emphasis on the abundance of the biological forms found in such places increases the sense that the lands at the edges of the earth are unruly and disorganised and therefore in need of 'conquering' by the Greeks in order to tame their strangeness.

3.3 *Thaumata* and the Ethnographic Tradition

relevant discussion of the wondrous nature of Arabia's zoology to his wider description of spice collection in order to present a forceful image of this region's abundance in every sort of marvel belonging to the natural world. The effect of these complex transitions is crucial in creating the escalating sense of wonder which binds the description of Arabia to the historian's wider argument about the earth's extremities.[42]

This becomes clearer when we examine each method of spice collection. The first spice to be gathered is frankincense (3.107). The action begins when storax, a fragrant tree resin, is burnt to ward off the 'winged snakes, small in size and multicoloured in form' (ὄφιες ὑπόπτεροι, σμικροὶ τὰ μεγάθεα, ποικίλοι τὰ εἴδεα, 3.107) which guard the frankincense: this then allows the spice to be collected safely. In passing, Herodotus notes that these winged snakes are 'the ones which attack Egypt' (οὗτοι οἵ περ ἐπ' Αἴγυπτον ἐπιστρατεύονται, 3.107) on a seasonal basis. This links back to an earlier moment in the *Histories'* Egyptian *logos* (2.75), where Herodotus makes a controversial autoptic claim concerning these same Arabian snakes:

ἔστι δὲ χῶρος τῆς Ἀραβίης κατὰ Βουτοῦν πόλιν μάλιστά κῃ κείμενος, καὶ ἐς τοῦτο τὸ χωρίον ἦλθον πυνθανόμενος περὶ τῶν πτερωτῶν ὀφίων· ἀπικόμενος δὲ εἶδον ὀστέα ὀφίων καὶ ἀκάνθας πλήθεϊ μὲν ἀδύνατα ἀπηγήσασθαι, σωροὶ δὲ ἦσαν ἀκανθέων καὶ μεγάλοι καὶ ὑποδεέστεροι καὶ ἐλάσσονες ἔτι τούτων, πολλοὶ δὲ ἦσαν οὗτοι. ἔστι δὲ ὁ χῶρος οὗτος, ἐν τῷ αἱ ἄκανθαι κατακεχύαται, τοιόσδε τις, ἐσβολὴ ἐξ ὀρέων στεινῶν ἐς πεδίον μέγα, τὸ δὲ πεδίον τοῦτο συνάπτει τῷ Αἰγυπτίῳ πεδίῳ. λόγος δὲ ἐστὶ ἅμα τῷ ἔαρι πτερωτοὺς ὄφις ἐκ τῆς Ἀραβίης πέτεσθαι ἐπ' Αἰγύπτου, τὰς δὲ ἴβις τὰς ὄρνιθας ἀπαντώσας ἐς τὴν ἐσβολὴν ταύτης τῆς χώρης οὐ παριέναι τοὺς ὄφις ἀλλὰ κατακτείνειν.

There is a place in Arabia very near the city of Buto, and I went to this region to learn about the winged snakes. When I arrived there I saw a huge number of bones and backbones of snakes, impossible to describe in full: there were heaps of backbones, some large, some smaller, and some smaller still: and these were very many. And this place where the backbones lie, is something like this: a pass out of the narrows of the mountains into a broad plain, and this plain joins with the plain of Egypt. It is said that at the start of spring winged snakes fly from Arabia towards Egypt, but the ibis birds meet them in the mountain pass and not only do they prevent the entry of the winged snakes, they kill them.

---

[42] See Pelling (2000a) 172 on the 'host of careful transitions' in book 2 of the *Histories*: Herodotus makes use of a similar method here.

The second mention in book 3 of these marvellous flying snakes thus adds to the sense that we are moving towards an increasingly wondrous sphere, as the narrative moves geographically to the southernmost limit of the world. If – Herodotus almost seems to say to us – the mere remains of these dead winged Arabian snakes caused me to stop and wonder in Egypt, that 'land more full of marvels than any other' (πλεῖστα θωμάσια ἔχει ἢ ἡ ἄλλη πᾶσα χώρη, 2.35), then how much *more* marvellous is Arabia, home to trees full of live winged snakes? Arabia here becomes the producer and point of origin of one of Egypt's most bizarre zoological wonders, and the overall point is clear: the further out from the Hellenic centre of the world one travels, the more marvellous the natural phenomena one witnesses or hears about are likely to be.

The tendency of *thoma* to provide opportunities for continued, rolling excursuses is also manifested in Herodotus' mention of these creatures within his broader description of Arabia's rare and wondrous spices, for the reappearance of the winged snakes now provides him with the opportunity to transition smoothly into an impressive display of Ionian scientific thinking as the historian suddenly embarks upon a complex discussion of several important principles underpinning the broader biological balance of relative numbers of predators and prey in the animal world. In relation to the winged snakes in particular he tells us that, according to the Arabians, such is the ferociousness and mobility of these creatures that, if nature failed to intervene and instead left their reproduction unchecked, 'the entire land would be filled up with these snakes' (ὡς πᾶσα ἂν γῆ ἐπίμπλατο τῶν ὀφίων τούτων, 3.108), inevitably leading to the presence of too many of the fearsome predators in the world as a whole. But as it is the proportion of predators and prey remains balanced because of the fact that the female winged snake kills the male during mating and is in turn then killed when 'her young, exacting vengeance for their father, gnaw through their mother while still in her stomach' (τῷ γονέϊ τιμωρέοντα ἔτι ἐν τῇ γαστρὶ ἐόντα τὰ τέκνα διεσθίει τὴν μητέρα, 3.109).[43] The

---

[43] On this passage, see Thomas (2000) 139–50. On account of the zoological focus of Herodotus' discussion at 3.108–9 his reports of two further wondrous examples of unusual and violent animal parturition in this passage – the first involving the reproduction of vipers, the second about lionesses and the birth of lion cubs – are among the very

3.3 Thaumata and the Ethnographic Tradition

theoretical and scientific nature of this discussion about the reproductive peculiarities of winged snakes and other, more conventional predators only serves to make the zoology of Arabia seem both simultaneously familiar and strange, as well as giving an impression of scientific accuracy and authority far removed from the increasingly fabulous descriptions about to come.

After this zoological meditation Herodotus moves swiftly back to the theme of Arabian spice collection, shifting from winged snakes to other unconventional 'winged creatures, very much like bats in form, which squeak dreadfully' (θηρία πτερωτά, τῇσι νυκτερίσι προσείκελα μάλιστα, καὶ τέτριγε δεινόν, 3.110) and attack men bound in protective ox-hides as they collect the spice cassia. The vague description of the winged animal is important because there is a gradual movement in this section from the winged snake – a creature which is definitely not a bird but nevertheless happens to have wings – to this bat-like creature, which has more in common with a true bird than a winged snake, but still does not seem to be a bird proper. The reason why Herodotus focuses above all else on the winged nature of this ambiguous bird-like creature becomes clear when we reach the description of the next method of obtaining an exotic Arabian spice: the collection of cinnamon with the help of giant birds.[44] Wings are once more at the forefront of our attention, as Herodotus describes in detail (3.111) how the giant Arabian birds first carry the cinnamon off to nests which men cannot reach. These birds are soon lured back down to the ground by men who placed dead oxen, asses and beasts of burden below the nests. After flying down the birds collect these offerings and carry them back to the cinnamon-filled nests, which cannot bear the extra weight and fall down, cinnamon in tow. This method of spice-collection is even explicitly marked as an event which is 'even more wondrous than the previous methods' (ἔτι τούτων θωμαστότερον, 3.111), highlighting Herodotus' concern to create

few *thaumata* that are explicitly cited from his work in later paradoxographical collections: see Antigonus *Collection* 21 on both the lioness and the viper and Ps-Arist. *Mir. ausc.* 165 on the viper.

[44] Detienne (1994) 14–20 emphasises the contrasts and similarities between the collection of cassia and cinnamon through the use of specifically bird-like animals, but does not focus on the use of winged creatures as a means of transitioning from marvel to marvel in the Arabian excursus as a whole.

63

an ongoing escalation of wonder in his narrative of the earth's edges.

This sense of escalating wonder is further reinforced when the collection and production of the next spice, a fragrant gum called ledanon, is once more explicitly marked as 'even more wondrous than the previous one' (ἔτι τούτου θωμασιώτερον, 3.112). Unlike the previous methods of spice-collection, the gathering of Arabian ledanon does not involve a wondrous winged creature: the substance is instead 'found in the beards of male goats just like gum from trees' (τῶν γὰρ αἰγῶν τῶν τράγων ἐν τοῖσι πώγωσι εὑρίσκεται ἐγγινόμενον, οἷον γλοιός, ἀπὸ τῆς ὕλης, 3.112). At first this sudden movement away from wondrous winged creatures might strike the reader as rather arbitrary, but the placement of this specific method of collection at the very end of Herodotus' catalogue of spicy Arabian marvels is actually an important point of transition into the next segment of the broader Arabian excursus.[45] This is because fragrant-gum-producing goats span across (and can be included within) the two very specific – and very diverse – categories of Arabian *thaumata* found in Herodotus' ethnographic catalogue of marvels: marvellous spices and wondrous caprids. The significance of this skilful placement of this specific marvel at this precise moment in the catalogue becomes even clearer when we examine how this choice permits the seamless narrative shift from spice-bearing goats to two astonishing kinds of sheep (3.113):

δύο δὲ γένεα ὀίων σφι ἔστι θώματος ἄξια, τὰ οὐδαμόθι ἑτέρωθι ἔστι. τὸ μὲν αὐτῶν ἕτερον ἔχει τὰς οὐρὰς μακράς, τριῶν πήχεων οὐκ ἐλάσσονας, τὰς εἴ τις ἐπείη σφι ἐπέλκειν, ἕλκεα ἂν ἔχοιεν ἀνατριβομένων πρὸς τῇ γῇ τῶν οὐρέων· νῦν δ' ἅπας τις τῶν ποιμένων ἐπίσταται ξυλουργέειν ἐς τοσοῦτο· ἁμαξίδας γὰρ ποιεῦντες ὑποδέουσι αὐτὰς τῇσι οὐρῇσι, ἑνὸς ἑκάστου κτήνεος τὴν οὐρὴν ἐπὶ ἁμαξίδα ἑκάστην καταδέοντες. τὸ δὲ ἕτερον γένος τῶν ὀίων τὰς οὐρὰς πλατέας φορέουσι καὶ ἐπὶ πῆχυν πλάτος.

They have two kinds of sheep worthy of wonder which are found nowhere else. One type has a long tail, no less than three cubits long. If one were to allow them to drag these tails, they would wound themselves through rubbing them on the

---

[45] These wondrous cinnamon birds also turn up as a *thauma* at Antigonus *Collection* 43, an entry which cites Aristotle's discussion of these strange creatures at *Hist. an.* 616a6–12.

3.3 *Thaumata* and the Ethnographic Tradition

ground. But instead every shepherd there knows at least this much carpentry: enough to make little carts which they tie under the tail, binding each sheep's tail to its own cart. The other kind of sheep has a tail a full cubit broad.

With these final examples of Arabia's natural marvels Herodotus' excursus on the southernmost limit of the world ends. Subsequent brief surveys of the world's westernmost limits in Ethiopia (3.114) and northernmost limits in the land of the Arimaspians (3.116) are then followed by Herodotus' final conclusion that 'the edges of the earth possess those things which seem to be finest and rarest' (τὰ κάλλιστα δοκέοντα ἡμῖν εἶναι καὶ σπανιώτατα ἔχειν αὐταί, 3.116). With this statement – a very clear echo and ring composition of Herodotus' opening declaration that 'the furthest edges of the known world possess the finest goods' (αἱ δ' ἐσχατιαί κως τῆς οἰκεομένης τὰ κάλλιστα ἔλαχον, 3.106) – the discussion of the nature of the inherently wondrous properties of the earth's edges concludes.

The collection of multiple marvels narrated in a dense, almost catalogue-like style and connected through oblique transitional motifs which we find in Herodotus' Arabian excursus is a literary form echoed in the structure of later paradoxographical collections. In these texts the connections between entries are also often not as arbitrary as they may at first appear.[46] On closer inspection, most paradoxographical collections can be seen to link *thaumata* together in loose thematic clusters which enable the reader to consider the possible relationships between each marvel.[47] Moreover, when entries are viewed in relation to one another, and within the wider context of the work as a

---

[46] Priestley (2014) 84 notes that paradoxographical works bear some resemblance in their structure to Herodotus' marvel-passages, but I would go much further and suggest that the effect upon the reader shows similarities in both cases, as does the use of complex transitional techniques. Cf. Romm (1992) 91 for the suggestion that the catalogic effect of listing ethnographic *thaumata* was a key aspect of Ctesias' writings on distant lands, though the fragmentary nature of his extant work makes it difficult to ascertain fully how this effect was created in practice. Nichols' suggestion (2018: 3–16) that Ctesias' *Indica*, with its inclusion of many marvels and focus on a single geographical area, can be seen as a 'bridge' between fifth-century BCE historiography and third-century paradoxographical collections is certainly compelling, though the fragmentary state of the *Indica* once again makes detailed comparison difficult.

[47] Jacob (1983) 128, Hansen (1996) 4–5 and Krevans (2011) 125 have recognised the importance of thematically connected sequences of *thaumata* within Antigonus' paradoxographical collection.

Reading *Thauma*

whole, it is usually possible to discern more complicated principles of arrangement, whereby certain keywords are used to create implicit and explicit links which allow skilful transitions between entries.

A fresh example, a sequence of zoological *thaumata*, taken this time from the pseudo-Aristotelian *On Marvellous Things Heard*, demonstrates these principles of loose thematic ordering and shows how one of the aims of the paradoxographical collection is to allow new and unexpected connections to be drawn between previously disparate *thaumata* (9–12):

9. αἱ ἐν Κεφαλληνίᾳ αἶγες οὐ πίνουσιν, ὡς ἔοικεν, ὥσπερ καὶ τἆλλα τετράποδα, καθ' ἡμέραν δὲ πρὸς τὸ πέλαγος ἀντία τὰ πρόσωπα ποιήσασαι χάσκουσιν εἰσδεχόμεναι τὰ πνεύματα. — The goats in Cephallenia do not drink, it seems, as other quadrupeds do. Instead, every day, after turning their faces towards the sea, they open their mouths wide and take in the air.

10. φασὶν ἐν Συρίᾳ τῶν ἀγρίων ὄνων ἕνα ἀφηγεῖσθαι τῆς ἀγέλης, ἐπειδὰν δέ τις νεώτερος ὢν τῶν πώλων ἐπί τινα θήλειαν ἀναβῇ, τὸν ἀφηγούμενον θυμοῦσθαι, καὶ διώκειν ἕως τούτου ἕως ἂν καταλάβῃ τὸν πῶλον, καὶ ὑποκύψας ἐπὶ τὰ ὀπίσθια σκέλη τῷ στόματι ἀποσπάσῃ τὰ αἰδοῖα. — They say that in Syria one wild ass within the herd is the leader. And whenever one of the younger ones mounts a female, the leader of the herd becomes angry, and he chases the young ass until he catches him, and stooping under his hind legs he tears off his genitals with his mouth.

11. τὰς χελώνας λέγουσιν, ὅταν ἔχεως φάγωσιν, ἐπεσθίειν τὴν ὀρίγανον, ἐὰν δὲ μὴ θᾶττον εὕρῃ, ἀποθνῄσκειν. πολλοὺς δ' ἀποπειράζοντας τῶν ἀγραυλούντων εἰ τοῦτ' ἀληθές ἐστιν, ὅταν ἴδωσιν αὐτὴν τοῦτο πράττουσαν, ἐκτίλλειν τὴν ὀρίγανον· τοῦτο δὲ ὅταν ποιήσωσι, μετὰ μικρὸν αὐτὴν ὁρᾶσθαι ἀποθνῄσκουσαν. — They say that tortoises, whenever they eat vipers, eat wild marjoram afterwards, and if they do not find any quickly, they die. And many rural people, making trial of this to see whether it is true, pull up wild marjoram whenever they see a tortoise, and whenever they do this they see the tortoise die within a short space of time.

3.3 *Thaumata* and the Ethnographic Tradition

12. τὸ τῆς ἰκτίδος λέγεται αἰδοῖον εἶναι οὐχ ὅμοιον τῇ φύσει τῶν λοιπῶν ζῴων, ἀλλὰ στερεὸν διὰ παντὸς οἷον ὀστοῦν, ὅπως ἄν ποτε διακειμένη τύχῃ. φασὶ δὲ στραγγουρίας αὐτὸ φάρμακον εἶναι ἐν τοῖς ἀρίστοις, καὶ δίδοσθαι ἐπιξυόμενον.

It is said that the penis of the marten is not like that of other animals. Instead it is hard at all times, like a bone, no matter what the circumstances are. And they say that the penis of the marten is the best remedy for strangury and is given in powdered form.

In the above examples several key themes are reiterated in different ways, in order to bind together the otherwise disparate entries. The unexpectedly airy diet of goats in Cephallenia is most obviously paralleled by the tortoise's strange dietary habit of washing down vipers with marjoram. In between these entries concerning odd zoological eating habits, we are told about the propensity of the angry adult ass to castrate his younger rivals. The sudden intrusion of genitalia is echoed by the focus on the marten's endless erection, which comes after we are told of the tortoise's dietary requirements. At the most obvious level there is an alternating arrangement of theme here. But on another level all four of these marvels can be linked together under an alternate heading of 'unexpected things animals put in their mouths': goats gape with their mouths open to drink the sea air, an ass tears off genitals 'with his mouth' (τῷ στόματι) specifically, tortoises can only put snakes into their mouths if they are well-seasoned, and even humans occasionally take in powdered marten penis (presumably orally?) when suffering from strangury.[48]

---

[48] Similar connections spread out and ripple through the other entries in the initial section (entries 1–30) of zoological marvels in Ps. Arist. *On Marvellous Things Heard*. Just before we reach the examples discussed here, we are told in entry 4 that goats seek out a certain herb when injured (cf. the tortoise needing wild marjoram); birds eat things from the mouths of crocodiles in entry 7 (cf. the unexpected eating habits on display in 9–12); hedgehogs can tell which way the wind is blowing and change direction as a result in entry 8 (cf. goats turning their faces to the air in entry 9); after entries 9–12 (cited in full above), we return to the eating habits of birds in entry 13, which tells us that woodpeckers peck so far into trees in search of food that the trees collapse (cf. birds and food in entry 7, and the following description of another bird eating in entry 14: pelicans swallow mussels and then vomit up the shells).

When viewed in this way, the careful transitions and connections between entries echo those in Herodotus' descriptions of ethnographic *thomata*, as well as being reminiscent of some of the ordering principles discerned in later miscellanistic texts. In these, a 'latching-on' technique allows seemingly disparate material to hang together, as one bizarre subject somehow tumbles effortlessly into another.[49] This sense of one marvel tumbling into another is essential to the aesthetic of paradoxography as a whole: the ability of texts to communicate back and forth in unexpected dialogue with one another is key to the creation of surprising continuities and discontinuities which arouse the bafflement and wonder that the paradoxographical collection is aiming for. This effect is further reinforced by the paradoxographer's methods of excerpting his source texts, as the next section will demonstrate.

3.4 Reactivating *Thauma*: Paradoxography and the Aristotelian Tradition

The ethnographic tradition is not the only mode of writing from which paradoxography draws. As mentioned earlier in Section 3.1, the strong connection between the traditions of Peripatetic philosophy and science and the work of the Hellenistic paradoxographers has often been noted, especially in respect of the themes and content of their works. But the significance of the place of *thauma* within Aristotle's conceptual framework of philosophy and science as a whole on the paradoxographers' conception of

---

[49] See Pelling (2000a) 171–90 on this 'latching-on' technique and the sophisticated principles of arrangement in Athenaeus' *Deipnosophistae*. In terms of this 'latching-on' technique in particular, the paradoxographical collection should be seen as an important precursor of later 'miscellanistic' styles of writing, which often reveal the presence of complex structures on closer examination of the author's presentation of material. For recent reassessments of the complicated structural strategies adopted in miscellanistic texts, often in the face of implicit or explicit authorial denials of such ordering, see e.g. König (2007) 43–68, Klotz and Oikonomopoulou (2011) 22–7 and Morgan (2011) 70–3 on the miscellanistic quality and ordering principles of Plutarch's *Quaest. conv.*; Vardi (2004) 169–86 and Howley (2018) on Gellius' *NA*; Smith (2014) 47–66 on Aelian's *NA*; Wilkins (2000) 23–37, Jacob (2000) 85–110 and Jacob (2013b) on Athenaeus' *Deipnosophistae*. See also König and Whitmarsh (2007) 31–4 on strategies for ordering disorderly miscellanistic knowledge in Imperial prose more generally.

3.4 Paradoxography and the Aristotelian Tradition

their texts has not yet been examined fully. The most explicit and significant Aristotelian discussion of the place and purpose of *thauma* in philosophy comes in the passage from the opening of the *Metaphysics* (982b12–21) which has already been mentioned at the very beginning of this book, now cited here at greater length:

διὰ γὰρ τὸ θαυμάζειν οἱ ἄνθρωποι καὶ νῦν καὶ τὸ πρῶτον ἤρξαντο φιλοσοφεῖν, ἐξ ἀρχῆς μὲν τὰ πρόχειρα τῶν ἀτόπων θαυμάσαντες, εἶτα κατὰ μικρὸν οὕτω προϊόντες καὶ περὶ τῶν μειζόνων διαπορήσαντες, οἷον περί τε τῶν τῆς σελήνης παθημάτων καὶ τῶν περὶ τὸν ἥλιον καὶ ἄστρα καὶ περὶ τῆς τοῦ παντὸς γενέσεως. ὁ δ' ἀπορῶν καὶ θαυμάζων οἴεται ἀγνοεῖν (διὸ καὶ ὁ φιλόμυθος φιλόσοφός πώς ἐστιν· ὁ γὰρ μῦθος σύγκειται ἐκ θαυμασίων)· ὥστ' εἴπερ διὰ τὸ φεύγειν τὴν ἄγνοιαν ἐφιλοσόφησαν, φανερὸν ὅτι διὰ τὸ εἰδέναι τὸ ἐπίστασθαι ἐδίωκον καὶ οὐ χρήσεώς τινος ἕνεκεν.

Through wonder men now begin, and once first began, to philosophise: from the beginning they have wondered at strange things which were near at hand, and then progressed forward step-by-step in this way, raising questions about greater matters, such as the changes of the moon and the sun and the constellations and the origin of everything. And the man who is perplexed and who wonders feels that he is ignorant (and for this reason the lover of myth is in some way a philosopher, for myth is composed of wonders). As a result, if it was to escape ignorance that men philosophised, it is clear that they pursued understanding for the sake of knowing, rather than for some practical use.

For Aristotle, *thauma* is thus able to motivate the pursuit of knowledge itself by encouraging the recognition of one's own ignorance concerning the object, matter or phenomenon which is the cause of such wonder.[50] Wonder acts as a sort of protreptic to philosophy and the attainment of knowledge: a spur to curiosity which is initially useful, but is to be discarded and replaced by knowledge once the causes of a given phenomenon have been understood. Philosophy therefore stems from *thauma*, and it is possible to wonder at and philosophise concerning matters both big and small (in size and significance), near and far.

Aristotle makes this point again in a slightly different way in his *De partibus animalium* (645a15–17), where he issues a protreptic

---

[50] The relationship between *thauma*, recognition, ignorance and knowledge in Aristotle's work will be discussed again in greater detail in Chapter 5, Section 1. On *thauma* and *thaumata* in *Metaphysics*, see e.g. Schaeffer (1999) 641–56, Cambiano (2012) 34, Broadie (2012) 62–7 and Bowe (2017) 50–72.

towards the study of animal bodies by arguing that it is easier for us to begin inquiring and gaining knowledge of creatures which are familiar and accessible to us, before turning to weightier matters concerning the heavens, which are much further away and therefore more difficult to contemplate and understand fully. For this reason, 'the study of even the lowest animals' (τὴν περὶ τῶν ἀτιμοτέρων ζῴων ἐπίσκεψιν) is worth undertaking because of the fact that 'there is something wondrous in every aspect of the natural world' (ἐν πᾶσι γὰρ τοῖς φυσικοῖς ἔνεστί τι θαυμαστόν).[51] For Aristotle, the *thauma* generated by the contemplation of even the smallest biological problem affords the chance to philosophise and ultimately, in due course, to move towards the understanding of greater and more impressive phenomena.

There are indications that this Aristotelian conception of *thauma* as a crucial starting point for further inquiry lies in the background of the production of Hellenistic paradoxographical collections. In this regard it is particularly striking that the connection between *thauma* and inquiry seems to have influenced Callimachus, the first named producer of a marvel collection of whom we are aware. To judge from the surviving fragments of his *Collection of Marvels from Every Land Arranged According to Places*, Callimachus' marvel-collection focused primarily upon geological and geographical *thaumata*, especially wondrous bodies of water. But his paradoxographical collection is not the only work to exhibit such an interest in unique geographical features in particular locations: his *Aitia* also deals with such features in connection with cultural and historical particularities.[52] This sense of a connection between Callimachus' interest in paradoxography and aetiology is further strengthened if we turn to the *Aitia* itself and note the role which wonder plays at a crucial

---

[51] See Lennox (2001) 172, Nightingale (2004) 262–5, Poulakos and Crick (2012) 301–4, Thein (2014) 217–18 and Tipton (2014) 68–9 on the place of wonder within Aristotle's defence of and protreptic towards the study of lower animals. See Balme (1972) 122–4 on the unusual nature of this passage in the *De partibus animalium*.

[52] See Prioux (2009) 121 on the parallelism between the *Aitia* and Callimachus' paradoxographical collection in terms of the pronounced interest which both works exhibit in the geography (especially rivers) of the West (especially Magna Graecia). The continuities between Callimachus' interest in aetiology and paradoxography have also been noted by Fraser (1972a) 774, Krevans (2004) 173, and Acosta-Hughes and Stephens (2012) 17.

3.4 Paradoxography and the Aristotelian Tradition

transitional point between two discussions of cultic practices in book 2 of the poem. In the first *aition* (fr. 43–43a Harder) of this book, Callimachus, apparently conversing with and questioning the Muses, exhibits his own scholarly knowledge by providing a catalogue of Sicilian cities before Clio answers the poet's question about the foundation cult of Zancle. The transition into the next *aition* then begins (fr. 43b1–4 Harder):

ὥς] ἡ μὲν λίπε μῦθον, ἐγὼ δ' ἐπὶ καὶ τ[ὸ πυ]θέσθαι
ἤ]θελον – ἦ γάρ μοι θάμβος ὑπετρέφ[ε]το – ,
Κ]ισσούσης παρ' ὕδωρ Θεοδαίσια Κρῆ[σσαν ἑ]ορτὴν
ἡ] πόλις ἡ Κάδμου κῶς Ἁλίαρτος ἄγ[ει

In this way she ended her account, but I was full of desire to learn this as well – for truly my wonder was nourished – why near the waters of Kissousa does the city of Cadmus, Haliartus, celebrate the Theodaisia, a Cretan festival ...

The poet's astonishment at Zancle's cult, and Clio's explanation of its provenance, here fuels a further desire for aetiological answers, this time in connection with a seemingly unrelated question concerning the reasons why the Theodaisia is celebrated both on Crete and at Haliartus in Boeotia. Crucially, it is wonder which here feeds the scholar-poet's child-like curiosity, and becomes the starting point for renewed inquiry, as well as being the impulse which encourages the transition from one *aition* to the next.[53] Like Aristotle's philosophical inquiries, Callimachus' aetiological questions find their starting point in wonder, and the contemplation of one small point of cultural interest has the potential to nurture a pursuit of knowledge concerning what may at first seem radically separate matters.[54]

---

[53] On *thambos* as a response to Clio's answer to Callimachus' obscure question, see Hutchinson (1988) 44. Cf. Fantuzzi and Hunter (2004) 59 on the use of wonder to link the Haliartus episode to the seemingly unrelated discussion of Sicilian cities which precedes it; see also Harder (2012) 303 and 362 on *thambos* as a transitional device which reveals 'how Callimachus pretended that amazement and curiosity were the impulses that accounted for his choice of subjects'. Cf. Cozzoli (2011) 424–7 on the significance of *thambos* in fr. 43a Harder, and on the narrator's pose of child-like curiosity and wonder in the *Aitia* as a whole. On the general significance in the poem of the child-like posturing of the *Aitia*'s narrator, see Snell (1953) 271–6.

[54] See Fantuzzi and Hunter (2004) 59–60 on the similarity between Callimachus' inquiries and the Platonic/Aristotelian notion that philosophical inquiry originates in wonder.

There is, however, an additional complication when it comes to nurturing the reader's curiosity about those very problems of Aristotelian inquiry that the paradoxographical collections tend to focus on, which is precisely that the works of Aristotle and his Peripatetic followers had already provided a ready-made explanatory framework in which to contextualise many natural *thaumata*. This had the potentially disastrous effect of curtailing the budding philosopher's ability to start with small and unexplained natural marvels near at hand, before moving on to weightier matters of philosophy. Due to the assiduous scientific and philosophical work of scientific thinkers from the Ionian school down to Aristotle, certain natural *thaumata* had perhaps already become *too* familiar. A process of defamiliarisation was therefore necessary before nature might seem sufficiently strange again. This is precisely what the paradoxographical collection offers to the reader. Rather than building up and explaining the causes and context behind a given phenomenon in order to nurture a desire for further knowledge – a process which we see enacted somewhat comically in Callimachus' *Aitia* – the writer of paradoxography adopts an almost diametrically opposed strategy in order to achieve the same effect. Phenomena which are already relatively well-contextualised and explained are stripped back, pared of their explanatory framework, and made to astonish again.

With this in mind, the seemingly puzzling methods which the paradoxographer adopts with respect to his source texts begin to make more sense. Luckily for us, some of the source texts which lurk in the background of certain sections of some extant paradoxographical collections survive, allowing us to examine the intricacies of the paradoxographer's excerpting art in closer detail. Perhaps the most fascinating example is a large central section of Antigonus' *Collection of Marvellous Investigations* (26–115) which makes extensive use of Aristotle's *Historia animalium*, and permits us a close-up view of paradoxography's relationship to Aristotelian biology. This is because many of the *thaumata* which Antigonus culls and adapts from the *Historia animalium* are part of much longer zoological discussions in

3.4 Paradoxography and the Aristotelian Tradition

which Aristotle has contextualised, classified and often at least partially explained the biological phenomena which he is documenting. In almost every case in Antigonus' *Collection*, however, the paradoxographer neglects to adapt any of this wider contextual padding in his own work.[55]

In fact, Antigonus actually emphasises that the removal of Aristotle's explanations of the causes of phenomena relating to the animal world is an integral aspect of his own paradoxographical art in a brief authorial comment in his text, a rare moment where he explicitly discusses his principles of selection and composition. After relating a marvel excerpted from the *Historia animalium* Antigonus notes (*Collection* 60) that Aristotle 'took great care in his works' (πάνυ πολλὴν ἐπιμέλειαν πεποιημένος) and explained things 'without including extraneous information in his interpretation' (οὐ παρέργῳ χρώμενος τῇ περὶ τούτων ἐξηγήσει). He also comments that Aristotle 'wrote almost seventy books about animals and endeavoured to focus more on explaining matters rather than narrating them in each of these works' (τὰ γοῦν πάντα σχεδὸν ἑβδομήκοντα περὶ αὐτῶν καταβέβληται βιβλία, καὶ πεπείραται ἐξηγητικώτερον ἢ ἱστορικώτερον ἐν ἑκάστοις ἀναστρέφεσθαι). In contrast, Antigonus notes that his 'own collection focuses only on the selection of strange and incredible content from these Aristotelian works and passes up on other types of content' (πρὸς τὴν ἡμετέραν ἐκλογὴν ἐκποιεῖ <τῶν> προῃρημένων αὐτῷ τὸ ξένον καὶ παράδοξον ἔκ τε τούτων καὶ τῶν ἄλλων ἐπιδραμεῖν). As this explicit comment makes clear, Antigonus' primary aim within his marvel-collection is the evocation of a sense of the strange and incredible through the deliberate curtailment of Aristotelian explanation.

---

[55] I am grateful to one of the anonymous readers for drawing my attention to the fact that this stripping of contextual padding is somewhat aided by Antigonus' choice to use the *Historia animalium* as his source text, rather than any of Aristotle's other biological works, because the focus of that text is mostly on the classification, collection and grouping of animals rather than on large-scale causal explanation. The paradoxographer's task of finding wondrous material buried within Aristotle's wider contextualised discussion is therefore made easier by the variety of the phenomena recorded and classified in the first place. For summaries of various positions relating to the distinctiveness of the aim, focus and purpose of the *Historia animalium* in Aristotle's biological corpus, see Gotthelf (2012) 261–92, 309–24.

Reading *Thauma*

The deliberate effects of Antigonus' striving for the strange through this method of excerption and adaptation can be seen more clearly if we examine some of his *thaumata* alongside Aristotle's original discussions in the *Historia animalium*. The three short successive marvels which form the seventy-third to seventy-fifth entries in Antigonus' collection are good examples of the paradoxographer's typical treatment of his source texts:

73.	τῶν δ' ἰχθύων τὸν σκάρον μόνον μηρυκάζειν.	[And Aristotle says that] the parrotfish is the only fish which chews the cud.
74.	τοῦ δὲ λέοντος οὕτως εἶναι τὰ ὀστᾶ στερεά, ὥστε πολλάκις κοπτομένων πῦρ ἐκλάμπειν.	[And Aristotle says that] the bones of the lion are so hard that often fire flashes forth from them when they are struck.
75.	ἐν Φρυγίᾳ δὲ βοῦς εἶναι, οἳ κινοῦσι τὰ κέρατα.	[And Aristotle says that] there are oxen in Phrygia which wiggle their horns.

When stated in this bare form these enigmatic and puzzling statements encourage the reader to marvel at the peculiarities of the natural world, while simultaneously testing the boundaries of credulity. Do we really believe that a trip to Phrygia could result in an encounter with cow horns of a type we have never experienced before, or are we to doubt the veracity of this claim despite the fact that Aristotle himself supposedly said it?

In fact, Aristotle really did say all of these things, as well as all the other claims attributed to him in Antigonus' paradoxographical collection. If, however, we turn to Aristotle's biological works we find that the paradoxographer has always been very careful to cherry-pick his *thaumata* out of the vast zoological discussion in a way which distorts their original meaning. Two mutually reinforcing strategies are employed to achieve this goal. The paradoxographer either selects the unusual exceptions to various biological rules which Aristotle lays out carefully in the first place, or he strips away the complicated reasoning which the philosopher builds up to explain away an apparent inconsistency or anomaly. The cud-chewing parrotfish is a good example of the combination of these two methods. In Antigonus' *Collection* the creature's

3.4 Paradoxography and the Aristotelian Tradition

strange status as the 'only fish which chews the cud' (μόνον μηρυκάζειν) transforms it into a unique marvel, since cud-chewing is naturally associated with large land animals such as cows rather than fish. None of Aristotle's reasoning or carefully collected contextual information about the parrotfish's digestive system is preserved: only the bare fact of this creature's seemingly strange behaviour remains.

However, if we turn to the precise mention of the cud-chewing parrotfish in the *Historia animalium* (508b10–12) and examine its wider context, we quickly see how crucial Antigonus' careful curtailment of Aristotle's wider reasoning is to the creation of a sense of wonder in his marvel-collection. In Aristotle's text the fish's unusual masticatory habit is mentioned in a long discussion about different types of animal stomach. This wider discussion makes clear why Aristotle sees fit to mention the parrotfish's strange status here, since one element which he consistently comments on in this work in relation to the form of an animal's stomach and digestive processes is its dentition. At 507a34–6 Aristotle declares a general rule that 'horned viviparous quadrupeds which do not have teeth in both jaws possess four-chambered stomachs: these are the animals said to 'chew the cud'' (τῶν τετραπόδων καὶ ζωοτόκων ὅσα μὴ ἔστιν ἀμφώδοντα τῶν κερατοφόρων, τέτταρας ἔχει τοὺς τοιούτους πόρους· ἃ δὴ καὶ λέγεται μηρυκάζειν). He also establishes that cud-chewing animals, having teeth in only one jaw, do not have straight guts since 'animals without teeth in both jaws do not possess a straight gut' (εὐθυέντερον δ' οὐδέν ἐστι μὴ ἀμφώδουν, 507b34). Aristotle then moves on to the assessment and classification of the digestive systems of oviparous animals, starting with snakes and then moving onto fish, which he declares 'have one simple stomach' (μίαν γὰρ καὶ ἁπλῆν ἔχουσι, 508b10). By this point in the discussion Aristotle has thus established that all cud-chewing animals have four-chambered stomachs, non-straight guts and teeth in only one jaw, while all fish possess only one stomach.

It is at this point that the parrotfish, the 'only fish which seems to chew the cud' (δοκεῖ μόνος ἰχθῦς μηρυκάζειν, 508b12) and a potential outlier in the careful taxonomy of stomachs which has just been laid out, is mentioned. According to Aristotle's system, if the parrotfish really did chew the cud it would possess a four-chambered stomach, only one jaw full of teeth, and a non-straight gut. The issue is quickly settled when it is revealed that, despite its apparent cud-chewing capabilities, the parrotfish possesses a single 'gut-like stomach' (ἐντεροειδῆ ἔχουσιν, 508b11) which is simple in form along its whole length (τὸ τοῦ ἐντέρου δὲ μέγεθος ἁπλοῦν, 508b12). The verb 'seems' (δοκεῖ) in Aristotle's initial statement about the animal's apparent cud-chewing thus takes on its full force here, since on closer inspection it turns out that the parrotfish, with its singly-formed gut-like stomach, must be a fish after all – even if the action of scraping at coral with its beak-like protrusion does make the creature look as if it is chewing the cud when eating.[56] But all of these complexities are very deliberately elided in Antigonus' *Collection*. According to the paradoxographer's account, Aristotle does not say that the parrotfish *seems* to eat in this way, he simply asserts that 'the parrotfish is the only fish which chews the cud' (τῶν δ' ἰχθύων τὸν σκάρον μόνον μηρυκάζειν). With the removal of a few crucial words, Aristotle's careful and informative discussion of fish stomachs is obliterated, and in its place a baffling *thauma* arises.

A similar paradoxographical manoeuvre takes place when it comes to the pyrotechnical potential of lion bones. In the *Historia animalium* the unusual qualities of the bones of the lion receive a special mention during a much longer discussion on the nature of animal bones when Aristotle notes that 'the lion possesses bones which are harder than those of any animal; they are so hard that fire flashes out of them when they are rubbed together, just as it does from flint' (στερεὰ δὲ πάντων μάλιστα ὁ λέων ἔχει τὰ ὀστᾶ· οὕτω γάρ ἐστι σκληρὰ ὥστε συντριβομένων ὥσπερ ἐκ λίθων ἐκλάμπειν πῦρ, 516b9–11). Aristotle is very much concerned with the relative hardness of animal bones in this part of his discussion, rather than their inherent flame-producing potential, but from Antigonus' truncated and context-free adaptation of this wider

---

[56] See also Aristotle's mention of the parrotfish at *Part. an.* 675a4, which makes the unique aspect of this fish clearer: it does have teeth in only one jaw, just as viviparous four-stomached cud-chewing ruminants do, hence the *apparent* chewing motion that the fish makes. The animal's stomach, however, confirms that the parrotfish is really a fish, at least according to Aristotle's taxonomy.

3.4 Paradoxography and the Aristotelian Tradition

discussion it is not clear how hard lion bones are in relation to those of other animals, or why they might be able to give off sparks at all.[57] Once again, we see that the paradoxographer's careful act of adaptation manages to shift the emphasis of the original source text by focusing on an unusual zoological example which constitutes a definite exception to the more general rules and principles being outlined in the broader discussion as a whole.

The mobility of cattle horns in Phrygia also turns out to be a more logical phenomenon than first imagined, as Aristotle's longer discussion of the general composition of animal horns makes clear. At *Historia animalium* 517a20–3 he observes that 'most horns are hollow from the point they attach to the bone inside them growing out from the head, but solid at the tip' (τῶν δὲ κεράτων τὰ μὲν πλεῖστα κοῖλά ἐστιν ἀπὸ τῆς προσφύσεως περὶ τὸ ἐντὸς ἐκπεφυκὸς ἐκ τῆς κεφαλῆς ὀστοῦν, ἐπ' ἄκρου δ' ἔχει τὸ στερεόν). There are some types of horned animal, however, which are exceptions to this general rule, like certain cattle 'from Phrygia and elsewhere' (ἐν Φρυγίᾳ εἰσὶ βόες καὶ ἄλλοθι, 517a28–9), whose horns attach to the skin of the head rather than to the solid bone of the skull. For this reason they freely 'move their horns just as they move their ears' (κινοῦσι τὰ κέρατα ὥσπερ τὰ ὦτα, 517a29–30).[58] In Antigonus' paradoxographical version of this observation, however, the relatively straightforward explanation that horns are able to move if they are attached to movable skin as opposed to fixed bone is completely excised. Moreover, Aristotle's note that such animals are found in Phrygia *and elsewhere* (ἐν Φρυγίᾳ εἰσὶ βόες καὶ ἄλλοθι) is also carefully neglected, giving the impression that the wiggly-horned Phrygian

---

[57] Aristotle does in fact elaborate upon the reasons why lion bones are naturally so exceptionally hard in even more detail at *Part. an.* 655a12–16. There it is explained that the bones of bulky male flesh-eating animals are naturally hard because these creatures must obtain food by fighting: as perhaps the fiercest flesh-eating animal, the lion's bones are therefore naturally the hardest.

[58] Aristotle may be referring to cattle with scurs (known as *Wackelhörner* in German), movable 'horns' created by incomplete horn growth which is not attached to the skull (see Kyselý (2010) 1241–6 for a discussion of the 'loose horns' phenomenon in cattle and archaeological evidence for such bovids in Eneolithic central Europe). For other ancient accounts of the movable horns of Phrygian cattle, see Oppian, *Cynegetica* 2.90–5 and Plin. *HN* 11.125; cf. Ael. *NH* 2.20 (describing the movable horns of cattle in Erythrae) and 17.45 (on the movable horns of Ethiopian flesh-eating bulls; cf. also Diod. Sic. 3.35.7).

animals are a truly exceptional *thauma* worthy of particular wonder. As these examples show, Antigonus has not arbitrarily plucked sentences from his source text in an unexamined fashion. Instead, the paradoxographer has carefully chosen his *thaumata* by picking up on natural exceptions and then systematically stripping them of their carefully constructed explanatory framework. As suggested above, this deliberate stripping of explanation and context acts to heighten a sense of paradox and wonder through the deliberate suppression of any sense of the causes of each given phenomenon, acting in turn as a means of restimulating the primordial Aristotelian wonder felt at the initial observation of strange and inexplicable zoological specimens or processes. If we read Hellenistic paradoxographical collections with this kind of deliberate treatment of their source texts in mind, these marvel-collections begin to make more sense as interlocutors in a philosophical tradition which situates its origins in *thauma* itself.

3.5 Textual *Thaumata*: Paradoxography and the Poetics of Hellenistic Literature

There is one other important respect in which the paradoxographical collection can be seen as echoing contemporary Hellenistic intellectual and literary trends. The brevity and lack of any contextual framework associated with the *thaumata* created by the paradoxographer's preferred methods of excerption also align the paradoxographical collection with another contemporary textual genre: the literary epigram collection. In Chapter 2, it was noted that the connections between the *content* of Hellenistic paradoxographical collections and the Posidippus epigrams on the Milan Papyrus have recently been recognised, although the similarities of *form* apparent between the epigram collection and the paradoxographical collection have not yet been explored.[59] In many respects the systematic stripping away of any contextual information that surrounded the *thaumata* of paradoxography in their source texts is akin to the manner in which the literary epigram's relative concision and absence of a clear context of utterance or

---

[59] See Chapter 2, Section 4.

3.5 Textual *Thaumata*

inscription encourages the reader to fill in resulting interpretative gaps, deriving pleasure from the imaginative engagement which the supplementation of contextual knowledge provokes: a process which Bing has termed *Ergänzungsspiel* (supplementation game) in relation to Hellenistic epigram.[60] The restimulation of inquiry which the paradoxographical collection encourages through its manipulation of *thauma* bears many similarities to the response provoked by the *Ergänzungsspiel* of epigram, with the reader prompted to speculate about the possible causes of each marvel, and encouraged to try to fill in the now renewed gaps in explanation. This potentially starts the chain of philosophical inquiry afresh, with the possibility of eventually moving on to the contemplation of even weightier philosophical matters lying ahead.

Far from representing the shoddy end-product of an inadequate Hellenistic scientist trying and failing to produce a set of usable 'research notes', or of a shambolic historian missing the point when it comes to framing a coherent historical narrative, the paradoxographical collection becomes yet another manifestation of a complex engagement with intellectual, philosophical and literary trends on the part of Hellenistic scholars and poets. Furthermore, by entering the world of the paradoxographers, we witness a change in the conception of what an appropriate object of *thauma* might be in the Hellenistic age: now the text itself has cemented its place as possibly the most marvellous object of all. Far from being a manifestation of decline, the emergence of paradoxography as a mode of writing in the third century BCE attests to changing attitudes concerning the effects and causes of wonder itself.

---

[60] See Bing (1995) 115–31 on *Ergänzungsspiel* in relation to Hellenistic epigram; cf. also Hunter (1992) 114 on the use of literary epigrams as 'a provocation to speculation'; this speculation becomes a hallmark of the genre as a whole; see also Meyer (2007) 187–210. For the act of supplementation as an essential aspect of the aesthetics of Hellenistic art as well as poetry, see Zanker (2004) 72–102.

4

THE SOUND OF *THAUMA*: MUSIC AND THE MARVELLOUS

ἴδιον δὲ καὶ τὸ περὶ τὰ ἔντερα τῶν προβάτων· τὰ μὲν γὰρ τῶν κριῶν ἐστιν ἄφωνα, τὰ δὲ τῶν θηλέων εὔφωνα. ὅθεν καὶ τὸν ποιητὴν ὑπολάβοι τις εἰρηκέναι, πολυπράγμονα πανταχοῦ καὶ περιττὸν ὄντα:

ἑπτὰ δὲ θηλυτέρων ὀΐων ἐτανύσσατο χορδάς.

οὐχ ἧττον δὲ τούτου θαυμαστόν, καθωμιλημένον δὲ μᾶλλον τὸ περὶ τὴν ἐν τῇ Σικελίᾳ ἄκανθαν τὴν καλουμένην κάκτον· εἰς ἣν ὅταν ἔλαφος ἐμβῇ καὶ τραυματισθῇ, τὰ ὀστᾶ ἄφωνα καὶ ἄχρηστα πρὸς αὐλοὺς ἴσχει. ὅθεν καὶ ὁ Φιλητᾶς ἐξηγήσατο περὶ αὐτῆς εἴπας:

γηρύσαιτο δὲ νεβρὸς ἀπὸ ζωὴν ὀλέσασα,
ὀξείης κάκτου τύμμα φυλαξαμένη.

This property of the entrails of livestock is also strange: the entrails of rams are unmelodious, while those of ewes are melodious. From this it is possible to understand what the poet [i.e. Homer], who is in all respects desirous of knowledge[1] and painstaking, said: 'He strung it with seven gut-strings from female sheep' [= *hHerm.* 51]

And no less marvellous than this, but even better known, is this fact concerning the prickly plant in Sicily called 'cactus'. Whenever a deer treads upon this plant and is wounded, its bones become unmelodious and useless for the manufacture of *auloi*. For this reason Philitas expounds on this plant when he says: 'Let the fawn which has lost its life sing, the fawn which has avoided the sting of the sharp cactus' [= Philitas fr. 18 Sb.]

Antigonus of Carystus, *Collection of Marvellous Investigations* 7–8

---

[1] While the adjective *polupragmon* most often denotes the quality of being 'meddlesome' or 'a busybody' in a negative sense, in certain cases, usually in the context of scholarly activity as in this example from Antigonus, it points to a more positive sense of curiosity and desire for further knowledge: see Leigh (2013) on these various shades of meaning.

The Sound of *Thauma*: Music and the Marvellous

In the opening of Antigonus' *Collection of Marvellous Investigations* it is not the scientific intricacies of Aristotle's zoological works which are thrust to the forefront of the reader's attention, but rather the world of the music and poetry of the past. A group of eight thematically connected marvels speak back and forth to each other on the subjects of music, voice and voicelessness. The first entry is derived from Timaeus, who reports that 'cicadas sing on the Locrian side of the river Halex, but remain silent on the Rhegian side' ("Άληκος καλουμένου ποταμοῦ τῶν τεττίγων τοὺς μὲν ἐν τῇ Λοκρικῇ ᾄδειν, τοὺς δὲ ἐν τῇ Ῥηγίνων ἀφώνους εἶναι), and that the Locrian citharode Eunomus was aided in a contest at Delphi with the Rhegian citharode Ariston when 'a cicada flew onto his lyre and began to sing' (τέττιξ ἐπὶ τὴν λύραν ἐπιπτὰς ᾖδεν, *Collection* 1). This marvel is followed by two further reports about these singing insects. The first also relates to Rhegion and informs us that 'when he was somewhere in this region Heracles, who was trying to sleep, was annoyed by the sound of the cicadas and prayed for them to become voiceless' (Ἡρακλῆς ἔν τινι τόπῳ τῆς χώρας κατακοιμηθεὶς καὶ ἐνοχλούμενος ὑπὸ τῶν τεττίγων ηὔξατο αὐτοὺς ἀφώνους γενέσθαι, *Collection* 2). The next marvel moves away from south Italy, informing us that 'in Cephallenia too a river separates out two banks: on one bank cicadas are present, on the other they are absent' (καὶ ἐν Κεφαλληνίᾳ δὲ ποταμὸς διείργει, καὶ ἐπίταδε μὲν γίνονται τέττιγες, ἐπέκεινα δὲ οὔ, *Collection* 3). Wondrous zoological silences remain the focus of the next entry, which tells us that 'frogs in Seriphus do not make a sound' (οὐδ' ἐν Σερίφῳ δὲ οἱ βάτραχοι φθέγγονται, *Collection* 4). This focus on silence strongly contrasts with the subsequent entry, a report from Myrsilus of Methymna concerning marvellously noisy birds in Lesbos near the tomb of Orpheus' head in Antissa: in this place 'the nightingales are more tuneful than those found elsewhere' (τὰς ἀηδόνας εἶναι εὐφωνοτέρας τῶν ἄλλων, *Collection* 5). The focus on the tunefulness of certain birds continues in the next entry about partridges in Attica and Boeotia: 'some are melodious while others are completely weak-voiced' (ὧν τοὺς μὲν εὐφώνους, τοὺς δὲ τελείως ἰσχνοφώνους, *Collection* 6).

The Sound of *Thauma*: Music and the Marvellous

The final two entries (7–8) in Antigonus' initial grouping of marvels, cited in full above, demonstrate in an especially pointed form the paradoxographer's multi-layered engagement with the thaumatic power of both the oral and written poetry of the past. The successive citations from the *Homeric Hymn to Hermes* and from the work of the early Hellenistic poet Philitas of Cos once again reveal the paradoxographer's typically Hellenistic interest in literary games involving his source texts, a phenomenon which was explored in the previous chapter. At the beginning of the present chapter I want to build on this discussion further by examining the reasons behind Antigonus' inclusion and juxtaposition of these two particular poetic citations within the opening section of his paradoxographical collection.

Antigonus is interested in the *hHerm.* as a text which allows him to play upon the connection between *thauma* and music as it is reflected in both the poetic *and* the scientific traditions. The hymn is an especially apt text for Antigonus to include in his marvel-collection. Out of all the texts in our extant corpus of Homeric hymns, this one is by far the most explicitly thaumatic. *Thauma* is an almost constant reaction to Hermes' activities and achievements, starting from the moment of his birth, and it is the ability to see the marvellous potential of the familiar material of the world around him, and to make use of the marvellous in the everyday, which enables the infant god to prove his divine parentage. Hermes' most marvellous invention of all, the lyre, is inherently imbued with the ability to provoke *thauma* in an audience in every single performance. As an instrument created out of the everyday familiar material of nature, which goes on to produce exceptional marvels of culture, the lyre is depicted as an object which transcends established boundaries and simultaneously creates new links between previously unconnected realms. Perhaps the most important areas which the lyre is able to connect in new ways within the *Hymn* are the separate realms of god and man. We see this in action in the poem itself during Hermes' two musical performances, each of which has an explicitly marvellous effect within the narrative, hinting at the complex interrelationship between musical performance, *thauma* and the boundaries between gods and mortals.

This effect is complicated in the second half of the *Hymn*, when Hermes' second musical performance even manages to provoke wonder in a fellow god, his elder brother Apollo. Mortals often marvel, especially at divine epiphanies, but this portrayal of a god's marvelling response is extremely unusual. It hints at the significant place the lyre is presented as occupying not only in the relationship between gods and humans but within the everyday experience of both. As I will show below, by the end of the narrative the *Hymn* has thus given us an aetiology not only of the lyre's existence but also of its intensely thaumatic effect. In fact, the effect of *thauma* is continually associated with aetiological accounts of the origins of various musical and choral genres in the Greek tradition. This is a theme which will be explored further in this chapter's final section as I move onto the broader connections between *thauma*, music, song and *choreia* (song-dance) in *Odyssey* 8 and the Delian half of the *Homeric Hymn to Apollo* as case studies of the interconnections between all of these elements in the Greek poetic and musical tradition. The importance of *thauma* in Greek conceptions of music and song will become even clearer in the final case study at the end of this chapter, which turns to the presentation of another wondrous musical performance: Herodotus' epiphanic and godlike vision of the citharode Arion in the *Histories*. But before reaching back and further examining the relationship between *thauma*, music and song from early Greek hexameter poetry onwards, I will now return to Antigonus' reception and appropriation of the intensely thaumatic impact of music in his own marvel-collection.

4.1 Homer the Proto-Paradoxographer: Poetry, Music and Science in Antigonus' *Collection of Marvellous Investigations*

For Antigonus, *hHerm.* is an ideal text through which to explore how familiar, everyday aspects of the natural world around us are able to induce *thauma*. In this respect, the paradoxographer has picked up on the potential of this poem to stand as an antecedent to his own poetics: just as the *Hymn* describes the combination of disparate parts of everyday nature to produce a stunning instrument of thaumatic effect, so too does Antigonus' own work involve the dismemberment and reassembly of previous poetic and scientific texts, which are then bound together to induce wonder in the reader. Perhaps this is why Antigonus is so keen

The Sound of *Thauma*: Music and the Marvellous

to cast the poet of *hHerm*. – whom he here designates as Homer – as a sort of 'proto-paradoxographer'.[2] In one of the relatively rare explicit authorial comments in his *Collection* Antigonus here praises the poet as 'in all respects desirous of knowledge and painstaking' (πολυπράγμονα πανταχοῦ καὶ περιττὸν ὄντα). As Matthew Leigh has recently pointed out, these two terms take on an unusually positive sense here: rather than denoting a pedantic and useless sort of scholarship, as they do often elsewhere, they have become terms of approbation, reflecting a sense of intellectual and scholarly rigour on the part of the poet which could equally be extended to the art of the paradoxographer himself.[3] In this way, Antigonus tries to cast Homer in his own image, making the poet into a sort of (accidental or otherwise) *protos heuretes* (first inventor) of paradoxography itself. Furthermore, by casting the poet in his own image in this way, Antigonus lays claim to the authority of the Homeric poetic tradition for the sort of inquisitive Aristotelian interest in natural wonders which the paradoxographer's collection espouses, almost as if the poet of the *Hymn* understood that there is 'something wonderful in all aspects of the natural world', even in the 'study of the lowest animals', long before Aristotle formulated it as such in his *De partibus animalium* (645a15–17).[4]

Antigonus is helped in his aim of fusing the Homeric and Aristotelian traditions by the fact that the line he cites does exhibit a sort of scientific concern prescient of the interests shown in Aristotle's biological works. The thing which allows Antigonus to link the poet to his claim that ewes produce more melodious gut-strings than rams is the detail that Hermes chose 'female sheep' (θηλυτέρων ὀΐων) rather than rams to string the first lyre. There is no other extant source for this claim about the relation between sex, gut-strings and sound, with the exception of a mention in a later paradoxographical collection, the *Paradoxographus*

---

[2] It is not uncommon for ancient authors to attribute *Homeric Hymns* to Homer, as Antigonus does here. See e.g. Thuc. 3.104 and Ar. *Av.* Σ ad. 575. On the widespread attribution of *Homeric Hymns* to Homer in antiquity, see Faulkner (2011) 175–8.
[3] Leigh (2013) 189–90 on Antigonus' citation of the *hHerm.* here, and pp. 188–94 on Antigonus and 'the aesthetic of the paradoxographer' in general.
[4] On this Aristotelian formulation in the *De partibus animalium*, see Chapter 3, Section 4.

4.1 Homer the Proto-Paradoxographer

Palatinus (c. third century CE?), which uses Antigonus' collection as one of its sources.[5] Despite the lack of evidence for this precise claim about the nature of gut-strings according to sex, this idea does have a sort of plausible Aristotelian flavouring. There is certainly plenty of interest in the differences between ewes and rams, and the differences between the sounds created by the voices of male and female animals, in Aristotle's biological works.[6] Theophrastus of Eresus is even said to have produced a treatise entitled *On the Different Sounds Produced by Animals of the Same Species* (Περὶ ἑτεροφωνίας ζῴων τῶν ὁμογενῶν).[7] Antigonus seems to have extended this Peripatetic interest here in order to make his claim even more marvellous: according to Homer, there is apparently not only a difference between the voices of male and female animals but even between the sounds their bodies make when used to provide the 'voice' of an instrument.[8]

The juxtaposition of the presentation of Homer as a sort of 'proto-paradoxographer' with the next marvel concerning

---

[5] *Paradoxographus Palatinus* 20: ἐπὶ τῶν ἐντέρων τῶν προβάτων φησὶν Ἀντίγονος τὰ μὲν τῶν κριῶν ἄφωνα εἶναι, τὰ δὲ τῶν θηλέων ἔμφωνα· οὐ λεληθέναι δὲ τοῦτο τὸν ποιητήν. φησὶ γάρ· ἑπτὰ δὲ θηλυτέρων οἴων ἐτανύσσατο χορδάς (On the entrails of livestock Antigonus says that those of rams are unmelodious, while those of ewes are melodious. Nor did this escape the notice of the Poet [i.e. Homer]. For he says: 'He strung it with seven gut-strings from female sheep'). Clearly the author of the *Paradoxographus Palatinus* is using Antigonus' paradoxographical collection in order to present the same claim in a truncated form.

[6] On the differences between the sounds created by the voices of male and female animals in general, cf. e.g. Arist. *Hist. an.* 538b12 (female animals have sharper and thinner voices than male animals, except for the cow, which has a deeper voice than the bull); 544b32 (the female animal has a sharper voice than the male, and the younger animal has a sharper voice than the elder); 545a22 (male animals which are gelded assume the voices of their female equivalents); 581a17 (the voices of male humans begin shrilly but deepen upon maturation); 581b6 (women have higher voices than men, younger women have higher voices than older women, boys have higher voices than men, and as a result girls' *auloi* are tuned more sharply than those of boys).

[7] This treatise is mentioned as a work of Theophrastus at Athenaeus, *Deipnosophistae* 320a and Diog. Laert. 5.2.43.

[8] Antigonus' claim that Homer really wrote θηλυτέρων ὄιων has been subject to some doubt. It is intriguing that all of the manuscript copies of the poem read συμφώνους (harmonious) rather than θηλυτέρων (female), a reading which only Antigonus transmits. Most editors and commentators have dismissed Antigonus' reading, usually on the basis that συμφώνους makes more thematic sense in relation to a lyre (see e.g. Càssola (1975) 520; West (2003) 116; Thomas (2020) 170–3; Richardson (2010) 162). Vergados ((2007) 737–42 and (2013) 269–70) has recently proved the exception to this general tendency, supporting Antigonus' reading on the basis that paradoxographers tend to transmit their texts fairly faithfully.

Philitas of Cos' knowledge about the type of deer bone needed for the manufacture of melodious *auloi* again demonstrates that the connections between entries in Antigonus' paradoxographical collection are both sophisticated and thematically motivated. Moreover, this entry also focuses on the wondrous creation of a 'living' voice out of a dead and voiceless animal.[9] In contrast to the positioning of 'Homer' in the previous entry, the presentation of Philitas as another kind of 'proto-paradoxographer' with scientific interests which dictate his poetic output is perhaps less surprising, given the Hellenistic poet's reputation for scholarly activity. Famed in antiquity as a 'poet and scholar' (ποιητὴς ἅμα καὶ κριτικός, Strabo, *Geography* 14.2.19), Philitas certainly did exhibit an interest in philological and grammatical scholarship in the testimonia and fragments of writings relating to his work which remain to us.[10] But even so, Antigonus slightly exaggerates the Coan's status as a writer who prefigures his own paradoxographical and natural scientific interests, since there is no evidence from these relatively meagre remains that Philitas was chiefly interested in natural science in the same way as, for example, Aristotle was. That is not to say that Philitas was not at all interested in this kind of technical or scientific material concerning the natural world, just as many subsequent Hellenistic poets were, but it is clear that he cannot be held up as an obvious paradoxographical predecessor for Antigonus in the same way as a figure such as Aristotle or Callimachus can be.[11]

---

[9] Antigonus may also be drawing a connection between the *hHerm.* and Philitas' poem here: both Spanoudakis (2002) 209 and Lightfoot (2009) 49 n. 12 suggest that Philitas' words may be from a sympotic context, as they seem to constitute a call for music on the *aulos* in a riddling form; the *hHerm.* can itself be seen as a sort of aetiological narrative for the future place of the lyre at the symposium. At the end of the first group of entries of his *Collection* Antigonus thus juxtaposes two examples of instruments which derive from the natural world and yet find a home in a later sympotic context.

[10] On Philitas' life, works and famed status as the archetypal Hellenistic scholar-poet, see e.g. Pfeiffer (1968) 88–93, Sbardella (2000) 3–75, Dettori (2000) 19–49 and Spanoudakis (2002) 19–74.

[11] For example, in the fragment cited by Antigonus the use of τύμμα for thorn has been regarded as indicative of an interest in the use of medical terminology (see Sbardella (2000) 148, Spanoudakis (2002) 215 and Manakidou (2012) 115). But, as Bing (2003) 342–3 points out, Philitas' interest in the relationship between the dead fawn and the cactus thorn in this fragment is probably predominantly lexical, and not paradoxographical or 'scientific' as Antigonus seems to suggest.

4.1 Homer the Proto-Paradoxographer

Antigonus is nevertheless keen to reinforce this impression: soon after the mention of the deer-bone *auloi*, the paradoxographer is even more explicit in his praise of his predecessor's supposed scholarly and scientific interests. A little later in the *Collection of Marvellous Investigations*, Philitas is again mentioned in connection with Antigonus' discussion of 'unusual similarities and differences between animal species and their ways of birth' (ἴδια δὲ καὶ περὶ τὰς συγκρίσεις καὶ ἀλλοιώσεις τῶν ζῴων, ἔτι δὲ γενέσεις, 19). As his first example of this type of marvel, he plunges into a lengthy entry on a topic which is a staple of both paradoxographical collections proper and texts which aim at inducing a temporary paradoxographical flavour: the process known as *bugonia*, the spontaneous generation of bees from dead oxen.[12] Antigonus begins this entry about the spontaneous generation of living creatures from dead animals by noting that 'if you bury an ox in certain locations in Egypt so that its horns protrude out from the ground, and then saw the horns off later, people say that bees fly out' (ἐν Αἰγύπτῳ τὸν βοῦν ἐὰν κατορύξῃς ἐν τόποις τισίν, ὥστε αὐτὰ τὰ κέρατα τῆς γῆς ὑπερέχειν, εἶθ' ὕστερον ἀποπρίσῃς, λέγουσιν μελίττας ἐκπέτεσθαι, 19).[13] He then notes that Philitas took a particular interest in this phenomenon precisely because he 'took trouble over things' (ὧν περίεργος, 19) – like a paradoxographer himself, or so Antigonus seems to hint. Once again, we see that by using the literary texts of the past in this way to cast their authors as proto-paradoxographers, Antigonus is taking pains to invent a tradition for his own miscellanistic mode of writing. At the same time, this return to and reuse of familiar texts of the literary past allows the paradoxographer to offer a wondrous new view on these works which potentially surprises and stimulates our interest anew. Moreover, for Antigonus, the presence of these marvels buried within the texts of the past is itself part of the *thauma* of his own collection: the opening section

---

[12] Virgil's two versions of the generation of ox-born bees at *Georgics* 4.281–314 and 4.538–58 are of course the best-known poetic descriptions of the phenomenon in ancient literature: on Virgil and *bugonia*, see e.g. Kitchell (1989) 193–206, Habinek (1990) 209–23 and Morgan (1999) 105–49.

[13] For other epigrams on spontaneous generation attributed to Archelaus which Antigonus transmits along with Philitas' verses at *Collection of Marvellous Investigations* 19, see Chapter 3, Section 2.

of the *Collection of Marvellous Investigations* thus not only hits upon the thaumatic potential of music but implicitly promotes the world of the text itself as an equally wondrous realm capable of preserving the paradoxographical interests of the past, present and future.

4.2 Giving Voice to the Dead: *Thauma* and the Lyre in the *Homeric Hymn to Hermes*

It seems then that Antigonus clearly saw the thaumatic potential of the *hHerm.* while compiling his collection of marvels. But what can we say about the place of *thauma* in the *hHerm.* itself? Hermes' stringing of the lyre with seven melodious (and possibly distinctly female) strings in line 51 of the *Hymn*, which Antigonus cites, is the culmination of a long description of the tortoise's wondrous transformation from voiceless living animal to inanimate, yet articulate object. This process begins with Hermes' first address to the tortoise at the moment he stumbles upon it by chance (30–8):

> σύμβολον ἤδη μοι μέγ' ὀνήσιμον, οὐκ ὀνοτάζω.
> χαῖρε φυὴν ἐρόεσσα χοροιτύπε δαιτὸς ἑταίρη,
> ἀσπασίη προφανεῖσα· πόθεν τόδε καλὸν ἄθυρμα
> αἰόλον ὄστρακον ἔσσο χέλυς ὄρεσι ζώουσα;
> ἀλλ' οἴσω σ' εἰς δῶμα λαβών· ὄφελός τί μοι ἔσσῃ,
> οὐδ' ἀποτιμήσω· σὺ δέ με πρώτιστον ὀνήσεις.
> οἴκοι βέλτερον εἶναι, ἐπεὶ βλαβερὸν τὸ θύρηφιν·
> ἦ γὰρ ἐπηλυσίης πολυπήμονος ἔσσεαι ἔχμα
> ζώουσ'· ἢν δὲ θάνῃς τότε κεν μάλα καλὸν ἀείδοις.

Here's a sign in front of me, a great source of profit: I do not dismiss it! Hail my companion of the feast who beats out the dance, lovely in form, welcome is your manifestation! Where did you get this beautiful plaything from, this dappled shell you have put on, tortoise living in the mountains? But taking you up I shall carry you into the house. You will be of some benefit to me, I shall not dishonour you. You will profit me first of all. 'Better to be at home, since outside is harmful' [= Hesiod, *Works and Days* 365]. For you will be a defence against woeful attack while you live, but if you die, then you will be able to sing beautifully.

Hermes' persistent anthropomorphisation of the tortoise is immediately clear from his initial address to the animal as his

4.2 Thauma and the Lyre in the Homeric Hymn to Hermes

'companion of the feast who beats out the dance' (χοροιτύπε δαιτός ἑταίρη). This hints at the future status of the dead tortoise: she will 'beat out the dance' as a lyre in symposia yet to come, a paradoxically energetic manoeuvre for a lifeless animal, and encourage dancing in others. There is a hint here as well that the tortoise has been eroticised and already cast as a sort of sympotic *hetaira* when Hermes first bumps into her seductively 'sashaying along' (σαῦλα ποσὶν βαίνουσα, 28) outside Maia's cave.[14]

This anthropomorphisation of a living animal which will become a strangely vocal inanimate object reflects Hermes' famed ability to cross boundaries, since the lyre itself is an object which embodies the transgression of various conceptual borders.[15] The tortoise suits Hermes' purpose in this respect since it is already an animal which skirts boundaries by its very nature, as the infant god's speech makes clear. As a creature which paradoxically carries its own home on its back, the tortoise is constantly poised on the boundary between inside and outside, as Hermes' bantering use of the Hesiodic line 'better to be at home, since outside is harmful' (οἴκοι βέλτερον εἶναι, ἐπεὶ βλαβερὸν τὸ θύρηφιν, 36 = *Works and Days* 365) draws out.[16] Moreover, Hermes' promise to take the living tortoise which dwells outside in the mountains (χέλυς ὄρεσι ζώουσα, 33) into the house (οἴσω σ' εἰς δῶμα, 34), for Hesiod a place of safety, is undercut by the fact that the animal's transition into a lyre which is played indoors at the feast will involve prising it forcibly away from the home on its back.

The antithesis between inside and outside is not the only one which is overturned here. The tortoise is by definition a liminal animal which also hovers between the status of animal/*hetaira* and living/dead from the very moment of Hermes' first encounter with his future lyre. But it is the animal's ability to provide a living voice through its death that is emphasised most in the next section

---

[14] See Thomas (2015) 364–5 and (2020) 156; cf. Vergados (2013) 248. For the continued eroticisation of the tortoise lyre later on in the *Hymn*, see lines 475–8.
[15] On Hermes' ability to cross borders in general, see Vernant (1983) 127–75; on borders and Hermes in the *hHerm*. specifically, cf. Kahn (1978) and Clay (2006) 98–103.
[16] See Vergados (2013) 24 on Hermes' citation of the *Works and Days* and how it relates to the distinction between outside and inside which the tortoise inherently blurs in this *Hymn*.

of *hHerm*, as Hermes sets about turning his 'lovely plaything' (ἐρατεινὸν ἄθυρμα, 40) into a singer once he has first 'gouged out the life of the mountain-dwelling tortoise' (αἰῶν' ἐξετόρησεν ὀρεσκώιοιο χελώνης, 42).[17] This strange transition from silent living animal to singing dead instrument is reinforced by the repetition of the phrase 'lovely plaything' (ἐρατεινὸν ἄθυρμα) in line 52 at the moment Hermes begins to play the lyre for the very first time. Hermes' opening address to the tortoise therefore clearly hints at her future function as an instrument. The importance of the tortoise's ability to sing beautifully in death, a quality which the infant god predicts on their first encounter (ἢν δὲ θάνῃς τότε κεν μάλα καλὸν ἀείδοις, 38), becomes clearer as the *Hymn* goes on, since we will see that the lyre possesses a voice which can be used in variety of contexts to make even the gods marvel, and which turns Hermes himself into a source of wonder. The *hHerm*. seems to suggest that the lyre inspires this thaumatic response at least in part due to its inherently paradoxical nature as a dead animal which is able to replicate the voice of an animate creature.[18]

The marvellous paradoxes surrounding the lyre's creation remain an important aspect of the literary tradition surrounding the instrument's invention by Hermes. Sophocles picks up on this in his version of the story of Hermes' theft of Apollo's cattle in the satyr-play *Ichneutai*. In this play the satyr-chorus' astonished and fearful reaction to the lyre is stressed several times. After being

---

[17] Burkert (1983) 39 places an even greater significance on the connection between death and song here, claiming that '[a]ny new creation, even the birth of music, requires ritual killing. Underlying the practical use of bone-flutes, turtle-shell lyres, and the tympanon covered with cowhide is the idea that the overwhelming power of music comes from a transformation of and overcoming of death.' The paradox of the beautiful 'living voice' of an instrument emanating from the dead body of an animal is also present in the riddling lines referring to a conch-shell trumpet which Athenaeus cites (*Deipnosophistae* 457a) and attributes to Theognis (1229–30): ἤδη γάρ με κέκληκε θαλάσσιος οἴκαδε νεκρός, | τεθνηκὼς ζωῷ φθεγγόμενος στόματι (For already a corpse from the sea has called me homewards, speaking with a living mouth though dead).

[18] There is perhaps a further note of irony here if the author of the *Hymn* is implicitly contrasting the unimpressive voices of real-life tortoises with the beautiful future voice of the tortoise-lyre. The nature of the voice of the tortoise was certainly a matter of interest in later Greek texts: Aristotle, for example, discusses animal voices at *Hist. an.* 536a and claims that all oviparous quadrupeds have weak voices, and the tortoise's voice in particular consists of a low hiss; on this and later Greek views concerning the tortoise's voice, see Vergados (2013) 258.

4.2 *Thauma* and the Lyre in the *Homeric Hymn to Hermes*

frightened by the overwhelming new sound of Hermes' instrument, the satyrs beg the nymph Cyllene to tell them 'who in the regions below the ground spoke wondrously with a divine voice' (ἐν τόποις τοῖσ[δε τίς νέρθε γᾶς ὧδ' ἀγαστῶς | ἐγήρυσε θέσπιν αὐδά[ν, 249–50).[19] Cyllene replies that the contrivance they heard making the noise belongs to Hermes, whose astonishing abilities and incredibly swift growth over the course of six days are 'amazing', so much so that they have left the goddess gripped with 'wonder and fear' (ἀγα]στός, ὥστε θαῦμα καὶ φόβος μ' ἔχει, 278). This *thauma* at Hermes himself is paralleled by the satyrs' wonder at the lyre, a reaction caused in part by the paradox of the instrument's status as an inanimate object with a voice (299–300):

ΧΟ: καὶ πῶς πίθωμαι τοῦ θανόντος φθέγμα τοιοῦτον βρέμειν;
ΚΥ: πιθοῦ· θανὼν γὰρ ἔσχε φωνήν, ζῶν δ' ἄναυδος ἦν ὁ θήρ.

CHORUS: Yet how am I to believe that such a voice roars out of something dead?
CYLLENE: Believe it! The creature possesses a voice while dead, but while living it was voiceless.

The lyre even has the ability to create wonder by transforming the satyrs themselves into an astonishing visual and aural spectacle, as Cyllene's labelling of the satyr-chorus' new, unexpected and wild lyre-inspired *choreia* as a *thauma* suggests.[20] In *Ichneutai* as in the *hHerm.* the lyre floats between various antitheses – living/dead, animate/inanimate, voiced/voiceless, animal/instrument – in a way which accounts to a great extent for its thaumatic effect. As noted in Chapter 2, the strange collapse of boundaries between animate and inanimate, and living and dead, is a primary means of creating wonder when it comes to gazing at *visual* objects; here the transgression of that boundary stretches into the *aural* realm as well.

---

[19] As noted by Lämmle (2013) 432–5, the wonder and fear of the *Ichneutai*'s satyr-chorus at the acoustic effects of this 'voice from below the ground', and the riddling effect of their subsequent stichomythia with Cyllene, is at times suggestive of ancient mystery cult.
[20] *Ichn.* 229–30: ποῖ στροφαὶ νέαι | μανιῶν στρέφουσι; θαῦμα γάρ (To where are the new whirlings of madness whirling you? It is a wonder!). I am grateful to Rebecca Lämmle for drawing my attention to the significance of these lines. On the satyr-chorus' novel *choreia* here, see Lämmle (2013) 232–3 and (2019) 34–5.

4.3 Hermes' Signs and Songs: *Thaumata and Semata*

But how is the potentially wondrous aural effect of the lyre articulated in the *hHerm.*? Over the course of the *Hymn*, the marvellous results of Hermes' performances with the lyre are increasingly emphasised. Immediately following the description of the stretching of the sheep-gut strings which Antigonus later cites in his paradoxographical collection comes the account of Hermes' first performance (52–9):

> αὐτὰρ ἐπεὶ δὴ τεῦξε φέρων ἐρατεινὸν ἄθυρμα
> πλήκτρῳ ἐπειρήτιζε κατὰ μέλος, ἡ δ' ὑπὸ χειρὸς
> σμερδαλέον κονάβησε· θεὸς δ' ὑπὸ καλὸν ἄειδεν
> ἐξ αὐτοσχεδίης πειρώμενος, ἠΰτε κοῦροι
> ἡβηταὶ θαλίῃσι παραιβόλα κερτομέουσιν,
> ἀμφὶ Δία Κρονίδην καὶ Μαιάδα καλλιπέδιλον
> ὡς πάρος ὠρίζεσκον ἑταιρείῃ φιλότητι,
> ἥν τ' αὐτοῦ γενεὴν ὀνομακλυτὸν ἐξονομάζων.

But when he had crafted it, after taking up the lovely plaything he started to try it out in a tuned scale with a plectrum, and by his hand it resounded terrifyingly. And the god tried it out improvisationally and sang beautifully in accompaniment, just as young men in the prime of youth taunt each other with banter at feasts: he sang about how Zeus son of Cronus and Maia with beautiful sandals used to flirt with friendly intimacy, and named his own renowned lineage.

The simile describing Hermes' first experimental song again hints at a possible sympotic context for the future use of the lyre, just as Hermes' initial teasing address to the tortoise prefigured the future use of the instrument. Now during the god's first performance his extempore singing is compared to the impromptu sung banter which young men hurl at each other at the symposium. It is not such banter, however, which Hermes goes on to offer in this case, but a hymn very much like the *hHerm.* itself.[21] Hermes must sing for himself because as an infant god who has not yet confirmed his place among the Olympians (at least in the eyes of the other gods), he does not seem, at least at this point in the narrative of the poem, to have anyone (human or otherwise) to sing praises of what the poet will soon come

---

[21] For example, Hermes' hymn here begins with his own conception and an account of his lineage, just as the *hHerm.* itself begins with the conception of the god (see lines 3–12). On the strongly hymnic features of Hermes' first song, see Vergados (2013) 4–12 and Thomas (2020) 177–81.

4.3 Hermes' Signs and Songs: *Thaumata and Semata*

to term his *thaumata erga* ('wondrous deeds', 80, 440). His own description of Maia's seduction by Zeus thus provides him with a weighty genealogy and acts as implicit self-praise which justifies his claim to a place on Olympus.[22] This also creates a *mise en abyme* effect, as the poet of the *hHerm.* describes Hermes performing nothing other than the present hymn to Hermes. I will return to the significance of this *mise en abyme* effect for the thaumatic power of the *Hymn* as a whole below, but for now it is worth turning to the other *thaumata erga* which Hermes undertakes before he picks up his lyre and sings for the second time.

Before we reach Hermes' second thaumatic performance it is made clear that the young god's verbal *thaumata* are repeatedly and explicitly paralleled by his ability to manipulate visual *semata* (signs) throughout the narrative. This ability to exploit *semata* is enabled by Hermes' facility for the creation of marvellous inventions which combine previously disparate familiar objects of the natural world: first the lyre, and then the deceptive sandals which allow the infant god to mislead Apollo in the search for his cattle by further confusing the twisting tracks which Hermes has forced the livestock to create by walking backwards.[23] The sandals are ingeniously created through the connection of disparate parts and specifically parallel the lyre in their wondrous effect as objects of Hermes' skill (*metis*).[24] In fact, they are first explicitly named as *thaumata* at the very moment of their creation (79–81):

σάνδαλα δ' αὐτίκα ῥιψὶν ἐπὶ ψαμάθοις ἁλίῃσιν
ἄφραστ' ἠδ' ἀνόητα διέπλεκε, θαυματὰ ἔργα,
συμμίσγων μυρίκας καὶ μυρσινοειδέας ὄζους.

Immediately on the sands of the seashore he began to weave together sandals, unthought of and unimaginable, marvellous works, mixing together tamarisk and myrtle twigs.

Hermes' *thaumata erga* and the poet's own art are here aligned, as innovative and unusual compound words (ἄφραστ' ἠδ' ἀνόητα)

---

[22] See Vergados (2013) 4–5.
[23] On the relationship between Hermes' wondrous inventions, see Clay (2006) 113: 'Hermes' sandals, the θαυματὰ ἔργα, resemble the god's other inventions in that disparate things ... are joined together ... to produce something new and unheard of.'
[24] On *thauma* as a natural reaction to *metis* in the *hHerm.*, see Kahn (1978) 106–9 and Clay (2006) 131–2.

are used to express the novelty of Hermes' invention.[25] By this point in the narrative we might already begin to suspect that the bard of the *hHerm*. is as inventive as Hermes: the creation of the sandals is one of the first hints that we are meant to wonder at the bard's *thaumata erga* most of all in this *Hymn*.

The parallel created between the wondrous sandals and the wondrous lyre is reinforced further by the fact that a few lines later Hermes is said to have 'improvised' (αὐτοτροπήσας, 86) the sandals, just as his invention of hymnic song on the lyre arises in an improvisatory manner (cf. ἐξ αὐτοσχεδίης πειρώμενος, 55). It is Hermes' ability to make something appear out of nothing, to metamorphose a product of culture out of nature, which creates a sense of wonder in those who are on the receiving end of such transformations. But it is not only the inventions themselves but also the products and the effects they facilitate that cause *thauma* in this *Hymn*. In the case of the lyre, these products consist of the instrument's melodies and the vocal performance it enables; in that of the sandals, the concealment of the cow tracks and the increase of confusion this entails.

We see this in action when Apollo is explicitly struck by wonder at the *semata* which Hermes' invention has created during the cattle rustling (218–25):

> ἴχνιά τ' εἰσενόησεν Ἑκηβόλος εἶπέ τε μῦθον·
> ὢ πόποι ἦ μέγα θαῦμα τόδ' ὀφθαλμοῖσιν ὁρῶμαι·
> ἴχνια μὲν τάδε γ' ἐστὶ βοῶν ὀρθοκραιράων,
> ἀλλὰ πάλιν τέτραπται ἐς ἀσφοδελὸν λειμῶνα·
> βήματα δ' οὔτ' ἀνδρὸς τάδε γίγνεται οὔτε γυναικὸς
> οὔτε λύκων πολιῶν οὔτ' ἄρκτων οὔτε λεόντων·
> οὔτε τι κενταύρου λασιαύχενος ἔλπομαι εἶναι
> ὅς τις τοῖα πέλωρα βιβᾷ ποσὶ καρπαλίμοισιν.

And the god who shoots from afar noticed the tracks and said: 'Oh! What a great marvel I see with my eyes! These are indeed the tracks of the straight-horned cattle, but they are turned backwards towards the asphodel meadow. And these footsteps come from neither a man nor a woman nor grey wolves nor bears nor

---

[25] Shelmerdine (1981) 111 suggests that the poet is using deliberately novel adjectives to describe Hermes' novel invention here seeing as neither ἄφραστος nor ἀνόητος appear anywhere else in Homer, Hesiod or any of the other *Hymns*.

4.3 Hermes' Signs and Songs: *Thaumata and Semata*

lions. Nor do I think that a shaggy-necked centaur is the one who makes such monstrous tracks with his swift feet'.

Apollo's exclamation at the sight of the tracks plays with *thauma* in an especially rich manner. The formulaic line 'Oh! What a great marvel I see with my eyes!' (ὦ πόποι ἦ μέγα θαῦμα τόδ' ὀφθαλμοῖσιν ὁρῶμαι) is uttered only by mortals in the *Iliad* and the *Odyssey*, often as a result of the recognition of divine presence.[26] Throughout the *hHerm*. Apollo's ceaseless wonder at Hermes' works is reminiscent of the marvelling response of mortals at the actions or presence of gods.[27] As well as contributing to the humorous tone of the *Hymn* as a whole, the fact that Apollo reacts to Hermes' actions in a typically 'mortal' way emphasises that the young god is actually worthy of his place on Olympus after all, as his fellow god reacts to his deeds with awe. This is later confirmed when Apollo's initial astonishment at the misleading *semata* created by the cattle and Hermes' marvellous shoes is reiterated by his later description (342–3) of the confusing cattle's trail created by the infant god: 'the tracks were doubly monstrous, the sort of thing worthy of wonder, the work of a glorious god' (τὰ δ' ἄρ' ἴχνια δοιὰ πέλωρα | οἷά τ' ἀγάσσασθαι καὶ ἀγαυοῦ δαίμονος ἔργα). The monstrous and wondrous tracks thus prompt Apollo's recognition of Hermes' non-mortal nature for the first time by creating a feeling of wonder reminiscent of the way mortals react to divine epiphanies.[28] It is by wielding the power of *thauma*, then, that Hermes is able to turn the tables on his elder brother and firmly

---

[26] Cf. *Il.* 15.286, where this line is uttered by the Achaean Thoas, who is amazed that Hector has survived Ajax's attack and realises that one of the gods has saved him (τις αὖτε θεῶν ἐρρύσατο καὶ ἐσάωσεν, 15.290); cf. *Il.* 20.344, where Achilles has just had a mist shed over his eyes by Poseidon and is amazed that his spear has missed Aeneas, whom he (rightly) assumes must be dear to one of the immortal gods. Cf. also the slight variant of this line at *Od.* 19.36, where Telemachus says 'Oh father! What a great marvel I see with my eyes!' (ὦ πάτερ, ἦ μέγα θαῦμα τόδ' ὀφθαλμοῖσιν ὁρῶμαι) when, led by Athene, he sets off with Odysseus to remove the shields and helmets from the hall before they kill the suitors and sees the house glowing, with the result that he supposes that there is 'surely one of the gods who hold wide heaven inside' (ἦ μάλα τις θεὸς ἔνδον, οἳ οὐρανὸν εὐρὺν ἔχουσι, 19.40).

[27] On the unusual nature of the way in which Apollo reacts with *thauma* not only at the *visual* effect of Hermes' deeds but even to the very sound of Hermes' performance on the lyre, see Lather (2017) 140–4.

[28] See Vergados (2013) 463–4; cf. Turkeltaub (2003) 31–2 on *thauma* as an element of epiphany scenes in epic poetry and Platt (2011) 56–7, 64–5, 68–72 on *thauma* and divine epiphany in general, especially in the *Homeric Hymns*.

assert himself as the more powerful god at this point in the *Hymn* – a paradoxical achievement given that Hermes is still only one day old.

The marvellous *semata* created by the combination of the deceptively reversed cow tracks and Hermes' wonderful shoes are structurally parallel with the marvellous product of his other thaumatic invention in the poem: the music of the lyre and the song which accompanies it.[29] Both the visual *semata* and the musical performances are *thaumata* produced by Hermes, and both are types of epiphanic manifestations of the god's power. The effect of Hermes' first performance on an audience is not made clear to us within the *Hymn*, as no internal audience is present. This is possibly a reflection of his stature at this early point in the poem, since the infant god has not yet gained enough power to command an audience of his fellow gods.[30] This is not the case, however, after Hermes' second performance, where we find the lyre's future patron, Apollo, praising the astonishing musical performance in the strongest terms (439–46):

> νῦν δ' ἄγε μοι τόδε εἰπὲ πολύτροπε Μαιάδος υἱὲ
> ἦ σοί γ' ἐκ γενετῆς τάδ' ἅμ' ἕσπετο θαυματὰ ἔργα
> ἦέ τις ἀθανάτων ἠὲ θνητῶν ἀνθρώπων
> δῶρον ἀγαυὸν ἔδωκε καὶ ἔφρασε θέσπιν ἀοιδήν;
> θαυμασίην γὰρ τήνδε νεήφατον ὄσσαν ἀκούω,
> ἣν οὔ πώ ποτέ φημι δαήμεναι οὔτε τιν' ἀνδρῶν,
> οὔτε τιν' ἀθανάτων οἳ Ὀλύμπια δώματ' ἔχουσι,
> νόσφι σέθεν φηλῆτα Διὸς καὶ Μαιάδος υἱέ.

But now come on and tell me this, son of Maia with many wiles: did these marvellous works follow straight from your birth, or did one of the immortals or one of mortal men bestow this glorious gift and show you divine singing? For I hear this marvellous newly-spoken/newly-slain voice, which I say that no mortal or immortal who holds Olympus has ever yet learnt, with the exception of you, tricky son of Zeus and Maia.

Apollo's first mention of Hermes' 'marvellous works' relates both to his preceding song, as the reference to his 'divine singing'

---

[29] Cf. Steiner (1994) 44 on the lyre and the cattle tracks as the two 'message-bearing tokens of the first half of the poem'.
[30] See Clay (2006) 103–51 and Vergados (2013) 4–5 on Hermes' process of maturation and its relation to his two songs in the *hHerm*.

4.3 Hermes' Signs and Songs: *Thaumata and Semata*

(θέσπιν ἀοιδήν) in the following lines makes clear, and also to the 'glorious gift' (δῶρον ἀγαυόν) of the lyre itself. It also covers all of the infant Hermes' other inventions and actions in the *Hymn*. But at this point, the particular cause of Apollo's present wonder is the 'wondrous voice' (θαυμασίην ... ὄσσαν) of the instrument he has just heard.[31] The quality of this wondrous voice is described as νεήφατον, a word which, as Oliver Thomas has pointed out, could mean both 'newly-slain' and 'newly-spoken'.[32] Once again, the lyre's ability to straddle boundaries is what lends it its thaumatic power. In the *hHerm.*, this power is something that affects even gods. This is important, since elsewhere in the *Homeric Hymns thauma* is a *topos* of the human response to, and recognition of, the epiphanic revelation of god to man.[33] The *hHerm.* self-reflexively turns this *topos* on its head: Hermes' powerful performance is the final piece of evidence which ensures Apollo's recognition of his younger half-brother as a god truly deserving of his place on Olympus. The very end of Apollo's long praise of Hermes reinforces the importance of *thauma* in this process of quasi-epiphanic revelation and recognition when the god once again returns to the astonishing nature of the performance he has just experienced in line 455: 'I am astonished, son of Zeus, at how lovely your lyre-playing is' (θαυμάζω, Διὸς υἱέ, τάδ' ὡς ἐρατὸν κιθαρίζεις). Wonder, then, is certainly the keynote effect of Hermes' musical performances as a whole, as Apollo's repeated emphasis on his astonished response demonstrates. Furthermore, since this is an aetiological narrative about the invention of the lyre, the *hHerm.* suggests that this wonder carries over into every subsequent divine or human performance with the instrument. This, I suggest, is really where the power of wonder and divine

---

[31] On the particular association of the word ὄσσα with the divine, see Ford (1992) 175–6.
[32] See Thomas (2020) 389.
[33] On *thauma* as a usual response to divine epiphany in the *Homeric Hymns*, see especially Platt (2011) 64–70 and Richardson (2010) 102 on *hAp.* 134–9. For examples from the *Hymns*, cf. Anchises' sense of wonder at Aphrodite's sudden appearance before him (despite the fact that she initially presents herself in human form) at *hAph.* 84–5, Dionysus' wondrous manifestations (line 34) and the pirates astonished response (line 50) in the *hDion.*, and the Cretan sailors' wonder at Apollo in dolphin guise at *hAp.* 414–5.

epiphany in the *hHerm.* comes into play, as the next section will demonstrate.

4.4 Collapsing Boundaries: Epiphanic *Thauma, Choreia* and Song

Unlike the other major *Homeric Hymns*, the *hHerm.* does not describe to its audience a moment of epiphanic and wonder-inducing revelation of god to mortal within the narrative itself.[34] In other *Homeric Hymns*, in particular those to Demeter (2), Apollo (3), Aphrodite (5), and Dionysus (7), epiphanic *thauma* is indeed a constant keynote of the meetings of gods and mortals. Why, then, is *thauma* not explicitly connected to the epiphanic revelation of the titular god to mortals in the *hHerm.*? It seems that the answer lies in the nature of Hermes himself in this *Hymn*. Since Hermes is a figure who delights in boundaries and who has not yet quite proven his own place on Olympus at the beginning of the narrative, it is fitting that he is hymned in a way which probes the boundaries between mortal and divine much more intensely and self-referentially than other hymns through the *mise en abyme* effect employed, which also makes the god's wondrous inventions obvious paradigms for ritual and sung praise of the gods in the real world. Another way in which the *Hymn* self-referentially explores the boundaries between the realms of gods and mortal is by depicting *thauma* as a paradigmatic response to music and as a signifier of the meeting point between the divine and human realms.

We also see this in the *Odyssey* when the poet describes Odysseus' wonder at the skilful dancing of the Phaeacian youths, accompanied by the bard Demodocus' lyre-playing. This scene becomes an archetypal depiction of the astonishing effects of marvellous *choreia* on its audience (8.261–5):

> κῆρυξ δ' ἐγγύθεν ἦλθε φέρων φόρμιγγα λίγειαν
> Δημοδόκῳ· ὁ δ' ἔπειτα κί' ἐς μέσον· ἀμφὶ δὲ κοῦροι
> πρωθῆβαι ἵσταντο, δαήμονες ὀρχηθμοῖο,

---

[34] On the unusual treatment of the epiphany theme in this poem, see Vergados (2011) 82–104 and Cursaru (2012) 42–8.

4.4 Epiphanic *Thauma, Choreia* and Song

πέπληγον δὲ χορὸν θεῖον ποσίν. αὐτὰρ Ὀδυσσεὺς
μαρμαρυγὰς θηεῖτο ποδῶν, θαύμαζε δὲ θυμῷ.

And the herald approached bearing the clear-voiced lyre for Demodocus. And he then moved into the middle, and the boys in the prime of youth, skilled in dancing, took up their positions around him, and they struck the sacred dancing floor with their feet. And Odysseus was gazing at the flashing of the feet, and he was marvelling in his heart.

The Phaeacians' excellence and frequent indulgence in *choreia*, like their love of constant and carefree feasting, is one of the most notable manifestations of their suprahuman qualities and uncanny closeness to the gods.[35] The wondrous effect that the blurring of the boundaries between the mortal and human realms is able to provoke is similarly depicted in the *Homeric Hymn to Apollo*, where the description of the marvellous performance of the Delian Maidens depicts the potential which the *thauma* of successful human choral activity has to mediate between the realms of men and gods (149–64):

>οἳ δέ σε πυγμαχίηι τε καὶ ὀρχηστυῖ καὶ ἀοιδῆι
>μνησάμενοι τέρπουσιν, ὅταν καθέσωσιν ἀγῶνα.
>φαίη κ' ἀθανάτους καὶ ἀγήρως ἔμμεναι ἀνήρ,
>ὃς τότ' ἐπαντιάσει', ὅτ' Ἰάονες ἀθρόοι εἶεν·
>πάντων γάρ κεν ἴδοιτο χάριν, τέρψαιτο δὲ θυμόν
>ἄνδράς τ' εἰσορόων καλλιζώνους τε γυναῖκας
>νῆάς τ' ὠκείας ἠδ' αὐτῶν κτήματα πολλά.
>πρὸς δὲ τόδε μέγα θαῦμα, ὅου κλέος οὔποτ' ὀλεῖται,
>κοῦραι Δηλιάδες Ἑκατηβελέταο θεράπναι·
>αἵ τ' ἐπεὶ ἄρ πρῶτον μὲν Ἀπόλλων' ὑμνήσωσιν,
>αὖτις δ' αὖ Λητώ τε καὶ Ἄρτεμιν ἰοχέαιραν,
>μνησάμεναι ἀνδρῶν τε παλαιῶν ἠδὲ γυναικῶν
>ὕμνον ἀείδουσιν, θέλγουσι δὲ φῦλ' ἀνθρώπων.
>πάντων δ' ἀνθρώπων φωνὰς καὶ κρεμβαλιαστὺν
>μιμεῖσθ' ἴσασιν· φαίη δέ κεν αὐτὸς ἕκαστος
>φθέγγεσθ'· οὕτω σφιν καλὴ συνάρηρεν ἀοιδή.

And mindful of you [Apollo] they [the Ionians] delight you with boxing and dancing and song, whenever they have set up a gathering. A man present then when the Ionians are gathered would think that they were immortal and unaging:

---

[35] On Demodocus' lyre-playing and the dance of the Phaeacians as the archetypal scene of wonder-inducing *choreia*, see e.g. Power (2011) 82–5, Kurke (2012) 228 and (2013) 153–4, and Olsen (2017) 5–11.

he would see the charm of everything, and be delighted in his heart while looking at the men and the women with beautiful girdles, and the swift ships and their many possessions. And in addition there is this great wonder, the fame of which will never come to an end: the Delian Maidens, servants of the Far-Shooter. After they have first hymned Apollo, they then in turn hymn Leto and Artemis pourer of arrows, and then mindful of the men and women of the past they sing a song, and they enchant the tribes of men. And they know how to imitate the voices and rhythmic rattling of castanets of all men. Each man would think he himself is speaking – so beautifully does their song hang together.[36]

In the *hAp.* the events of the Ionian festival on Delos are focalised through the eyes of a deliberately anonymous 'everyman', a hypothetical spectator who demonstrates the desired and ideal effect that witnessing the festival and the accompanying performance of the Delian Maidens would have on anyone who happened to be present. Within the ritual space of the festival, the Ionian participants seem to become 'immortal and unaging' (ἀθανάτους καὶ ἀγήρως, 151), two attributes which only the gods, or objects created by the gods, can truly possess.[37] The Ionians are thus portrayed as closer to the gods than mortals ordinarily are during the festival itself, seemingly occupying a liminal space between gods and men (similar to the state of the Phaeacians in the *Odyssey*) which the ritual activity in honour of Apollo has opened up.[38] Moreover, the Delian Maidens' wonder-provoking performance creates an impression of divine presence which draws the audience in and causes the Ionian spectators to 'fuse' or 'merge' in some sense with the *choreuts* themselves.[39]

This ability which the *thauma* arising from song, dance and music for the gods has to create a space within which the divine and human realms might touch upon one another is thus essential to the self-reflexive workings of the *hHerm.* as a narrative which both describes and enacts the confirmation of the young Hermes'

---

[36] Here reading κρεμβαλιαστύν ('rhythmic rattling of castanets') rather than the common variant βαμβαλιστύν ('chatter, incomprehensible babble') in line 162: for summaries of the arguments for the former and against the latter, see Peponi (2009) 41–60.
[37] See Kurke (2012) 225 on the overtones of divinity associated with this phrase in early hexameter poetry.
[38] On the features of Phaeacia in the *Odyssey* which suggest a festival setting involving poetic contests, see especially Ford (1992) 116–20.
[39] See especially Kurke (2012) 223–4 and (2013) 146–60 on the significance of *thauma* in the *hAp.* for the creation of this kind of impression of divine presence.

4.4 Epiphanic *Thauma, Choreia* and Song

status as a divinity. This is because a human performance is conceived of as a fragment or echo of an eternal, divine music – just as the Phaeacians' endless dance, song and feasting echo the enviable and marvellous lifestyle of the gods, so too does mortal *choreia*, especially in a festival context, simultaneously represent and provide a form of vicarious access to the gods' wondrous musical activities. For this reason Hermes' wondrous lyre-playing, with its ability to astonish even the gods, is simultaneously one of the means by which he eventually proves his right to inhabit the divine rather than the mortal realm, and a mode of playfully signalling the young god's temporarily indeterminate status, as he partakes of an activity seemingly more befitting the human realm and hymns himself with the lyre. Furthermore, *thauma* is associated within the narrative of the *hHerm.* not with the description of a god's revelation to a mortal, but with the inventions and actions of Hermes himself. Since the lyre is the foremost of these inventions it becomes visually manifest evidence of Hermes' power and symbolic of the thaumatic power of the entire bardic tradition. The *thauma* associated with the manifestation of a god is thus transferred to the instrument itself, and the aetiological nature of the *Hymn* makes clear that all subsequent lyre performances partake of this effect. Moreover, the *mise en abyme* effect created by the two wondrous performances described in the narrative further reinforces this effect. For this reason, as the *Hymn* progresses, it becomes clear that we are ultimately supposed to wonder at the epiphanic embodiment of Hermes we see made manifest before us as the *Hymn* is performed: the singer himself. By performing the *Hymn* the bard brings the realms of men and gods closer together by becoming a visually manifest stand-in for Hermes the lyre player. The audience's marvelling response to the bard is thus a reflection of Apollo's wondering response to Hermes, and vice versa.[40]

This sense that a solo performer may in some manner represent a wondrous epiphanic manifestation of a god through the medium of musical or poetic performance is not confined to the *hHerm.*

---

[40] Cf. Vergados (2013) 13: 'If the god's song causes wonder in his audience, the poet's performance lays claim to a similar effect.'

alone. In Herodotus' *Histories*, this wonder-inducing aspect of music and song is strongly hinted at in another literary representation of lyre-playing: the famous story of Arion and the dolphin (1.23–4). At the very beginning of this account, Herodotus describes the well-known narrative concerning the abduction, sea dive and subsequent rescue of the citharode Arion by dolphins as a 'very great wonder' (θῶμα μέγιστον, 1.23).[41] The reasons for this wonder become clear in the description of Arion's musical performance at *Histories* 1.24. Here the marvellous collapse of firm boundaries between humans, gods and animals is described in a way which makes us reflect further on the nature and effect of musical performance in Greek thought. This begins when Arion beseeches the pirates to allow him to dress himself in his citharodic costume and sing on the quarter deck of the ship's stern before killing himself as they have demanded:

τοὺς δὲ ἐν τῷ πελάγεϊ ἐπιβουλεύειν τὸν Ἀρίονα ἐκβαλόντας ἔχειν τὰ χρήματα. τὸν δὲ συνέντα τοῦτο λίσσεσθαι, χρήματα μέν σφι προϊέντα, ψυχὴν δὲ παραιτεόμενον. οὔκων δὴ πείθειν αὐτὸν τούτοισι, ἀλλὰ κελεύειν τοὺς πορθμέας ἢ αὐτὸν διαχρᾶσθαί μιν, ὡς ἂν ταφῆς ἐν γῇ τύχῃ, ἢ ἐκπηδᾶν ἐς τὴν θάλασσαν τὴν ταχίστην· ἀπειληθέντα δὴ τὸν Ἀρίονα ἐς ἀπορίην παραιτήσασθαι, ἐπειδή σφι οὕτω δοκέοι, περιιδεῖν αὐτὸν ἐν τῇ σκευῇ πάσῃ στάντα ἐν τοῖσι ἑδωλίοισι ἀεῖσαι· ἀείσας δὲ ὑπεδέκετο ἑωυτὸν κατεργάσασθαι. καὶ τοῖσι ἐσελθεῖν γὰρ ἡδονὴν εἰ μέλλοιεν ἀκούσεσθαι τοῦ ἀρίστου ἀνθρώπων ἀοιδοῦ, ἀναχωρῆσαι ἐκ τῆς πρύμνης ἐς μέσην νέα. τὸν δὲ ἐνδύντα τε πᾶσαν τὴν σκευὴν καὶ λαβόντα τὴν κιθάρην, στάντα ἐν τοῖσι ἑδωλίοισι διεξελθεῖν νόμον τὸν ὄρθιον, τελευτῶντος δὲ τοῦ νόμου ῥῖψαί μιν ἐς τὴν θάλασσαν ἑωυτὸν ὡς εἶχε σὺν τῇ σκευῇ πάσῃ.

But when they were at sea, the pirates plotted to throw Arion overboard and take his money. When he realised this, he entreated them and offered his money to them, begging for his life. But he did not persuade them: instead the sailors ordered him to either kill himself, so that he might be buried on land, or to cast himself into the sea immediately. Arion, being between a rock and hard place, begged them (since their will was such) to allow him to stand on the quarterdeck in his full citharodic costume and sing. And after singing, he promised, he would finish himself off. The sailors, pleased by the opportunity of hearing the best singer in the world, withdrew from the stern to the middle of the ship. Arion, after putting on his full garb and taking up his cithara, stood on the quarterdeck and went through the *nomos orthios* [a high-pitched song in honour of Apollo] in full,

---

[41] On the significance of wonder in Herodotus' account of the Arion story, see Munson (2001) 251–5.

4.4 Epiphanic *Thauma, Choreia* and Song

and after finishing the *nomos* he cast himself into the sea clad in his full citharodic costume.

The emphasis placed on Arion's appearance in this passage is striking. The fact that Arion performs these actions in his complete citharodic costume (*skeue*) is stressed no fewer than three times (τῇ σκευῇ πάσῃ ... πᾶσαν τὴν σκευὴν ... τῇ σκευῇ πάσῃ) in a few lines.[42] This suggests that his visual appearance is as significant as the music which emanates from the lyre.[43] Here we once again catch sight of the original visual reference of *thauma*: it is not the aural aspect of Arion's song alone which provides its wondrous impact, impressing the pirates and drawing the dolphin towards him, but the whole sensory experience of the citharodic performance.

The importance of the combination of the visual and aural aspects of Arion's performance becomes clear once the potential meaning of his citharodic *skeue* is examined. Timothy Power has suggested that the citharode's *skeue* is not only essential in marking the performer out from other people and signifying that he is 'a musical magician capable of wonders' but that the *skeue* even suggests that the musician is to be seen for the duration of the performance as some sort of epiphanic manifestation of a god (in this case, Apollo).[44] Several details in Herodotus' description of Arion's reappearance after his marvellous dive and rescue reinforce this suggestion (1.24):

καὶ τοὺς μὲν ἀποπλέειν ἐς Κόρινθον, τὸν δὲ δελφῖνα λέγουσι ὑπολαβόντα ἐξενεῖκαι ἐπὶ Ταίναρον. ἀποβάντα δὲ αὐτὸν χωρέειν ἐς Κόρινθον σὺν τῇ σκευῇ, καὶ ἀπικόμενον ἀπηγέεσθαι πᾶν τὸ γεγονός. Περίανδρον δὲ ὑπὸ ἀπιστίης Ἀρίονα μὲν ἐν φυλακῇ ἔχειν οὐδαμῇ μετιέντα, ἀνακῶς δὲ ἔχειν τῶν πορθμέων. ὡς δὲ ἄρα παρεῖναι αὐτούς, κληθέντας ἱστορέεσθαι εἴ τι λέγοιεν περὶ Ἀρίονος. φαμένων δὲ ἐκείνων ὡς εἴη τε σῶς περὶ Ἰταλίην καί μιν εὖ πρήσσοντα λίποιεν ἐν Τάραντι, ἐπιφανῆναί σφι τὸν Ἀρίονα ὥσπερ ἔχων ἐξεπήδησε· καὶ τοὺς ἐκπλαγέντας οὐκ ἔχειν ἔτι ἐλεγχομένους ἀρνέεσθαι.

And the pirates sailed away to Corinth, but they say that the dolphin picked Arion up on its back and dropped him off at Taenarum. After landing there he went to

---

[42] On the unusual nature of Herodotus' repeated emphasis on Arion's *skeue*, see Power (2010) 25–7, Gray (2001) 14–15 n. 15 and Herington (1985) 16–17.
[43] Cf. Power (2010) 11: 'A powerful visual impact is made even before the music begins. The *kithara* alone inspires wonder and curiosity.'
[44] See Power (2010) 25.

Corinth with his citharodic costume and on arrival narrated everything that had happened. Periander, being of a naturally suspicious disposition, put him under guard and did not release him, and kept a careful eye out for the sailors. When they arrived, they were summoned and asked if they had anything to say about Arion. After they said that he was safe in Italy and that they had left him doing well at Taras, Arion appeared, looking just as he did when he had leapt overboard. And the pirates were astonished and, being confuted, were not able to deny it any longer.

It seems then that Herodotus is playing here with various senses and causes of wonder in his description of this 'very great wonder' (θῶμα μέγιστον, 1.23). First, he explores the nature of seemingly unbelievable stories and the marvelling reaction they provoke. Periander's explicit disbelief of Arion's story (Περίανδρον δὲ ὑπὸ ἀπιστίης), and his testing of both Arion and the pirates, echo the reader's potential scepticism concerning Herodotus' own narration of *thaumata* in the *Histories*. The fact that Arion's story turns out to be true, despite the seemingly unbelievable element of his rescue by a dolphin, is a warning to us at this early point in the *Histories* to be careful about our own potential disbelief of Herodotus' more unlikely accounts.[45]

Furthermore, Herodotus again draws attention to the citharodic *skeue* here (ἀποβάντα δὲ αὐτὸν χωρέειν ἐς Κόρινθον σὺν τῇ σκευῇ). It is specifically as a citharode with all his accoutrements that Arion approaches Periander's court, and it is in his citharodic *skeue* that he will confront the pirates once again. The sense that there is something godlike in the appearance of the musician is also emphasised by the fact that the moment of Arion's reappearance is explicitly staged as a sort of quasi-divine epiphany (ἐπιφανῆναί σφι τὸν Ἀρίονα); at the same time, his sudden reappearance causes a natural sense of astonishment purely due to the fact that the pirates think that he is already dead – are they afraid because they think Arion is a god, or a ghost, or both?[46]

---

[45] On the way in which Periander's initial disbelief tallies with the reader's (and possibly Herodotus' own) initial scepticism about Arion's story, see Packman (1991) 400; cf. also Munson (2001) 252.

[46] See Power (2010) 27: 'The second surprise appearance of Arion in front of the sailors is configured as a divine epiphany – specifically, Arion in the fullness of his citharodic persona resembles none other than Apollo *kitharoidos*.' Cf. Lonsdale (1993) 93–4 on the 'quasi-divine status' of Arion in Herodotus' tale and Munson (2001) 253 on Arion's status as 'an almost sacral figure' in Herodotus' account.

4.4 Epiphanic *Thauma, Choreia* and Song

Arion therefore transgresses several seeming boundaries with his sudden epiphany here, being both alive and dead, human and divine. No wonder the pirates are astonished. Moreover, the result of Arion's sudden appearance is the same as the archetypal response to divine epiphany itself: astonished wonder and paralysing fear, as the pirates' reaction (τοὺς ἐκπλαγέντας) makes clear. Arion is not just a human singer in the moment of his citharodic performance of a *nomos* to Apollo, but a representation of the god himself, who allows those watching and listening to access, in some sense, the divine realm.

This becomes clear from another aspect of the Arion story. Just as *thauma* is presented as an integral aspect of the birth of both the hymnic genre and the later sympotic uses of the lyre in the *hHerm.*, so too is it shown to be an essential aspect of the aetiology of dithyramb itself in book 1 of the *Histories*. In Herodotus' account Arion is presented as the *protos heuretes* of this mode of song: 'the first man of those we know who made and named the dithyramb and taught it in Corinth' (διθύραμβον πρῶτον ἀνθρώπων τῶν ἡμεῖς ἴδμεν ποιήσαντά τε καὶ ὀνομάσαντα καὶ διδάξαντα ἐν Κορίνθῳ, 1.23).[47] Arion's status as a marvellous performer in Herodotus' account suggests that *thauma* implicitly bleeds over into the genre of dithyramb itself.[48] As both an emotion and cognitive state which, in Richard Neer's terms, inherently acts as a 'synapse' between outside and inside, wonder becomes in this way the paradigmatic response to music and song which brings gods and men into closer contact with one another. *Thauma* is the response

---

[47] See D'Alessio (2013) 113–18 for a discussion of what this passage means in relation to the genesis of dithyramb; on the relation between Herodotus' passage about Arion and his aetiology of the dithyrambic genre, see Lonsdale (1993) 93–4, Csapo (2003) 91–2, Csapo and Miller (2007) 10–11, Steiner (2011) 304, Pavlou (2012) 517–18, Kowalzig (2013) 34, and Hedreen (2013) 187.

[48] In Bacchylides 17, *thauma* plays a similarly important role in the aetiological account of the paean, with Theseus' wonder-inducing reappearance on the deck of the ship after his dive into the sea framed as a marvellous quasi-divine epiphany. Theseus' astonishing reappearance, like the typical epiphanic appearance of a god, is a cause of 'wonder for everyone' (θαῦμα πάντεσσι, 123) who witnesses it and can be read as an aetiology of the paean itself because it acts as the immediate cause of the outbreak of the Athenians' choral song within the poem and casts Theseus as a *de facto choregos* (see Calame (1996) 207–8, Fearn (2007) 255, and Pavlou (2012) 537 n. 95 on Theseus as *choregos* in Bacchylides 17; cf. also Hedreen (2011) 494 on the depiction of Theseus leading a dance as *choregos* on his arrival in Crete on the François Vase).

that this blurring of the boundaries between mortal and divine provokes, and as a result it becomes integral to all subsequent acts of ritual music-making, dance and song.[49]

---

[49] See also Ford (1992) 6, 55, 91, 195–6, 200 on the audience's experience of epic performance as a kind of 'divine epiphany'.

5

THE EXPERIENCE OF *THAUMA*: COGNITION, RECOGNITION, WONDER AND DISBELIEF

γέρων δ' ἰθὺς κίεν οἴκου,
τῇ ῥ' Ἀχιλεὺς ἵζεσκε διίφιλος· ἐν δέ μιν αὐτὸν
εὗρ', ἕταροι δ' ἀπάνευθε καθήατο· τὼ δὲ δύ' οἴω,
ἥρως Αὐτομέδων τε καὶ Ἄλκιμος, ὄζος Ἄρηος,
ποίπνυον παρεόντε· νέον δ' ἀπέληγεν ἐδωδῆς
ἔσθων καὶ πίνων· ἔτι καὶ παρέκειτο τράπεζα.
τοὺς δ' ἔλαθ' εἰσελθὼν Πρίαμος μέγας, ἄγχι δ' ἄρα στὰς
χερσὶν Ἀχιλλῆος λάβε γούνατα καὶ κύσε χεῖρας
δεινὰς ἀνδροφόνους, αἵ οἱ πολέας κτάνον υἷας.
ὡς δ' ὅτ' ἂν ἄνδρ' ἄτη πυκινὴ λάβῃ, ὅς τ' ἐνὶ πάτρῃ
φῶτα κατακτείνας ἄλλων ἐξίκετο δῆμον,
ἀνδρὸς ἐς ἀφνειοῦ, θάμβος δ' ἔχει εἰσορόωντας,
ὣς Ἀχιλεὺς θάμβησεν ἰδὼν Πρίαμον θεοειδέα·
θάμβησαν δὲ καὶ ἄλλοι, ἐς ἀλλήλους δὲ ἴδοντο.
τὸν καὶ λισσόμενος Πρίαμος πρὸς μῦθον ἔειπε·
μνῆσαι πατρὸς σοῖο, θεοῖς ἐπιείκελ' Ἀχιλλεῦ,
τηλίκου ὥς περ ἐγών, ὀλοῷ ἐπὶ γήραος οὐδῷ.

And the old man went straight to the house where Achilles dear to Zeus was accustomed to sit. He found him there, but his companions sat far off; two of them alone, warrior Automedon and Alkimos, scion of Ares, were busily attending to him. And Achilles had just turned away from his food, from eating and drinking, and the table still lay beside him. Unnoticed by them great Priam came in, and then after standing next to him took Achilles' knees in his hands and kissed his hands, the terrible man-slaying hands which had slaughtered many of his sons. And just as when suffocating madness has come over a man, who has killed someone in his own country and comes to the country of other people, to the house of a wealthy man, and wonder takes hold of those who look at him, in this way Achilles wondered seeing godlike Priam, and the others wondered as well, and looked at each other. And Priam entreated him, and said this to him: 'Remember your father, godlike Achilles, of similar age to me, on the deadly threshold of old age'.

Iliad 24.471–87

The climactic meeting of Achilles and Priam in the middle of the *Iliad*'s final book has long been considered one of the most moving episodes in the entire Greek literary tradition. Wrath (μῆνις), the emotion which is held up in the poem's first line as the essential motivation of the *Iliad*'s entire narrative, and which is at the forefront of Achilles' mind from the moment he loses Briseis, finally gives way to pity over the course of this encounter. The emergence of pity as the foremost emotion aroused in Achilles, and by extension in us the audience, has been emphasised by recent critics as perhaps the most essential element in the success of book 24 as a fitting closure to the action of the *Iliad* as a whole.[1] But pity is not the only emotional keynote which this scene explores. Before pity is provoked by Priam's supplicatory actions and words, it is wonder which is thrust to the forefront of our attention. Achilles first marvels at Priam's sudden quasi-epiphanic appearance, but as the scene draws on it becomes clear that this is not the only aspect of their mutual wonder which these lines draw to our attention. For wonder is also one of the predominant emotional responses which the young warrior and the old king feel in each other's presence at the mutual recognition of the similarities which exist between them, as well as an effect of the cognitive realisation that their current situations are perhaps not as diametrically opposed as they might have appeared at first glance. It is precisely the double-edged impact of *thauma* as both an emotional and cognitive response that this chapter explores in more detail.

Recognition (*anagnorisis*) is configured from Homer onwards as producing an inherently astonishing effect on both an emotional and cognitive level. Not only is *thauma* consistently conceived of as an emotional reaction to the recognition that what was initially perceived to be radically 'other' is in some sense uncannily familiar, and vice versa; it is also seen as a sort of catalyst which kickstarts the cognitive processes of realisation and learning

---

[1] Especially in the influential reading of the *Iliad* as a poem with pity at its heart which Macleod (1982) 14 puts forth: cf. his thoughts on the place of the final book within Homer's overall conception (p. 8): 'if the description of suffering and the evocation of pity are the very essence of poetry as Homer conceives it, then Book 24 is a proper complement and conclusion to the rest'.

The Experience of *Thauma*

which potentially ensue as a result of this recognition. By the end of the fifth century BCE the potential impact of the emotional and cognitive effects of *thauma* are subject to an increasing level of scrutiny. On the one hand, *thauma* is increasingly seen to play a vital role within the realm of intellectual endeavour as a force which is able to highlight ignorance, provoke curiosity and act as a spur towards the acquisition of new or modified knowledge. But at the same time, it takes on an increasingly ambivalent aspect as the notion that *thaumata* can be fabricated by humans of their own accord, rather than being produced by and belonging to the natural world or divinely sanctioned by the gods, takes hold. It is in Plato's work that we can most clearly see the culmination of these two responses to *thauma*: on the one hand, wonder becomes the origin of the newly defined field of 'philosophy' itself, but at the same time it has also become a deeply questionable and potentially distracting effect in the hands of anyone but the 'true' philosopher.

But before returning in the following chapters to the significance of *thauma* in the newly codified genre of philosophical writing which Plato's work represents, certain aspects of the position of *thauma* in the intellectual climate of the late fifth and early fourth centuries BCE need to be examined in order to demonstrate how and why responses to *thauma* and *thaumata* started to shift over the course of the fifth century BCE. I will begin in this chapter by examining the place of pity and *thauma* in the meeting between Achilles and Priam in *Iliad* 24, a scene which has often been read as a precursor of Greek tragedy in its thematic focus and emotional intensity, before turning to Aristotle's later reading in the *Poetics* of the relationship between *thauma* and *anagnorisis* in fifth-century Athenian tragedy. This will be followed by an examination of how these themes work in Euripides' *Iphigenia among the Taurians* (henceforth *IT*) and *Ion*. Throughout the meeting between Achilles and Priam, the constant interplay between nearness and distance, familiarity and unfamiliarity, in both literal and metaphorical terms, contributes to the increasing sense of wonder which both men feel in each other's presence. In the recognition-scenes of tragedy the *thauma* provoked by this interplay between nearness and distance becomes even clearer, as the unfamiliar can suddenly appear familiar, or the familiar oddly unfamiliar. Of the Athenian tragedies which remain to us it is the work of Euripides that probes the potential of *thauma* and recognition in the theatre most intensely. Euripides' stance towards *thauma* is particularly illuminating for several reasons. His particular interest in and alignment with the most pressing trends in his contemporary intellectual climate is a *topos* of criticism on the tragedian, who was already called 'the philosopher of the stage' in antiquity.[2] By assessing his treatment of recognition and *thauma*, it becomes possible to discern some of the ways in which wonder fits into contemporary theatrical and intellectual thought.[3] Furthermore, Euripides' later plays seem to exhibit an intense interest in the workings of recognition, a tragic plot device which is almost always inherently wondrous. The most famous example of this interest is of course in Euripides' *Electra* (508–84), where he reworks the recognition scene between Electra and Orestes in Aeschylus' *Choephori* (164–245).[4] But as we shall see, several other Euripidean plays are equally concerned with recognition and its wondrous effects.

The power of the tragic recognition scene to provoke wonder, disbelief and questioning of even our most basic assumptions becomes one of Euripides' predominant concerns in his later plays, some of which are set in very unusual locations. Towards the end of the fifth century, Euripides probes the potential of distant settings most intensely in three plays which share certain similarities of theme, plot and setting: *IT* (c. 414 BCE), *Helen* and *Andromeda* (both first produced in 412 BCE). All three of these

---

[2] The description of Euripides as a 'philosopher of the stage' is first attested at Vitr. *De arch.* 8 pr. 1 (*Euripides ... quem philosophum Athenienses scaenicum appellaverunt*). The first attested uses of this appellation in Greek are found in Athenaeus' *Deipnosophistae* at 158e (ὁ σκηνικὸς οὗτος φιλόσοφος) and 561a (τοῦ σκηνικοῦ φιλοσόφου Εὐριπίδου). See Wright (2005) 226–337 for a comprehensive discussion of Euripides' designation as 'philosopher of the stage' and the influence of contemporary intellectual trends and philosophical ideas in his 'escape-tragedies' set in distant lands (*Helen, IT, Andromeda*).

[3] On aspects of Euripides' plays which are influenced by and reflective of contemporary intellectual trends more generally, see e.g. Reinhardt (1960) 227–56, Winnington-Ingram (1969) 127–42, Conacher (1998), Allan (1999–2000) 145–56 and Dunn (2017) 447–67.

[4] For recent treatments of the relationship between the recognition-scenes in Aeschylus' *Choephori* and Euripides' *Electra*, see e.g. Davies (1998) 389–403, Torrance (2011) 179–92 and (2013) 14–33 and Zeitlin (2012) 361–78.

The Experience of *Thauma*

plays begin with endangered female protagonists trapped in distant lands that lie towards the edges of the earth. Iphigenia has been transported from Aulis to the Taurian Chersonese in the north, Helen is residing in Egypt instead of Troy, while Andromeda is bound and awaiting rescue in Ethiopia near the south-western boundary of the known world.[5] In both *IT* and *Helen*, a heroic Greek male arrives in these distant locales and a series of complicated (mis)recognitions soon ensue; the fragmentary state of *Andromeda* makes it difficult to say much about the play with certainty, but it is clear that Perseus arrives in Ethiopia and encounters Andromeda there, just as Menelaus finds Helen in Egypt and Orestes meets Iphigenia on the Taurian shore.

This chapter examines the connection between recognition and *thauma* in the *IT* and shows how both of these themes touch upon another central Euripidean concern in that play: the mythic tradition. After examining these issues the chapter then turns to Euripides' *Ion* (c. 413 BCE), a work which was very probably produced within a few years of *IT*, *Helen* and *Andromeda*. *Ion* does not at first glance seem easily comparable with these three plays since, far from focusing on the plight of endangered women in distant lands, it concentrates on the life of a young man who dwells in Delphi, the very navel of the Greek world. But when examined more closely, *Ion* can be seen to share some of the most pressing concerns of other Euripidean plays of this period. Ion may live at the very centre of the world, but he has been abandoned by his absent parents in the same way that Helen, Iphigenia and Andromeda have been left stranded at the edges of the earth, and his own identity turns out to be anything but fixed and well-centred, as the uncanny familial recognitions (and misrecognitions) of the play gradually reveal. Both *IT* and *Ion* are concerned with astonishing familial recognitions in unexpected locations. Both focus on a paradoxical interplay between spatial nearness and distance. This interplay results in *thauma*, which brings the

---

[5] The Ethiopian setting of *Andromeda* is situated in the far west, as fr. 145 *TrGF* Kannicht, which describes the monster approaching Andromeda 'from the Atlantic sea' (ἐξ Ἀτλαντικῆς ἁλός), suggests. On the distant western setting of *Andromeda*, see Klimek-Winter (1993) 259, Wright (2005) 128–9 and Collard and Cropp (2008) 151 n. 1.

The Experience of *Thauma*

veracity and reliability of mythic discourse itself into question while simultaneously mediating between self and other, near and far, and familiar and unfamiliar. But before turning to Euripides, it is worth examining the wonder-inducing meeting between Achilles and Priam more closely.

5.1 Recognition, Realisation and *Thauma*: The Meeting of Priam and Achilles

During the climactic meeting between Priam and Achilles in *Iliad* 24 the wonder provoked by Priam's unexpected arrival provides the main point of contact between the tenor and vehicle of the strangely paradoxical simile that follows even before the marvelling reactions of Achilles and his fellow comrades and spectators (ὡς Ἀχιλεὺς θάμβησεν ἰδών ... θάμβησαν δὲ καὶ ἄλλοι, 483–4) are explicitly noted by the narrator. Just as a murderer arriving in a foreign land causes those present to wonder because of the unexpectedness of his arrival and the sense of awe and dread which surrounds a person who has polluted themselves with such a deed, so too does Priam's arrival provoke a natural sense of astonishment. The paradoxes of this simile are multiple. Priam is compared to a murderer, and yet it is the hands of his son's murderer (δεινὰς ἀνδροφόνους, 479) that he is kissing; he is like a man in the land of strangers after fleeing far from home (ὅς τ' ἐνὶ πάτρῃ | φῶτα κατακτείνας ἄλλων ἐξίκετο δῆμον, 480–1), when in fact he is already in his homeland, which is occupied by hostile strangers. The poet dwells on these paradoxes and the resulting wonder they provoke at the very beginning of the meeting between these two enemies to hint towards the ensuing reversals (of Achilles' wrath and, temporarily, of Priam's fortunes) which are about to take place. This also ensures that, in addition to pity, the sense of astonishment apparent at the very opening of this momentous encounter continues to make itself felt in the rest of the episode.

The wonder which arises in this scene has two main causes. The first is the way in which Priam's unseen entry to Achilles' hut and sudden appearance in front of the assembled company is

5.1 Recognition, Realisation and *Thauma*

deliberately framed as a sort of divine epiphany.[6] The second is the inherently wondrous impact of processes of recognition and self-realisation which depend upon an interplay of various kinds of nearness and distance, both literal and metaphorical. I begin with the epiphanic aspect of the passage. As a rule, when a guest visits a host in the *Iliad* or the *Odyssey* they are immediately noticed on approach by those present.[7] Unusually, this is not the case here: Priam's initial entry completely escapes the attention of Achilles and his attendants (τοὺς δ' ἔλαθ' εἰσελθὼν Πρίαμος μέγας, 477), so that he is able to creep up on the greatest Achaean warrior completely unawares and stand beside him (ἄγχι δ' ἄρα στάς, 477), like the unexpected arrival of a god beside a mortal. The epithets used to describe Priam as he appears in front of Achilles further reinforce the sense that his sudden manifestation is somehow akin to a divine epiphany. Before the simile, Priam is described as 'great' (μέγας, 477). This is the only use of this epithet in connection with Priam in the *Iliad*. It is well-chosen in this context as it both hints at his nobility and emphasises the stunning visual impact of his arrival, since magnitude is an aspect of astonishing visual objects which is often presented as a prime cause of their wondrous effect.[8] After the impact of the unexpected sight of the 'great' old man has been conveyed by the paradoxical simile about a murderer arriving in a foreign land, Achilles is then explicitly said to wonder at the sight of 'godlike' Priam before him (Ἀχιλεὺς θάμβησεν ἰδὼν Πρίαμον θεοειδέα, 483). This is not a redundant epithet at this point in the narrative: Priam is godlike in Achilles' eyes precisely because of the manner of his surprising, unexpected and almost supernatural

---

[6] On divine epiphanies and *thauma*, see Chapter 4, sections 3 and 4.

[7] See Macleod (1982) 126 and Richardson (1993) 320–1 on the departure from the usual Homeric motifs associated with the entrance of guests here. The only real parallel to this sudden and unseen approach in Homer is Odysseus' sudden appearance from his goddess-given cloud during the supplication of Arete at *Od.* 7.142–5. In this passage it is significant that Odysseus' unseen entrance is heavily aided by Athene: his arrival is thus, like Priam's, a sort of divine epiphany by proxy which provokes a similar reaction of wonder among onlookers (θαύμαζον δ' ὁρόωντες, 7.145) when the goddess chooses to make Odysseus manifest.

[8] Richardson (1993) 322 correctly recognises the weightiness of this epithet at this moment and connects it to Priam's unseen entrance: 'At this momentous point it is appropriate to speak of "mighty Priam" entering unseen, and it helps to prepare for the shock of surprise when he is suddenly seen, present in all his greatness.'

entrance.[9] The sudden epiphanic *thauma* which explicitly opens the encounter between the young Achaean warrior and the Trojan king continues implicitly through the whole scene. It is connected to the sense that the gods are somehow present in the background of this meeting, and that the reversals which ensue as a result of it are divinely sanctioned. This is not surprising given that the meeting has indeed been encouraged and enabled by the gods. In fact, Priam's unusual epiphanic and wonder-provoking appearance has itself already been prefigured by Hermes' similar disguised appearance to him earlier on in the book (24.352–467), an encounter between god and mortal which acted as a catalyst for the old king's successful journey across the empty battlefield towards his younger foe, and which proleptically echoes the encounter between an older and a younger man which will take place once Priam reaches Achilles' dwelling.

Already in this passage, in the very first moments of the meeting between the two enemies, there are hints of the mutually respectful and reciprocal relationship which is about to be established between Priam and Achilles. These relate to the combination of vision, *thauma* and the implied presence of the gods' power which Priam's epiphanic appearance suggests. In the old man's opening words, Achilles is addressed as 'similar to the gods' (θεοῖς ἐπιείκελ' Ἀχιλλεῦ, 486). On the one hand, this apostrophe is a rhetorical *captatio benevolentiae* of the most basic kind which aims to flatter Achilles through the common enough comparison of warrior to god – though of course Achilles really is as close to a god as any mortal can be. But at the same time, this epithet gives us a hint of how the scene might be focalised from Priam's perspective: just as Priam seems to approach godhood from Achilles' point of view due to his wondrous ability to appear where he is not expected, from Priam's Achilles has already repeatedly demonstrated his ability to loom large in his enemy's life by snatching away the

---

[9] On the significance of θεοειδέα at *Il.* 24.483, see Macleod (1982) 127: this epithet is 'more than a generic and decorative one' because '[i]t corresponds to Achilles; and it makes Priam his equal (cf. 629–32): Priam in his turn addresses him as "god-like" (486)'. I would go even further and suggest that this epithet brings out the similarities between the effect of Priam's unseen entrance and the effects of divine epiphanies on their audiences.

5.1 Recognition, Realisation and *Thauma*

lives of his nearest and dearest. Already then, in the initial glimpses exchanged between the two, we can discern the traces of that explicit and mutual wonder at each other's godlikeness which will increasingly envelope both characters until the point when we reach the end of their initial interaction (24.629-32):

ἦ τοι Δαρδανίδης Πρίαμος θαύμαζ᾽ Ἀχιλῆα,
ὅσσος ἔην οἷός τε· θεοῖσι γὰρ ἄντα ἐῴκει·
αὐτὰρ ὁ Δαρδανίδην Πρίαμον θαύμαζεν Ἀχιλλεύς,
εἰσορόων ὄψίν τ᾽ ἀγαθὴν καὶ μῦθον ἀκούων.

Then indeed Priam son of Dardanus wondered at Achilles, at how big he was and what sort of man he was: for he was like the gods. But Achilles wondered at Priam son of Dardanus, looking upon his noble appearance and hearing his speech.

This mutual wonder at the end of the climactic meeting creates an effect of ring composition; it also emphasises the importance of *thauma* to the process of mutual recognition and realisation which both Priam and Achilles have undergone. The initial wonder which Achilles feels towards Priam imbues the old man with an aura of divine sanctity and power that finally helps to unlock the young man's sense of pity, and allows this one supplication to be successful, unlike all the many previous supplications of the *Iliad*, which are immediately and coarsely rejected.[10]

The constant interplay of nearness and distance during the central meeting of book 24 is the second central cause of the *thauma* which this scene as a whole provokes. Achilles' initial astonishment is caused by the literal proximity of someone who has previously been, and should by all rights remain, far away from him. At the start of their meeting, Priam is his enemy and he is the killer of the old man's sons; his own friend Patroclus' death can be attributed to Priam's son Hector and in some sense to Priam personally as the foremost leader of the Trojans. His wonder at Priam's appearance is not only because of its unexpected suddenness but also because the person in front of him, as a result of their enmity, is a manifestation of extreme otherness. And yet it does not take long before both men find they have more in common than

---

[10] Before this moment, every supplication made in the *Iliad* has been rejected: see Macleod (1982) 15–16 for examples.

The Experience of *Thauma*

first anticipated. The paradoxes and inversions of the opening simile, which casts Priam as a young man who has slaughtered others and found himself in a foreign land – a young man who, like Achilles, has blood on his hands and is unable to return home – provides perhaps the first hint of this. The most striking and wonder-provoking collision of nearness and distance in this passage, however, is surely the way in which Achilles seems to recognise his own father in the father of his enemy. Priam's exhortation to 'remember your father' (μνῆσαι πατρὸς σοῖο, 486) explicitly encourages Achilles in some way to recognise his own father's plight, not least because Peleus was both a famous provider for the exiled (most obviously Patroclus), and a notorious exile himself, banished by his father for the murder of his half-brother Phocus.[11] Achilles does indeed think of his own father after the old man's opening speech, as the fact that Priam's words 'roused a desire to weep for his father in him' (τῷ δ' ἄρα πατρὸς ὑφ' ἵμερον ὦρσε γόοιο, 24.507) makes very clear. It is worth remembering as well that Achilles has already configured his own grief for Patroclus as 'like that of a father who wails aloud for his son as he burns his bones' (ὡς δὲ πατὴρ οὗ παιδὸς ὀδύρεται ὀστέα καίων, 23.222): another unexpected similarity between the two men. By the end of their meeting, both Achilles and Priam have recognised the similarity of their mutual suffering and have discovered that they are closer to one another than they first envisaged. This sort of recognition is not just a renewed understanding of the other, but can be termed a kind of tragic 'realisation' enabled by *thauma* – a form of recognition which encompasses a discovery of the universality of death, suffering and grief in the human condition and one's place in it. This provokes a renewed sense of wonder at the closeness of an object which was once thought of as being radically distant.[12]

This type of wonder, especially in cases where it is caused by the unexpected recognition or recollection of familial relationships, prefigures some of the uses of *thauma* in later Greek poetic genres, especially Attic tragedy. For this reason, Homer's attention

---

[11] See Heiden (1998) 4–6.
[12] See Rutherford (1982) 159–60 on the tragic realisation which takes place in the scene between Achilles and Priam in *Il.* 24, especially p. 147 on 'realisation' as a broader form of *anagnorisis* which is involved in the attainment of self-knowledge in later Athenian tragedy.

5.1 Recognition, Realisation and *Thauma*

to the evocation and effects of *thauma* in the middle of book 24 is another way in which Richardson's assessment of the meeting between Priam and Achilles as 'the most dramatic moment in the whole of the *Iliad*' seems especially apt.[13] In the way this episode exposes the uncanny similarities between the two enemies, and in its movement from an initial sense of surprised astonishment (which we might term 'wondering at difference') through to pity, empathy and back to astonishment again (which we might term 'wondering at similarity'), it certainly seems to resemble some of the most moving confrontations between tragic characters in the later dramatic tradition.

Furthermore, the wondrous recognition of the self in the other, and the other in the self, accounts to some extent for the general power and appeal of fifth-century Athenian tragedy to its audience. Often mythical events placed at a spatial and temporal remove from contemporary Athenian life nevertheless show themselves in tragedy to be directly relevant to everyday life. For example, the action may be set over there, in Thebes, in the past, but somehow it applies (often uncomfortably, almost never simply) to the here and now in Athens as well.[14] The *thauma* which this process of recognition involves operates on a cognitive level as a means of forcing an audience to reconsider its own perspective, though the emotional impact of the strange and dislocating effects which this type of unexpected wonder produces is equally significant.

Aristotle well recognised the importance of the dual cognitive and emotional role of wonder in tragedy. Within his wider discussion in the *Poetics* of the connection of tragic *anagnorisis* to the creation of pity and fear, he repeatedly emphasises the importance of the astonishment which ensues from unexpected recognitions in tragic theatre.[15] For Aristotle, the type of wonder aroused by sudden and

---

[13] Richardson (1993) 323.
[14] See e.g. Zeitlin's (1990) 130–67 seminal work on Thebes as a *topos* in Athenian tragedy.
[15] Aristotle first introduces an explicit connection between *anagnorisis* and *ekplexis* at *Poetics* 1454a2–4. Here he suggests that a better, 'astonishing sort of recognition' (ἡ ἀναγνώρισις ἐκπληκτικόν) arises when a play's characters commit actions out of ignorance rather than knowingly and then later recognise the truth of their situation. The impression that *ekplexis* is the effect which a skilful portrayal of *anagnorisis* naturally causes is reinforced by Aristotle's later suggestion that 'the best recognition of all is the one which comes out of the events themselves, since astonishment arises through the probable series of events, just as in Sophocles' *Oedipus* and the *Iphigenia* [i.e.

unexpected *anagnorisis* has both a cognitive and emotional effect on the audience which is intimately connected to a person's supposed ability to learn from mimetic representations.[16] Aristotle's insistence on the potential cognitive as well as emotional power of the evocation of *thauma* in the tragic theatre is in line with his views in the *Metaphysics* (982b12–21) about wonder's status at the beginning of philosophy as a crucial spur to curiosity which causes someone to become aware of their initial ignorance and strive to replace it with knowledge. In that work Aristotle even goes so far as to suggest that 'the philosopher and the lover of myth' – and presumably those who enjoy viewing tragedy can be termed lovers of myth – are naturally the same person, since 'myth is composed of wonders' (ὁ φιλόμυθος φιλόσοφός πώς ἐστιν· ὁ γὰρ μῦθος σύγκειται ἐκ θαυμασίων, *Metaphysics* 982b18–19).[17]

In the time that elapsed between Homer's portrayal of the wondrous and pitiful meeting of Achilles and Priam and Aristotle's formulation of the place of *thauma* in tragic theatre and in philosophical endeavour, wonder has taken on a double-sided and potentially contradictory role in the Greek intellectual tradition. On the one hand, *thaumata* are the natural material of mythic and other types of discourse, such as ethnographic accounts, which relate to spatially or temporally distant domains.[18] The spatial or temporal distance of *thaumata* often causes the reliability and believability of accounts

---

Euripides' *IT*]' (πασῶν δὲ βελτίστη ἀναγνώρισις ἡ ἐξ αὐτῶν τῶν πραγμάτων, τῆς ἐκπλήξεως γιγνομένης δι' εἰκότων, οἷον ἐν τῷ Σοφοκλέους Οἰδίποδι καὶ τῇ Ἰφιγενείᾳ, 1455a16–18). Lucas (1968) 172 argues that the use of the article in τῆς ἐκπλήξεως points to the possibility that Aristotle is here suggesting that *ekplexis* is caused by the process of *anagnorisis* in general, rather than solely by the specific 'best type' of *anagnorisis* mentioned in the previous clause. On *ekplexis* in the *Poetics* and its connection to *anagnorisis*, see Halliwell (2011) 228–30.

[16] Halliwell (1987) 111–12 well describes the broader conception of the relationship between wonder, recognition and understanding which underpins Aristotle's thoughts about the place of *thauma* in tragic plots and actions at *Poetics* 1452a4 ff: 'The "sense of wonder" to which he refers is an experience which startles and challenges our capacity to understand what we witness in a play, but it is not one which allows for a deep or final inscrutability: wonder must give way to a recognition of how things do after all cohere "through probability or necessity"'. Cf. also Cave (1988) 43–6 on the connection Aristotle draws between wonder and recognition in the *Poetics*.

[17] See Chapter 3, Section 4, for further discussion of this important passage of the *Metaphysics*.

[18] For more on *thauma* and the Greek ethnographic tradition, see Chapter 3, Section 3, and Chapter 6, sections 1 and 2.

which purport to describe such objects or phenomena to be questioned. This tendency manifests itself in different ways in different genres over the course of the fifth century BCE. For example, in Herodotus' work accounts of marvels must be carefully discussed in relation to the relative weight of personal autopsy and the reliability of hearsay – though the later reception of Herodotus' discussions of the 'great and wondrous deeds' (ἔργα μεγάλα τε καὶ θωμαστά, *Histories* 1.1) associated with both Greeks and barbarians in the past and/or in distant lands shows that his handling of marvels was a major contributing factor to the historian's reputation for lies, despite his open consideration of the relative reliability of his various sources.[19] Elsewhere we begin to see evidence of an increased self-consciousness about the believability of the mythical tradition in general: perhaps the most famous example being Pindar's First *Olympian*, where the 'many marvels' (θαύματα πολλά, 28) of a potentially deceptive tradition of poetic myth are put under the spotlight. It is all of these varying reactions to *thauma* which Euripides focuses on in his *IT*, as the next two sections will demonstrate.

5.2 Marvels at the Margins: Geographical and Mythic Innovation in Euripides' *Iphigenia among the Taurians*

It is significant that Euripides seems to have turned his attention to astonishing recognitions in unexpected locations over the course of a few consecutive years, 414–412 BCE. Both *Helen* and *Andromeda* can be securely dated to the City Dionysia of March 412, from comments found in Aristophanes' parodic reworking of central scenes from both plays in *Thesmophoriazusae* (411 BCE), and from further information found in the scholia to that play and also to *Frogs* (405 BCE), where Dionysus makes reference to 'reading [Euripides']

---

[19] See Chapter 6, Section 1, for further discussion of some of the earliest evidence for Herodotus' reputation as a liar by the end of the fifth century in Aristophanes' *Birds*, where it is precisely the language of Herodotean ethnographic *thauma* which the comedian parodies in order to expose the fantastic and unbelievable nature of the new utopian society of Nephelococcygia. See also Priestley (2014) 209–22 on the development of the 'Herodotus the liar' theme in the historian's reception in antiquity more generally.

The Experience of *Thauma*

Andromeda to myself' (ἀναγιγνώσκοντί μοι | τὴν Ἀνδρομέδαν πρὸς ἐμαυτόν, 52–3).[20] It is not possible to date either *IT* or *Ion* with such pinpoint precision, though the current consensus favours placing the first production of both plays in the approximate period 414–412.[21] The stylistic and thematic similarities which these plays share have led to suggestions that either *IT* or *Ion* might have been the third play in Euripides' trilogy of 412, along with *Helen* and *Andromeda*, though there is no firm way to confirm or exclude either suggestion.[22]

It is no coincidence that Euripides should have turned his attention to the wondrous and often simultaneously disturbing effects and problems of the near and far over the course of this period. It was a tumultuous time, as the imperial might of Athens pivoted westwards and embarked upon an ambitious invasion of Sicily, an aggressive act which ultimately proved disastrous by the winter of 413. Over the course of this crucial period, in which Athenian imperial hopes veered from wildly optimistic to crushingly pessimistic, Euripides' continual, pronounced interest in the

[20] At *Thesm.* 1060–1 Echo, a character in Euripides' *Andromeda*, appears and declares that last year in the very same place (presumably the Theatre of Dionysus) she joined with Euripides and aided him in the dramatic contest; cf. Σ ad. *Thesm.* 850, which confirms that *Thesmophoriazusae* was produced when *Helen* was still a very recent play. We know that *Andromeda* and *Helen* were produced together in the previous year in the same trilogy from Σ ad. *Thesm.* 1012, while Σ ad. *Ran.* 53 confirms that *Andromeda* was produced in the eighth year before *Frogs*, a play we know was performed at the Lenaia in 405. This gives a date (with inclusive counting) of 413/12 for *Helen* and *Andromeda* and 412/11 for *Thesmophoriazusae*: further evidence from Aristophanes' play supports a date of 411 (see Austin and Olson (2004) xxxiii–vi for full discussion).

[21] In his edition, Diggle (1981a) 242, 306 suggests a date of c. 414 for *IT* and c. 413 for *Ion*. See Kyriakou (2006) 39–41 on the *IT*'s possible date range; cf. Parker (2016) lxxvi–lxxx on the metrical basis for dating *IT* to c. 414. For a more speculative approach to the metrical dating of *IT* which argues that the play is a pre-415 work, see Marshall (2009) 141–56 and (2014) 11–12. For summaries of the more complicated issues surrounding the precise dating of the *Ion*, see Martin (2018) 24–32 and Gibert (2019) 2–4.

[22] Wright (2005) 44–55 argues at length for a Euripidean 'escape-trilogy' in 412 BCE consisting of *Helen*, *Andromeda* and *IT*; this position is also supported by Jordan (2006) 20. See also Wright (2006) 23–48 for the suggestion that *Helen*, *Andromeda*, *IT* and *Cyclops* were performed as a tetralogy in 412 BCE. Wright (2005) 50 supports his argument for an 'escape-trilogy' in 412 with the suggestion that the final scenes of Aristophanes' *Thesmophoriazusae* subtly parody aspects of Euripides' play, just as early scenes had contained more obvious parodic references to *Helen* and *Andromeda*. For similar suggestions about potential references to the *IT* at the end of *Thesmophoriazusae*, see Hall (1989) 52 n. 71, Bobrick (1991) 67–76, Sommerstein (1994) 237, Cropp (2000) 62 and Kosak (2017) 215. For an alternate possibility, a trilogy consisting of *Helen*, *Andromeda* and *Ion* in 412 BCE, see Zacharia (2003) 3–7.

5.2 Marvels at the Margins

relationship of the Hellenic centre of the world to its more distant and potentially astonishing peripheries reflects, in no simple manner, contemporary concerns about the relationship of Athens to other places and societies which at one moment appear very different, and at another similar.

The complicated relationship between centre and periphery is one of the concerns which lies at the heart of Euripides' *IT*. It is no coincidence that this play also thrusts questions concerning the nature of wonder and its effects to the forefront of the audience's attention. Language connected to *thauma* appears more frequently in the *IT* than in any other surviving Euripidean work.[23] Throughout the play Euripides consistently emphasises the inherent wonder of distant and exotic geographical locations through the repeated appearance of *thauma* and its effects. By the end of the prologue, the unusual and potentially wondrous nature of the play's geographical setting, and its treatment of conventional mythical tradition, has already become self-evident to the audience. Usually the immediate geographical frame of a Euripidean play is made clear in the first few opening lines, but it is not until Iphigenia reveals in line thirty of her opening speech that she is currently in 'the land of the Taurians' (Ταύρων χθόνα) that the *IT*'s setting is revealed – unprecedentedly late for a Euripidean prologue.[24] Before we reach this point, however, Iphigenia begins her speech by focusing first on Aulis, the location most intimately connected to her past fate (1–9):

> Πέλοψ ὁ Ταντάλειος ἐς Πῖσαν μολὼν
> θοαῖσιν ἵπποις Οἰνομάου γαμεῖ κόρην,
> ἐξ ἧς Ἀτρεὺς ἔβλαστεν· Ἀτρέως δὲ παῖς
> Μενέλαος Ἀγαμέμνων τε· τοῦ δ' ἔφυν ἐγώ,
> τῆς Τυνδαρείας θυγατρὸς Ἰφιγένεια παῖς,
> ἣν ἀμφὶ δίνας ἃς θάμ' Εὔριπος πυκναῖς
> αὔραις ἑλίσσων κυανέαν ἅλα στρέφει
> ἔσφαξεν Ἑλένης οὕνεχ', ὡς δοκεῖ, πατὴρ
> Ἀρτέμιδι κλειναῖς ἐν πτυχαῖσιν Αὐλίδος.

With swift horses, Pelops the son of Tantalus, after going into Pisa, wedded the daughter of Oenomaus who gave birth to Atreus. And Menelaus and Agamemnon

---

[23] See Budelmann (2019) 289–304 on the prevalence of *thauma* in *IT*.
[24] Wright (2005) 129.

The Experience of *Thauma*

were Atreus' children. From Agamemnon I was born, Iphigenia, the child of the daughter of Tyndareus. Near the eddies which the Euripus with numerous breezes often turns about, making the dark-blue sea roll, my father – so it's claimed – for the sake of Helen sacrificed me to Artemis, in the famous mountain clefts of Aulis.

The delay before the revelation that Iphigenia is in fact no longer in Greece at all allows the audience's geographical expectations to be manipulated. Iphigenia focuses at the very beginning of the prologue on the idea of swift movement and travel from one location to another, not only with respect to her own swift dislocation from the famous clefts of Aulis, which she describes at length before revealing her current location, but also by picking out the episode in her own ancestral history which is most strongly related to the idea of travel: Pelops' journey to Pisa for his famous chariot race (1–2). The connection between geographical dislocation and mythical innovation, and the surprising effects which ensue from the combination of these two factors, is in this way made immediately apparent from the play's opening lines.

Euripides certainly did not invent the story of Iphigenia's presence in the Taurian land wholesale, as Herodotus' description of Scythia and other northern lands in book four of the *Histories* demonstrates. In Herodotus' account, however, Iphigenia herself is not said to have carried out sacrifices of Greeks washed up on the shore while she was among the Taurians: instead, 'the Taurians themselves say that Iphigenia the daughter of Agamemnon is the deity to whom they make sacrifices' (τὴν δὲ δαίμονα ταύτην τῇ θύουσι λέγουσι αὐτοὶ Ταῦροι Ἰφιγένειαν τὴν Ἀγαμέμνονος εἶναι, 4.103). There is also one other play we know about which may have focused on Iphigenia's presence among the Taurians. This is Sophocles' *Chryses* (frs. 726–9 *TrGF* Radt). The play possibly depicted the events which occurred after Orestes and Iphigenia fled from the north with a statue of Artemis in tow and the Taurian king Thoas in pursuit. But even if we accept that Sophocles' play focused on this later stage of the escape – and the fragmentary remains do not make the events of the

5.2 Marvels at the Margins

plot at all clear – the action of *Chryses* is certainly not set in the far-off land of the Taurians.[25]

The precise location of the distant Taurian territory which Iphigenia and Orestes find themselves inhabiting in Euripides' play was itself a matter of dispute in the fifth century, though it seems to be located somewhere towards the north-eastern edges of the known world, with the Taurians themselves conceived of as a sort of 'semi-mythical' race.[26] This setting is certainly unusual, if not unique, for a tragedy, as is the placement of both Iphigenia *and* Orestes in the Taurian land. In fact, it is highly probable that Orestes' rescue of his sister and the Taurian statue of Artemis is a mythical innovation on the part of Euripides, who seems to combine accounts of Iphigenia's escape from Aulis and removal to the far north-eastern edges of the world with Orestes' famous wanderings in order to depict a novel and unexpected familial recognition in an unfamiliar setting.[27]

Over the course of the play various questions about the novelty of myth and the general reliability of the mythical tradition – in both its previous incarnations in the poetry of the past, and in its present Euripidean form – become some of the *IT*'s most pressing and self-conscious concerns. Euripides lays the groundwork of this incessant questioning from the play's first word: Pelops. Putting the name of Iphigenia's somewhat dubious ancestor into

---

[25] The Roman Republican tragedian Pacuvius produced a play entitled *Chryses* which may be based on the plot of Sophocles' *Chryses* (see Warmington 1936: 192–209). Its remaining fragments suggest that the plot follows the version of the story concerning the aftermath of Iphigenia and Orestes' escape which is related by Hyginus (*Fabulae* 120–1). He tells us that after fleeing from the Taurian land with the Artemis statue, the siblings arrive at Sminthe (location unknown, but probably in the Troad), where Chryses, the child of Agamemnon and Chryseis, helps his newly-discovered half-brother Orestes to kill the pursuing Taurians. Iphigenia, Orestes and Chryses then go to Mycenae together with the statue of Artemis. On this version of the myth and its possible relation to Sophocles' *Chryses*, as well as other possible versions of the story involving Chryses, Orestes and Iphigenia, see e.g. Wilamowitz (1883) 257–8, Lloyd-Jones (1996) 340–3 and Slater (2000) 315–16. A probable allusion to Sophocles' *Chryses* in Aristophanes' *Birds* (see Σ ad. *Av.* 1240) suggests a *terminus ante quem* of 414 BCE for Sophocles' play, meaning that his *Chryses* may predate Euripides' *IT*, though this is by no means certain: on these issues, see Marshall (2009) 141–56.

[26] See Hall (1987) 427–33 on Euripides' conception of the location of the Taurians in the *IT*. On ancient confusion over the identity and location of the Taurians, see Cropp (2000) 48 and Hall (2012) 66.

[27] On Euripides' probable mythical innovations in the *IT*, see e.g. Wright (2005) 113–15, O'Brien (1988) 98, Zeitlin (2011) 451 and Burnett (1971) 48, 73–5.

her mouth as her very first word is not a thoughtless detail on Euripides' part. Throughout the play Pelops' grisly fate at the hands of his father Tantalus, as well as his own sometimes morally questionable actions, are repeatedly called to mind with special reference to Iphigenia's own position as a Tantalid who now has a very special connection to human sacrifice, since Pelops' past parallels Iphigenia's own situation in one fundamental way: both were involved in a form of failed sacrifice at the hands of their own fathers.[28] The importance of Pelops for Iphigenia's own thinking about her unexpected position in the Taurian land is made clear not long after the prologue. Here Iphigenia ponders the supposed fate of her ancestor by questioning the received accounts of the mythical tradition concerning Tantalus' supposed gory banquet for the gods (380–91):

> τὰ τῆς θεοῦ δὲ μέμφομαι σοφίσματα,
> ἥτις βροτῶν μὲν ἤν τις ἅψηται φόνου
> ἢ καὶ λοχείας ἢ νεκροῦ θίγῃ χεροῖν
> βωμῶν ἀπείργει, μυσαρὸν ὡς ἡγουμένη,
> αὐτὴ δὲ θυσίαις ἥδεται βροτοκτόνοις.
> οὐκ ἔσθ' ὅπως ἔτεκεν ἂν ἡ Διὸς δάμαρ
> Λητὼ τοσαύτην ἀμαθίαν. ἐγὼ μὲν οὖν
> τὰ Ταντάλου θεοῖσιν ἑστιάματα
> ἄπιστα κρίνω, παιδὸς ἡσθῆναι βορᾷ,
> τοὺς δ' ἐνθάδ', αὐτοὺς ὄντας ἀνθρωποκτόνους,
> ἐς τὴν θεὸν τὸ φαῦλον ἀναφέρειν δοκῶ·
> οὐδένα γὰρ οἶμαι δαιμόνων εἶναι κακόν.

But I censure the clever contrivances of the goddess. For any mortal who has come into contact with slaughter or who touches childbirth or a corpse with his hand, she [i.e. Artemis] keeps away from her altars, thinking that he is polluted. But she herself delights in man-slaying sacrifices! It is not possible that Leto, the consort of Zeus, gave birth to such great stupidity. But no: Tantalus' banquet for the gods, that they enjoyed eating a child – that I judge to be unbelievable. Instead I think that the people who live here, who are themselves man-slaughterers, attribute their own low deed to the goddess. For I believe that no god is wicked.

---

[28] The significance of Pelops in the *IT* is generally acknowledged, but the degree to which he can be seen as a model for any single character in particular is debated. Unlike Sansone (1975) and O'Brien (1988), Kyriakou (2006) denies that there is an overall similarity between the escape plot of the *IT* and the escape of Pelops and Hippodameia from Oenomaus, but agrees that there is an affinity between Iphigenia and Pelops in particular throughout the play, since his connection to (potentially failed) sacrifices is strong (see esp. 12–13, 276); cf. also Hartigan (1991) 90.

5.2 Marvels at the Margins

This moment is a crucial one in the action of the *IT*, since Iphigenia has been informed of the arrival of Greek strangers on the shore and is beginning to steel herself for her part in the sacrifice, unaware that her brother is among those newly-arrived men. In this passage Iphigenia refuses to ascribe a lust for human sacrifice to the goddess Artemis herself, blaming instead the bloodthirsty Taurians for the supposed necessity of the planned slaughter. A key part of Iphigenia's argument about the nature of Artemis is that the story that her ancestor Tantalus sacrificed and served his son Pelops to the gods is completely 'unbelievable' (ἄπιστα). The thrust of Iphigenia's argument seems to be that Artemis cannot be desirous of human sacrifices from the Taurians because the human sacrifice element of the Tantalus episode itself cannot possibly have happened. These lines, however, have long raised questions over what precisely it is in the Tantalus episode that Iphigenia is judging to be incredible. Is she denying that Tantalus' feast ever took place? Or that even if the feast did take place, the gods certainly did not eat Pelops? Or that even if the feast took place, and the gods ate Pelops, they did not enjoy it?[29]

As it turns out, Iphigenia's declaration at this point in the *IT* has a very specific antecedent which is also concerned with this supposed failed sacrifice: Pindar's first *Olympian*.[30] The use of the word 'incredible' (ἄπιστα) at *IT* 388 with reference to the feast of Tantalus specifically recalls lines 25–40 of Pindar's poem, where the well-known account of Tantalus' crime is completely rejected, first with the seeming denial of Pelops' dismemberment and subsequent acquisition of an ivory shoulder as something untrue (28–9):

ἦ θαύματα πολλά, καί πού τι καὶ βροτῶν
φάτις ὑπὲρ τὸν ἀλαθῆ λόγον

---

[29] Burnett (1971) 63–4 sees this as a simple case of Iphigenia clearing Tantalus' name 'with her explicit repudiation of his banquet', but there is more ambiguity involved than this. For the various possible interpretations of these lines, see Sansone (1975) 288–9 and Kyriakou (2006) 143–5.

[30] Platnauer (1938) 93 notes that *Ol.* 1.35 ff. is a relevant comparison here, while Whitman (1974) 10 goes further and suggests that *IT* 380–91 contains an 'echo of Pindar's First *Olympian* Ode'. Wolff (1992) 310 n. 5 and Parker (2016) 142–3 suggest that Iphigenia's version here explicitly recalls Pindar's *Ol.* 1.36–53.

The Experience of *Thauma*

δεδαιδαλμένοι ψεύδεσι ποικίλοις
ἐξαπατῶντι μῦθοι.

Yes, truly, marvels are many, and even, I suppose, what mortals say too (that is, stories elaborated above the true account with variegated lies) deceives us.

Pindar goes on to claim that *Charis* (Grace), is the specific cause that makes the unbelievable believable in such cases (30–5):

Χάρις δ', ἅπερ ἅπαντα τεύχει τὰ μείλιχα θνατοῖς,
ἐπιφέροισα τιμὰν καὶ ἄπιστον ἐμήσατο πιστόν
ἔμμεναι τὸ πολλάκις·
ἁμέραι δ' ἐπίλοιποι μάρτυρες σοφώτατοι.
ἔστι δ' ἀνδρὶ φάμεν ἐοικὸς ἀμφὶ δαι-
μόνων καλά· μείων γὰρ αἰτία.

But Grace, who fashions all gentle things for mortal men, through bestowing honour, contrives to make even the unbelievable believable most of the time. But future days are wisest witnesses. It is right for a man to speak well of the gods: the blame is less.

After this, Pindar purports to present the true version of the myth – one which does not attribute the evil of eating human flesh to the gods (36–40):

υἱὲ Ταντάλου, σὲ δ' ἀντία προτέρων φθέγξομαι,
ὁπότ' ἐκάλεσε πατὴρ τὸν εὐνομώτατον
ἐς ἔρανον φίλαν τε Σίπυλον,
ἀμοιβαῖα θεοῖσι δεῖπνα παρέχων,
τότ' Ἀγλαοτρίαιναν ἁρπάσαι ...

Son of Tantalus, contrary to tradition I will say of you that when your father invited the gods to that most well-ordered feast and to his dear Sipylus, providing to the gods a feast in return for previous hospitality, then the god with the shining trident seized you ...

In the *IT*, Iphigenia's rejection of the report of Tantalus' feast similarly echoes Pindar's reluctance to attribute deeds to the gods which may force him to speak ill of them. Furthermore, Pindar's rejection of the well-known version of Pelops' fate anticipates Euripides' own practice in this play: previous versions of myth are rejected because of their potential to cause wonder and thereby provoke questions of belief and disbelief, while innovative new versions of mythic stories which seem in some sense to correct the previously dominant versions are presented as authoritative and truthful. Although it seems that wonder is an obvious response to the more unbelievable aspects of a given mythical story, there is also a suggestion – both in *Olympian* 1 and in the *IT* – that even the seemingly believable version of any given account only succeeds in substituting wonders of its own for the discredited wonders of the previous, rejected variant of the tale.[31] It is this potentially problematic aspect of mythic discourse which Euripides thrusts into the spotlight in the recognition scene of the *IT* in a starker form than in any other scene in his surviving plays.

5.3 Wonders beyond *Mythoi*: Recognition and *Thauma* in Euripides' *Iphigenia among the Taurians*

The *IT*'s prolonged and surprising recognition scene (636–901) goes on to reinforce the sense that the supposed 'real world' of the action presented in the theatre is just as wondrous and unbelievable as the version of Pelops' story which Iphigenia objected to so vehemently earlier in the play. In antiquity the fact that the action of the play is completely dominated by Euripides' complicated handling of the recognition theme is noticed by Aristotle, who holds up the *IT* in the *Poetics* as one of the two tragedies which deserve to be admired most for their treatment and handling of tragic *anagnorisis* (the other being Sophocles' *Oedipus Tyrannus*).[32] Aristotle's admiration for Euripides' treatment of *anagnorisis* in this play is related to the sheer length of the emotionally heightened recognition scene between Iphigenia and Orestes in which two separate recognitions are portrayed in two separate ways. Orestes first realises that the Greek-speaking priestess on the Taurian shore is actually his sister after a letter is read

---

[31] On the way in which the version of Pelops' story favoured by Pindar can itself be viewed only as a different type of *thauma* as opposed to a complete banishment of the thaumatic, see Howie (1983) 190 and Bundy (1986) 9.

[32] See *Poet.* 1455a16–21; cf. 1452a32–b7 and 1454a3–7. In line with general critical responses to both plays modern critics and scholars have tended to lavish their attention on Aristotle's admiration for Sophocles' *OT* while almost completely neglecting his praise for Euripides' *IT*: see Belfiore (1992) 359–77 and White (1992) 221–40 on reasons for Aristotle's intense interest in the *IT*, despite the play's relative lack of appeal to modern critics and audiences.

The Experience of *Thauma*

out loud, a device which Aristotle thought especially skilful and wonder-inducing because of the fact that Euripides manages to insert this recognition token naturally into the plot.[33] Iphigenia then comes, by alternate means, to realise that one of the shipwrecked Greek travellers is in fact her own brother when she questions Orestes about items relating to their youth in Argos about which only her brother could know (798–826), culminating with a final piece of information relating to the siblings' grandfather Pelops which forces Iphigenia to believe what initially seemed to be unbelievable.

Orestes' recognition of his sister begins to take shape from line 636 onwards. After learning from a conversation between Orestes and Pylades that her brother is actually alive, Iphigenia, not realising that Orestes is one of the two strangers in front of her, decides to send a writing tablet home to Argos, where she thinks he is now located. Orestes and Pylades realise who Iphigenia is after she returns with the writing tablet and decides to recite its contents aloud for the two strangers to hear and remember as a precaution in case of the physical loss of the tablet and its message on the long sea journey home (759–87). Orestes' initial recognition of his sister emphasises the wonder and disbelief which this realisation causes (793–7):

> δέχομαι· παρεὶς δὲ γραμμάτων διαπτυχὰς
> τὴν ἡδονὴν πρῶτ' οὐ λόγοις αἱρήσομαι.
> ὦ φιλτάτη μοι σύγγον', ἐκπεπληγμένος
> ὅμως σ' ἀπίστωι περιβαλὼν βραχίονι
> ἐς τέρψιν εἶμι, πυθόμενος θαυμάστ' ἐμοί.

---

[33] *Poet.* 1455a16–19: πασῶν δὲ βελτίστη ἀναγνώρισις ἡ ἐξ αὐτῶν τῶν πραγμάτων, τῆς ἐκπλήξεως γιγνομένης δι' εἰκότων, οἷον ἐν τῷ Σοφοκλέους Οἰδίποδι καὶ τῇ Ἰφιγενείᾳ· εἰκὸς γὰρ βούλεσθαι ἐπιθεῖναι γράμματα (The best recognition of all is the one which comes out of the events themselves, since astonishment arises through the probable series of events, just as in Sophocles' *Oedipus* and the *Iphigenia* [i.e. Euripides' *IT*]; for desiring to despatch a letter is probable). Aristotle has also alluded to the belief that only events or actions which seem probable and convincingly believable are able to cause the greatest *thauma* in audiences earlier in the *Poetics* (1452a5-11), when he notes that even when it comes to unexpected events, 'the most wondrous of those things that happen by chance seem to have happened by design' (τῶν ἀπὸ τύχης ταῦτα θαυμασιώτατα δοκεῖ ὅσα ὥσπερ ἐπίτηδες φαίνεται γεγονέναι, 1452a6–7), such as when a statue of Mitys falls purely by chance but nevertheless kills Mitys' murderer as if this were an intended outcome.

5.3 Wonders beyond *Mythoi*

I accept it. But leaving aside the folding leaves of the letter, I shall choose first pleasure without words. O sister dearest to me, though I am astonished, nevertheless, embracing you with disbelieving arm, I shall come to delight, having learnt things which are wondrous to me.

The utter astonishment which Orestes feels on the recognition of a familiar relative in an unfamiliar location is soon paralleled by Iphigenia's own response once she overcomes her disbelief and accepts that the Greek stranger who has washed up on the Taurian shore is actually her brother. But before Iphigenia can come to recognise that this is the case, an elaborately-structured stichomythia takes place in which Pelops, the relative whose situation most closely echoes Iphigenia's own circumstances, plays a crucial part (806–9):

Ιφ.   ἀλλ' ἡ Λάκαινα Τυνδαρίς σ' ἐγείνατο;
Ορ.   Πέλοπός γε παιδὶ παιδός, οὗ 'κπέφυκ' ἐγώ.
Ιφ.   τί φῄς; ἔχεις τι τῶνδέ μοι τεκμήριον;
Ορ.   ἔχω· πατρῴων ἐκ δόμων τι πυνθάνου.

IPHIGENIA: But did the Spartan woman, the daughter of Tyndareus, bear you?
ORESTES: Indeed, she did: to the child of Pelops' child, whose son I am.
IPHIGENIA: What are you saying? Do you have some proof of this for me?
ORESTES: I have it. Inquire about something from our father's house.

The first two proofs – the story of the golden ram of Atreus and Thyestes told through Iphigenia's weaving, and the report of Iphigenia's Aulis bath and the removal of a lock of hair – are known to Orestes through 'hearsay' (ἀκοῇ, 811) alone, from his other sister, Electra. The third piece of evidence – the one which actually clinches the successful recognition – is the only one which is thoroughly autoptic, and thereby presumably more reliable, than the rest (822–6):

ἃ δ' εἶδον αὐτός, τάδε φράσω τεκμήρια·
Πέλοπος παλαιὰν ἐν δόμοις λόγχην πατρός,
ἣν χερσὶ πάλλων παρθένον Πισάτιδα

The Experience of *Thauma*

ἐκτήσαθ' Ἱπποδάμειαν, Οἰνόμαον κτανών,
ἐν παρθενῶσι τοῖσι σοῖς κεκρυμμένην.

But the things which I myself have seen, these proofs I will tell to you: [I have seen] hidden in your maiden bedroom the ancient spear of Pelops in the house of our father, the one which he brandished in his hands when he obtained the maiden from Pisa, Hippodameia, killing Oenomaus.

The link between Iphigenia and Pelops is thus strengthened yet again by the mention of this important ancestral object, which simultaneously becomes a catalyst for the realisation that the two siblings are intimately connected, despite the previous distance which existed between them. Moreover, this final moment of recognition involving Pelops' spear leads to a recapitulation of the themes surrounding Iphigenia's discussion of the possibility of Tantalus' banquet for the gods, with the link between the unbelievable 'myth' and *thauma* once again highlighted. The idea that the wonder created by the recognition transgresses the very boundaries of what can be said in words is picked up again by Iphigenia's response at the moment she recognises her brother (838–40):

ὦ κρεῖσσον ἢ λόγοισιν εὐτυχοῦσά μου
ψυχά, τί φῶ; θαυμάτων
πέρα καὶ λόγου πρόσω τάδ' ἀπέβα.

O my soul, more good-fortuned than words can tell! What shall I say? Beyond wonders and beyond words these events have turned out!

These words echo Orestes' recognition (793–7), quoted in full above. The importance of the meeting's unexpected geographical location helps to create an additional sense of wonder at this moment of *anagnorisis*. Throughout the *IT*, Euripides plays with familiar tropes of recognition in unfamiliar geographical locations to probe the nature and boundaries of *thauma* and its relation to belief and disbelief.[34] The traditional antitheses between familiar, unremarkable objects or events, and unfamiliar, wonder-inducing objects or events are continually inverted. The importance of the language of *thauma* to the impact of the recognition scene is further reinforced by the very end of the siblings' reunion, where

---

[34] See further Budelmann (2019) 296–9 on the language of (dis)belief in relation to *thauma* in the *IT*.

5.3 Wonders beyond *Mythoi*

we find the chorus offering a brief comment which picks up on the thaumatic language used by Orestes and Iphigenia throughout the recognition-scene (900–1):

> ἐν τοῖσι θαυμαστοῖσι καὶ μύθων πέρα
> τάδ' εἶδον αὐτὴ κοὐ κλύουσ' ἀπ' ἀγγέλων.

These events are wonders and beyond myths! And I myself have seen them, rather than hearing them from messengers!

The emphasis on the fact that these sights have really been seen by the chorus and not only heard by report has a further resonance here, as it reflects the audience's own experience of having witnessed the recognition scene immediately beforehand. The audience's response is also reflected at the end of the play in the reaction of Thoas, the hostile barbarian king of the Taurians, to the escape of Iphigenia and Orestes (1317–24):

> Θο. πῶς φήις; τί πνεῦμα συμφορᾶς κεκτημένη;
> Αγ. σώιζουσ' Ὀρέστην· τοῦτο γὰρ σὺ θαυμάσηι.
> Θο. τὸν ποῖον; ἆρ' ὃν Τυνδαρὶς τίκτει κόρη;
> Αγ. ὃν τοῖσδε βωμοῖς θεὰ καθωσιώσατο.
> Θο. ὦ θαῦμα· πῶς σε μεῖζον ὀνομάσας τύχω;
> Αγ. μὴ 'νταῦθα τρέψηις σὴν φρέν', ἀλλ' ἄκουέ μου·
> σαφῶς δ' ἀθρήσας καὶ κλύων ἐκφρόντισον
> διωγμὸν ὅστις τοὺς ξένους θηράσεται.

THOAS: What are you saying? What favourable gust of good luck did she obtain?
MESSENGER: She was rescuing Orestes. You will wonder at that!
THOAS: What Orestes? The one the daughter of Tyndareus bore?
MESSENGER: The one whom the goddess consecrated for herself at these altars.
THOAS: O wonder! How can I call you by a greater name and hit the mark?[35]

---

[35] Line 1321 has long troubled commentators uncomfortable with the idea of a vocative address to *thauma*. See Diggle (1981b) 89–91 for possible emendations, and Kyriakou (2006) 418–19 for a good summary of the various interpretations of this line. Markland's suggestion that μεῖζον should read μεῖον is defended by Diggle but rightly rejected by

MESSENGER: Don't turn your mind in that direction: listen to me instead! After observing clearly and hearing, think out a means of pursuit to hunt down the strangers.

The chorus' final judgement that the recognitions which they have just witnessed are 'beyond wonders', and Thoas' astonished response to the improbable events which have just taken place before his eyes, both raise questions about what the appropriate response to the mimetic power of drama – and to mythical stories in general – should be. Throughout the *IT* Euripides thus plays with familiar tropes of recognition in unfamiliar geographical locations to probe the power of tragic *thauma* on the audience of the theatre itself.

5.4 Marvels at the Centre: Delphi, Athens and *Thauma* in Euripides' *Ion*

In the action of Euripides' *Ion*, *thauma* is similarly presented as a natural reaction to the inversion of the familiar and the unfamiliar. In stark contrast to the *IT*, *Ion* is set at the very centre of the Hellenic world: the *omphalos* at Delphi. Throughout the action there is a constant interplay between Delphi and Athens, the location which would have seemed closest of all to the original audience. As the play draws on, each location appears to be sometimes near at hand, sometimes distant.[36] By the end of the play the manipulation of the near and the far exposes the uncanny familiarity of unexpected events right at the centre of the world. *Thauma* is again manipulated by Euripides in ways which intertwine with this dynamic. The centrality of this interplay between near and far is made most clear by Ion's response to his unexpected recognition of Xouthos, who claims (falsely) to be his father (585–6):

Cropp (1997) 40–1 and (2000) 254, who notes that the rhetorical point of this question is the suggestion that the very term and concept of wonder is insufficient to express the enormity of the events just described and witnessed in the theatre. See also Parker (2016) 322–3 for discussion of reasons why this vocative address to *thauma* should be maintained.

[36] On the constant interplay between the words ἐνθάδε (here) and ἐκεῖ (there) in the *Ion* (e.g. at 24, 251, 384–5, 645, 1278), see Loraux (1990) 177. On the play's near/far dynamic and its connection to Athens and Delphi, see Zacharia (2003) 22 and Griffiths (2017) 236.

5.4 Marvels at the Centre

οὐ ταὐτὸν εἶδος φαίνεται τῶν πραγμάτων
πρόσωθεν ὄντων ἐγγύθεν θ' ὁρωμένων.

The appearance of things at a distance is not the same as when they are seen close up.

These words – which anticipate later Platonic conceptions of the relationship between *thauma* and perspective – have been taken as a programmatic statement about the action of the play as a whole.[37] Certainly, this antithesis between the near and the far becomes one of the central structuring principles of Euripides' play. In some respects, the unique position of Delphi at the centre of the world suggests that the appearance of unfamiliar marvels in this location is unlikely if the customary geographical expectation that the further away from the Greek centre one travels, the more likely one is to encounter *thaumata* is adhered to rigidly. But in another, more paradoxical sense, the idea of Delphi as the rightful domain of the marvellous is not as bizarre as it might at first seem: its very status as the dead centre of the entire known world lends it a remarkable power of its own, symbolised not least by the wondrous nature of the *omphalos* itself – as Hesiod had already made clear with his description of the placement of the Delphic stone itself as 'a wonder for mortal men' (θαῦμα θνητοῖσι βροτοῖσι, *Theog.* 500).

Ion's two lengthy ekphrases reinforce the sense that in this play wonders lurk at the very centre of the world as opposed to the edges of the earth. The first ekphrasis (184–218) consists of the chorus' description of the images on the temple at Delphi. Despite the familiarity of the images the chorus is viewing, the recognition of these scenes is still able to provoke a marvelling response (190–200):

ἰδού, τᾷδ' ἄθρησον·
Λερναῖον ὕδραν ἐναίρει
χρυσέαις ἅρπαις ὁ Διὸς παῖς·
φίλα, πρόσιδ' ὄσσοις.

---

[37] See Lee (1997) 226 and Gibert (2019) 217 on the programmatic nature of this statement in the *Ion*. See Chapter 7, Section 3, for discussion of Platonic configurations of this sentiment and its connection with *thauma* and its effects.

The Experience of *Thauma*

> ὁρῶ. καὶ πέλας ἄλλος αὐ-
> τοῦ πανὸν πυρίφλεκτον αἴ-
> ρει τις· ἆρ' ὃς ἐμαῖσι μυ-
> θεύεται παρὰ πήναις,
> ἀσπιστὰς Ἰόλαος, ὃς
> κοινοὺς αἰρόμενος πόνους
> Δίῳ παιδὶ συναντλεῖ;

Look, observe this! The son of Zeus slays the Lernaian hydra with a golden sickle. Friend, look over here with your eyes.

I see. And near him another man raises a torch blazing with fire. Is it the man whose story is told at my loom, the shield-fighter Iolaus, who takes up common labours with the son of Zeus and endures them with him to the bitter end?

There are striking similarities between the chorus' viewing of the temple at the beginning of the play, and the later ekphrasis of the tent adorned with *thaumata* which Ion constructs, and within which he almost meets his end at his own mother's hands (1141–5):

> λαβὼν δ' ὑφάσμαθ' ἱερὰ θησαυρῶν πάρα
> κατεσκίαζε, θαύματ' ἀνθρώποις ὁρᾶν.
> πρῶτον μὲν ὀρόφωι πτέρυγα περιβάλλει πέπλων,
> ἀνάθημα Δίου παιδός, οὓς Ἡρακλέης
> Ἀμαζόνων σκυλεύματ' ἤνεγκεν θεῶι.

And after taking the sacred tapestries from the storeroom he began to spread them as coverings, marvels for men to see. First, he threw over a covering of robes as a roof, an offering from Zeus' son, which Heracles offered to the god as spoils from the Amazons.

The constant focus throughout the play on external, monstrous dangers points out the irony of Ion's real situation: that it is not dangers from without which are a threat to him, but his own family. In fact, it is the failure to recognise what is truly familiar which motivates the central action of the play.[38]

On the other hand, although Ion and Creusa do not explicitly recognise each other immediately, there are hints of an uncanny feeling of kinship from their very first meeting. The opening interaction between them reveals an implicit relationship between

---

[38] See Lee (1997) 22; cf. Danek (2001) 55.

5.4 Marvels at the Centre

the two in a way which is completely lacking in Ion's meetings with Xouthos. For Ion, his Athenian mother is immediately an object of wonder who is able to catch his attention. This is apparent at 247–8, when Ion is astonished by Creusa's tears, which for her shows his good upbringing:

> ὦ ξένε, τὸ μὲν σὸν οὐκ ἀπαιδεύτως ἔχει
> ἐς θαύματ' ἐλθεῖν δακρύων ἐμῶν πέρι.

O stranger, your behaviour – this coming to wonder at my tears – shows that you are not uneducated.

In contrast to Ion's cold and non-committal response to the revelation that Xouthos is his supposed father, mother and son seem to share an immediate concern for one another, suggesting elements of a wondrous subconscious *anagnorisis*.[39] On closer inspection, we find that throughout *Ion* the distant is much closer than it might at first glance seem.

One other strand of imagery contributes powerfully to the *Ion*'s representation of the multiple intersections between near and far, familiar and unfamiliar. Birds, always potential signifiers of the ability to travel to distant places, take on a particular significance in relation to Ion himself.[40] He mentions three birds during his temple-cleaning monody: first an eagle, which he terms 'herald of Zeus' (ὦ Ζηνὸς | κῆρυξ, 158–9), then a swan (κύκνος, 162), and finally a more ambiguous 'new bird' (ὀρνίθων καινός, 171). Here then at the beginning of the play we find a mixture of familiar and unfamiliar birds which cause the first of a series of unexpected avian intrusions into the play's action – intrusions which will eventually culminate in the recognition of mother and son.[41] The connection between bird imagery and Ion is strengthened when Ion himself is described as a 'new son' (ὁ καινός … γόνος) (1202) at the point towards the

---

[39] Lee (1997) 187. See also lines 262–3, where Creusa's Athenian lineage fills Ion with an immediate sense of respect and awe: ὦ κλεινὸν οἰκοῦσ' ἄστυ γενναίων τ' ἄπο | τραφεῖσα πατέρων, ὥς σε θαυμάζω, γύναι (O lady dwelling in a famous city and reared from noble ancestors, how I wonder at you!).

[40] Cf. Giraud (1987) 84 and Zeitlin (1989) 144 on the strong connections between Ion and birds in this play; see also Hoffer (1996) 297–9, Griffiths (2017) 238 and McPhee (2017) 475–89 on the significance of birds and bird imagery throughout the play.

[41] See Lee (1997) 174 on the *Ion*'s multiple 'surprising intrusions'.

end of the play where we find bird imagery returning most explicitly. The unwanted avian incursions into the temple precinct during Ion's temple-cleaning monody prefigure the paradoxically welcome intrusion of a dove, which saves Ion from certain death by preventing him from drinking poison at the play's climax (1202–6):

> ἣ δ' ἕζετ' ἔνθ' ὁ καινὸς ἔσπεισεν γόνος
> ποτοῦ τ' ἐγεύσατ'· εὐθὺς εὔπτερον δέμας
> ἔσεισε κἀβάκχευσεν, ἐκ δ' ἔκλαγξ' ὄπα
> ἀξύνετον αἰάζουσ'· ἐθάμβησεν δὲ πᾶς
> θοινατόρων ὅμιλος ὄρνιθος πόνους.

But the bird landed where the new son had made a libation and tasted the drink: immediately it shook its fair-winged body and became frenzied like a Bacchant, and wailing, it screeched out a voice hard to interpret. And the whole gathering of feasters wondered at the sufferings of the bird.

The wonder of the assembled crowd at the monstrous images of Ion's tent is transmuted into astonishment (θάμβησεν δὲ πᾶς, 1205) at the monstrous fate which overcomes the bird, a symbol of Ion himself – though the fact that the recognition of mother and son succeeds without disaster soon after this moment soon becomes the most wondrous aspect of the play as a whole.

Just as in the *IT*, in the *Ion* too Euripides inverts the antithesis between near and far to establish the wonder of the familiar as a category of experience which forces his characters – and the audience – to question their most basic and deeply held assumptions. The displacement of the familiar into unusual contexts can also have new and unexpected effects. This idea, namely that wonder can be something found near at hand, becomes particularly important when the concept of recognition is considered. Whereas the astonishment provoked by the distant often entails complete ignorance of the object provoking wonder, the wonder of the familiar often involves a recovery of knowledge, a recognition that in itself is able to provoke an often disconcerting sense of *thauma* due to the uncanny closeness of the object of wonder to its subject. Rather than associating *thauma* with the unusual or the unfamiliar, in this play we see a radically different

5.4 Marvels at the Centre

conception of what the wondrous might be: the ordinary as well as the extraordinary, the familiar as well as the unfamiliar. This type of *thauma*, based on the unexpected mutual entwining of near and far, holds just as much potential to surprise, delight, or disturb, as the next chapter will demonstrate.[42]

---

[42] Cf. Daston and Park (1998) 311 and Kareem (2014) 55 on the importance of viewing wonder not only as something associated with the unfamiliar, but as (in Kareem's words) 'a category within the aesthetics of ordinary experiences'.

6

NEAR AND DISTANT MARVELS: DEFAMILIARISING AND REFAMILIARISING *THAUMA*

ὥσπερ γὰρ πρὸς τοὺς ξένους οἱ ἄνθρωποι καὶ πρὸς τοὺς πολίτας, τὸ αὐτὸ πάσχουσιν καὶ πρὸς τὴν λέξιν· διὸ δεῖ ποιεῖν ξένην τὴν διάλεκτον· θαυμασταὶ γὰρ τῶν ἀπόντων εἰσίν, ἡδὺ δὲ τὸ θαυμαστόν ἐστιν. ἐπὶ μὲν οὖν τῶν μέτρων πολλά τε ποιεῖται οὕτω καὶ ἁρμόττει ἐκεῖ· πλέον γὰρ ἐξέστηκεν περὶ ἃ καὶ περὶ οὓς ὁ λόγος· ἐν δὲ τοῖς ψιλοῖς λόγοις πολλῷ ἐλάττω.

For just as men are affected in a certain way by strangers and in a certain way by their fellow citizens, they are affected in the same way by verbal style. Therefore it is necessary to make language 'strange': for people are wonderers at things which are distant, and the wondrous is pleasurable. In cases of verse, many things produce this effect and it suits that medium: for the things and people found in that discourse are more out of the ordinary. In prose this is true to a much lesser extent.

Aristotle, Rhetoric 1404b8–14

In his discussion of appropriate rhetorical style (*lexis*) in the third book of the *Rhetoric*, Aristotle sets forth a claim about the nature of effective rhetorical speech which will go on to reverberate through the subsequent literary critical tradition. He suggests that the task of the effective speaker is to make what is familiar to the listener appear somehow strange, unfamiliar and wondrous again. This claim makes one shift which takes place over the course of the fifth century BCE abundantly clear: *thauma* is no longer necessarily aroused by an externally visible physical object, event or action, but is now often a response to the effects of *language* alone. By the time Aristotle composes the *Rhetoric* in the latter half of the fourth century BCE, the conceptualisation of speech as something able to cause wonder has become concrete.[1]

---

[1] The treatise has been dated to 340–335 BCE since the latest historical events alluded to in this work fall in this period, though it is likely that Aristotle reworked his ideas about rhetoric over a longer period of time (see Kennedy (1991) 299–305).

In the above passage Aristotle uses a simile to explain the effect which he expects successful rhetorical style to provoke. He describes the sense of wonder created when language is 'made strange' as akin to that felt in the presence of a foreigner from far away, a feeling which differs greatly from that experienced in the presence of a fellow citizen. A little further on from this passage Aristotle contemplates how a wonder-inducing strangeness of language might be created by the successful rhetorician. He suggests that one of the primary means of making everyday language 'clear, pleasurable and strange is through the use of metaphor especially' (καὶ τὸ σαφὲς καὶ τὸ ἡδὺ καὶ τὸ ξενικὸν ἔχει μάλιστα ἡ μεταφορά, 1405a8–9).[2] Metaphor and wonder come to be associated together elsewhere in Aristotle's works in a way which exposes a complicated nexus of ideas surrounding the connection between *thauma*, learning, mimesis and pleasure. We can begin to untangle this web of associations if we turn to an earlier passage in the first book of the *Rhetoric* (1371a31–b8): here Aristotle claims that 'both learning and wondering are usually pleasurable, for wondering at something implies a desire to learn, with the result that the object of wonder is an object of desire ... and since learning and wondering are pleasurable, it makes sense that such things, acts of imitation like painting and sculpture and poetry and everything that is well-imitated, are pleasurable, even if the object imitated is not itself pleasurable'.[3] He posits a similar idea at *Poetics* 1448b4–17 when he suggests that mimetic objects are pleasurable to contemplate even if the objects they depict are inherently unpleasant. The reason Aristotle gives for this observation is that 'learning is pleasurable, not only for philosophers but

---

[2] See Moran (1996) 387–9 on the importance of the connection between strangeness and wonder here in light of Aristotle's subsequent argument in the *Rhetoric*. On the influence of these Aristotelian ideas about the connection between wonder and strangeness in Classical Arabic literary theory, see Harb (2020) 95–7, 119–22.

[3] καὶ τὸ μανθάνειν καὶ τὸ θαυμάζειν ἡδὺ ὡς ἐπὶ τὸ πολύ· ἐν μὲν γὰρ τῷ θαυμάζειν τὸ ἐπιθυμεῖν μαθεῖν ἐστιν, ὥστε τὸ θαυμαστὸν ἐπιθυμητόν ... ἐπεὶ δὲ τὸ μανθάνειν τε ἡδὺ καὶ τὸ θαυμάζειν, καὶ τὰ τοιάδε ἀνάγκη ἡδέα εἶναι, οἷον τό τε μιμούμενον, ὥσπερ γραφικὴ καὶ ἀνδριαντοποιία καὶ ποιητική, καὶ πᾶν ὃ ἂν εὖ μεμιμημένον ᾖ, κἂν ᾖ μὴ ἡδὺ αὐτὸ τὸ μεμιμημένον. For a detailed discussion of the interrelationships between pleasure, learning, wonder and recognition in Aristotle's thought (especially in the *Poetics*), see Halliwell (1986) 73–81. Cf. Warren (2014) 67–77 on the connections between learning, pleasure and *thauma* at *Rhet.* 1371a, *Poet.* 1448b and *Part. an.* 644b.

for everyone' (μανθάνειν οὐ μόνον τοῖς φιλοσόφοις ἥδιστον ἀλλὰ καὶ τοῖς ἄλλοις ὁμοίως), because it involves processes of learning, inference and recognition as the viewer 'pieces each thing together' (συλλογίζεσθαι τί ἕκαστον) and decodes what each element of the object viewed (e.g. an image) means.

Later in book 3 of the *Rhetoric*, Aristotle goes on to claim that metaphor is itself pleasurable precisely because it produces learning, since 'naturally learning easily is pleasurable for everyone ... all words that make us learn are pleasant ... and metaphor produces this effect most of all' (τὸ γὰρ μανθάνειν ῥᾳδίως ἡδὺ φύσει πᾶσιν ἐστί ... ὅσα τῶν ὀνομάτων ποιεῖ ἡμῖν μάθησιν, ἥδιστα ... ἡ δὲ μεταφορὰ ποιεῖ τοῦτο μάλιστα, 1410b10–13). This learning stems from metaphor's ability to elucidate similarities between previously disparate objects which have never been compared in this way before, and its power to encourage the recognition of the familiar within the unfamiliar.[4] In fact, this is not too dissimilar from the process of recognising similarities and connections which Aristotle considers to be essential to the practice of philosophising in general (*Rhetoric* 1412a11–13): 'it is necessary to make metaphors, as was said earlier, out of things which are related but not obviously so – just as in philosophy too sagacity is required to see what is similar in things far apart' (δεῖ δὲ μεταφέρειν, καθάπερ εἴρηται πρότερον, ἀπὸ οἰκείων καὶ μὴ φανερῶν, οἷον καὶ ἐν φιλοσοφίᾳ τὸ ὅμοιον καὶ ἐν πολὺ διέχουσι θεωρεῖν εὐστόχου).[5] For Aristotle, it is clear that the effect of recognising unexpected connections between things which do

---

[4] Aristotle hints at this in his discussion of metaphor at *Poetics* 1459a7, when he states that the ability to discern likenesses between things is something which cannot be taught, although it is an essential attribute of a good metaphor-maker: τὸ γὰρ εὖ μεταφέρειν τὸ τὸ ὅμοιον θεωρεῖν ἐστιν (to make metaphor well is to see what is similar). On the element of *anagnorisis* inherent in Aristotle's conception of metaphor, see Swiggers (1984) 44 and O'Rourke (2006) 158.

[5] The interplay between the familiar and unfamiliar, near and far, and the wonder caused by the recognition of potential connections between the two is also implied at the beginning of the *Metaphysics* (982b12–15) when Aristotle notes that wonder is the beginning of philosophy because it encourages us to move on to wondering at greater, more distant matters after first marvelling at the workings of things near at hand. This idea also underlies Aristotle's exhortation (*Part. an* 644b29–645a17) to study the nature and bodies of animals and plants before turning towards weightier matters relating to the divine, since we live near at hand among these organisms and can wonder at and therefore learn about them with less difficulty. On these passages, see further Chapter 3, Section 4. Thein (2014) 214–18 also notes the strong connection between Aristotle's thoughts on

Near and Distant Marvels

not normally belong together contributes to creating and sustaining wonder on both aesthetic and philosophical levels.[6] This wonder then goes on to encourage learning.

These observations concerning the power and potentially wonder-inducing effects of 'making language strange' certainly have a long afterlife in later critical discussions of literary and poetic style. One of the most obvious recapitulations of this idea occurs in the Romantic period, when Coleridge states that Wordsworth's aim in the *Lyrical Ballads* was 'to give the charm of novelty to things of every day, and to excite a feeling analogous to the supernatural, by awakening the mind's attention from the lethargy of custom, and directing it to the loveliness and the wonders of the world before us'.[7] But it is within Russian Formalist thought that by far the most influential revisiting of Aristotle's claims about the wonderful power of making language strange are found, with Viktor Shklovsky's concept of 'defamiliarisation' – i.e. the claim that '[t]he technique of art is to make objects unfamiliar' – explicitly based on Aristotle's comments at *Rhetoric* 1404b.

But where do the roots of Aristotle's own idea lie? Was he the first to suggest that language itself can produce wonder and make the familiar unfamiliar, and vice versa? These are the fundamental questions which this chapter will explore, turning first to Aristophanes' *Birds* and then to Thucydides' *History*. In both of these works, the ability of language itself to cause its audiences to marvel, and the ease with which words can alter perceptions as a result, are shown to be issues of great importance in Athens, a society which is itself now held up as an object of *thauma*. In these texts this has a radically dislocating effect, since the rhetoric of wonder which begins to inform Athens' view of its own political and military predominance contributes to distorted

---

knowledge, learning, pleasure and wonder at *Rhet.* 1404b, 1460a, *Met.* 982b and *Part. an* 644b–45a.

[6] O'Rourke (2006) 171–2 aptly summarises Aristotle's conception of wonder as an integral effect of metaphor: 'Vital to metaphor is the contrast between the familiar and the strange, which is the hallmark of wonder ... Metaphor is a continual reminder of the strangeness of things all around: the marvellous in the quotidian ... With its power of estrangement metaphor arrests our habitual relationship with the world. The miracle of metaphor is its power to evoke marvel and astonishment.'

[7] Coleridge describes Wordsworth's poetic practice thus in chapter XIV of his *Biographia Literaria* (1817).

perceptions of the true extent of the imperial might of the city state, leading the Athenians (at least, in Thucydides' view) to overreach themselves. In both of these authors, the unease caused by the sense that *thaumata* are no longer simply exceptional objects of the natural world or of divine craftsmanship, but are now the result of man-made (often deceptive, and often linguistic) craft, is articulated through continual shifts and reassessments of the relationship between the near and the far, both in literal, spatial terms and in more metaphorical senses. Aristotle's use of an image concerning foreigners and citizens to express processes of linguistic defamiliarisation thus draws upon a deeper and more complex view in this culture of the changing role of language itself – a role which *thauma* now finds itself an ever more important part of, as the next two chapters will demonstrate. But first, to begin to explore the status of *thauma* in Athenian society and culture in the last quarter of the fifth century BCE, it is necessary to turn to a work which, on the face of it, has very little to do with Athens as a real-world location at all.

6.1 The Wonder of Nephelococcygia: Aristophanes' *Birds* and the Edges of the Earth

In Euripides' *Ion*, as we saw at the end of the last chapter, birds become ideal signifiers of the confusion between the near and far, the familiar and unfamiliar. At around the same time as Euripides wrote that play, Aristophanes' *Birds*, performed at the City Dionysia of 414 BCE, also hits upon the figure of the bird as a means of exploring spatial transgression and its effects. One such effect is the ability to bridge easily the gap between the human and the divine, since birds are capable of crossing not only terrestrial geographical boundaries at will but are even able to move vertically between the mortal realm of earth and the sky, the preserve of the gods. In *Birds*, the geographical and conceptual transgression linked to these creatures is firmly connected to *thauma*, as Aristophanes indulges in a humorous form of paraethnography to emphasise, at least initially, just how radically different and distant the fantastic utopian society of Cloudcuckooland supposedly is from the corrupt world of

6.1 Aristophanes' *Birds* and the Edges of the Earth

contemporary Athens. Towards the end of the play, however, Aristophanes takes advantage of the spatial inversions which the natural movement of birds allows to turn the radically distorting lens of *thauma* back upon Athenian society itself.

The groundwork for this eventual inversion of 'near' and 'far' is laid from the very opening words of the play. Euelpides' first complaint that the confusion caused by the protagonists' constant 'wandering up and down' (ἄνω κάτω πλανύττομεν, 3) has already reached the point that he no longer knows where on earth he is (ἀλλ' οὐδὲ ποῦ γῆς ἐσμὲν οἶδ' ἔγωγ' ἔτι, 9) hints at the spatial and linguistic inversions which are to follow; despite referring to travel over the surface of the earth at this point, the words 'up and down' (ἄνω κάτω) will soon be shown to refer to literal vertical as well as horizontal movement.[8] The sense of spatial inversion is further reinforced by the gradual realisation that the expected locations of the protagonists' longed-for escape – the wondrous and pleasing edges of the earth – must in their turn be rejected. At the beginning of the play the edges of the earth are initially presented as the expected location of *thaumata*. Peisetairus' ludicrous claim, when interrogated by Tereus' bird-slave, that he is an unusual 'Libyan bird' (Λιβυκὸν ὄρνεον, 65) seems to hint at Africa as a proverbial location of exotic animals, while Euelpides' claim to be a 'Phasian bird' (Φασιανικός, 68) from the opposite side of the world, the region around the Black Sea, reinforces the sense that, initially at least, the world's extremities are to be regarded as the home of the exotic and unusual.[9] But this assumption quickly breaks down once Tereus' house is finally reached. When asked to use his birdly experience of travel to suggest a location free from Athenian meddling (*polypragmosyne*), Tereus automatically recommends 'a blessed city beside the Red Sea' (εὐδαίμων πόλις | παρὰ τὴν ἐρυθρὰν θάλατταν, 144–5), which here seems to mean the furthest edges of the Persian empire. But this suggestion is immediately

---

[8] Cf. Rusten (2013) 314 on the new vertical perspective of space which the play establishes.

[9] On Libya as the location of exotic animals, cf. Ronca (1992) 147 and Dunbar (1995) 156. On the proverb 'Libya always brings forth some new thing' (ἀεὶ Λιβύη φέρει τι καινόν, first attested in Aristotle's biological works and already described by him as a proverb (*paroimia*), see Arist. GA 746b8 and HA 606b19), see Ronca (1992), Romm (1992) 88–9 and D'Angour (2011) 109.

rejected by Euelpides on the basis that Athenian power is able to reach everywhere by sea these days (145–8) – as a result, escape to the marvellous ends of the earth is no longer possible.[10]

The sense of spatial collapse between periphery and centre is emphasised still further by the entrance of the chorus, where we find familiar Mediterranean birds flocking together with their more far-flung cousins. Euelpides expresses amazement at the unusual sight, but Peisetairus remains unmoved. Of course, this fits with Euelpides' role as comic buffoon in this play; still, it is notable that Peisetairus never seems to wonder at anything, even going so far as to demand that the birds 'do not fly around everywhere with beaks agape' (μὴ περιπέτεσθε πανταχῇ κεχηνότες, 165), as if they are constantly in a state of wonder at everything.[11] Peisetairus' consistent lack of wonder seems to be connected to his increasingly dominant role as the play proceeds. Euelpides, however, seems to reflect the audience's likely reaction to the sight of the comic chorus. His exclamation on the entrance of the Persian Mede bird that 'this bird has an out of place colour' (χοῦτος ἔξεδρον χρόαν ἔχων, 275) hints at the wonder-inducing literal and metaphorical dislocations which the play will increasingly delight in as the action goes on, since these words echo a line from Sophocles' *Tyro* which relates to the literal unusual position of a bird in the sky when a witness asks 'what is this bird in an out of place position?' (τίς ὄρνις οὗτος ἔξεδρον χώραν ἔχων, fr. 654 *TrGF* Radt).[12] Here the Sophoclean sense of religious awe connected with an ill-omened bird has been suddenly displaced and transmuted into an Aristophanic sense of wonder at the exotic, a transformation which renders Euelpides' reuse of the tragedian's expression just as out of place as the bird he is describing.

It seems then that even before Peisetairus' plan begins properly to unfold, the familiar distinctions between the world's centre and

---

[10] For more on Euelpides' comment about the seemingly boundless reach of Athenian imperial power, see Section 3 below. On the apparent impossibility of escape from Athenian imperial power in the *Birds*, see Amati (2010) 215 and Bowie (1993) 106.

[11] On the birds' wondering response here, see Konstan (1997) 9: 'The gaping mouth is a standard Aristophanic image for dumb wonder'; cf. Arrowsmith (1973) 143, who attributes the fact that the birds are 'agape with wonder and desire' to their zeal for 'the unknown frontiers of boundless conquest'.

[12] See Dunbar (1995) 232 and Sommerstein (1987) 214.

6.1 Aristophanes' *Birds* and the Edges of the Earth

its peripheries have already started to crumble, and the process of playing with the familiar and unfamiliar has already begun. This is reinforced by the strong Herodotean echoes that surround the most important structural aspect of Nephelococcygia: the city wall.[13] At 550–2, Herodotus is recalled when Peisetairus instructs the birds to build a wall around the city out of baked bricks:

> καὶ δὴ τοίνυν πρῶτα διδάσκω μίαν ὀρνίθων πόλιν εἶναι,
> κἄπειτα τὸν ἀέρα πάντα κύκλῳ καὶ πᾶν τουτὶ τὸ μεταξὺ
> περιτειχίζειν μεγάλαις πλίνθοις ὀπταῖς ὥσπερ Βαβυλῶνα.

Well then, I instruct this first of all: make a single city of birds, and then surround all of the air and everything which lies between heaven and earth in a circle with big kiln-baked bricks just like Babylon.

The detail 'kiln-baked bricks' (πλίνθοις ὀπταῖς) specifically recalls Herodotus' description of the construction of Babylon's massive external wall, a structure similarly made out of 'bricks baked in kilns' (πλίνθους ... ὤπτησαν αὐτὰς ἐν καμίνοισι, *Histories* 1.179), making clear that the historian's account of one of the proverbial seven wonders of the world is what Peisetairus has in mind for Nephelococcygia here.[14] The wondrous nature of the Herodotean wall is made even clearer by the messenger speech narrating its construction. The messenger begins by emphasising the structure's tremendous dimensions (1125–9):

> κάλλιστον ἔργον καὶ μεγαλοπρεπέστατον·
> ὥστ' ἂν ἐπάνω μὲν Προξενίδης ὁ Κομπασεὺς
> καὶ Θεογένης ἐναντίω δύ' ἅρματε,
> ἵππων ὑπόντων μέγεθος ὅσον ὁ δούριος,
> ὑπὸ τοῦ πλάτους ἂν παρελασαίτην.

---

[13] On the general importance of the wall as a boundary marker and the spatial ramifications this has in the play, see Kosak (2006) 173–80. I am grateful to one of the anonymous readers for drawing my attention to the fact that in addition to the wall the geometry and organisation of the city as a whole can be considered a source of potential *thauma*, especially since the proposed regular organisation of the city contrasts with the comparatively unruly natural development of real cities. On conceptions of various schemes of ordered spatial organisation in Nephelococcygia, see Amati (2010) 213–27.

[14] See Dunbar (1995) 374 and Sommerstein (1987) 233 on the Herodotean echo. Fornara (1971) 28–9 argues (rightly) that this is a rare specific verbal parody of a particular Herodotean passage, rather than just a vague allusion to the historian's style. See also Nesselrath (2014) 58–60 on the possibility that Aristophanes had access to a written edition of Herodotus' *Histories*.

Near and Distant Marvels

A most fine and most magnificent work, so wide on top that Proxenides of Boasttown and Theogenes could drive two chariots past each other with horses as big as the Wooden Horse [i.e. the Trojan Horse] attached to them.

Here we are immediately thrust into the Herodotean rhetoric of wonder, with the focus on extreme size (μέγεθος ... πλάτους), and the labelling of the structure as a 'most fine and most magnificent work' (κάλλιστον ἔργον καὶ μεγαλοπρεπέστατον), which recalls the proem of the *Histories* and its stated claim of keeping alive 'great and wondrous works' (ἔργα μεγάλα τε καὶ θωμαστά, 1.1). In fact, the messenger even once again makes explicit reference to Herodotus' description of Babylon's wall at *Histories* 1.178–9 by claiming that the birds' structure allows *two* chariots to be driven around the top of the wall by Proxenides and Theogenes (apparently a pair of well-known braggarts); in Herodotus' version the fact that space was left on top of Babylon's wall 'for the driving around of *one* four-horse chariot' (τεθρίππῳ περιέλασιν, 1.179) is a prime cause of the overwhelming magnitude and *thauma* of the wall's construction as a whole.[15]

Furthermore, the description which the messenger then gives of thirty thousand cranes from Libya and ten thousand storks helping to build the wall only increases the sense that Herodotus' focus on measurement, scale, large numbers and supposed extreme accuracy is being parodied here (1130–41):

<blockquote>
Αγ. τὸ δὲ μῆκός ἐστι, καὶ γὰρ ἐμέτρησ' αὔτ' ἐγώ,
    ἑκατοντορόγυιον.
Πει.   ὦ Πόσειδον, τοῦ μάκρους.
τίνες ᾠκοδόμησαν αὐτὸ τηλικουτονί;
Αγ. ὄρνιθες, οὐδεὶς ἄλλος, οὐκ Αἰγύπτιος
πλινθοφόρος, οὐ λιθουργός, οὐ τέκτων παρῆν,
ἀλλ' αὐτόχειρες, ὥστε θαυμάζειν ἐμέ.
ἐκ μέν γε Λιβύης ἧκον ὡς τρισμύριαι
γέρανοι θεμελίους καταπεπωκυῖαι λίθους·
τούτους δ' ἐτύκιζον αἱ κρέκες τοῖς ῥύγχεσιν.
ἕτεροι δ' ἐπλινθούργουν πελαργοὶ μύριοι·
ὕδωρ δ' ἐφόρουν κάτωθεν εἰς τὸν ἀέρα
οἱ χαραδριοὶ καὶ τἆλλα ποτάμι' ὄρνεα.
</blockquote>

---

[15] See Dunbar (1995) 595 on this instance of Aristophanes' intensely allusive Herodotean language.

6.1 Aristophanes' *Birds* and the Edges of the Earth

MESSENGER: And the height – for I measured it myself – is a hundred fathoms.
PEISETAIRUS: O Poseidon! That's high! Which people built this to such a height?
MESSENGER: Birds, and no one else: no Egyptian brick-bearer, no stonemason, no carpenter was present; instead they built it with their own hands, with the result that I marvel. From Libya thirty thousand cranes who had gulped down foundation stones arrived, and the corncrakes were working them with their beaks. Another ten thousand storks were making bricks, and the curlews and the other river birds were bringing water up to the sky.

Again, Aristophanes has picked up on Herodotus' penchant for detailing large measurements when designating a distant man-made object as something to be marvelled at.[16] The messenger's asides concerning his own response to witnessing the marvel of the wall also manipulate the stance of the Herodotean narrator in a new and humorous way, first through the use of a Herodotean-style autoptic verification of detail in the aside that the height of the wall is one hundred fathoms, then by the announcement that the effect on the eyewitness of the wall and its construction was one of wonder.[17]

These humorous references to the importance of autoptic accounts of distant marvels are not the only instances in which Herodotean-style rhetoric of ethnographic *thauma* is exposed to ridicule in the *Birds*. Aristophanes again takes a swipe at ethnographic descriptions of *thaumata* when Tereus warns his fellow birds that they are about to hear plans about the wall from Peisetairus which are completely 'unbelievable and beyond listening to' (ἄπιστα καὶ πέρα κλύειν, 416), even before the first foundations of the marvellous wall of Nephelococcygia are laid. From the very moment of its initial conception, the wondrous nature of

---

[16] On Herodotus' frequent recourse to large numbers and the language of measurement to describe the magnitude of *thomata* in the *Histories*, see Hartog (1988) 230–7, Welser (2009) 375 and Priestley (2014) 57.
[17] On the Herodotean phraseology here, see Sommerstein (1987) 274–5 and Dunbar (1995) 596–9.

Nephelococcygia is constantly undercut, even by Peisetairus himself, as a sense of scepticism regarding the very believability of any object labelled as a marvel gradually arises. This becomes clearest when the chorus' exhortation to wonder at the speed with which the fortifications were erected is quickly taken up by Nephelococcygia's founder, who equates the fact that the wall is worthy of wonder with its utterly fictitious nature (1164–7):

> Χο. οὗτος, τί ποιεῖς; ἆρα θαυμάζεις ὅτι
> οὕτω τὸ τεῖχος ἐκτετείχισται ταχύ;
> Πε. νὴ τοὺς θεοὺς ἔγωγε· καὶ γὰρ ἄξιον·
> ἴσα γὰρ ἀληθῶς φαίνεταί μοι ψεύδεσιν.

CHORUS: You there, what are you doing? Are you astonished that the wall has been built up so swiftly?
PEISETAIRUS: I am indeed, by the gods: because it's worthy of astonishment. For truly it seems to me to be equal to lies.

Peisetairus' words here provide a concrete hint that the marvellous wall which is being described may in fact be marvellous not because of its size, but because of the fact that it does not exist at all: this is a structure created purely with words, a discursive wall which comes into being, when required, through language itself. This interpretation becomes more likely when the structure's seeming defensive purpose is undercut almost as soon as it has been completed, during a scene (1199–224) in which the messenger Iris does not even notice the wall's existence, passing through it completely unhindered and ending up confused by Peisetairus' insistence that she has transgressed this new boundary.[18]

Through these consistent parodic references to Herodotean *thauma* during the scenes of the new city's construction, Aristophanes deliberately aligns this novel society of birds and metamorphosed humans with those of fantastic peoples situated at the edges of the earth in Greek thought. Seeing as Peisetairus' new city is supposedly located at a distant geographical boundary in the sky, in one sense Aristophanes' use of unusual and often

---

[18] See Amati (2010) 217, Kosak (2006) 175 and Sommerstein (1987) 4 on Iris' complete ignorance of the supposedly insurmountable wall's presence in this scene.

6.2 Familiar *Thaumata*: The Bird-Chorus' Wondrous Travels

far-fetched reports of marvels which may be encountered in reports of lands distant from Greece is fitting, and it is easy to create humour through the simple inversion of usual notions of centre and periphery: the edges of the known world now stretch upwards on a vertical axis, rather than simply expanding out on a horizontal axis from the Hellenic centre. At the same time, however, the injection of ethnographic *thauma* into his play's construction of a supposedly novel society allows Aristophanes to critique the general believability of objects designated as *thaumata*, and the reliability of the ethnographic tradition as a whole. This becomes an increasingly pressing issue as the play draws on and the audience is gradually refamiliarised with the greatest *thauma* of all: Athens.

6.2 Familiar *Thaumata*: The Bird-Chorus' Wondrous Travels

In the final scenes of the *Birds* it becomes clear that it is not really Nephelococcygia with its wondrous wall which is truly deserving of *thauma*, but rather the city of Athens itself. Aristophanes transfigures Athens into an object of wonder through the repeated transformation of metaphor and other familiar figures of speech into unexpected and often troubling literalisations as the play draws on.[19] This becomes most evident in the play's final scenes as the bird-chorus perform a song describing the *thaumata* they have seen on their travels over Peisetairus' new sphere of influence. The song's stanzas, despite being non-consecutive (1470–81; 1482–93; 1553–64; 1694–1705), are nevertheless clearly connected structurally, thematically and metrically.[20]

Within this song about seemingly distant *thaumata* Aristophanes combines two main generic influences. The first is the ethnographic *periodos ges*, which systematically describes the route and geographical features of a (distant)

---

[19] On the importance of verbal artifice and the literalisation of metaphor in the *Birds*, see especially Dobrov (1997) 95–132; cf. Sommerstein (1987) 3, Bowie (1993) 173, Slater (1997) 85–6 and Rothwell (2007) 175.
[20] See Parker (1997) 346–50 on the metrical correspondence of these four stanzas, which she terms 'lampoon-songs', and their use as a means of marking out the dramatic structure of the play's end. Cf. Moulton (1981) 32, 45–6, Dunbar (1995) 688 and Rusten (2013) 298 on the structure and thematic unity of the song as a whole.

journey.[21] The second, of course more common in Aristophanic comedy, is tragedy. In particular, in this specific choral song Aristophanes parodies the tendency of certain Euripidean choruses to sing of how they wish to become birds so that they can flee from whatever troubles are unfolding in front of them.[22] The contrast drawn in these odes between the unpalatable situation faced by the chorus in their present location, and the potentially happier life to be found in far-off places towards the edges of the earth is something Aristophanes repeatedly picks up on and reinvents in the *Birds* in order to critique the norms of contemporary Athenian society.

The most pertinent extant example we possess of the type of imagery which Aristophanes is parodying is found in the second stasimon of Euripides' *Hippolytus*, first performed in 428 BCE, long before the first performance of *Birds* in 414. After the shocking revelation that Phaedra has hit upon death as a remedy for her shame (715–31), the geographical scope of Euripides' play is radically expanded in this ode as the chorus react with an anguished wish for a sudden avian transformation (732–4):

ἠλιβάτοις ὑπὸ κευθμῶσι γενοίμαν,
ἵνα με πτεροῦσσαν ὄρ-
νιν θεὸς ἀμφὶ ποταναῖς ἀγέλαις θείη.

If only I were in the steep mountain clefts, where a god might make me into a winged bird among the flying flocks.

The chorus go on to emphasise their longing for escape by imagining themselves soaring away from their distressing situation in Troezen, and winging their way instead towards the world's very western edges. The geographical movement of the ode tends increasingly towards the fantastic, as the chorus first envisage flying over the Adriatic gulf (τὰς Ἀδριηνὰς | ἀκτάς, 736–7) before they reach 'the water of the Eridanus' (Ἠριδανοῦ θ' ὕδωρ, 737). The river Eridanus, the location of Phaethon's fiery chariot crash, was thought to be located towards the westernmost edge of the

---

[21] See Rusten (2013) 308.
[22] On Euripidean 'escape odes' and their tendency to evoke distant places, see Padel (1974), especially pp. 228–31 on bird imagery; cf. Swift (2009) 364 on the Euripidean choral 'escape fantasy'.

6.2 Familiar *Thaumata*: The Bird-Chorus' Wondrous Travels

world, flowing into the outermost sea on the western side of Europe.[23] But the chorus' fantastic journey does not stop there: their distress is such that only the garden of the Hesperides, near the Pillars of Heracles, the western end point of the world – or the 'sacred boundary of the sky' (σεμνὸν τέρμονα... οὐρανοῦ, 746–7) as the chorus term it – seems to offer a potential haven from the horror of Phaedra's shocking revelations.

As might be expected, in the later so-called 'escape-plays' this Euripidean imagery is transformed in line with the surprising geographical inversions common in those works. Since these plays are set in locations near the edges of the earth, it is Hellas itself which becomes an idealised distant space which the chorus longs to escape to, as we see in the second stasimon of the *IT* (1089–152). After learning that Iphigenia has gained the opportunity to break free from her current plight and return home, the chorus long to escape captivity in the Taurian land and similarly return to Hellas and their maiden choral dances. The first strophe, a single lyrical period, is framed by bird imagery as the desire to flee away is outlined (1089–105):

> ὄρνις ἃ παρὰ πετρίνας
> πόντου δειράδας ἀλκυών
> ἔλεγον οἶτον ἀείδεις,
> εὐξύνετον ξυνετοῖς βοάν,
> ὅτι πόσιν κελαδεῖς ἀεὶ μολπαῖς,
> ἐγώ σοι παραβάλλομαι
> θρηνοῦσ', ἄπτερος ὄρνις,
> ποθοῦσ' Ἑλλάνων ἀγόρους,
> ποθοῦσ' Ἄρτεμιν λοχίαν,
> ἃ παρὰ Κύνθιον ὄχθον οἰ-
> κεῖ φοίνικά θ' ἁβροκόμαν
> δάφναν τ' εὐερνέα καὶ
> γλαυκᾶς θαλλὸν ἱερὸν ἐλαί-
> ας, Λατοῦς ὠδῖνι φίλον,
> λίμναν θ' εἱλίσσουσαν ὕδωρ
> κύκλιον, ἔνθα κύκνος μελῳ-
> δὸς Μούσας θεραπεύει.

---

[23] The actual location of the Eridanus was a matter of debate in antiquity: for example, in his discussion of the earth's edges Herodotus famously (*Histories* 3.115) dismisses the geographical veracity of the claim that the Eridanus actually exists and issues forth into the sea on the westernmost edges of Europe. On ancient ideas about the river's location see Barrett (1964) 300–1.

Halcyon bird, you who sing lamenting your fate, beside the rocky ridges of the sea, a cry well-understood by those who understand that you loudly mourn your husband ceaselessly with songs like mine – I, a wingless bird, compete with you in wailing, longing for the meeting places of the Hellenes, longing for Artemis of childbirth, who lives beside the Cynthian hill and the delicate-leaved palm and the flourishing laurel and the sacred shoot of the grey olive, dear to the birth-pains of Leto, and the lake which swirls its water in a circle, where the tuneful swan serves the Muses.

The chorus begin by comparing their lamentation with that of the halcyon, whose humanlike cry of mourning is explained by the myth that she is the metamorphosed form of Alcyone, who bewails her dead husband Ceyx. The distant land which the chorus particularly longs for is the centre of the Athenian empire, Delos, home to Apollo and Artemis. There they might resume their native worship of a Delian Artemis who is much less bloodthirsty than the Taurian goddess in whose cult practices the women are currently forced to participate. Specific markers of the landscape in Delos which relate to Greek cult practices there are picked out as objects of the women's particular longing: the palm associated with the birth of Apollo and Artemis, the laurel sacred to Apollo, and the olive tree. The olive appears for the first time in our extant texts in connection with Delos here; as Athens' sacred tree, undoubtedly it reminds the audience of current Athenian influence over the island.[24] The long lyrical sentence ends with the appearance of another bird: this time a species associated with Apollo rather than Artemis, the tuneful swan.

In their opening address to the halcyon/Alcyone, the chorus bemoan the fact that they currently resemble a 'wingless bird' (ἄπτερος ὄρνις, 1095), but as the ode progresses their desire to overcome this difference becomes clear. This culminates in another explicit wish to undergo an avian metamorphosis (1138–42):

> λαμπροὺς ἱπποδρόμους βαίην,
> ἔνθ' εὐάλιον ἔρχεται πῦρ·
> οἰκείων δ' ὑπὲρ θαλάμων
> ἐν νώτοις ἁμοῖς πτέρυγας
> λήξαιμι θοάζουσα.

---

[24] On the intrusion of the olive tree into the traditional Delian scene as a marker of Athenian influence, see Cropp (2000) 240, Kyriakou (2006) 355 and Hall (2012) 55.

6.2 Familiar *Thaumata*: The Bird-Chorus' Wondrous Travels

If only I could travel along the bright chariot-tracks where the fire of the fine sun goes! But I would cease the quick movement of the wings of my back above the rooms of my home.

In fact, these choral addresses to birds seem to have been a technique which Euripides particularly favoured: another example can be found in the first stasimon of *Helen*, where the chorus 'cry out' to the melodious 'tearful nightingale' (ἀναβοάσω ... ἀηδόνα δακρυόεσσαν, 1108–10) just as the *IT*'s chorus call out to the halcyon bird.[25]

Aristophanes makes fun of Euripides for this tendency most explicitly in the *Frogs* (405 BCE) by portraying Aeschylus mocking Euripidean choral lyric with a song which opens with an address to halcyons (1309–12):

> ἀλκυόνες, αἳ παρ' ἀενάοις θαλάσσης
> κύμασι στωμύλλετε,
> τέγγουσαι νοτίοις πτερῶν
> ῥανίσι χρόα δροσιζόμεναι

O halcyons, who chatter beside the ever-flowing waves of the sea, moistening and besprinkling the skin of your wings with rainy drops!

On a much larger scale Aristophanes parodies the tragic avian wishes of these Euripidean choruses in the *Birds* as well. For example, just before the bird-chorus begin their song about distant *thaumata* Peisetairus' new city is approached by a succession of unpalatable Athenians (a father-beater at 1337–71, Cinesias the dithyrambic poet at 1372–409 and a sycophant at 1410–69), all of whom desperately long for a pair of wings to enable them to escape Athens and enjoy the riches of the new utopia in the sky. The approach of the sycophant, the final Athenian longing for wings, is immediately followed by Aristophanes' own take on tragic choral bird imagery: a chorus of actual birds singing about

---

[25] Euripides also turned to the conceit of inverting the conventional wish to flee away from danger towards the world's peripheries in *Helen*. There the chorus sing of Helen and Menelaus' prospective return to Sparta, and add their own wish to flee from Egypt by becoming birds (1478–9). More specifically, they long to join migrating cranes as they fly over the known world, fleeing from the wintry weather of the north and heading toward Libya in the far south (1479–82), passing over Sparta and bringing news of Menelaus' homecoming (1491–4). On the significance of this bird imagery, see Steiner (2011) 310–15.

the fantastic lands and *thaumata* they have overflown. Aristophanes thus reifies the familiar lyrical wish of this type of Euripidean chorus, metamorphosing the figurative language of tragic lyric into a comedic spectacle, as the actors literally don wings in front of the audience.[26]

This paratragic take on Euripidean choral lyric is exuberantly fused with a parodic rewriting of Herodotean-style ethnography, as the first two stanzas of the *Birds'* travel narrative demonstrate (1470-93):

> πολλὰ δὴ καὶ καινὰ καὶ θαυ-
> μάστ' ἐπεπτόμεσθα καὶ
> δεινὰ πράγματ' εἴδομεν.
> ἔστι γὰρ δένδρον πεφυκὸς
> ἔκτοπόν τι Καρδίας ἀ-
> πωτέρω Κλεώνυμος,
> χρήσιμον μὲν οὐδέν, ἄλ-
> λως δὲ δειλὸν καὶ μέγα.
> τοῦτο τοῦ μὲν ἦρος ἀεὶ
> βλαστάνει καὶ συκοφαντεῖ,
> τοῦ δὲ χειμῶνος πάλιν τὰς
> ἀσπίδας φυλλορροεῖ.
>
> ἔστι δ' αὖ χώρα πρὸς αὐτῷ
> τῷ σκότῳ πόρρω τις ἐν
> τῇ λύχνων ἐρημίᾳ,
> ἔνθα τοῖς ἥρωσιν ἄνθρω-
> ποι ξυναριστῶσι καὶ ξύν-
> εισι πλὴν τῆς ἑσπέρας.
> τηνικαῦτα δ' οὐκέτ' ἦν
> ἀσφαλὲς ξυντυγχάνειν.
> εἰ γὰρ ἐντύχοι τις ἥρῳ
> τῶν βροτῶν νύκτωρ Ὀρέστῃ,
> γυμνὸς ἦν πληγεὶς ὑπ' αὐτοῦ
> πάντα τἀπὶ δεξιά.

Many things both new and wondrous have we flown over and strange acts have we seen. For there is a certain extraordinary tree that grows somewhat far away from Heart-ford,[27] called Kleonymos – useful for nothing, but in other respects

---

[26] See Dobrov (1997) 100 and 117 on how the literalisation of the 'would that I were a bird!' *topos* of Euripidean choral lyric is a central underpinning of the *Birds'* plot.

[27] A pun suggested by Sommerstein (1987) 295 which aptly captures the double meaning of the Greek wordplay.

6.2 Familiar *Thaumata*: The Bird-Chorus' Wondrous Travels

cowardly and big. In spring this tree always buds and blooms with vexatious litigation (lit. 'shows forth figs'), while in wintertime it sheds its shields like leaves.

There is a land far off at the edge of darkness, in a lampless wasteland, where men have lunch and meet with heroes – but not in the evening. At that time it's no longer safe to meet together. For if any mortal met with the hero Orestes by night, he would be stripped naked and paralysed all down his right side.

The programmatic placement of 'new and wondrous' (καινὰ καὶ θαυμάστ') at the beginning of the song sets up an expectation that we are about to hear a catalogue of distant ethnographic *thaumata*. But it soon becomes obvious that Aristophanes has something different in mind, as exotic *thaumata* from unfamiliar lands are substituted with the defamiliarised practices, people and objects of quotidian Athenian life. The first real *thauma* is the so-called Kleonymos tree – but rather than the expected botanical marvel, the punning on Kardia as both a place name (referring to a colony in the Thracian Chersonese) and as a simple noun ('heart', 'courage') soon lets us recognise that what is really being described is less a wondrous tree than a cowardly Athenian citizen. The bizarre imagery created through the transposition of man and plant in this first description of the wondrous Kleonymos tree (e.g. the use of the verb συκοφαντεῖ as a legal term which simultaneously puns on the word's etymological relationship with the word 'fig') is one way in which the familiar meanings of words are shed, and unfamiliar nuances unexpectedly taken up.

The antistrophe continues to play on the conventional imagery of the earth's edges by purporting to describe a land so distant that it lies at the edge of darkness itself. This dark land is reminiscent of the scene of Homer's *Nekyia* in the *Odyssey*: the territory of the Cimmerians, a distant people imagined as living in the north, situated by Homer (*Od.* 11.13–15) near the far-off boundary of the world formed by Ocean in a place which is gripped by perpetual night because of the sun's absence (*Od.* 11.15–19).[28] At first glance, it seems that Aristophanes is describing a typical distant and wondrous semi-mythical locale in which gods and men are close and able to dine together, just as the gods are described as

---

[28] See Dunbar (1995) 691 for further references to the earth's sunless northern edges in Greek literature.

sharing feasts with the Phaeacians at *Odyssey* 7.203. He goes on to suggest that mythical heroes, such as Orestes, might also lurk in such far-off places, perhaps referring here to the Greek conceptualisation of distant islands (such as the Isles of the Blessed) as fitting locations for deceased heroes.[29] It soon becomes clear, however, that this is not really a description of the sunless extremities of the earth but rather a description of the dangers of wandering around Athens at night: Orestes is not a mythical hero, but a common thief liable to strip the unwary of their clothes.[30]

Aristophanes continues to build on this unflattering vision of Athens through the lens of ethnographic *thauma* in the third stanza of the bird-chorus' song as a pseudo-ethnographic tone combines with play on the literal and metaphorical meanings of words (1553–64):

> πρὸς δὲ τοῖς Σκιάποσιν λί-
> μνη τις ἔστ', ἄλουτος οὗ
> ψυχαγωγεῖ Σωκράτης·
> ἔνθα καὶ Πείσανδρος ἦλθε
> δεόμενος ψυχὴν ἰδεῖν ἢ
> ζῶντ' ἐκεῖνον προὔλιπε,
> σφάγι' ἔχων κάμηλον ἀ-
> μνόν τιν', ἧς λαιμοὺς τεμὼν ὥσ-
> περ ποθ' οὑδυσσεὺς ἀπῆλθε,
> κᾆτ' ἀνῆλθ' αὐτῷ κάτωθεν
> πρὸς τὸ λαῖτμα τῆς καμήλου
> Χαιρεφῶν ἡ νυκτερίς.

And near the Shadowfeet there is a certain swamp, where Socrates – never bathing – raises dead spirits. And there Peisander went asking to see the soul which had abandoned him while he was still alive. He had a baby camel as a sacrificial offering; after cutting its throat, just like Odysseus did, he stepped back, and up to him from below, attracted to the deep pool of camel's blood, came Chaerephon the bat.

The description of Socrates raising ghosts as the chief marvel of the land of the Shadowfeet is humorous not only due to the

---

[29] See Rusten (2013) 309–10 for the suggestion that this stanza refers to distant islands as fitting locations for heroes such as the mythical Orestes.

[30] Orestes seems to have been the name or nickname of a notorious cloak thief in Athens: the chorus have already complained of his thieving exploits in line 712; cf. Euelpides' complaint about being mugged and stripped of his cloak after being clubbed over the head at night in lines 492–8.

6.2 Familiar *Thaumata*: The Bird-Chorus' Wondrous Travels

ludicrousness of the image in itself, but also because it plays with the literal and metaphorical meanings of the verb for 'soul-leading' or 'spirit-raising' (ψυχαγωγεῖ). Here the term refers to Socrates' actual ghost-raising, at the same time as it reminds us of its growing use as a term referring to the beguiling and seductive nature of rhetoric itself.[31] This sense that rhetorical language is increasingly bound up with the effect of *thauma* becomes even more obvious in the final stanza (1694–705):

> ἔστι δ' ἐν Φάναισι πρὸς τῇ
> Κλεψύδρᾳ πανοῦργον Ἐγ-
> γλωττογαστόρων γένος,
> οἳ θερίζουσίν τε καὶ σπεί-
> ρουσι καὶ τρυγῶσι ταῖς γλώτ-
> ταισι συκάζουσί τε·
> βάρβαροι δ' εἰσὶν γένος,
> Γοργίαι τε καὶ Φίλιπποι.
> κἀπὸ τῶν Ἐγγλωττογαστό-
> ρων ἐκείνων τῶν φιλίππων
> πανταχοῦ τῆς Ἀττικῆς ἡ
> γλῶττα χωρὶς τέμνεται.

In Denunciation-land, near the Waterclock, there are the tricky Tongue-Belly people, who reap and sow and gather in vintages with their tongues – and they unscrupulously prosecute with them too. They are a barbarian people, Gorgiases and Philippuses. And after the fashion of these Philippic Tongue-Belly people everywhere in Attica the tongue is cut out separately.

Wordplay again stretches familiar lexical meanings into unfamiliar territory: 'Denunciation-land' (Φάναισι, 1694) refers to a literal harbour on Chios while hinting at the verb φαίνειν, which in this case means 'to inform against someone' and is supposed once again to bring the practice of sycophancy to mind; 'Waterclock' (Κλεψύδρᾳ, 1695) is often a name for springs with concealed sources (one such was at the foot of the Acropolis), as well as referring to the clock used to time speeches in the law courts.[32] The 'Tongue-Belly people' are not an exotic, distant tribe, but orators in Athens who live and fill their bellies as a result of words,

---

[31] On the play with the meaning of ψυχαγωγεῖ, see Dunbar (1995) 711–12 and Moulton (1981) 40.
[32] For the wordplay in this stanza, see Hubbard (1997) 31 and Dunbar (1995) 740–4.

the product of their tongues. These people are said to be 'barbarians', a charge which contemptuously hints at the famous rhetorician Gorgias' non-Athenian, Sicilian origins, while at the same time maintaining the ethnographic tone of this description of everyday Athenian life. It is not known for certain who Philippus might be, though clearly he is another Gorgianic orator.[33] Aristophanes completes this fantastic vision with another reference to the overwhelming importance of both literal and metaphorical tongues in Athens, focusing on the separate cutting-out of the tongue from the sacrificial animal, an Athenian religious custom familiar from everyday life which sounds plausibly exotic when defamiliarised and presented with a bizarre origin (*aition*) through the ethnographer's lens, while simultaneously offering yet another coded insult against the power of rhetoricians' tongues in the Attic lawcourts.

As we can see, as the *Birds* draws to a close and the final scenes reveal that this is a play about Athens after all, despite the opening claims to the contrary, there is one aspect of Athenian society in particular which is presented as the ultimate *thauma*: the use and abuse of language itself. By approaching everyday Athenian life with the eye of an ethnographer hungry for *thaumata*, Aristophanes manages to defamiliarise the audience's well-known surroundings, simultaneously encouraging renewed assessments of Athens, her imperial ambitions, their causes, and their potentially dislocating effects. In the play's final choral songs, the focus on *thauma* in unexpected contexts continues to draw attention to the place of wonder in ethnographic accounts, but there is perhaps also a concomitant and increasing sense that comedy as a genre can itself be framed as a sort of ethnography of Aristophanes' own society.

6.3 The Wonder of Athens: Thucydides and *Thauma*

This redefinition of *thauma* as a concept which can now be associated primarily with one's own society is a key effect of the

---

[33] Cf. Bdelykleon's reference to 'Philippus son of Gorgias' (Φίλιππον ... τὸν Γοργίου) at Arist. *Vesp.* 421: it is not clear if Philippus was literally a son of Gorgias or, more likely, his student. See Dunbar (1995) 743 for a detailed discussion of Philippus' possible identity.

6.3 The Wonder of Athens: Thucydides and *Thauma*

process of linguistic defamiliarisation and refamiliarisation which the *Birds* presents to its audience. For Aristophanes, this redefinition of the potential boundaries and meaning of wonder is strongly connected to Athens' imperialistic drive, with the fantastic colonisation of the marvellous expanses of the sky presented as the final frontier of Athenian dominance. The real-world engagement of the Athenians in ambitious political and military activity at the time of the *Birds*' first performance in 414 BCE lends an additional power to Aristophanes' focus on the ambivalent nature of Peisetairus' colonisation of the sky. In the summer of 415 the Athenians set out on an expedition against Sicily, which aimed both at quashing Syracusan influence and establishing Athenian control over the island as a whole. Aristophanes clearly makes reference to the contemporary situation in Sicily at three points within the play, all of which relate to the generals in command of the expedition. At 145–7, Alcibiades' recall to Athens on charges relating to the mutilation of the Herms is hinted at when Euelpides rejects the suggestion of fleeing to the shore of the Red Sea on the basis that the *Salaminia*, the sacred state trireme which was sent to arrest and retrieve Alcibiades, might appear there and haul him off too. The role of Nicias in contemporary politics is also referred to twice: first when Euelpides tells Peisetairus that 'in terms of clever devices you've outdone Nicias already' (ὑπερακοντίζεις σύ γ' ἤδη Νικίαν ταῖς μηχαναῖς, 363), and then later when Peisetairus declares that his plan should be put into action at once since there is 'no time for faffing about like Nicias' (ὥρα 'στὶν ἡμῖν οὐδὲ μελλονικιᾶν, 639) – an obvious reference to the older statesman's reluctance to sail against Syracuse.

It is important to stress, however, that the eventual disastrous outcome of the expedition would not yet have been apparent to the *Birds*' original audience.[34] The overall outcome of the enterprise still hung in the balance at the moment of the play's writing and first production, but that is not to say that contemporary debate

---

[34] See e.g. Pelling (2000b) 126, Asper (2005) 6–18 on contemporary attitudes towards the expedition at the moment of the *Birds*' production; cf. Dunbar (1995) 2–4 on *Birds* and the contemporary political situation regarding Sicily. For a more sceptical approach about the significance of Sicily see now Hall (2020) 187–213, which draws out the importance of Athens' relationship with Thrace and its influence on the play.

over the nature and role of Athenian imperialism in relation to Sicily is not in the background of Aristophanes' vision of Peisetairus' quest to colonise the sky. Certainly, the connection between conquest, imperial expansion and *thauma*, and the potential lure of the acquisition and control of objects which can be labelled as *thaumata*, seems to form one strand of contemporary discourse concerning Athenian imperial power which the *Birds* picks up on. The importance of *thauma* becomes apparent when we compare Aristophanes' conceptualisation of the newly marvellous nature of Athens during the Sicilian expedition with Thucydides' retrospective vision of the power and effects of wonder in relation to Athens and Athenian self-fashioning during the Peloponnesian War.

Thucydides' view of the place of wonder in Athenian society during this period is, of course, complicated by the importance the concept of *thauma* had assumed in the ethnographic and historiographical tradition. There is undeniably a relative paucity of words relating to wonder and astonishment in Thucydides' work compared to the frequency of such terms in Herodotus' *Histories*. When *thaumata* in the *History* are examined in detail, it soon becomes clear that very different types of objects are labelled as marvels in this work in comparison to Herodotus' writing, and that the concept of *thauma* is itself now configured in transformed terms. It is certainly not the case, however, that Thucydides' interest in wonder functions as a means of subtly maligning Herodotus' work, or that *thauma* has become an unimportant concept and force in Thucydides' historiographic vision.[35] Instead, the relative infrequency of thaumatic language in Thucydides' *History* only renders its occasional appearances more striking.

The significance of wonder to Thucydides' narrative becomes clearest when the appearances of *thauma* and *ekplexis* within the narrative of the expedition to Sicily in books 6 and 7 are analysed.

---

[35] See Priestley (2014) 61–8 on how a divergent attitude towards *thauma* is one of the ways in which Thucydides differentiates himself from Herodotean historiography. Cf. Scanlon (1994) 165–71, who reads Thucydides' references to *thauma* as examples of direct engagement with, and even verbal allusions to, Herodotus' *Histories*. On the relative paucity of *thauma* and cognate terms in Thucydides, see also Mette (1960) 67–8.

6.3 The Wonder of Athens: Thucydides and *Thauma*

Just as *thauma* assumes an important place in Peisetairus' founding of a city in the sky, which is portrayed as an imperialistic colonisation, so too does wonder play a key role in the portrayal of Athenian motivation for the Sicilian expedition, a voyage which is framed by Thucydides as a similar sort of colonising venture.[36] The potential for wonder is emphasised by the fact that the Athenians are presented as almost entirely ignorant of the reality of the situation in the west before they set out on their expedition. They believe that Sicily is a far-off, mysterious land which sustains a society radically different from their own. At the very beginning of book 6, Thucydides stresses that 'most of the Athenians were unfamiliar with the size of the island and the number of its inhabitants, both Greek and barbarian, and unaware that they were undertaking a war which was not much inferior to the one which they were waging against the Peloponnesians' (ἄπειροι οἱ πολλοὶ ὄντες τοῦ μεγέθους τῆς νήσου καὶ τῶν ἐνοικούντων τοῦ πλήθους καὶ Ἑλλήνων καὶ βαρβάρων, καὶ ὅτι οὐ πολλῷ τινι ὑποδεέστερον πόλεμον ἀνῃροῦντο ἢ τὸν πρὸς Πελοποννησίους, 6.1.1). This claim cannot be literally true: it is clear that contact between Athens, Sicily and Italy more broadly had been significant and sustained throughout the fifth century long before 415 BCE: for example, a large contingent of Athenians had visited the island already in 426.[37] This apparent ignorance of the west takes on a wider metaphorical significance over the course of books 6 and 7, as it becomes increasingly clear that the Athenians are just as unfamiliar with the true extent of their own power as they are of the true nature of the Syracusans. The geographical inversion of the customary location of *thaumata* is part of this distorting process: Athens itself is now more marvellous than the seemingly distant land of Sicily – though Thucydides soon shows that the Syracusans are more similar to the Athenians than the latter could ever have imagined. By mapping the way in which *thauma* intersects with this constant

---

[36] See Green (1970) 131, Avery (1973) 8–13 (who draws explicit parallels between the colonisation theme in *Birds* and Thucydides) and Kallet (2001) 25 on Thucydides' presentation of the Sicilian expedition as a colonising venture.

[37] For the strict factual impossibility of Thucydides' opening claim, see D. G. Smith (2004) 33–70, Hornblower (2002) 41–3, 163 and (2008) 5–12, 260.

inversion of the concepts of the near and far, the familiar and unfamiliar, Thucydides' conception of the radically distorting and dangerous effects that ensue when people's capacity for wonder is manipulated becomes apparent. It is this new conception of *thauma* which becomes predominant in the fourth century BCE, as wonder's ability to connect self and other through potentially distorting processes of (verbal and/or visual) representations seemingly becomes a matter of increasing interest and anxiety.

But before we can understand the role which *thauma* plays in the historian's vision of the origins and eventual failure of the Sicilian expedition, it is necessary to examine the other most notable passage in which Thucydidean *thauma* plays a vital role: Pericles' Funeral Oration. For it is here, during Pericles' famous speech in book 2, that we see *thauma* most transparently associated with Athenian society itself for the very first time.[38] Whereas Aristophanes' *Birds* presents us with the prospect of Athens as the ultimate *thauma* more obliquely, as the paradoxical punchline of a joke, Pericles is unequivocal in his vision of Athens' ability to induce wonder in all who witness or contemplate the *polis* and her power (2.41.3–4):

μόνη γὰρ τῶν νῦν ἀκοῆς κρείσσων ἐς πεῖραν ἔρχεται, καὶ μόνη οὔτε τῷ πολεμίῳ ἐπελθόντι ἀγανάκτησιν ἔχει ὑφ' οἵων κακοπαθεῖ οὔτε τῷ ὑπηκόῳ κατάμεμψιν ὡς οὐχ ὑπ' ἀξίων ἄρχεται. μετὰ μεγάλων δὲ σημείων καὶ οὐ δή τοι ἀμάρτυρόν γε τὴν δύναμιν παρασχόμενοι τοῖς τε νῦν καὶ τοῖς ἔπειτα θαυμασθησόμεθα, καὶ οὐδὲν προσδεόμενοι οὔτε Ὁμήρου ἐπαινέτου οὔτε ὅστις ἔπεσι μὲν τὸ αὐτίκα τέρψει, τῶν δ' ἔργων τὴν ὑπόνοιαν ἡ ἀλήθεια βλάψει, ἀλλὰ πᾶσαν μὲν θάλασσαν καὶ γῆν ἐσβατὸν τῇ ἡμετέρᾳ τόλμῃ καταναγκάσαντες γενέσθαι, πανταχοῦ δὲ μνημεῖα κακῶν τε κἀγαθῶν ἀίδια ξυγκατοικίσαντες.

For Athens alone of cities today is even greater, when put to the test, than reports suggest, and it is Athens alone which no enemy who comes up against her feels angry about when he suffers defeat, and none of her subjects resent her, thinking they are ruled by those who are unworthy. And with mighty monuments, and because of the power which we have put forth not without witnesses, we shall be wondered at by people today and by those in the future. We do not at all need a Homer, nor anyone else, to praise us with verses which give pleasure for a moment, but whose interpretation of events will be destroyed by the truth.

---

[38] The association of *thauma* with Athens is something which very much differentiates Thucydides from Herodotus and his conception of the role and place of *thauma* in historiography, as Priestley (2014) 64–6 points out.

6.3 The Wonder of Athens: Thucydides and *Thauma*

Instead, we have forced every sea and every land open with our daring, and have established everywhere eternal monuments of our vengeance and our benefactions.

At this point in his oration, Pericles substantiates his earlier claim that Athens is an 'educational example to the whole of Greece' (τῆς Ἑλλάδος παίδευσιν, 2.41.1) by confirming that the reports of her greatness which have so far circulated have not been exaggerated. The now clichéd claim that hearsay leads to false and misleading statements relating to marvels in far-off lands is firmly turned on its head, as Pericles paradoxically claims that in Athens' case, the reality is more astonishing than rumour. Even when put to the test, which in this case seems to imply the autoptic witnessing of great monuments or proofs of great deeds relating to Athenian power, Athens will remain marvellous.[39]

The wondrous reality of Athens is linked to her empire, mentioned explicitly here for the first and only time in the Funeral Oration, in Pericles' claim that those subjected to Athenian hegemony can bear no grudges in the face of such conspicuous strength and worthiness, and even her enemies cannot complain about being beaten by such a power. The present and future wonder inspired by the visible indications of this power is reminiscent of the present and future *kleos* which a god-crafted object, Achilles' shield, is able to provide to the individual warrior in the *Iliad* through the past and future wonder of many men.[40] But in this case a poet, even a Homer, is not needed to ensure the present and future fame of Athens: the obvious signs and memories of the city's marvellous power at home and abroad will ensure that of their own accord. This power now stretches over every land and sea, with the result that the mysterious and potentially wondrous nature of far-off lands is no longer a geographical certainty, seeing

---

[39] Cf. also the fleeting reference to the wondrous nature of Athens just before Pericles' statement here, when he claims that the Lacedaemonians are inferior to the Athenians because they have to cultivate their courageous and manly behaviour by training themselves intensely from a young age, whereas the Athenians do not need to undergo such training because they are born this way. The city is thus worthy to be wondered at for these reasons, as well as those which Pericles will elaborate in the rest of the speech (καὶ ἔν τε τούτοις τὴν πόλιν ἀξίαν εἶναι θαυμάζεσθαι καὶ ἔτι ἐν ἄλλοις, 2.39.4).

[40] *Il.* 18.467: ἀνθρώπων πολέων θαυμάσσεται, ὅς κεν ἴδηται (anyone among the multitude of men will marvel at it [i.e. the shield], whoever sees it).

as Athens herself is now the natural domain of *thaumata*. Furthermore, Homer, and the mythical marvels which the sort of poetry he created contain, are no longer needed.

But there have already been hints in Thucydides' previous narrative that the potentially distorting and falsifying effects which Pericles claims Homer and the poets produce might also be created by Pericles' own speech. Although he claims that the mighty and wonder-inducing monuments of Athens attest to the power of the *polis*, we have already been warned early on in book I that the physical remains of the city are a misleading standard by which to judge Athens' power (1.10.2–3):

Λακεδαιμονίων γὰρ εἰ ἡ πόλις ἐρημωθείη, λειφθείη δὲ τά τε ἱερὰ καὶ τῆς κατασκευῆς τὰ ἐδάφη, πολλὴν ἂν οἶμαι ἀπιστίαν τῆς δυνάμεως προελθόντος πολλοῦ χρόνου τοῖς ἔπειτα πρὸς τὸ κλέος αὐτῶν εἶναι ... Ἀθηναίων δὲ τὸ αὐτὸ τοῦτο παθόντων διπλασίαν ἂν τὴν δύναμιν εἰκάζεσθαι ἀπὸ τῆς φανερᾶς ὄψεως τῆς πόλεως ἢ ἔστιν.

For if the city of the Lacedaemonians was abandoned, and only the temples and the traces of the infrastructure remained, I think that after a great length of time had passed people in the future would be in complete disbelief that their power matched their renown ... But if the same thing befell the Athenians their power would seem double what it is in reality from the visible remains of the city.

This retrospective view of the inequalities between the most obvious visible traces of Athenian and Lacedaemonian power colours Pericles' claims about Athens' capacity to inspire wonder through great monuments and achievements which bear witness to her greatness. Personal autopsy may be held up as a superior means of forming epistemological judgements, but appearances can, of course, be deceiving.

In fact, as Thucydides' narrative goes on to reveal, the visual manifestations of Athenian power in which Pericles places such trust turn out to guarantee nothing of the sort. *Thauma*, however, is a crucial means by which this sort of optical illusion occurs. As wonder takes over, the potential for misjudgements and miscalculations of magnitude increases. Funeral speeches (*epitaphioi logoi*), such as the one delivered by Pericles, naturally overmagnify the objects of their praise, with speakers painting verbal pictures of the city and her people which aim at the glorification and memorialisation of the community and its past and present

6.3 The Wonder of Athens: Thucydides and *Thauma*

citizens above all else. We find a humorous yet telling critique of the potential dangers which this sort of intense focus on the city's marvellous nature might produce in Plato's *Menexenus*. Before embarking on his own version of an *epitaphios logos*, Socrates describes how such speeches change his visual and mental perceptions of the city, and even of himself (235a–b):

καὶ τὴν πόλιν ἐγκωμιάζοντες κατὰ πάντας τρόπους καὶ τοὺς τετελευτηκότας ἐν τῷ πολέμῳ καὶ τοὺς προγόνους ἡμῶν ἅπαντας τοὺς ἔμπροσθεν καὶ αὐτοὺς ἡμᾶς τοὺς ἔτι ζῶντας ἐπαινοῦντες, ὥστ' ἔγωγε, ὦ Μενέξενε, γενναίως πάνυ διατίθεμαι ἐπαινούμενος ὑπ' αὐτῶν, καὶ ἑκάστοτε ἕστηκα ἀκροώμενος καὶ κηλούμενος, ἡγούμενος ἐν τῷ παραχρῆμα μείζων καὶ γενναιότερος καὶ καλλίων γεγονέναι. καὶ οἷα δὴ τὰ πολλὰ ἀεὶ μετ' ἐμοῦ ξένοι τινὲς ἕπονται καὶ ξυνακροῶνται, πρὸς οὓς ἐγὼ σεμνότερος ἐν τῷ παραχρῆμα γίγνομαι· καὶ γὰρ ἐκεῖνοι ταὐτὰ ταῦτα δοκοῦσί μοι πάσχειν καὶ πρὸς ἐμὲ καὶ πρὸς τὴν ἄλλην πόλιν, θαυμασιωτέραν αὐτὴν ἡγεῖσθαι εἶναι ἢ πρότερον, ὑπὸ τοῦ λέγοντος ἀναπειθόμενοι.

And they [i.e. the speakers of the *epitaphioi logoi*] extol the city in every possible way, praising both those who died in the war and our ancestors before us and ourselves, who are still living. As a result of this, Menexenus, I end up thinking of myself as extremely noble when I am praised by them. And each time, listening to them and being enchanted, I am raised up: right there on the spot I think I am bigger and nobler and handsomer. And often some foreign visitors tag along with me and listen: right there on the spot I become more awe-inspiring to them. For they seem to me to be affected in just the same way as I am with respect to me and the rest of the city, believing her to be more wonderful than before after being seduced by the speaker.

Socrates picks up on the potentially skewed effect which the verbal images crafted by orators have the power to create by claiming that he feels his own physical proportions increase as he listens to the praise of the city and its citizens, describing precisely the kind of distortion which the creation of *thauma* is able to induce. Although Socrates is obviously exaggerating here, this humorous portrayal of the effects of *epitaphioi logoi* nevertheless contains a more serious critique of the conceptual illusions which wonder-inducing language may help to encourage.[41] It is this aspect of the power of *thauma* that Thucydides also engages

---

[41] On the dangerous effects of the rhetoric of the *epitaphios logos* which Plato outlines in the *Menexenus*' prologue, and on the place of *thauma* in this passage, see Loraux (1986) 264–70.

with in his portrayal of Pericles' wonderful vision of Athens in his own Funeral Oration.

But it is only as Thucydides' account of the Peloponnesian War progresses that the risk of unreflectively falling prey to the distorting power of *thauma* truly becomes apparent. One of the ways in which the danger of *thauma* is demonstrated is through the increasing importance of the idea of skewed and distorted perceptions over the course of the narrative of the expedition to Sicily. In connection with this, we find that the antithesis between the near and the far is continually turned on its head over the course of books 6 and 7. Just as Euripides' *Ion* demonstrates the risk of simultaneously wondering at and fearing potential threats from far-off when it is matters close at hand which constitute true hazards, the dangers which might be thought to lurk in the west at the beginning of the narrative of the Sicilian expedition actually turn out to be situated at home, with mistakes in Athens ultimately leading to disaster abroad.[42]

Before the expedition even sets sail, the ability of wonder to skew perceptions is explored by Nicias in his first speech. Nicias cautions the Athenians to use their capacity to inspire wonder wisely, arguing that the idea of wondrous power far-off is more awe-inspiring than the reality of *thaumata* close up once they are put to the test (6.11.4):

ἡμᾶς δ' ἂν οἱ ἐκεῖ Ἕλληνες μάλιστα μὲν ἐκπεπληγμένοι εἶεν εἰ μὴ ἀφικοίμεθα, ἔπειτα δὲ καὶ εἰ δείξαντες τὴν δύναμιν δι' ὀλίγου ἀπέλθοιμεν· τὰ γὰρ διὰ πλείστου πάντες ἴσμεν θαυμαζόμενα καὶ τὰ πεῖραν ἥκιστα τῆς δόξης δόντα.

But the Hellenes there would be especially astonished if we did not turn up at all; second best would be to depart after making a display of our power for a short time. For we all know that the things which are furthest off and which give the least opportunity to put their reputation to the test are wondered at.

These words echo those of Pericles' Funeral Oration on the subject of *thauma*. While Pericles claims that the wonder-inspiring aspects of Athens can be put to the test and not found wanting, Nicias suggests that *thaumata* can lose their power by becoming

---

[42] See Rood (1998) 133–82 on the connections between mistakes at home and results abroad in the Sicilian narrative; cf. Taylor (2010) 135–87 on the frequent inversion of what is near/far within the narrative of the Sicilian expedition.

6.3 The Wonder of Athens: Thucydides and *Thauma*

familiar when seen close up. In contrast to Pericles' view that Athens alone can withstand intense scrutiny at close quarters and remain impressive, Nicias grasps the fact that it is through distance that the potentially thaumatic power of Athens retains its mystique in the eyes of others.

What Nicias does not grasp, however, is the fact that it is this same alluring fascination with the distant which enthuses the Athenians in the build-up to the Sicilian expedition. He may be correct in his contention that 'the things furthest off are wondered at and give the least opportunity to put their reputation to the test', but he does not take account of the fact that this inability to put matters to the test can also increase desire, if the imagination is gripped by a longing for *thaumata* rather than a fear of the unknown. In fact, Nicias' constant reminders (and exaggerations) of the extreme distance of Sicily only inflame Athenian desire for the acquisition of potentially marvellous far-off lands, rather than dissuading the *polis* from the difficult enterprise which has been proposed. Nicias seems aware that longing for the distant is a risk in his first speech when he appeals to the older citizens to not be seized by 'a harmful desire for things far away' (δυσέρωτας εἶναι τῶν ἀπόντων, 6.13.1), but he fails to recognise the danger his own rhetoric creates, as it repeatedly places the idea of Sicily as a distant land into the minds of his listeners. Ironically, and quite inadvertently, these words create a marvellous distorting effect of their own. Although Nicias expects that his speech will either dissuade the Athenians from the expedition, or at least make them more cautious about it because of 'the great number of issues' (τῷ πλήθει τῶν πραγμάτων, 6.24.1) he has taken pains to outline, his words have the very opposite effect, with the result that 'those desirous of sailing' (οἱ δὲ τὸ μὲν ἐπιθυμοῦν τοῦ πλοῦ, 6.24.2) are only encouraged by his speech rather than deterred. Nicias even misjudges the effect of his words on the older Athenian citizens whom he expects to side with him against the youthful impetuousness of Alcibiades and his followers. In fact, his rhetoric only serves to remind the *polis* of the wondrous potential of Athenian martial glory and achievements like those described in Pericles' Funeral Oration, with the result that these warnings inflame the desire (*eros*) for conquest of both young and old alike (6.24.3):

καὶ ἔρως ἐνέπεσε τοῖς πᾶσιν ὁμοίως ἐκπλεῦσαι· τοῖς μὲν γὰρ πρεσβυτέροις ὡς ἢ καταστρεψομένοις ἐφ' ἃ ἔπλεον ἢ οὐδὲν ἂν σφαλεῖσαν μεγάλην δύναμιν, τοῖς δ' ἐν τῇ ἡλικίᾳ τῆς τε ἀπούσης πόθῳ ὄψεως καὶ θεωρίας, καὶ εὐέλπιδες ὄντες σωθήσεσθαι.

And a passionate desire to set sail gripped everyone equally: the elder men believed that either they would trample upon the places they were sailing against, or that the great force would suffer no disaster, while a longing for far-off spectacles and sights fell upon the younger men, and they were all extremely confident that they would be alright.

Despite Nicias' warnings against the potentially damaging effects of harmful desire, his warning again increases the Athenians' daring and desperate desire for the possession of far-off lands and the attainment of unknown glory.

The language of longing for the far-off here is reminiscent of the sentiment expressed in Pindar's *Pythian* 3, which describes Coronis' punishment because 'she was in love with things far-off' (ἤρατο τῶν ἀπεόντων, 20) – i.e. she takes a mortal lover despite the fact that she is already pregnant with Apollo's child Asclepius. As a result of this, Coronis becomes one of the many foolish people 'who despise what is near at hand and set their sights on things far away' (ὅστις αἰσχύνων ἐπιχώρια παπταίνει τὰ πόρσω, 22). The near/far dynamic in this poem creates a paradox: a mortal lover should be much closer to the mortal Coronis than a god, but in this instance her longing for what should be much more familiar to her has become strangely transgressive after Apollo's previous attentions. The Athenian situation in Thucydides presents a similar sort of paradox: on the one hand, the Syracusans are continually presented as exotic, distant and desirable, yet as books 6 and 7 progress it becomes clear that the Athenians and Syracusans are actually now very similar to each other in many ways. It is this paradoxical longing for something unfamiliar yet familiar which causes disaster for the Athenians, just as it does for Coronis in Pindar's poem.[43]

Even more paradoxically, this increased longing for far-off sights is further inflamed by the astonishing spectacles of

---

[43] On the near/far theme in *Pyth*. 3, see Young (1968) 27–68; on the closeness of Thucydides' language to this Pindaric parallel, see Cornford (1907) 206, Rood (1998) 177 n. 68, Hornblower (2004) 73 and (2008) 335.

6.3 The Wonder of Athens: Thucydides and *Thauma*

Athenian power at home, which Thucydides suggests distort Athenian conceptions of the true strength of their hegemony. It is through the figure of Alcibiades that we gain an increasing awareness of the nature of these types of distortion. After warning the Athenians about the dangers of diluting their capacity for inspiring wonder by making themselves overfamiliar to the enemy, Nicias turns to the danger that Alcibiades poses to the *polis*. He condemns the younger man for considering only his own interest while exhorting the Athenians to sail, and for thinking about how he might profit from the expedition and be 'wondered at for his habit of keeping horses' (τὸ ἑαυτοῦ μόνον σκοπῶν, ἄλλως τε καὶ νεώτερος ὢν ἔτι ἐς τὸ ἄρχειν, ὅπως θαυμασθῇ μὲν ἀπὸ τῆς ἱπποτροφίας, 6.12.2). This hint that Alcibiades has set himself up as a distracting object of wonder to the Athenians is soon confirmed by the younger man's reply to Nicias. Rather than refuting his criticism, Alcibiades instead embraces the suggestion that his life and conduct are an impressive and marvellous sight to behold, and suggests that this approach to his personal life has already yielded results for the *polis*. Nicias may have disparaged the way in which he has set himself up as an object of wonder because of his love of horses, but Alcibiades retorts (6.16.2) that the rest of the Hellenes now think that Athenian power is even greater than it really is as a result of his decision to enter seven chariots into the races at Olympia. He goes on (6.16.3) to claim that his other displays of wealth and brilliance in the city also produce an impression of strength in the eyes of foreigners, even if fellow citizens become jealous as a result. The brilliant, wonder-inducing exterior appearance of power is here confused with power itself, as Alcibiades concentrates on the external appearance and trappings of command throughout his speech.[44]

It is this sense of wonder, and its distorting effects, which Thucydides goes on to suggest are one of the causes of the subsequent negative outcome in Sicily, and nowhere is the potential confusion between the trappings of power and power itself more apparent than in the fleet's embarkation from Athens at

---

[44] On the focus on appearances in Alcibiades' speech and its distinction from the reality of the situation, see Macleod (1983) 86 and Jordan (2000) 70–1.

6.30–1.[45] Like Alcibiades' conspicuous display at Olympia, the Athenian fleet itself is 'a spectacle' (θέαν, 6.31.1), and its embarkation 'more resembled a displayof power and wealth aimed at all the other Hellenes than an expedition against enemies' (ἐς τοὺς ἄλλους Ἕλληνας ἐπίδειξιν μᾶλλον εἰκασθῆναι τῆς δυνάμεως καὶ ἐξουσίας ἢ ἐπὶ πολεμίους παρασκευήν, 6.31.4).[46] In fact, the astonishment caused by the sight of the Athenians setting off echoes, on a broader civic level, the external brilliance of the sight of Alcibiades' lifestyle (6.31.6):

καὶ ὁ στόλος οὐχ ἧσσον τόλμης τε θάμβει καὶ ὄψεως λαμπρότητι περιβόητος ἐγένετο ἢ στρατιᾶς πρὸς οὓς ἐπῇσαν ὑπερβολῇ, καὶ ὅτι μέγιστος ἤδη διάπλους ἀπὸ τῆς οἰκείας καὶ ἐπὶ μεγίστῃ ἐλπίδι τῶν μελλόντων πρὸς τὰ ὑπάρχοντα ἐπεχειρήθη.

And the expedition became no less famous for astonishment at its boldness and the brilliance of its spectacle, than for the disproportionate strength of the force compared to those whom it was directed against, and also because it was the lengthiest voyage away from home yet attempted and there was such great hope for the future in relation to their present resources.

The powerful astonishment (*thambos*) which the fleet inspires here is misplaced, aimed at those in Athens watching the spectacle, rather than at the enemy, as Nicias previously advised. Thucydides portrays the effects of this misplaced sense of astonishment as disastrous: by wondering at the sight of power close to home, it now becomes impossible to judge the true capabilities of Athenian influence abroad.

An important aspect of this misjudgement turns out to be the inability to appreciate how *close*, rather than distant, the military capabilities of Syracuse and the other Sicilian cities are to those of the Athenians. Although Nicias seems to grasp this and warn his fellow citizens that the Sicilian cities are 'equipped with everything in a manner very similar to our force' (παρεσκευασμέναι τοῖς πᾶσιν ὁμοιοτρόπως μάλιστα τῇ ἡμετέρᾳ δυνάμει, 6.20.3), his constant talk of the geographical distance of Sicily from Athens

---

[45] Cf. Jordan (2000) 63–79 and Kallet (2001) 21–84 on the specious nature of Athenian power which the spectacle of embarkation exposes.
[46] On the connection between the astonishment inspired by the appearance of Alcibiades' wondrous lifestyle and the spectacle of the Athenian fleet setting sail, see Jordan (2000) 65 and Kallet (2001) 64.

6.3 The Wonder of Athens: Thucydides and *Thauma*

perhaps dilutes this aspect of his message, encouraging his fellow Athenians to confuse spatial distance with cultural difference by inadvertently exoticising the distant regions to the west. Only in book 7, at the point when it has become clear to the Athenians that the expedition is a disastrous miscalculation, does the reality of Syracusan similarity become apparent to the attackers: the Sicilian cities are the only places the Athenians have encountered which are 'similar in manner' (ὁμοιοτρόποις, 7.55.2) to their own city in terms of their culture and democratic way of life – as well as being 'powerful in terms of ships, cavalry and size' (ναυσὶ καὶ ἵπποις καὶ μεγέθει ἰσχυούσαις, 7.55.2).[47]

In fact, uncanny similarities between the two powers continue to arise as Syracuse takes on the mantle of Athens in the Persian Wars, becoming a brave and free city resisting the Athenians' increasingly tyrannical (and Persian-looking) imperialistic overreach.[48] The sense of paradoxical similarity and simultaneous reversal is complete when the Syracusans, encouraged by their growing military success, resolve to continue to press their advantage over the Athenians until they have utterly destroyed them on land and on sea to ensure that they are 'wondered at by everyone at the present and in future time' (ὑπό τε τῶν ἄλλων ἀνθρώπων καὶ ὑπὸ τῶν ἔπειτα πολὺ θαυμασθήσεσθαι, 7.56.2). With these words the ironic reversal of the sentiment of Pericles' Funeral Oration (2.41.3–4), which set up the image of Athens as the ultimate *thauma*, is now almost complete. This reversal is made fully clear when Nicias, before the final battle in the harbour, exhorts his dispirited sailors to continue fighting hard and praises the fleet's metic sailors, rather than Athenian citizens, for being 'wondered at through the whole of Greece' (ἐθαυμάζεσθε κατὰ τὴν Ἑλλάδα, 7.63.3) as a result of learning the Athenians' language and way of life. Again, the Athenians' notions of near and far have been skewed in relation to the effects of *thauma*, as non-native

---

[47] See Rood (1999) 162 and Hornblower (2008) 21–2 on the similarities and parallels Thucydides draws between the Athenians and Syracusans as the Sicilian narrative progresses.

[48] On the similarity of Athens' imperial ambitions in the *History* to those of Persia against Greece in Herodotus, see Rood (1998) 197 and (1999) 141–68, Cornford (1907) 201–20 and Rogkotis (2006) 57–86.

metics are now objects of wonder through their association with Athens, and might even now be seen as objects of competitive emulation for the dejected citizens of Athens themselves.[49] From this point on, Athens and her native Athenian citizens are no longer able to inspire *thauma*. The confident and admiring (yet ultimately deceptive) *thauma* and *thambos* which the Athenian fleet attracted as it set sail on this expedition is replaced instead with a different type of astonishment: panicked and disbelieving *ekplexis* twice grips the Athenians (7.70.6 and 7.71.7) as they contemplate the battle and its disastrous effects and recognise the true status of their power away from home.[50]

The vision of Athens which Pericles' Funeral Oration paints in words does not stand up to scrutiny in the long run after all. In both Aristophanes' *Birds* and Thucydides' *History*, wonder is now one of the most powerful envisaged effects of the images which the successful rhetorician is able to plant in the minds of his audience. In both of these authors, we can see that there has been a marked change in the way in which the power and effect of *thauma* is conceptualised over the course of the Classical period. Objects which provoke *thauma* are no longer presented as potentially disconcerting because of the strangeness and otherness caused either by their association with the divine realm, or with unfamiliar peoples and locations. Nor is *thauma* used to describe the positive effects of shared experiences between mortals and gods. Instead, an encounter with *thauma* is often imbued with increasingly negative overtones of deception and trickery. Wondrous experiences may be both desirable and enjoyable, but they are also potentially misleading, even dangerous on occasion. *Thauma* has

---

[49] There are further echoes of Pericles' Funeral Oration here at 7.63.3 as well: see Rood (1998) 193; cf. also Joho (2017) 16–48 on the echoes and reversals of Pericles' Funeral Oration in books 6 and 7 more generally.

[50] See Jordan (2000) 77 on the transformation of the wonder inspired by Alcibiades and the sight of the fleet setting sail in book 6 into the shocked and panicked *ekplexis* of book 7. Cf. Hunter (1986) 418 on the importance of *ekplexis* in conveying the scale of the Athenian reversal in book 7, and Allison (1997) 62–5 on the particular association of *ekplexis* with the Sicilian expedition. Cf. also the ironic reversal of the earlier misguided *ekplexis* of the Athenian envoys at the deceptive sight of the Egestans' supposed wealth (μεγάλην τὴν ἔκπληξιν, 6.46.4) to the astonishment of the Athenians in book 7 (see Kallet (2001) 78 on this reversal), and Rogkotis (2006) 68–9 on the verbal analogies between the Egestan deception at 6.46 and the astonishing spectacle of the fleet's departure.

6.3 The Wonder of Athens: Thucydides and *Thauma*

become associated with the act of representation itself, with the arousal of a marvelling response now a means of inverting (and often subverting) an audience's conventional perspectives on their most familiar surroundings and beliefs.[51] It is a powerful effect of mimetic acts of representation which somehow involve the defamiliarisation and refamiliarisation of reality, especially through the use of rhetoric, which often distorts language for its own ends. It is this notion of the potential power of *thauma* which the next chapter will explore in further depth.

---

[51] A crucial aspect of the potentially radical effect of *thauma* which is rightly noted by D'Angour (2011) 149: 'Even if an object of wonder is familiar, the experience of *thauma* may create a new perspective which transports the observer into new realms of emotion, thought or feeling.'

7

MAKING MARVELS: *THAUMATOPOIIA* AND *THAUMATOURGIA*

μετὰ ταῦτα δή, εἶπον, ἀπείκασον τοιούτῳ πάθει τὴν ἡμετέραν φύσιν παιδείας τε πέρι καὶ ἀπαιδευσίας. ἰδὲ γὰρ ἀνθρώπους οἷον ἐν καταγείῳ οἰκήσει σπηλαιώδει, ἀναπεπταμένην πρὸς τὸ φῶς τὴν εἴσοδον ἐχούσῃ μακρὰν παρὰ πᾶν τὸ σπήλαιον, ἐν ταύτῃ ἐκ παίδων ὄντας ἐν δεσμοῖς καὶ τὰ σκέλη καὶ τοὺς αὐχένας, ὥστε μένειν τε αὐτοῦ εἴς τε τὸ πρόσθεν μόνον ὁρᾶν, κύκλῳ δὲ τὰς κεφαλὰς ὑπὸ τοῦ δεσμοῦ ἀδυνάτους περιάγειν, φῶς δὲ αὐτοῖς πυρὸς ἄνωθεν καὶ πόρρωθεν καόμενον ὄπισθεν αὐτῶν, μεταξὺ δὲ τοῦ πυρὸς καὶ τῶν δεσμωτῶν ἐπάνω ὁδόν, παρ' ἣν ἰδὲ τειχίον παρῳκοδομημένον, ὥσπερ τοῖς θαυματοποιοῖς πρὸ τῶν ἀνθρώπων πρόκειται τὰ παραφράγματα, ὑπὲρ ὧν τὰ θαύματα δεικνύασιν.

Plato, *Republic* 514a–b

'After these things', I said, 'compare our nature, with respect to education and the lack of it, to such an experience as this one. See, as it were, men in a cave-like subterranean dwelling, with a long entrance facing towards the light along the entire length of the cave. The men have been in this cave from childhood, bound by their legs and their necks, so that they remain in the same place and see only what is before them, unable to turn their heads around in a circle because of the bonds. The light of a burning fire is above them and a long way off behind them, and in between the fire and the bound men there is a path going upwards, beside which see a little built-up wall, just like the screen which hides the marvel-makers (θαυματοποιοῖς), above which they show their marvels (θαύματα δεικνύασιν)'.

Plato's Cave Allegory, found at the very beginning of the seventh book of the *Republic*, is possibly the most famous single passage of text in Western philosophy. Plato's wider attitude towards wonder in this passage plays a role in this image which has often been underestimated. *Thauma* occupies a complex and multifaceted position in Plato's philosophical thought. On the one hand, he often portrays the effects of falling prey to the marvellous displays of sophists, poets, rhapsodes, actors and politicians as inherently negative, particularly for the young. But on the other hand, *thauma* also simultaneously seems to be an unparalleled catalyst to philosophical inquiry, as the young mathematician (and in many ways Socratic doppelgänger) Theaetetus demonstrates in

Making Marvels: *Thaumatopoiia* and *Thaumatourgia*

the dialogue named after him.[1] This attitude hints that the presence of marvels in Plato's Cave Allegory is not an idle throw-away detail. In fact, the *thaumata* mentioned in the final sentence of this passage provide an interpretative key to the image as a whole.

My purpose in this chapter is twofold. I want to examine the introduction and use of the concepts of 'marvel-making' (*thaumatopoiia*) and 'wonder-working' (*thaumatourgia*) in Plato and elsewhere as a means of assessing the way attitudes towards wonder have shifted between Herodotus' *Histories* and the early fourth century BCE. In the process, I take Plato's Cave as a case study, and suggest a reading of the image through the lens of *thauma* which offers new perspectives on some of the passage's familiar problems. In particular, I want to approach one of the most commented-upon interpretative difficulties in this section of the *Republic*, namely our inability to map each element of the Cave image onto each outlined section of the preceding and interconnected image of the Divided Line in a precise one-to-one fashion, from a different angle.[2] Rather than pointing to some sort of flawed philosophical planning on Plato's part, the fact that these images do not map precisely onto one another actually turns out to be essential to the argument Socrates is making in *Republic* 6 and 7. If we take the cues about how to read this image given to us by Socrates, we discover that the Cave is itself held up as a marvel of sorts, and that distorted mapping, strange perspectives and changing views are at the very heart of the effect of the marvel-maker's art and its effects.

But before returning to the Cave, it is necessary to explore the cultural context of 'marvel-making' much more broadly. The questions I want to raise have been surprisingly neglected in modern scholarship.[3] What exactly is a *thaumatopoios*, and what

---

[1] See Chapter 2, Section 2, on the parallels between Socrates and Theaetetus as philosophical *thaumata*.

[2] Cf. the comprehensive recent discussions of this issue in e.g. Annas (1981) 252 ff., Karasmanis (1988) 147–71, Brunschwig (2003) 145–77 and Schofield (2007) 216–31.

[3] Kroll (1935) 1278–82 remains the most comprehensive overview of *thaumatopoiia*. Milanezi (2004) 191–3 provides the best brief discussion of the role of the real-life *thaumatopoios* while discussing various other types of minor paratheatrical entertainers (see also the very useful tables listing the appearances of terms for entertainers which appear in Athenaeus and on inscriptions on pp. 204–6). Cf. also the brief discussions concerning *thaumatopoiia* in Dickie (2001a) 601–2 and (2001b) 72–3.

175

does his or her art – *thaumatopoiia* – consist of? Why do we start to find these two terms in the extant literature towards the end of the fifth and the beginning of the fourth centuries BCE? These questions will be at the heart of my discussion of marvel-making below. I will first try and establish what kind of actions fall under the umbrella terms *thaumatopoiia* (marvel-making) and *thaumatourgia* (wonder-working), another synonymous compound word which begins to appear in this period; I will then return to the Cave Allegory to show just how complex and philosophically loaded the use of the marvellous has become in Plato's hands in this passage.

7.1 The Meaning of Marvel-Making: Theatrical *Thaumatopoiia*

Compound words denoting artificial man-made marvel-making begin suddenly to appear in extant literature in the first half of the fourth century BCE, in Demosthenes, Isocrates and Plato. It is clear from looking at late Classical and Hellenistic uses of the term, as well as uses in later texts which refer back to marvel-making in this period, that a variety of actions fall under the umbrella terms *thaumatopoiia* and *thaumatourgia*. The *madness* inherent in both terms, and the fact the term is itself *made* by being compounded together, is important: artificiality is at the heart of the marvel-maker's art. Unlike the divine, natural and cultural marvels of the past, the *thaumata* described here are somehow worked by ordinary human hands, as opposed to appearing spontaneously in the landscape, or being somehow linked to the power of divine craftsmanship, or to artists with creative powers approaching those of the gods.

The word *thaumatopoiia* appears much more frequently than *thaumatourgia*. Perhaps the defining feature of a *thaumatopoios* is the fact that he or she specialises in performances in front of a captive audience, particularly in venues such as the theatre or symposium. The actual content of these performances could vary greatly. Variety (*poikilia*) is of course intimately connected to the aesthetic impact of *thaumata*, so it is no surprise that the versatility of the marvel-maker becomes one of the prime causes of the

7.1 Theatrical *Thaumatopoiia*

thaumatic impact of their performances.[4] Mime actors, dancers and musicians are strongly linked to the art of the *thaumatopoios*: this reinforces the sense that the ability to perform spectacles of varying types is a key aspect of the role.[5] Athenaeus provides us with perhaps the most interesting evidence concerning all of these aspects of the *thaumatopoios*' art.[6] In a prolonged discussion (*Deipnosophistae* 19e) of well-known performers of the past, the apparently famous *thaumatopoios* Xenophon is mentioned, along with his pupil Cratisthenes of Phlius, who astonished the crowds with baffling tricks, such as making fire spontaneously flare up. These two *thaumatopoioi* are mentioned immediately after two other famous figures who made their name in the theatre: Potheinus the puppeteer (*neurospastes*), who performed in the same theatre as Euripides, and Eurycleides, who was honoured with a statue in the theatre next to that of Aeschylus.

Many other sources situate the *thaumatopoios* within a theatrical or paratheatrical context. Particularly intriguing is the mention of *thaumatopoioi* alongside other theatrical artists in numerous choregic inscriptions from Delos in the third and second centuries BCE, which seems to have had a particularly flourishing marvel-mongering scene.[7] On multiple inscriptions, *thaumatopoioi* are listed alongside figures such as tragic poets and actors, comic poets and actors, and *aulos* and cithara players, including several

---

[4] On the variable nature of the activities which the term *thaumatopoiia* denotes from the fifth century BCE onwards, see Milanezi (2004) 192.

[5] For the association between *thaumatopoioi* and *mimoi*, see Milanezi (2004) 192–3; cf. the brief discussion of the relation between Imperial stage-pantomimes and *thaumatopoioi* at Lada-Richards (2007) 31.

[6] Stephanis (1988) lists literary and epigraphic evidence of twenty-five potential *thaumatopoioi* in antiquity (see numbers 262, 320, 408, 419, 766, 984, 1031, 1092, 1225, 1304, 1451, 1496, 1785, 1890, 1894, 1914, 2002, 2257, 2285, 2508, 2520, 2258, 2748, 2976, 2989). Of these, nine are mentioned in Athenaeus, the rest in inscriptions.

[7] It is interesting that the epigraphic evidence for *thaumatopoioi* at festivals clusters around Delos in particular, although it is difficult to know what to make of this in terms of specific Delian performance contexts. Given the lack of epigraphic evidence for the inclusion of *thaumatopoioi* in festivals alongside other theatrical performers in other parts of the Hellenistic world, it is hard to agree with Milanezi (2004) 200–1 that *thaumatopoioi* are firmly attached to groups of *technitai* of Dionysus; Lightfoot's (2002) 212 assessment that mimes and conjurors in the Hellenistic world were 'no less part of the festivals, if on their fringes', seeing as these figures 'are not shown as members of guilds in the Hellenistic period', is surely closer to the mark. Cf. also Slater's (2004) 155 view that one of the key differences between the Artists of Dionysus and *thaumatopoioi* is that the former are regulated whereas the latter are not.

examples relating to one particular *thaumatopoios*, Kleopatra or Kleupatra (*IG* XI, 2 110, dated 268 BCE; *IG* XI, 2 112, dated c. 264 BCE; *IG* XI, 2 113, dated 263 BCE). Other named *thaumatopoioi* are mentioned on single occasions (cf. e.g. *IG* XI, 2 115, dated 259 BCE; *IG* XI, 2 120, dated 236 BCE; *IG* XI, 2 129, dated 192 BCE; *IG* XI, 2 133, dated 169 BCE).[8] The use of the actual theatre as the scene of *thaumatopoiia* is hinted at in later sources as well, such as an anecdote found in Plutarch (*Vit. Lyc.* 19.2):

Ἆγις μὲν οὖν ὁ βασιλεύς, σκώπτοντος Ἀττικοῦ τινος τὰς Λακωνικὰς μαχαίρας εἰς τὴν μικρότητα, καὶ λέγοντος ὅτι ῥᾳδίως αὐτὰς οἱ θαυματοποιοὶ καταπίνουσιν ἐν τοῖς θεάτροις, καὶ μὴν μάλιστα, εἶπεν, ἡμεῖς ἐφικνούμεθα τοῖς ἐγχειριδίοις τῶν πολεμίων.

When a certain Attic man mocked Laconian swords for their shortness, and said that the marvel-makers in the theatres swallow them easily, King Agis replied: 'And yet we certainly reach the enemy with these daggers'.

But the question of how exactly the displays of *thaumatopoioi* related to other kinds of performance within the theatre itself is impossible to answer from the evidence that remains. Did these spectacles compete with the large-scale theatrical performances of tragedy and comedy for the audience's attention, or operate entirely separately from these productions?

There is some evidence that displays of *thaumatopoiia* often functioned as more strictly paratheatrical endeavours, competing with the more established and prestigious forms of performance. The sense that displays of *thaumata* competed with other types of theatrical performance is perhaps strongest in one intriguing passage from Plato's *Laws*. Unsurprisingly, given his attitude towards even the more conventionally educative types of performance, the ability of theatrical *thaumata* to distract and dazzle the minds of spectators is a particular concern of Plato here. In a passage which focuses on the differing appeal of various pleasures to various people depending upon their age, the Athenian Stranger argues that in a contest of different types of performances, where the 'the contest was over pleasure alone' (ἀγωνιούμενον ἡδονῆς πέρι μόνον, 658a), somebody

---

[8] See Robert (1929) 427–38 on this group of inscriptions dealing with the theatre at Delos.

7.1 Theatrical *Thaumatopoiia*

would naturally put on a display of *thaumata* in an attempt to delight an audience (658b–c):

εἰκός που τὸν μέν τινα ἐπιδεικνύναι, καθάπερ Ὅμηρος, ῥαψῳδίαν, ἄλλον δὲ κιθαρῳδίαν, τὸν δέ τινα τραγῳδίαν, τὸν δ' αὖ κωμῳδίαν. οὐ θαυμαστὸν δὲ εἴ τις καὶ θαύματα ἐπιδεικνὺς μάλιστ' ἂν νικᾶν ἡγοῖτο.

I suppose it is likely that one man would put on a recitation of epic poetry, just as Homer did, and another would stage a citharodic performance, someone else would put on a tragedy, and someone else a comedy. And it would be no marvel if someone thought they might win by putting on a display of marvels.

The Athenian Stranger goes on to add that he can already predict the winner of this pleasure contest depending on the age of the judges in charge of making the final decision. Displays of *thaumata* are said to appeal more than any other sort of entertainment to young people, with the seemingly inevitable result that 'if the very smallest children are judges, they will judge in favour of the person putting on a display of *thaumata*' (εἰ μὲν τοίνυν τὰ πάνυ σμικρὰ κρίνοι παιδία, κρινοῦσι τὸν τὰ θαύματα ἐπιδεικνύντα, 658c).[9] In contrast, the more solemn and weighty performances of tragedy will appeal to 'educated women and young men and the majority of the population in general' (τραγῳδίαν δὲ αἵ τε πεπαιδευμέναι τῶν γυναικῶν καὶ τὰ νέα μειράκια καὶ σχεδὸν ἴσως τὸ πλῆθος πάντων, 658d), while 'old men would take pleasure in listening to a fine rhapsodic performance of the *Iliad* and *Odyssey* or a recitation from Hesiod and will declare that to be the definite

---

[9] Theophrastus also makes vague mention of such displays of *thaumata* twice in his *Characters*: the man who possesses 'shamelessness' (ἀπόνοια) is said to be the sort who goes around 'collecting money from each person watching *thaumata*' (ἐν θαύμασι δὲ τοὺς χαλκοῦς ἐκλέγειν, 6.4) and argues with those who claim they already have a ticket or do not need to pay, while the man who possesses 'lately-obtained learning' (ὀψιμαθία), which seems in the *Characters* to mean a liking for things appropriate for boys but inappropriate for anyone in an older age group, enjoys 'sitting through three or four performances of *thaumata* and learning the songs' (ἐν τοῖς θαύμασι τρία ἢ τέτταρα πληρώματα ὑπομένειν τὰ ᾄσματα ἐκμανθάνων, 27.7) which presumably accompanied the shows. The first mention implies that displays of *thaumata* were put on with the aim of collecting money (cf. the Syracusan dancing master's purveyance of sympotic *thaumatopoiia* in Xenophon's *Symposium* in Section 2 below), while the second suggests that such displays sometimes involved a musical element and were deemed appropriate for, or thought to appeal appropriately to, younger audience members rather than older male citizens. I will discuss what type of display Plato is thinking of when he refers to *thaumata* here when I return to the *thaumata* of the Cave in *Republic* 7 in Section 4 below.

winner' (ῥαψῳδὸν δέ, καλῶς 'Ιλιάδα καὶ 'Οδύσσειαν ἤ τι τῶν Ἡσιοδείων διατιθέντα, τάχ᾽ ἂν ἡμεῖς οἱ γέροντες ἥδιστα ἀκούσαντες νικᾶν ἂν φαῖμεν πάμπολυ, 658d).[10]

Public displays of *thaumata* to large-scale audiences are therefore portrayed in the *Laws* as a particularly dangerous prospect, due to the fact that they provide pleasure without much educative content to match. It is difficult to assess how much truth there is in Plato's worries here, since it is only when we turn to the Roman world in the second century BCE that we encounter an obvious comparandum. In the first and second prologues of Terence's *Hecyra* the failures of the comedy's first attempted performances are explicitly blamed on a 'disaster which prevented the play from being seen or understood' (*calamitas | ut neque spectari neque cognosci potuerit*, 2–3): a disaster which led to the theatrical production at hand being ignored when the 'amazed audience were distracted by their enthusiasm for a tightrope-walker' (*populus studio stupidus in funambulo | animum occuparat*, 4–5). The second prologue hints at yet another theatrical failure: this time the crowd are distracted again by the sudden emergence of a rumour concerning the potential appearance of boxers and 'the expectation of a tight-rope walker' (*funambuli... exspectatio*, 34).[11] The distracting acrobatic feats of the tightrope-walker are precisely the sort of spectacles associated with *thaumatopoioi*. Although it is of course impossible to say whether a similar incident could have occurred in the context of Greek theatrical festivals, it is nonetheless not difficult to imagine that the spectacles of *thaumatopoioi* could prove equally distracting if offered at the same time as theatrical performances with weightier themes, narrative complexity, and potentially edifying content – as Plato has indeed hinted while mentioning displays of *thaumata* in the *Laws*.

---

[10] See Folch (2013) 342–5 and (2015) 131–6 on the relationship between pleasure and the diverse genres and forms included in this hypothetical competition in the context of the wider argument about the necessary nature of the hypothetical society of Magnesia in the *Laws*.

[11] For good discussions of the play's supposed initial failure and its relation to the potential appearance of rival distracting spectacles in the vicinity of its performance, see e.g. Gilula (1981) 29–37, Sandbach (1982) 134–5, Parker (1996) 592–601, Lada-Richards (2004) 55–82 and Goldberg (2013) 15–18, 86–96.

7.2 Sympotic *Thaumatopoiia*: Wonder-Working in Xenophon's *Symposium*

Theatrical or paratheatrical settings are not the only areas in which the *thaumatopoios* frequently plies his or her trade: the symposium is an equally common venue for marvellous performances. The sense that these smaller-scale displays of *thaumata* also aim at distracting and capturing the minds of their spectators with amazement is also very clear. There is one extant text which explores the effect of wondrous performative marvels in a sympotic context in great depth: Xenophon's *Symposium*. The dialogue is set in 422 BCE, at the house of the famously rich Athenian Callias. Throughout Xenophon's Socratic dialogue, an antithesis arises between spectacular displays of feats held up as 'marvels' and philosophical questions about 'marvellous' natural phenomena. This suggests that there are now important differences to be drawn between wonder provoked by the gods or the natural world, and wonder provoked by the dazzling – and often deceptive – actions of our fellow humans.

Performative marvels involving bodily display are of particular interest in Xenophon's dialogue, becoming a prime topic of conversation over the course of the drinking party.[12] The serious philosophical conversation at Callias' symposium is provoked in no small part by the acrobatic feats of a beautiful dancing girl provided by a Syracusan dancing master, who is on hand to provide entertainment at the host's house from the very beginning of the symposium proper (2.1):

ὡς δ' ἀφῃρέθησαν αἱ τράπεζαι καὶ ἔσπεισάν τε καὶ ἐπαιάνισαν, ἔρχεται αὐτοῖς ἐπὶ κῶμον Συρακόσιός τις ἄνθρωπος, ἔχων τε αὐλητρίδα ἀγαθὴν καὶ ὀρχηστρίδα τῶν τὰ θαύματα δυναμένων ποιεῖν, καὶ παῖδα πάνυ γε ὡραῖον καὶ πάνυ καλῶς κιθαρίζοντα καὶ ὀρχούμενον. ταῦτα δὲ καὶ ἐπιδεικνὺς ὡς ἐν θαύματι ἀργύριον ἐλάμβανεν.

When the tables had been taken away and they had poured a libation and sung a paean, a Syracusan man on a *komos* arrived. He was accompanied by a girl, an excellent *aulos* player and dancer, one of those able to make marvels, and a boy

---

[12] Wohl (2004) 337–63 and Gilula (2002) 207–13 discuss the wider connections between the pronounced interest in bodily display and the philosophical concerns of the dialogue.

who was very good-looking and very talented at playing the cithara and dancing. The Syracusan made money by exhibiting them as something to marvel at.[13]

The girl's art is here described as that of 'making marvels', and she is clearly some kind of female *thaumatopoios*.[14] With the Syracusan dancing master's ability to make wondrous amounts of money from the marvellous displays he directs, Xenophon here links thaumatic display and pecuniary gain in a manner reminiscent of Plato's frequent cynical wordplay on this theme. The *Hippias Major* is a good example. At the beginning of the dialogue, Socrates mentions to Hippias that his fellow sophist Prodicus is well known for obtaining a wondrous amount of money (χρήματα ... θαυμαστὰ ὅσα, 282c) through his sophistic *epideixis* and association with the young. Hippias goes on to confirm that contemporary sophists are marvelled at not only for their performances but also for the absurdly large amounts that they are able to make. He tells Socrates that even though he is already aware of how much money Prodicus is said to make, and therefore would not be surprised at the fact Hippias makes money

---

[13] There is considerable debate about the precise meaning of ταῦτα δὲ καὶ ἐπιδεικνὺς ὡς ἐν θαύματι ἀργύριον ἐλάμβανεν. Bowen (1998) 94 notes that this phrase is difficult to interpret and suggests that the meaning is that the Syracusan makes money 'in remarkable sums' rather than that the performers are exhibited 'as something to marvel at' because the former interpretation also hints at Callias' wealth (and presumably his ability to pay the Syracusan wondrous sums) by extension. Huss (1997) 43–4 and (1999) 121 makes a strong case for emendation of the singular θαύματι to the plural, reading ὡς ἐν θαύμασιν ἀργύριον, suggesting that the meaning of this phrase becomes something along the lines of 'he showed them as in performances at a fair'. The phrase is still, however, deliberately ambiguous in meaning and it is clear that the Syracusan means to suggest here both that he displays his performers as something for others to marvel at, and that he makes a marvellous amount of money by doing so.

[14] As Huss (1999) 121 points out. See Schäfer (1997) 79–81 on what these scenes in Xenophon's *Symposium* suggest about the emergence of professional sympotic entertainers in the second half of the fifth century BCE. The connection between *thaumatopoiia* and sympotic eroticism which Xenophon draws out here is an enduring one if Matro's parodic epic poem *Attic Dinner Party* (late fourth century BCE), quoted by Athenaeus, is anything to go by. As soon as dinner has ended in that poem the necessary preparations for the symposium are made: hands are washed, garlands are distributed, wine is mixed and the flat cake arrives. This is swiftly followed by the introduction of 'two marvel-making prostitutes' (πόρναι ... δύο θαυματοποιοί, fr. 1.121 Olson-Sens). See Olson and Sens (1999) 143 on the use of *thaumatopoioi* here as a humorous suggestion that these prostitutes are not simple dancing girls, but actually able to perform wondrous acts in bed. Cf. also Athenaeus' report (*Deipnosophistae* 129d) of the wedding feast of Caranus the Macedonian, which allegedly involved naked female *thaumatopoioi* tumbling amongst swords and breathing fire.

7.2 Sympotic *Thaumatopoiia*

too, he would marvel (θαυμάσαις ἄν, 282d) nevertheless if he knew just how great that sum of money was. Hippias even goes so far as to claim that when he gives the money he has made on the road to his father back home in Elis, 'both his father and the other citizens marvel and are dumbstruck' (ἐκεῖνον καὶ τοὺς ἄλλους πολίτας θαυμάζειν τε καὶ ἐκπεπλῆχθαι, 282e).

The bitter irony here directed at the abilities of sophists to make ludicrous amounts of money is increased by the fact that the same terms are used elsewhere in Plato for the effect of the actual displays of sophistic or rhapsodic performances on their audiences. The astonishment which grips those who view Hippias' sophistic displays – and the piles of money he makes from them – is remarkably similar to that which rhapsodes are said to have on their audiences in another of Plato's aporetic dialogues, *Ion*.[15] This is most obvious when we reach the rhapsode Ion's own discussion of the audience's response to his art, after Socrates has first suggested to him that 'whenever you recite epic well astonishment very much comes over your audience' (ὅταν εὖ εἴπῃς ἔπη καὶ ἐκπλήξῃς μάλιστα τοὺς θεωμένους, 535b). Ion quickly agrees with Socrates and goes on to describe the experience from his point of view (535d–e):

ΣΩ: οἶσθα οὖν ὅτι καὶ τῶν θεατῶν τοὺς πολλοὺς ταὐτὰ ταῦτα ὑμεῖς ἐργάζεσθε;

ΙΩΝ: καὶ μάλα καλῶς οἶδα· καθορῶ γὰρ ἑκάστοτε αὐτοὺς ἄνωθεν ἀπὸ τοῦ βήματος κλαίοντάς τε καὶ δεινὸν ἐμβλέποντας καὶ συνθαμβοῦντας τοῖς λεγομένοις. δεῖ γάρ με καὶ σφόδρ' αὐτοῖς τὸν νοῦν προσέχειν· ὡς ἐὰν μὲν κλαίοντας αὐτοὺς καθίσω, αὐτὸς γελάσομαι ἀργύριον λαμβάνων, ἐὰν δὲ γελῶντας, αὐτὸς κλαύσομαι ἀργύριον ἀπολλύς.

SOCRATES: And so do you think that you produce the same effects on most of the spectators as well?

---

[15] See González (2013) 290 on the 'direct line' between rhapsodic *hypokrisis* and sophistic *epideixis*. See Ford (1992) 54–5 on the significance of Plato's *Ion* 535b–e as a conceptualisation of the vivid and astonishing experience which the audience experiences in the presence of the rhapsode during a performance of epic poetry.

Making Marvels: *Thaumatopoiia* and *Thaumatourgia*

ION: Yes, I know this full well: for each time from up on the platform I look down at them weeping and glaring formidably and totally astonished at my words. For it is very much necessary for me to pay attention to them, since if I make them cry, I myself will laugh at the money I make, but if I make them laugh, I myself will cry at my lost income.

The effect of viewing a sophistic *epideixis*, watching one of Ion's vivid and emotionally manipulative rhapsodic re-enactments of epic poetry, or glimpsing a huge pile of money is precisely the same: they induce a stultifying sense of astonishment.

Xenophon too is playing on this same idea in the *Symposium* as the troupe of entertainers arrives; already we have hints of the negative associations between marvel-making and moneymaking which go on to affect our view of the displays of *thaumatopoiia* proper later in the dialogue.[16] The main discussion of *thaumatopoiia* and its effects comes at 7.2–4. This passage first describes how in the middle of the symposium 'a potter's wheel was brought in for the dancing girl, on which she was about to work her wonders' (εἰσεφέρετο τῇ ὀρχηστρίδι τροχὸς τῶν κεραμικῶν, ἐφ' οὗ ἔμελλε θαυματουργήσειν, 7.2). The compound word *thaumatourgia* is being used in the same way as *thaumatopoiia* here; the two are clearly synonyms denoting the types of spectacular display which are deliberately worked by men or women in an effort to astonish an audience.[17] We have evidence for the type of thaumatic acrobatic feat described here on fourth-century BCE South Italian vases: a red-figure Paestan skyphos in the Ashmolean Museum (Oxford 1945.43) depicting a naked young woman performing a handstand upon a potter's wheel which is being rotated by a Phlyax actor, is the example which perhaps comes closest to

---

[16] The emphasis on the Sicilian provenance of the dancing master in the *Symposium* also perhaps hints at the spectacles which will go on to be served up at the symposium later in the dialogue. There is certainly an awareness of Sicilian performance traditions in Plato's dialogues: see e.g. Monoson (2012) 156–72 on the importance of Sicilian theatrical traditions in Plato's philosophical and political thought in the *Republic*. More generally, see Morgan (2012) 48–54 on the rise of Syracuse as a flourishing literary and theatrical centre over the course of the fifth century BCE.

[17] See Milanezi (2004) 187 on the use of *thaumatourgia* and *thaumatopoiia* as synonyms which denote the same sorts of action in the fourth century BCE; cf. Huss (1999) 348 on the equivalence of *thaumatourgia* and *thaumatopoiia* in this passage.

7.2 Sympotic *Thaumatopoiia*

Xenophon's description of the dancing girl's *thaumatourgia* in the *Symposium*.[18] Far from being rare marvels, these sorts of manoeuvres seem to have become performative commonplaces, as Socrates' subsequent response to this display of the dancing girl suggests (7.3–4):

δοκεῖ οὖν μοι τὸ μὲν εἰς μαχαίρας κυβιστᾶν κινδύνου ἐπίδειγμα εἶναι, ὃ συμποσίῳ οὐδὲν προσήκει. καὶ μὴν τό γε ἐπὶ τοῦ τροχοῦ ἅμα περιδινουμένου γράφειν τε καὶ ἀναγιγνώσκειν θαῦμα μὲν ἴσως τί ἐστιν, ἡδονὴν δὲ οὐδὲ ταῦτα δύναμαι γνῶναι τίν' ἂν παράσχοι. οὐδὲ μὴν τό γε διαστρέφοντας τὰ σώματα καὶ τροχοὺς μιμουμένους ἥδιον ἢ ἡσυχίαν ἔχοντας τοὺς καλοὺς καὶ ὡραίους θεωρεῖν. καὶ γὰρ δὴ οὐδὲ πάνυ τι σπάνιον τό γε θαυμασίοις ἐντυχεῖν, εἴ τις τούτου δεῖται, ἀλλ' ἔξεστιν αὐτίκα μάλα τὰ παρόντα θαυμάζειν, τί ποτε ὁ μὲν λύχνος διὰ τὸ λαμπρὰν φλόγα ἔχειν φῶς παρέχει, τὸ δὲ χαλκεῖον λαμπρὸν ὂν φῶς μὲν οὐ ποιεῖ, ἐν αὐτῷ δὲ ἄλλα ἐμφαινόμενα παρέχεται· καὶ πῶς τὸ μὲν ἔλαιον ὑγρὸν ὂν αὔξει τὴν φλόγα, τὸ δὲ ὕδωρ, ὅτι ὑγρόν ἐστι, κατασβέννυσι τὸ πῦρ.

It seems to me that to somersault into swords is a dangerous showpiece, something not fit for a symposium. Perhaps writing and reading on a potter's wheel while it whirls around is something of a marvel, but I can't think what pleasure it might provide. Nor is it more pleasurable to observe young and good-looking people twisting their bodies out of shape and imitating the wheels of potters than it is to watch them at rest. Of course, it's not at all a rare thing to encounter marvels, if somebody feels a need, rather it's possible to marvel just this very minute at the things right in front of you. For example, why does the lamp provide light with its bright flame, but the bright bronze lamp bowl does not provide light,

---

[18] This skyphos is attributed to Asteas (or his workshop) and dated to the third quarter of the fourth century BCE. For plates and discussion see *PPSupp* p. 34, no. 116, pl. V b; *PhV*² p. 58, no. 96; and *RVP* p. 69, no. 33, pls. 24 f–g. Vickers (1999) 74 notes the particular similarities between the scene depicted on this vase and the description of the wonder-working dancing girl's performance in Xenophon's *Symposium*: cf. also Dearden (1995) 81–6. See Marshall (2000) 13–25 for a discussion of this vase and what it might tell us about women and the theatre; cf. Hughes (2008) 11–12 on vases with depictions of acrobats on potters' wheels more generally. Among several other vases which portray a female acrobat either performing on a potter's wheel, or apparently gearing up to do so, the closest to the scene described in Xenophon include: (1) Sydney, Nicholson Museum 95.16 (c. 325–310 BCE, attributed to an artist related to the Woman-Eros Painter), which depicts a female acrobat doing a handstand on a potter's wheel along with two large birds (see *CVA* Australia I 64–5, pls. 84–5); (2) British Museum F 232 (c. 340–330 BCE, attributed to the Foundling Painter), which shows a scantily clad female acrobat performing a handstand next to a potter's wheel and tympana (see *CVA* British Museum 2 (Group IV Ea, Red-Figured Vases of Campania and Paestum) p. 6 and pl. 8.4 and *LCS* I 3/112 (p. 375) with *LCS* II pl. 143.3); (3) Naples, Museo Archeologico Nazionale 509 (SA 405), which depicts a female acrobat on a potter's wheel accompanied by an *auletris* (see *CVA* Naples III, p. 16, pl. 70.4). On the iconography of vases such as these, and for results of recent experiments to recreate the postures of the female *thaumatopoioi* upon them, see Pulitani et al. (2017) 35–56.

instead giving out onto itself only the reflections of other things? And how does olive oil increase a flame, though it is wet, while water, which is also wet, extinguishes fire?

Socrates is clearly not impressed by the dancing girl's *thaumatourgia*. His insistence here that it is not at all a rare event to encounter marvels makes clear that the sorts of questions provoked by not understanding the causes behind natural, everyday sights and processes in the world around us are what we should really be impressed and excited by, rather than the spectacles artificially developed by human performers.[19] The interplay between the near and the far which we have already seen to be increasingly connected to the marvellous towards the end of the fifth century BCE is obviously on Xenophon's mind here as well: once again, 'real' marvels are now considered to be found more often surprisingly close to home among familiar objects, rather than far away, or involving rare objects or actions. Moreover, as mentioned earlier, the acrobatic postures which the dancing girl performs in this dialogue are frequently encountered in later visual art, and from Socrates' weary mention of such feats here, it is no great stretch to posit that for Xenophon's contemporary readers, sword-dancing and whirling about on wheels while reading and writing were already familiar kinds of sympotic display.[20]

Socrates' view here is clear: it is the customary material of natural science – and of philosophy – that we should really be wondering about, not a girl whirling about on a potter's wheel.

---

[19] In this respect Socrates' words about near and distant objects and topics which provoke *thauma* here in Xenophon's *Symposium* are the closest antecedent of Aristotle's similar way of framing the issue at *Metaph.* 982b12–21 and *Part. an.* 644b–65a (for a more detailed discussion of these passages, see Chapter 3, Section 4).

[20] On the evident familiarity of these types of sympotic display, see Jones (1991) 190–1. Familiarity is certainly suggested at Pl. *Euthyd.* 294e, where Socrates challenges the sophist Dionysodorus and asks him if he even knows how 'to leap among swords and be whirled about on a wheel' (ἐς μαχαίρας γε κυβιστᾶν καὶ ἐπὶ τροχοῦ δινεῖσθαι), seeing as he claims to have knowledge of everything. It is no coincidence that Socrates implies that Dionysodorus is like a sympotic *thaumatopoios* here since his sophistic arguments, along with those of his brother Euthydemus, are strongly associated with *thauma* and *ekplexis* throughout the dialogue: see e.g. *Euthyd.* 271c (θαυμασία), 276d (ἐκπεπληγμένοι ... ἐκπεπληγμένους ... θαυμάζοιμεν), 283a–b (θαυμασίους ... θαυμαστὸν), 286b–c (θαυμάσας ... θαυμάζω), 288a–b (θαυμαστῆς ... θαυμάσιά ... θαυμασία), 294a (θαυμαστὸν), 295a (θαυμαστά).

7.3 *Thaumatopoiia* and Perspective in *Republic* and *Sophist*

Once again, we see that there is a division being made here between the type of wonder which spurs someone on to further inquiry and involves a mostly cognitive aspect, and that which is purely affective and as a result often leads to the sort of stunned cognitive stasis commonly associated with the term *ekplexis*. In Xenophon's *Symposium*, the fact that natural marvels provide the material for the former sort of wonder, while man-made marvels are associated with the latter, is laid out in perhaps its starkest form in Socrates' lengthy meditation upon the true nature of rare and familiar *thaumata* – the irony of course being that educated men such as himself would supposedly never find the sorts of acrobatic marvels displayed in Callias' house worthy of any astonishment. The risk of this type of stultifying astonishment, however, remains for the young, uneducated or foolish, and it is precisely for this reason that *thaumatopoiia* becomes such a worry for Plato and other contemporary thinkers, as the next section will demonstrate in more detail.

7.3 *Thaumatopoiia* and Perspective in Plato's *Republic* and *Sophist*

There is another aspect of Socrates' speech in Xenophon's *Symposium* which relates to connected concerns surrounding *thaumatopoiia*: the fact that the performance he refers to when he complains about young people twisting their bodies round and imitating the wheels of potters is a mimetic one.[21] Some of the problems associated with mimesis in Plato's work also come to be associated with marvel-making. One important aspect of Plato's treatment of *thaumatopoiia* is its relation to the discussion of

---

[21] Gilhuly (2009) 129 picks up on the thaumatic effect of the mimetic nature of the wonder-working girl's actions upon the potter's wheel: 'in this feat, mimesis closes in on itself. The girl enacts the process by which she is objectified, becoming the vessel that depicts her presence at a symposium. She is the material of her own representation – the clay and the pots and the knives and the image and the word. The real and representational realms collapse on each other in meaningless mimesis, and there is nothing for the spectators to do but marvel.' The importance of ideas about mimesis in this dialogue more generally has also been picked up on by Wohl (2004) 357–8 and Baragwanath (2012) 641, who note that the behaviour of the Syracusan's performers in the *Symposium* seems to shift from performative mimesis to supposedly 'real' actions in the mime depicting the relationship between Dionysus and Ariadne with which the dialogue ends.

Making Marvels: *Thaumatopoiia* and *Thaumatourgia*

artistic mimesis in book 10 of the *Republic*, and in the later dialogue *Sophist*. In these dialogues *thaumatopoiia* and mimesis both relate to problems which arise as a result of changes in distance, measurement, proportion and perspective. As we saw in earlier chapters, the relationship between the near and the far and *thauma* in Greek thought in the fifth century is a very complex one. As we might expect, *thauma* comes into Plato's discussions of the near and the far as well, in both a literal and a metaphorical sense.

In *Republic* 10, Socrates argues that mimesis is not the second stage distant from truth (i.e. the second stage away from the Forms), but in fact the 'third from the truth' (τρίτον μέν τί ἐστιν ἀπὸ τῆς ἀληθείας, 602c). He then states that the power of mimesis affects the same part of us as visual illusions. He explains this point by noting that the 'dimensions of the same object do not seem to be the same when viewed both from close up and from far away' (ταὐτόν που ἡμῖν μέγεθος ἐγγύθεν τε καὶ πόρρωθεν διὰ τῆς ὄψεως οὐκ ἴσον φαίνεται, 602c).[22] Even though the object does not actually change its magnitude in reality, it seems to be a different size depending on where the viewer is stood. Other errors of perception are similar to this kind of effect (602c–d):

καὶ ταὐτὰ καμπύλα τε καὶ εὐθέα ἐν ὕδατί τε θεωμένοις καὶ ἔξω, καὶ κοῖλά τε δὴ καὶ ἐξέχοντα διὰ τὴν περὶ τὰ χρώματα αὖ πλάνην τῆς ὄψεως, καὶ πᾶσά τις ταραχὴ δήλη ἡμῖν ἐνοῦσα αὕτη ἐν τῇ ψυχῇ· ᾧ δὴ ἡμῶν τῷ παθήματι τῆς φύσεως ἡ σκιαγραφία ἐπιθεμένη γοητείας οὐδὲν ἀπολείπει, καὶ ἡ θαυματοποιία καὶ ἄλλαι πολλαὶ τοιαῦται μηχαναί.

And the same things look bent within water and straight outside of it, and both concave and convex, again because of visual error concerning colours, and every single confusion like this is clearly inherent in the human soul. Three-dimensional painting (*skiagraphia*), which attacks this weakness in our nature, is nothing short of bewitchment, as is marvel-making (*thaumatopoiia*) and all other such artifices.

Skiagraphia and *thaumatopoiia* are here equated with the effect that mimesis itself supposedly has on the spectator. In Plato, both of these terms are interconnected in ways that suggest that a deceptive, spurious appearance of truth is the aim of mimesis.

---

[22] Cf. Ion's sentiments at Eur. *Ion* 585–6: see Chapter 5, Section 4.

7.3 *Thaumatopoiia* and Perspective in *Republic* and *Sophist*

Skiagraphia, often translated as 'shadow painting', seems to be the use of darker and lighter shades together in such a way as to give figures the impression of three-dimensionality.[23] Distance is key to *skiagraphia*: the lengths of lines and/or the colours used only look correct from a distance, and fail to stand up to detailed scrutiny when viewed up close. As Eva Keuls puts it, in the realm of painting, *skiagraphia* represents 'the epitome of illusionism ... the device which most intensively exploited the subjectivity and fallibility of human eyesight'.[24] The way in which *skiagraphia* exploits this power of illusion seems to be by making things look *more* real rather than less: objects on a flat plane somehow take on the appearance of three-dimensional objects, even though they are just flat depictions of real-life objects. Moreover, the sort of play with distance and magnitude in which the purveyors of *skiagraphia* and *thaumatopoiia* indulge is a key aspect of the sort of ekplektic wonder that these thaumatic objects provoke: this fits with the connection of *thauma* to the visual in general, and to extremes of magnitude (things which are either amazingly big or amazingly small) and distance (things which should be far away appearing closer to you than you imagined, or vice versa) which we find elsewhere long before Plato begins to manipulate these ideas.

But there is an important development in the way in which these ideas are wielded for philosophical purposes here. Rather than referring in a strictly literal manner to real-life material objects, Plato's discussion of distance and *thauma* also takes on an important metaphorical aspect. This is made clearer in a similar discussion in the later dialogue the *Sophist*. As one of the steps in the long conversation with Theaetetus which aims to define what, exactly, a sophist is, the Eleatic Stranger first, in a subsection of the argument beginning at 234b–c, pinpoints the ability to deceive people through the use of visual or verbal mimesis as a key aspect of the sophist's character:

---

[23] For a detailed discussion of *skiagraphia* see Bruno (1977) 37; cf. Rouveret (1989) 24–6, 50–9 and Burnyeat (1999) 223–4.
[24] See Keuls (1978) 80.

Making Marvels: *Thaumatopoiia* and *Thaumatourgia*

ΞΕ: οὐκοῦν τόν γ' ὑπισχνούμενον δυνατὸν εἶναι μιᾷ τέχνῃ πάντα ποιεῖν γιγνώσκομέν που τοῦτο, ὅτι μιμήματα καὶ ὁμώνυμα τῶν ὄντων ἀπεργαζόμενος τῇ γραφικῇ τέχνῃ δυνατὸς ἔσται τοὺς ἀνοήτους τῶν νέων παῖδων, πόρρωθεν τὰ γεγραμμένα ἐπιδεικνύς, λανθάνειν ὡς ὅτιπερ ἂν βουληθῇ δρᾶν, τοῦτο ἱκανώτατος ὢν ἀποτελεῖν ἔργῳ.
ΘΕ: πῶς γὰρ οὔ;
ΞΕ: τί δὲ δή; περὶ τοὺς λόγους ἆρ' οὐ προσδοκῶμεν εἶναί τινα ἄλλην τέχνην, ᾗ αὖ δυνατὸν ὂν αὖ τυγχάνει τοὺς νέους καὶ ἔτι πόρρω τῶν πραγμάτων τῆς ἀληθείας ἀφεστῶτας διὰ τῶν ὤτων τοῖς λόγοις γοητεύειν, δεικνύντας εἴδωλα λεγόμενα περὶ πάντων, ὥστε ποιεῖν ἀληθῆ δοκεῖν λέγεσθαι καὶ τὸν λέγοντα δὴ σοφώτατον πάντων ἅπαντ' εἶναι;

ELEATIC STRANGER: And so we recognise this I suppose about the person who professes to be able to do everything with a single art: that by producing imitations which have the same names as real things through the art of painting, and by displaying his pictures at a distance, he is able to deceive the unintelligent ones among young children into thinking that he is supremely able to carry out any deed he wishes to do in reality.
THEAETETUS: Yes, indeed.
ELEATIC STRANGER: Well then? Surely we should expect that there is another art concerning words, with which it is again possible to bewitch the young through their ears while they are still standing far-off from the reality of things, displaying images of all things to them, so as to make it seem that true things are said, and that the man saying them is indeed the wisest of all men about all things?

In this case it is specifically mindless young children who are at risk of believing that one man can make or do all things by virtue of a single art. These children are therefore the ones most at risk of being deceived by this type of man through his use of illusionistic

7.3 *Thaumatopoiia* and Perspective in *Republic* and *Sophist*

painting or similar mimetic arts. This deceptive use of visual art is shown to have an analogous counterpart in the deceptive use of verbal art; the sophist is further defined as one who can trick young people with words (234c). In this discussion, it is clear that a viewer's literal distance from a mimetic artistic object is parallel to a sort of metaphorical epistemic distance of the mind from truth itself.[25]

Given that the ability to dazzle someone with deceptive mimetic performances is a key aspect of marvel-making, it comes as no surprise when the Eleatic Stranger concludes that one of the key elements of the definition of the sophist is that he is a *thaumatopoios* as well.[26] At 235a–b, the idea of the sophist as a type of marvel-maker is first introduced:

ΞΕ:: ἄγε δή, νῦν ἡμέτερον ἔργον ἤδη τὸν θῆρα μηκέτ' ἀνεῖναι· σχεδὸν γὰρ αὐτὸν περιειλήφαμεν ἐν ἀμφιβληστρικῷ τινι τῶν ἐν τοῖς λόγοις περὶ τὰ τοιαῦτα ὀργάνων, ὥστε οὐκέτ' ἐκφεύξεται τόδε γε.
ΘΕ:: τὸ ποῖον;
ΞΕ:: τὸ μὴ οὐ τοῦ γένους εἶναι τοῦ τῶν θαυματοποιῶν τις εἶς.
ΘΕ:: κἀμοὶ τοῦτό γε οὕτω περὶ αὐτοῦ συνδοκεῖ.

ELEATIC STRANGER: Come on then, it's our task not to let the beast escape. For we nearly have him surrounded with one of those net-like instruments which words provide for such things, so he will not escape from the next point.
THEAETETUS: What point is that?
ELEATIC STRANGER: That he certainly belongs to the class of marvel-makers.
THEAETETUS: This seems to me too to be true about that man.

The sophist's art ultimately keeps the young far away from the truth in the same way as illusionistic effects in painting such as *skiagraphia* necessitate a literal distance from the artwork in order

---

[25] See Nightingale (2002) 228. Cf. also Socrates' very similar argument in relation to painting and mimesis at *Resp.* 598a–d.
[26] See Casadesús Bordoy (2012) 26 and Bernabé (2012) 53–5 on the importance of *thauma* in this definition of the sophist.

to create a convincing image. The sophist's ability to enthral the young and keep them far away from the truth turns him into a sort of *thaumatopoios*, a marvel-maker who constructs artificial thaumatic arguments which maintain the appearance of reality. Plato's discussion of nearness and distance in relation to *thaumatopoiia* and *thaumata* is therefore a distinctive element of his wider epistemological concerns.

7.4 Socratic Marvel-Making: *Thaumatopoiia* in the Cave

To return to the Cave. In this passage Plato again meditates upon the many associations surrounding displays of *thaumata* and mimesis, the relationship between the natural and the artificial, and familiar and unfamiliar wonders. Plato activates all these meanings in the Cave to warn against the potentially misleading and stultifying marvels of others – all the while having Socrates himself present a captivating image that does much to arrest and grab hold of the reader. If we focus on the use of wonder in this passage, Plato's wider message becomes clear: certain types of philosophical wonder can lead to educative and cognitive advancement, but in the hands of the wrong people *thauma*, though often pleasurable, can only lead to a state of cognitive stasis. This is a particular danger for the young person who is as yet not sufficiently educated to withstand the potential lure of deceptive thaumatic spectacles. This distinction is in fact made clear within the Cave Allegory itself. As we saw above, for Plato the concept of *thaumatopoiia* involves a series of interlinking issues involving perception, potential deception and mimesis. How then does this relate to the display of shadowy *thaumata* found in the Cave?

It is worth thinking further about how, exactly, the *thaumata* on display might appear to those watching the spectacle. From the description of the fire burning behind the prisoners from a long way off, and the low wall in front of them above which shadows are projected, it seems that we are dealing here with some form of shadow puppet theatre.[27] The choice of this particular variety of thaumatic spectacle is especially apt, as the issues involving

---

[27] See Gocer (1999) 119–29 on Plato's use of the idea of shadow puppetry in the Cave Allegory.

7.4 Socratic Marvel-Making: *Thaumatopoiia* in the Cave

perception and mimesis which Plato often associates with *thauma* and *thaumatopoiia* are massively accentuated by the way in which the composition of this spectacle is described. The prisoners in the Cave are not only forced to observe shadowy imitations of the objects being held up behind them rather than the objects themselves, they cannot even observe the true proportions of the shadows cast in front of them. This is the result of many factors: their distance from the wall of the Cave will affect their ability to measure the size of each shadow accurately, the use of a flickering fire as a light source presumably results in distorted and moving shadows, and the shadows may differ radically in size from the objects which cast them anyway depending on the relation between those objects and the fire itself.[28] The distortions always associated with *thaumatopoiia* are thus in play in the Cave Allegory as well.

The spectators in the Cave are thus not only deceived by the fact that they think that the shadows are real objects, but also by the fact that they cannot even grasp the real dimensions of these shadows. Nor can they understand the causes of the movements of these objects: instead of understanding that the shadows can only imitate the movements of animate beings, they think that the shadows themselves are alive, especially since the voices of the *thaumatopoioi*-like men rebound off the wall of the Cave and make the shadows seem to speak. The objects casting shadows are made to look like statues of men or other living things, but they are not living creatures. Instead they have all been constructed out of materials like wood and stone (514c–515a):

ὅρα τοίνυν παρὰ τοῦτο τὸ τειχίον φέροντας ἀνθρώπους σκεύη τε παντοδαπὰ ὑπερέχοντα τοῦ τειχίου καὶ ἀνδριάντας καὶ ἄλλα ζῷα λίθινά τε καὶ ξύλινα καὶ παντοῖα εἰργασμένα, οἷον εἰκὸς τοὺς μὲν φθεγγομένους, τοὺς δὲ σιγῶντας τῶν παραφερόντων.

---

[28] Schofield (2007) 226 notes that the dazzling and flickering nature of the fire would make it hard for the released prisoner to look at the objects casting shadows, but we can apply this principle further and note that even the shadows, especially their proportions, would be difficult to see clearly due to the moving nature of the light source. Cf. Harte (2007) 208 on potential distortions caused by the relation between the objects casting shadows and their light source. We might also note that the irregularity of the cave wall would presumably cause the shadows to appear even more distorted to their viewers.

Making Marvels: *Thaumatopoiia* and *Thaumatourgia*

And now picture this: along this wall there are men bearing all sorts of props which project above the wall, both images of men and other living creatures made out of wood and stone and all sorts of materials. As you would expect, some of the men carrying the props along utter sounds, and some are silent.

The fact that these objects have been constructed out of other materials is very important: these are not *thaumata* which are found in the natural world, the kinds of everyday marvels which provoke the types of questions which lead to philosophical thinking. Instead they are deceptive images which aim to deceive and dazzle the onlooker with *thauma* in the same way that artworks which look 'as if they are alive' or 'as if they are about to speak' provoke a similar sense of wonder in their viewers.[29] The effect of the shadows is comparable – except that the chained viewer in the Cave does not realise that they are caused by artificial and man-made objects.

If the shadows are the ultimate in deceptive mimetic spectacles, then the *thaumatopoioi*-like men must represent the type of people who create these kinds of mimetic sights. In general, the recent voluminous scholarship on this passage has subscribed to one of two views: either the men in control of the *thaumata* which enthral the prisoners are politicians and legislators, or they represent men who are prominent in the cultural sphere such as poets, artists, playwrights and painters.[30] There is no need to decide between these groups: both are covered by the designation of the figures controlling the objects in the Cave as being like *thaumatopoioi*, since politicians and demagogues by necessity harness the powers of *thauma* in their speeches to play to the crowd just as poets and artists do. In a similar fashion, *thaumatopoiia* is

---

[29] See Chapter 2, sections 1, 3 and 4 on wonder as the customary response to statues or other types of artworks which are rendered so realistically that they seem to be on the verge of moving or speaking as though truly alive.

[30] Wilberding (2004) 117–39 provides a comprehensive overview of the many recent suggestions regarding the identity of the people compared to *thaumatopoioi* in the Cave Allegory. Wilberding himself argues that all of these orthodox views are wrong and that the puppeteers are not orators, demagogues, politicians or poets. Instead, he suggests that the prisoners are meant to represent these groups, and that the shadows are the *demos*. Given the performative bent of *thaumatopoiia*, however, it seems clear that the more conventional readings of this passage cohere more easily with Plato's use of the language of *thauma* in *Republic* 7.

7.4 Socratic Marvel-Making: *Thaumatopoiia* in the Cave

being used metaphorically here in disparaging reference to the potentially seductive and deceptive art of any public figure who attempts to influence the thought and direction of the rest of society.[31]

The power of such representations over the spectator is made very clear by Socrates' vision of the Cave's prisoners. As we have seen in earlier chapters, intensely or excessively wondrous displays often run the risk of provoking stunned astonishment in their audiences, a dumbstruck response which often also leads to a (usually temporary) sort of somatic paralysis. It is not by accident then that the absolutely static state of the chained prisoners echoes the position of those who elsewhere in Plato's dialogues are described as subject to the pleasurable but damaging charms of ekplektic wonder, since Plato is referring precisely to the same types of figures – orators, poets, rhapsodes, demagogues – whom he elsewhere accuses of misleading the general public, and the young in particular, with ekplektic and wondrous displays. The fact that the prisoners are fettered only emphasises the paralysing and stultifying effect of the *thaumata* on show and demonstrates how extraordinarily difficult the task of ever escaping or overcoming the marvellous power of these superficially pleasurable spectacles really is.

Given the emphasis on visual illusion and the power of arresting sights (whether they be actual visual objects or verbal descriptions of visual objects) at which the introduction of *thaumatopoiia* in the Cave Allegory hints, is it necessary for us as readers of Plato to pause and question the power of Socrates' own verbal painting? I believe that we must do so, not least because of the way in which the necessity of actually *seeing* the image that Socrates is constructing is emphasised to his interlocutor Glaucon (and, by extension, to us). At the very beginning of the account, Glaucon is explicitly instructed to see (ἰδὲ γὰρ ἀνθρώπους, 514a) the men and their surroundings which Socrates is about to describe, and this exhortation is restated as the description progresses (ἰδὲ τειχίον, 514b). At the end of Socrates' initial illustration of the situation in the Cave, Glaucon responds by explicitly saying that he sees what

---

[31] Thus McCoy (2008) 130 is correct in noting that: '[w]hat is crucial in the use of this term here [i.e. θαυματοποιοῖς] is that the speakers are performers'.

Socrates has described (ὁρῶ, ἔφη, 514b). Socrates then exhorts him to see again (ὅρα, 514b), proceeding to recount how men carrying images of men and other living things cast shadows upon the wall of the Cave. Although Glaucon claims he can see what Socrates is describing, and we can also follow along and imagine what the Cave might look like, it is difficult to understand straightaway what this image is supposed to convey. Socrates has already told us at the very beginning of the Cave Allegory that what he is about to say relates explicitly to our education (ἀπείκασον τοιούτῳ πάθει τὴν ἡμετέραν φύσιν παιδείας τε πέρι καὶ ἀπαιδευσίας, 514a) – yet it is difficult to understand immediately how the situation of the prisoners bound in the Cave could relate to this theme. Likewise, although we can visualise various elements of Socrates' description in our minds, the significance of the image being built up in front of us is not easy to grasp. Just as the prisoners in the Cave fail to understand the true significance and causes of the moving shadows on the wall, so too do we fail to grasp the true purpose of the image built up by Socrates and its relation to our education until we are guided through the image by someone who already understands its meaning.

This point is emphasised further by Glaucon's initial response at the end of Socrates' description: 'This image you speak of is strange', he said, 'and these are strange prisoners too' (ἄτοπον, ἔφη, λέγεις εἰκόνα καὶ δεσμώτας ἀτόπους, 515a). In this case the spatial aspect of the word *atopos* – literally meaning 'out of place' – is also activated in Glaucon's comment, as he implies that both the space of the Cave and the people in it are 'out of place', spatially and conceptually distant from his own existence and consciousness.[32] But Socrates reveals that these men are surprisingly much closer to Glaucon than he has realised: 'they are like us' (ὁμοίους ἡμῖν, 515a), he bluntly replies. Socrates has thus managed to make the familiar strange and the strange familiar, to defamiliarise and then refamiliarise the supposed

---

[32] See Nightingale (2004) 97 on the importance of *atopia* later on in the Cave Allegory when the philosopher himself will eventually go on to become *atopos* among his own people; this later reversal of the application of *atopia* echoes and transforms Glaucon's use here.

7.4 Socratic Marvel-Making: *Thaumatopoiia* in the Cave

situation of those who are just like us.[33] Wonder is a frequent response to this kind of defamiliarisation and refamiliarisation, and it is precisely that response which Socrates' image is attempting to provoke, both in Glaucon and in us. The Cave Allegory is itself offered up to us here as an object of *thauma* – though one that potentially offers the possibility of cognitive advancement rather than stasis, as long as we are correctly guided through and eventually manage to move away from the alluring nature of images, whether they are visual or constructed verbally.

In this way, the potential danger of falling prey to wonder-inducing images is a theme which is itself encoded within the Cave Allegory. By making a marvel of his own, Socrates by necessity distorts certain elements of his image, increasing the magnitude of some aspects and minimising the importance of others. This causes particular problems when we attempt to harmonise the image of the Cave with what we have previously been told about the Line.[34] But the lack of precise harmonisation between these images in *Republic* 6 and 7 is itself no wonder: distortions and changing proportions are after all at the heart of *thaumatopoiia*. Any image which works to arrest our attention and make us marvel is bound to mislead us to some extent, as Plato frequently warns us.[35] The difference in Socrates' use of *thauma* in this case is that it makes us think; it sets us off on the process towards the realisation that it is mathematical and dialectical reasoning which is necessary for us to approach an understanding of the Form of the Good. This is something we only come to

---

[33] Cf. Nightingale (2004) 96 on Plato's 'rhetoric of estrangement' in this passage, which 'aims to uproot and displace us, portraying the familiar world as strange and the strange reality of the Forms as kindred to the human soul'.

[34] Schofield (2007) 230 best sums up the resulting problems: 'The assumption that we are being told to bludgeon everything in the Cave to fit whatever parallels could be identified in Sun and Line has caused much of the interpretative damage.'

[35] Even Socrates' own wonder-inducing words are not immune from *thauma*'s potentially double-edged effects in Plato's dialogues: see e.g. Alcibiades' description of the often astounding effects of Socrates' speech, arguments and behaviour in the *Symposium*, where *thauma* and *ekplexis* make very frequent appearances in relation to the older man's words and actions (see *Symp.* 215b, 215d, 216c, 216d, 217a, 219c, 220a, 220b, 220c, 221c); cf. the use of the famous stingray image in the *Meno* (80a–b), where the potentially stunned result of engaging in elenctic discussion with Socrates looks remarkably similar to the paralysing effects of ekplektic wonder.

realise as the Cave Allegory draws on: as Myles Burnyeat notes, 'it is only in retrospect that we learn that the Cave has to do with mathematics as well as cultural values (532b–c)'.[36] From a distance, at first glance, we might think the image of the Cave is only about cultural values. But as Socrates brings us (and Glaucon) closer and closer to his true meaning, we realise close up that the main purpose of this image is to impress the necessity of mathematical and dialectical reasoning upon us. The Cave Allegory thus itself embodies the way in which wonder is one of the most dangerous weapons in the arsenal of those who are pre-eminent in the cultural and political spheres in contemporary Athens, the *thaumatopoioi*-like men who construct crowd-pleasing marvels for their own ends. But the other face of *thauma* is present in the Cave as well, and its potential as an initial protreptic towards further philosophical endeavour becomes clear: in the right (Socratic) hands, 'wondering' truly does turn out to be the 'beginning of philosophy' (τὸ θαυμάζειν ... ἀρχὴ φιλοσοφίας, *Theaetetus* 155d).

[36] Burnyeat (1999) 243.

8

EPILOGUE: *THAUMATA POLLA*

This study has attested to the truth of Pindar's famous claim that 'marvels are many' (ἦ θαύματα πολλά, *Olympian* 1.28). In almost every genre and mode of ancient Greek literary writing, the significance of wonder as a category of experience can be probed in ways which provide radically new and defamiliarising perspectives on familiar material. But amidst this general polyphony, there remain continuities in how *thauma* and *thaumata* are defined, configured and conceived. In this concluding epilogue three case studies are presented with a twofold purpose in mind: to trace out and reiterate some of the main trends, tendencies, changes and continuities in the treatment of *thauma* in Greek literature from Homer to the early Hellenistic period, while simultaneously suggesting some further directions for the study of wonder and the marvellous in antiquity and beyond.

The first section builds on this study's discovery of the growing significance of *thauma* as a philosophical concept. Following on from the last chapter's examination of the place of wonder in the *Republic*'s Cave Allegory, the significance of *thauma* in Plato's last work, the *Laws*, is examined. The discussion then moves to Rome in the first century BCE to consider the rise of another philosophical principle relating to *thauma*: the idea of *not* marvelling at anything at all (*nil admirari*). In the second section, the growing impact of *thauma* on ancient discussions of the relationship between nature and artifice is again reassessed through an examination of the place of wonder in the mechanical treatises of the first-century CE engineer Hero of Alexandria. Finally, in the third section, the idea of the marvel as a textual phenomenon is revisited through an examination of the first extant description of the reading and use of Greek paradoxographical texts, an account

199

which appears in the *Noctes Atticae* of the second-century CE Roman miscellanist Aulus Gellius, whose work also provides an opportunity to begin to think about the reception of Greek wonder and wonders in Roman culture.

In each of these sections I am not aiming to be exhaustive or absolute, either in my summing up or in my suggestions for further questions of interest. Rather, in the same spirit of Plato and Aristotle with which I opened this study, I want once again to suggest that *thauma* is only a starting point for new and renewed inquiry.

8.1 *Thauma* as the Beginning of Philosophy – or *Nil Admirari*?

Over the course of this book, it has become apparent just how much the importance of *thauma* as a concept in Greek philosophical thinking has been underrated in previous scholarship. By the time one reaches the work of Aristotle and his Peripatetic followers, the significance of *thauma* as a concept is already well-established in the realm of aesthetic and rhetorical theory (see Aristotle's *Poetics* and *Rhetoric*), in biology, zoology and science more generally (see Aristotle's biological writings and the works of the paradoxographers), and also in relation to the notion of what philosophy itself is and does (see Aristotle's *Metaphysics*). The significance of *thauma* for the Peripatetics is not surprising, since it is in Plato's work that *thauma* really emerges for the first time as a fully conceptualised and complex term of philosophical hermeneutics. By the end of the fifth century BCE, the cultural discourse of *thauma* and *thaumata*, and particularly of their effects on audiences and viewers, is fully ready for the various philosophical uses to which Plato puts it. The fact that sight and vision, from the beginning of the Greek literary tradition, remain the sensory realm in which *thauma* exercises its greatest impact accounts to some extent for Plato's pronounced interest in the concept as a vehicle for expressing more general and complex concerns about human sensory experience of the phenomenal world, mimesis, thinking, and the origins of philosophy itself. At the same time, the fact that *thauma* exercises a simultaneous emotional *and* cognitive

8.1 *Thauma* as Beginning of Philosophy – or *Nil Admirari*?

effect on its subjects means that it becomes a vital concept in the philosopher's broader exploration of human psychology. For Plato, *thauma* is not only a response to the most unfamiliar and distant objects and experiences, or to experiences provoked by and related to the divine rather than the human realm, as it primarily was in the past – though these associations do remain. It is also the radically ambivalent effect of contemporary man-made spectacles which aim, above all else, to delight and distract. The inherent doubleness and variability which *thauma* possesses as a response to experiences which are able to provoke cognitive advancement, while at the same time risking a sort of dazzling cognitive stasis, is part of what makes wonder such a potent concept in Plato's philosophical arsenal.

This is nowhere clearer than in the *Laws*, Plato's final work. In this dialogue *thauma* plays a part in the explanation of the workings of human psychology itself. Plato presents us with three old men – an unnamed Athenian, a Cretan called Clinias and a Spartan named Megillus – who embark upon a discussion of the relative advantages and disadvantages of the legislative practices and constitutions of different cities and cultures in an attempt to define the best laws for the foundation of a new, *almost* ideal state, the 'second best' city (δευτέρως ἂν πόλις οἰκεῖσθαι πρὸς τὸ βέλτιστον, 739a) of Magnesia. As their discussion progresses, the question of what the best type of education might be for this new city's inhabitants soon arises. It is in the context of this question that, relatively early on in the discussion, the Athenian Stranger – the *Laws*' dominant, often Socrates-like guiding philosophical voice – returns to the image of *thaumata*, those puppet-like objects which we have seen being deployed by the strange *thaumatopoioi* who populate Plato's image of the Cave, to describe the workings of human psychology (644d–e):

περὶ δὴ τούτων διανοηθῶμεν οὑτωσί. θαῦμα μὲν ἕκαστον ἡμῶν ἡγησώμεθα τῶν ζῴων θεῖον, εἴτε ὡς παίγνιον ἐκείνων εἴτε ὡς σπουδῇ τινι συνεστηκός· οὐ γὰρ δὴ τοῦτό γε γιγνώσκομεν, τόδε δὲ ἴσμεν, ὅτι ταῦτα τὰ πάθη ἐν ἡμῖν οἷον νεῦρα ἢ σμήρινθοί τινες ἐνοῦσαι σπῶσίν τε ἡμᾶς καὶ ἀλλήλαις ἀνθέλκουσιν ἐναντίαι οὖσαι ἐπ' ἐναντίας πράξεις, οὗ δὴ διωρισμένη ἀρετὴ καὶ κακία κεῖται.

Epilogue: *Thaumata Polla*

Let us think this matter over in the following way. Let's suppose that each of us living creatures is a *thauma* belonging to the gods, put together to be either a toy of theirs or for some serious reason. We do not know why we were made, but we do know this much: that the feelings, like cords or strings inside us, both pull us along and, being opposed to one another, in mutual opposition they pull us towards opposite actions, where the dividing line between goodness and badness lies.

The Athenian Stranger goes on to explain that there is one particularly forceful cord pulling inside us which we should always try and follow over all others: 'the golden and holy cord of reason, which is called the common law of the state' (τὴν τοῦ λογισμοῦ ἀγωγὴν χρυσῆν καὶ ἱεράν, τῆς πόλεως κοινὸν νόμον ἐπικαλουμένην, 645a). The pull of this cord is, however, 'gentle rather than violent' (πρᾴου δὲ καὶ οὐ βιαίου, 645a), and so needs help to ensure that we follow it rather than the other impulses.

To begin to unpack this enigmatic image it is necessary to establish what kind of object the Athenian Stranger is comparing every human being to when he suggests that each and every one of us is similar to a '*thauma* belonging to the gods' (θαῦμα ... θεῖον). The most common interpretation of this phrase is something like 'puppet of the gods' or 'divine puppet', with the 'cords or strings' (νεῦρα ἢ σμήρινθοί) inside us corresponding to the cords which control a marionette-type object. It is important to understand the way in which the *thauma* is thought to function in relation to its cords and strings in this passage, as it affects our interpretation of the way in which human psychology, and the gods' influence on our psychology, is supposed to function. Although many previous commentators have built substantial readings of this passage by conceiving of the '*thauma* belonging to the gods' as a marionette controlled by external strings, the whole point of this image is that the cords and strings described are *internal* rather than *external*: as a result, the *thauma* described here functions like an automaton rather than an externally controlled marionette.[1] The fact that

---

[1] The issue is complicated by the fact that there is a degree of overlap between the categories of puppet and automaton in antiquity: see Cappelletto (2011) 325, Shershow (1995) 3–4 and Cambiano (1994) 622. For recent interpretations of the '*thauma* belonging to the gods' as a type of externally operated marionette see e.g. Kurke (2013) 123 n. 1, who suggests that the image describes puppets 'worked by strings or wires from above'; see also Moore (2014) 40: 'a marionette would seem to be the more appropriate image

202

8.1 *Thauma* as Beginning of Philosophy – or *Nil Admirari*?

cords and strings are involved is perfectly congruous with this interpretation of the Athenian Stranger's biological *thaumata* as automata, since we know that ancient automata and self-moving mechanisms were made to move through the use of a system of internal cords which were wound up and operated with the actions of weights, counterweights and pulleys.[2] In fact, it was the automaton's apparent ability to move itself and become animate without continued input from elsewhere that led to the use of *thauma* as a synonym for such objects, since, as discussed in Chapter 2, the transgression of the boundaries between animate and inanimate and nature and artifice in objects of art or craft which appear to be so lifelike that they almost move is often said to be a prime cause of wonder, and indeed becomes a *topos* of ancient art criticism and ekphrasis.

Moreover, it is important to note that the common identification of the *thaumata* in this passage with puppets or marionettes is to a great extent a result of the influence of the description of the *thaumata* in the *Republic*'s Cave Allegory. As discussed in the last chapter, in that passage it is clear that the men compared to 'marvel-makers' (*thaumatopoioi*) are certainly in charge of the objects described as *thaumata* that are causing the shadows being cast upon the wall of the Cave. These *thaumatopoioi*-like men therefore seem to be undertaking some sort of form of shadow puppetry. But it is essential to note that although the shadows in

---

rather than a wind-up toy'; cf. also Meyer (2015) 178 and Schofield (2016) 135–40. But the mention of cords and strings does not necessarily imply that the *thauma* is externally operated. In fact, the whole point of the image is that these cords and strings are internal impulses which act inside us. For this reason, the image necessarily refers to an object operated through the pull of internal cords. We are in fact dealing with the image of an automaton here: it is clear that the mechanisms of ancient automata would have depended on an internal system of cords which used weights and counterweights to cause various motions. Frede (2010) 116 discerns this point and its significance correctly: 'Although *thauma* is commonly translated as "puppet", this translation is misleading if it suggests that humans are mere marionettes whose strings are pulled by the gods. For, as the further descriptions show, the "puppet's" behaviour is not determined by the higher powers; it depends, rather, on the workings of its own strings. Hence, Plato seems to have in mind wind-up toys that move by themselves, rather than marionettes.' Annas (2011) 8 also gets it right: 'Plato is thinking, not of puppets on strings, but of toys which move around by themselves (a kind of clockwork wind-up toy).'

[2] See Section 2 below on the treatises of the engineer Hero of Alexandria for more detailed descriptions of how wondrous (and possibly real-life) automata actually worked in antiquity.

Epilogue: *Thaumata Polla*

this passage are made to appear through the external agency of the *thaumatopoioi*-like men, they are not seen as such by the people who are watching the performance in the Cave, since the shadows they see displayed before them seem to move *of their own accord*. This is what makes them *thaumata*: the effect is actually one of autonomous motion.

The Athenian Stranger's comparison of each living being to a '*thauma* belonging to the gods' thus returns us to questions concerning *thauma* which have their roots as far back as the Homeric poems: the divide between human and divine, animate and inanimate, natural and man-made. From Homer onwards, we find spontaneously moving, automatous objects of divine craft labelled as *thaumata*. For example, divine craft is inextricably linked to the creation of automata when Thetis visits Hephaestus in *Iliad* 18 and catches a glimpse of him in the act of making self-moving tripods (18.372–7):

> τὸν δ' εὖρ' ἱδρώοντα ἑλισσόμενον περὶ φύσας
> σπεύδοντα· τρίποδας γὰρ ἐείκοσι πάντας ἔτευχεν
> ἑστάμεναι περὶ τοῖχον ἐυσταθέος μεγάροιο,
> χρύσεα δέ σφ' ὑπὸ κύκλα ἑκάστῳ πυθμένι θῆκεν,
> ὄφρα οἱ αὐτόματοι θεῖον δυσαίατ' ἀγῶνα
> ἠδ' αὖτις πρὸς δῶμα νεοίατο, θαῦμα ἰδέσθαι.

She found him sweating as he rushed around his bellows; for he was making tripods, twenty in total, to stand around the wall of his well-built hall, and he put golden wheels under the base of each, so that they would be able to make their way into the assembly of the gods of their own accord and go back again to his house, a wonder to see.

The self-movement of these tripods lies at the heart of their marvellous effect and is what renders them a particular 'wonder to see' (θαῦμα ἰδέσθαι). These self-moving tripods become the archetypal examples of automata in the Greek literary tradition, along with similarly lifelike moving golden handmaidens, also made by Hephaestus, which aid the god in his work.[3] The particular connection of these objects to the god's craft is important: once again we see that early conceptions of the marvellous are linked

---

[3] *Il.* 18.417–18: 'And the golden handmaidens, like living girls, moved swiftly to support their lord' (ὑπὸ δ' ἀμφίπολοι ῥώοντο ἄνακτι | χρύσειαι, ζωῇσι νεήνισιν εἰοικυῖαι).

8.1 *Thauma* as Beginning of Philosophy – or *Nil Admirari*?

explicitly to the power of the divine. In Plato's *Laws*, the Athenian Stranger hits upon this image of automata-like *thaumata* as a means of suggesting that humans, like automata, are similarly created by the gods, and that each person also has the capability, if set moving in the right direction, to become an object of wonder. Plato is thus playing once again on the double-edged nature of *thauma* and thaumatic objects in this dialogue in a way which differs from his approach in the *Republic*. In the Cave Allegory there, *thaumata* represent a dangerous distraction from cognitive advancement when their powers of astonishment are wielded by the wrong hands; the *Laws*, in contrast, establishes that we ourselves might become objects of *thauma*, belonging to the gods themselves, if only we follow the pull of the 'golden cord' of reason which guides us correctly, like the motions of an automaton that are wisely and decorously programmed in advance in accordance with Reason.

The inherent potential doubleness of *thauma* and its effects thus accounts for Plato's use of the image of *thaumata* in the *Laws* and elsewhere. However, it was not always the case in antiquity that the positive potential of *thauma* as a philosophical concept was recognised. In fact, many Hellenistic philosophical schools went on not only explicitly to disavow the significance of *thauma*'s place within philosophy but even went so far as to advise against succumbing to wonder and its effects entirely. In these philosophical traditions, the potentially disturbing *emotional* effects of *thauma* on the mind and soul are clearly thought to outweigh any positive effects that wonder may produce as a catalyst for (re)cognition and inquiry. The most famous surviving summation of this response to the effects of wonder is surely Horace's *Epistle* 1.6, which begins with a warning about wonder which the rest of the poem goes on to elaborate in more detail (1–8):

> nil admirari prope res est una, Numici,
> solaque quae possit facere et servare beatum.
> hunc solem et stellas et decedentia certis
> tempora momentis sunt qui formidine nulla
> imbuti spectent: quid censes munera terrae,
> quid maris extremos Arabas ditantis et Indos,
> ludicra quid, plausus et amici dona Quiritis,
> quo spectanda modo, quo sensu credis et ore?

Epilogue: *Thaumata Polla*

> To marvel at nothing, Numicius, is almost the one and only thing which is able to make and keep you happy. Some men can view the sun up there, and the stars, and the seasons passing with the stars' predictable movements, untouched by any emotional disturbance: what do you think of the gifts of the earth, what of those of the sea, which enriches far-distant Arabians and Indians, what of the theatrical shows, the applause, or the favour of the friendly Roman citizen – in what manner, with what feeling and expression do you think they should be viewed?

Horace here warns his addressee Numicius against precisely the sorts of marvellous phenomena we have seen associated with wonder throughout this study. The warning against marvelling at the sight of phenomena such as the potentially distracting and specious spectacles of the theatre is conventional enough, but Horace goes further here. Even those experiences which philosophers such as Aristotle would encourage us to wonder at above all else – the marvellous phenomena of the natural world and the celestial realm – are classed as problematic causes of wonder precisely because they risk opening the viewer up to some degree of emotional disturbance.

This view, which denies wonder a place in both philosophy and everyday life, is very different from Platonic and Aristotelian attitudes towards *thauma* which have been outlined in the previous chapters. In choosing to examine the potential benefits and difficulties of the art of not marvelling in this *Epistle*, Horace is drawing on attitudes towards philosophical wonder which developed after Plato, Aristotle, and their respective schools.[4] The principle of not wondering in order to avoid emotional disturbance seems to share certain similarities with Epicurean ideas about *ataraxia* (imperturbability) and Stoic concepts of *apatheia* (equanimity), as other texts from the first century BCE onwards which mention the ideal of wondering at nothing make clear. For example, Cicero mentions this principle in his discussion of how best to alleviate grief in book 3 of the *Tusculan Disputations*. He argues that because evil is harder to bear when it comes unexpectedly, it is best to exercise foresight and be prepared for all

---

[4] On Horace's eclectic drawing together of the teachings of various contemporary philosophical schools with this injunction against marvelling, and on this *Epistle* more generally, see e.g. Rudd (1993) 70, Mayer (1994) 157, McCarter (2015) 107–15; see also Armstrong (2004) 284–5 on the relation of the maxim *nil admirari* to Epicureanism.

8.1 *Thauma* as Beginning of Philosophy – or *Nil Admirari*?

emotional disturbances. A key means of achieving this is wondering at nothing when it occurs, and being prepared for anything that might come to pass (*nihil admirari cum acciderit, nihil, ante quam evenerit, non evenire posse arbitrari*, 3.30). Strabo, who was roughly contemporaneous with Horace, offers a similarly Stoically-inflected take on this principle in relation to the natural world in his *Geography*. In the first book, he tells us (1.3.16) that he will discuss multiple examples of wonder-provoking natural phenomena, such as the creation of a new island after the eruption of a volcano under the sea, to encourage 'not wondering at such changes' (πρὸς δὲ τὴν ἀθαυμαστίαν τῶν τοιούτων μεταβολῶν) and to 'put an end to astonishment' (παύσει τὴν ἔκπληξιν) through familiarity with these aspects of nature and geography. Later in the first century CE, Seneca the Younger offers yet another such Stoic view of the virtues of not marvelling, when he argues (*Epistulae* 8.5) that nothing except the soul is worthy of wonder, since 'nothing seems great to a soul which is itself great' (*nihil praeter animum esse mirabile, cui magno nihil magnum est*).

As these texts suggest, the place of wonder remained a matter of considerable debate in Roman philosophy. In fact, it is possible that Plato himself may have been reacting to certain aspects of this tradition of *not wondering* which were discussed by previous thinkers. In later discussions of the thought of Pythagoras and Democritus there is evidence that wonder's place in philosophical thinking was already an issue of concern. For example, Plutarch reports (*Moralia* 44b) that many people in his day misinterpret the Pythagorean saying that philosophy had given him the advantage of 'wondering at nothing' (τὸ μηδὲν θαυμάζειν). There are other extant testimonia of the atomist Democritus' supposed advice to wonder at nothing which again point to the possible emotional disturbance which *thauma* causes as potentially problematic. In the *De finibus*, Cicero notes that Democritus said that the study of natural philosophy should result in a tranquillity of mind or a freedom from fear, a form of happiness which he termed *euthumia* (contentment) or *athambia* (freedom from

Epilogue: *Thaumata Polla*

wonder/imperturbability).[5] Strabo associates similar terminology with Democritus, noting that not marvelling at things was approved of by the atomist (and other philosophers) since it is associated with a concomitant lack of emotional disturbance and therefore with imperturbability.[6] Although it is difficult to assess precisely how widespread such views were before Plato's time due to the paucity and lateness of the testimonia, it is nevertheless clear that the potentially disturbing emotional effects of *thauma* were a matter of some concern even before Plato was writing, and were certainly of even greater concern in the thinking of many later Hellenistic philosophical schools. In this study, I have inevitably been so concerned with marvelling at things that the notion of *not* marvelling – which seems to become more fully developed in the later Hellenistic philosophical schools – is not one that I, constrained both by necessities of space and chronological focus, have been able to investigate in any great detail. But the place of *thauma* as a key term of the philosophical tradition after Plato and Aristotle is certainly an area that would reward further study.

8.2 Mediating between Gods and Men, Nature and Artifice: Automata and *Thauma* in Hero of Alexandria's Mechanical Treatises

One aspect of change in the conception of what *thauma* is and does between the Archaic and the Hellenistic periods which this

---

[5] Cic. *Fin.* 5.29.87: *tamen ex illa investigatione naturae consequi volebat bono ut esset animo; id enim ille summum bonum* εὐθυμίαν *et saepe* ἀθαμβίαν *appellat, id est animum terrore liberum* (Nevertheless he [i.e. Democritus] desired that a cheerful disposition would ensue from his inquiries into nature, since that man says that contentment, and often imperturbability (that is, a mind free from terror), is the greatest good).

[6] *Geography* 1.3.21: ... τὴν ἀθαυμαστίαν ἡμῖν κατασκευάζειν ἐθέλοντες, ἣν ὑμνεῖ Δημόκριτος καὶ οἱ ἄλλοι φιλόσοφοι πάντες· παράκειται γὰρ τῷ ἀθαμβεῖ καὶ ἀταράχῳ καὶ ἀνεκπλήκτῳ (... wishing to equip us with a freedom from wonder, which Democritus goes on about, as do all the other philosophers, for freedom from wonder is mentioned along with freedom from emotional disturbance and freedom from fear). Two fragments preserved in Stobaeus also mention *athambia* as a concept associated with Democritus. See D295 LM = 68 B216 DK: σοφίη ἄθαμβος ἀξίη πάντων τιμιωτάτη οὖσα (wisdom that is free from wonder is worthy, since it is the most honourable thing of all) and D322 LM = 68 B215 DK: δίκης κῦδος γνώμης θάρσος καὶ ἀθαμβίη (the glory of justice is the courage and freedom from wonder of thought).

8.2 Automata and *Thauma*

study has drawn out is the degree of its relation to the divine and to the natural world. *Thauma* is often strongly associated with the gods in Archaic poetry, as an effect of divine epiphany or of divinely-crafted artworks, and of music, song and poetry which somehow involves divine presence. Over the course of the Classical period, the association of *thauma* with human action becomes gradually stronger, with a concomitant rise in the perception that man-made objects or actions which aim at provoking *thauma* somehow inherently produce potentially deceptive effects. This is not to say, however, that the association between *thauma* and the divine sphere ever disappeared entirely. Instead, the relation of wonder to the gods, and its position as a mediating factor in mortal interactions with them, only became more complicated as time passed, rather than ebbing away completely.

As we saw above in the discussion of the divine *thauma* in the *Laws*, by Plato's time the long cultural association of *thauma* with objects created by and relating to the divine goes hand in hand with the simultaneous association of wonder with man-made marvel-making (*thaumatopoiia* or *thaumatourgia*), an art which produces pure spectacles that aim primarily to delight and distract. The fact that the '*thauma* belonging to the gods' (θαῦμα ... θεῖον) which is used to reflect upon the workings of human psychology in the *Laws* is an automaton-like object is also significant because it hints at another transgression of conceptual boundaries to which wonder has always been linked: the line between nature and artifice. Since *thauma* is often conceived of as an effect caused by the extreme mimetic verisimilitude of inanimate artworks which somehow seem to turn into animate, living creatures, it is no surprise that the figure of the marvellous automatous object of craft should become a potent means of exploring the dividing line between nature and artifice more generally. Perhaps the predominant reason for the sense of wonder provoked by automata seems to be connected to the fact that the *cause* of such a mechanism's initial movement is unknown, often leading to speculation about divine or supernatural influence, or a sense of uncertainty about whether a given object – usually a simulacrum of a living being – really is a natural or artificial one. Certainly, the widespread

Epilogue: *Thaumata Polla*

suspicion of divine agency on seeing actions which appear to occur of their own accord makes sense, since in the absence of a known physical cause for a given event, its attribution to the gods provides a customary and reliable explanatory framework for what would otherwise be inexplicable.

This tendency to posit divine agency remains a potent aspect of the automaton's thaumatic appeal throughout antiquity. By the late Hellenistic period, there is evidence that *thauma* played a central role in theoretical discussions concerning the purpose, construction and effects of self-moving devices. In this period, automaton-building becomes a branch of the newly emerging discipline of mechanics. The significance of *thauma* in the development of this scientific discipline's own self-fashioning becomes clear when we examine the mechanical treatises of the engineer Hero of Alexandria.[7] Hero's dates have long been disputed, but he is now generally placed in the latter half of the first century CE, although his writings on automata-making draw heavily on the work of an earlier Hellenistic predecessor, Philo of Byzantium (late third/early second century BCE).[8] Two of Hero's treatises, *Peri Automatopoietikes* and *Pneumatica*, focus in particular on the construction of automatous devices. *Peri Automatopoietikes* is concerned entirely with the construction of two complex and very different automata: a moving altar of Dionysus, and a mechanical theatre in which the actions of a Sophoclean tragedy play out in miniature form. In contrast, Hero's *Pneumatica* contains descriptions of various smaller automatous mechanisms. *Thauma* occupies an important position in the proems of both treatises. At the beginning of *Peri Automatopoietikes*, Hero explains why the

---

[7] On the importance of *thauma* and its connection to philosophy in Hero's work, see Tybjerg (2003) 443–66. Berryman (2009) 52–3 disagrees with Tybjerg regarding the importance that actual theorists such as Hero placed on *thauma* in the practice of mechanics, arguing that wonder was valued purely as an effect on the audience rather than something to strive towards for its own sake. On the importance of *thauma* within the discipline of mechanics in antiquity see also Cambiano (1994) 617–21.

[8] On the question of Hero's dates, which are based on the possible mention of an eclipse dated to 62 CE in his treatise *Dioptra*, see Murphy (1995) 2 and Berryman (2009) 134. See Berryman (2009) 123–30 on Philo of Byzantium's work; cf. Roby (2016) 266–7 on the relationship between the work of Philo and Hero on automata.

8.2 Automata and *Thauma*

making of automata appealed to the engineers of the past (1.1):

τῆς αὐτοματοποιητικῆς πραγματείας ὑπὸ τῶν πρότερον ἀποδοχῆς ἠξιωμένης διά τε τὸ ποικίλον τῆς ἐν αὐτῇ δημιουργίας καὶ διὰ τὸ ἔκπληκτον τῆς θεωρίας.

The field of automata-making was thought worthy of approval by previous authorities on account of the variety of the craftsmanship which it entails and because of the astonishing nature of the sight it provides.

In fact, Hero goes on to inform us that those engineers of the past who crafted automata were actually known as 'wonder-workers on account of the astonishing nature of the sight created' (θαυματουργοὺς διὰ τὸ ἔκπληκτον τῆς θεωρίας, 1.7).[9] Hero speaks in similar terms in the proem of the first book of his *Pneumatica*, when he notes the potentially astonishing effects which can be created when the powers of air, earth, fire and water are properly harnessed (1.proem.12–17):

διὰ γὰρ συμπλοκῆς ἀέρος καὶ πυρὸς καὶ ὕδατος καὶ γῆς καὶ τῶν τριῶν στοιχείων ἢ καὶ τῶν τεσσάρων συμπλεκομένων ποικίλαι διαθέσεις ἐνεργοῦνται, αἱ μὲν ἀναγκαιοτάτας τῷ βίῳ τούτῳ χρείας παρέχουσαι, αἱ δὲ ἐκπληκτικόν τινα θαυμασμὸν ἐπιδεικνύμεναι.

For various compositions are put in action through the combination of air and fire and water and earth and the joining of three or four elements, some of which supply the most necessary needs of life, while others put an astonishing wonder on display.

It is precisely through the combination of the powers produced by these four elements that the automatic devices which Hero goes on to describe in the *Pneumatica* will produce their wondrous effects.

Indeed, when we look more closely at the function and effects of the automatous mechanical devices described, it becomes clear that the claims in each proem for the significance of *thauma* in the

---

[9] It is possible that such wondrous automata-making engineers of the past actually existed, since in addition to the mention of automatous *thaumata* in Plato's *Laws*, discussed above, there are several other mentions of the past production of possibly real fourth-century BCE automata: for example, automata are mentioned by Aristotle at *Metaph.* 983a12–14, *Gen. an.* 734b9–14, *De motu an.* 701b1–17; Archytas of Tarentum was said to have produced a flying dove (see Gell. *NA* 10.12.8–10); a slime-exuding snail which moved of its own accord was said to have been included in a procession of Demetrius of Phaleron (see Polyb. 12.13.9). On the difficulties of assessing these accounts as evidence for the production of actual automata see Berryman (2003) 344–69.

Epilogue: *Thaumata Polla*

mechanical sphere are indeed borne out. One thing that immediately strikes us is the fact that a significant number of the automata in both treatises are explicitly connected to temples or to religious ritual more broadly.[10] The most spectacular example is the first automaton described in *Peri Automatopoietikes* (3.1–19.5): a moving altar of Dionysus which contains a figure of the god standing before an altar within a miniature shrine, surrounded by maenads and with a panther at his feet. Once the engineer has performed the necessary preparations and placed the automaton down its amazing actions begin: 'after a short time, although everyone is stood far off, it will wheel itself out to a predetermined position, and when it is still the altar in front of Dionysus will blaze up. And either milk or water will be squirted out of Dionysus' thyrsus, and wine will flow out of his wine cup onto the panther lying at his feet.'[11] Nor are wondrous aural effects neglected as the automatic display continues, as Hero's description of what happens next makes clear: 'and the Bacchants will go around the shrine in circles dancing and the din of drums and cymbals will arise'.[12] Once these actions are completed the automaton will then come to a natural stop. Despite the extreme complexity of these mechanical actions, no further human intervention is needed once the automaton has been set in place, since every movement takes place as a result of a complex system of unseen weights, counterweights, pulleys and cords within the device itself. This inability to see the inner workings of the automaton is a crucial element of the *thauma* created, since from the observer's point of view the automaton appears to be operating through its own – or perhaps Dionysus' – agency.

There are numerous other examples of automatous mechanisms which aim to evoke an epiphanic and wondrous sense of divine presence in Hero's *Pneumatica*. Again, many of these devices are

---

[10] Cf. Lebrère (2015) 31–53 on our evidence for the use of automata in the earlier Hellenistic world as an aspect of the religious practice of Ptolemaic monarchs.

[11] *Peri Automatopoietikes* 4.1: ἀποστάντων μετ' οὐ πολὺν χρόνον ὑπάξει τὸ αὐτόματον ἐπί τινα ὡρισμένον τόπον. καὶ στάντος αὐτοῦ ἀνακαυθήσεται ὁ κατὰ πρόσθεν τοῦ Διονύσου βωμός. καὶ ἐκ μὲν τοῦ θύρσου τοῦ Διονύσου ἤτοι γάλα ἢ ὕδωρ ἐκπιτυσθήσεται, ἐκ δὲ τοῦ σκύφους οἶνος ἐκχυθήσεται ἐπὶ τὸν ὑποκείμενον πανθηρίσκον.

[12] *Peri Automatopoietikes* 4.2: αἱ δὲ περικύκλῳ Βάκχαι περιελεύσονται χορεύουσαι περὶ τὸν ναΐσκον. καὶ ἦχος ἔσται τυμπάνων καὶ κυμβάλων.

8.2 Automata and *Thauma*

connected to temples. For example, Hero describes how to construct altars with various automatic effects, including some with 'surrounding figures which pour libations when the fire is lit' (πυρὸς θυμιαθέντος τὰ παρακείμενα ζῴδια σπένδειν, 1.12), others where 'a snake hisses when the figures set up beside the altar pour a libation' (τὰ μὲν παριδρυμένα ζῴδια σπένδειν, τὸν δὲ δράκοντα συρίζειν, 2.21), and still others upon which 'dancing figures become visible when the fire is lit' (πυρὸς ἀνακαυθέντος ζῴδια καταφανήσεται χορεύοντα, 2.3). He even describes how to set up complex mechanisms for a small shrine which cause 'the doors to open up automatically when sacrifices are burnt, and close up again when the burnt offerings are extinguished' (θυσίας γινομένης τὰς θύρας αὐτομάτως ἀνοίγεσθαι, σβεσθείσης δὲ τῆς θυσίας πάλιν κλείεσθαι, 1.38). No doubt the visitor's marvelling response was meant to be stimulated further still by additional sensory effects, such as the automatic sounding of 'the din of trumpets on the opening of the temple doors' (θυρῶν ἀνοιγομένων ναοῦ σάλπιγγος ἦχος γίνεται, 1.17). Again, the idea was surely to create an impression of a divine epiphany as a succession of escalating visual and aural *thaumata* potentially greeted the visitor to a temple decked out with automata and automatous devices.

But marvellous automata relating to the religious sphere are not the only type of automatic device which Hero describes in these two treatises. The second half of the *Peri Automatopoietikes* moves on to another location which this study has shown to be a potent source of *thauma*: the theatre. Hero begins by telling us that his earlier Hellenistic predecessor, Philo of Byzantium, was well known for small-scale static automata which displayed versions of theatrical performances in miniature theatres placed atop small pillars (20.1–5), before going on to describe one such display: a performance of the story of Nauplius, possibly based on Sophocles' *Nauplius Pyrkaeus*.[13] Hero first outlines how these miniature theatrical automata operate by describing how the

---

[13] On the miniature theatre's probable depiction of Sophocles' *Nauplius Pyrkaeus* see Marshall (2003) 261–79; cf. also Beacham (2013) 15–39. On the plot and remaining fragments of this Sophoclean play see Sutton (1984) 82–4 and Lloyd-Jones (1996) 218–25.

Epilogue: *Thaumata Polla*

small-scale performances begin when the theatre doors open and the action proceeds to play of its own accord (21.1). A painted backdrop at the back of the theatre changes periodically as figures move on and off the stage and perform assorted movements to narrate the actions of the play (22.1). The first scene (22.3–4) depicts Greeks repairing their ships, and includes individual figures moving around and using saws, axes and hammers along with accompanying appropriate noises – a great din, Hero explicitly tells us, which is 'just as would occur in real life' (καθάπερ ἂν ἐπὶ τῆς ἀληθείας γίνοιτο, 22.4). Hero once again emphasises the realistic nature of the automatic performance when he notes that the next scene goes on to show the recently repaired Greek ships being launched and sailing across the field of vision with 'dolphins often swimming alongside, sometimes diving into the sea, and sometimes appearing above, just as in real life' (καθάπερ ἐπὶ τῆς ἀληθείας, 22.5), demonstrating that mimetic verisimilitude is clearly an important aspect of these miniature performances, despite their reduced scale. After the dolphins have appeared beside the ships, the sea turns stormy and Nauplius appears, holding a torch, with Athene beside him (22.5). The ships are then wrecked and Locrian Ajax is shown swimming; Athene appears above him on a crane and a lightning bolt (accompanied by the sound of thunder) falls upon the Greek hero, who disappears from view. The climax of the story thus reached, the theatre doors close, and the miniature theatrical performance is over (22.6).

As these examples from Hero's mechanical treatises suggest, the questions which developed over the course of the Classical period surrounding the relationship between *thauma* and the gods, *thauma* and the products of human craft, and the dividing line between natural and artificial *thaumata* continued to develop in tandem with developments in scientific and philosophical thinking in the later Hellenistic period. As a result, the development of actual automatous mechanisms is an ideal area to focus on as a means of thinking about the continuing importance of *thauma* in religious, philosophical and scientific discourse in the later Hellenistic and Roman worlds.

8.3 *Mera Miracula*: *Thauma*, Textuality and the Marvels of Aulus Gellius' *Noctes Atticae*

The development of textual collections of *thaumata*, and the idea of the text itself as something capable of provoking *thauma*, has been one of the key shifts in the concept of what a marvel is and does traced out in this book. This final section returns to the significance of the entextualisation of Greek marvels through an examination of the earliest extant description of the reading and use of Greek paradoxographical collections which remains to us from antiquity. This intriguing account of an encounter with Greek marvels appears in Aulus Gellius' *Noctes Atticae*, a second-century CE miscellanistic work containing, among many other things, varied discussions concerning Greek and Roman culture, literature, language, grammar, history and philosophy. Throughout this miscellanistic work Gellius frequently scatters autobiographical accounts and anecdotes relating to his own life and education, and also occasionally to the exploits of his group of learned and aristocratic friends. It is in one such autobiographical passage that he recounts a seemingly formative encounter with Greek paradoxographical collections when he describes himself stumbling across a battered and slightly seedy job lot of Greek book rolls at the stall of a bookseller in the Italian port town of Brundisium (9.4.1–5):

cum e Graecia in Italiam rediremus et Brundisium iremus egressique e naui in terram in portu illo inclito spatiaremur, quem Q. Ennius remotiore paulum, sed admodum scito uocabulo 'praepetem' appellauit, fasces librorum uenalium expositos uidimus. atque ego auide statim pergo ad libros. erant autem isti omnes libri Graeci miraculorum fabularumque pleni, res inauditae, incredulae, scriptores ueteres non paruae auctoritatis: Aristeas Proconnesius et Isigonus Nicaeensis et Ctesias et Onesicritus et Philostephanus et Hegesias; ipsa autem uolumina ex diutino situ squalebant et habitu aspectuque taetro erant. accessi tamen percontatusque pretium sum et, adductus mira atque insperata uilitate libros plurimos aere pauco emo eosque omnis duabus proximis noctibus cursim transeo; atque in legendo carpsi exinde quaedam et notaui mirabilia et scriptoribus fere nostris intemptata eaque his commentariis aspersi, ut qui eos lectitarit ne rudis omnino et ἀνήκοος inter istiusmodi rerum auditiones reperiatur.

When we were coming back to Italy from Greece and reached Brundisium, after disembarking from the ship onto land we were strolling about in that famous harbour, which Quintus Ennius – using an epithet which is somewhat obscure,

215

Epilogue: *Thaumata Polla*

but extremely erudite – called 'auspicious'.[14] We saw bundles of books placed out for sale. Straightaway I eagerly went over to the books. Now, all of these books were in Greek, full of marvellous stories, unheard of things, unbelievable things, by ancient writers of no little authority: Aristeas of Proconnesus and Isigonus of Nicaea and Ctesias and Onesicritus and Philostephanus and Hegesias. But the rolls themselves were filthy from long decay, repulsive in condition and appearance. Even so I approached and asked their price, and attracted by their marvellous and unexpected cheapness I bought very many books for very little money, and I went through them all swiftly over the course of two nights. And in the course of reading I picked out certain things from them and noted them down, marvellous things almost completely unexplored by Latin writers, and I scattered these things in these writings of mine, so that anyone who reads them will not be found to be completely uncultivated and ἀνήκοος [= not having heard something, ignorant] when hearing matters of this type.

One of the most striking aspects of the way in which the encounter with books containing marvels is framed here is the manner in which wonders are presented as distinctly Greek. For some reason, Gellius takes the time in the middle of his own miscellanistic collection to provide a supposedly autobiographical sketch which emphasises that the practice of composing books entirely full of wonder-provoking stories is something that Greek writers might do, but certainly not Roman ones. All of the texts Gellius purports to stumble across are in Greek, and they do not contain the occasional smattering of *mirabilia* – these books are absolutely stuffed full of marvels (*omnes libri Graeci miraculorum fabularumque pleni*). Furthermore, this kind of material is supposedly almost impossible to find in native Latin writers: unlike Greek writers, those fashioning Latin texts have scarcely attempted to compose this kind of material (*scriptoribus fere nostris intemptata*) – at least according to Gellius.

This emphasis on the Greekness of this marvellous material is clearly an attempted distancing effect on Gellius' part. The fact that the books are by ancient writers (*scriptores ueteres*), and that the rolls are themselves clearly so old that they have become filthy and decayed through long neglect (*uolumina ex diutino situ*

---

[14] Gellius had already cited the full Ennian line in which this word is found ('Brundisium encircled with a beautiful, auspicious (*praepete*) harbour' = Enn. *Ann.* 457) earlier on in his work during a lengthy discussion at *NA* 7.6 of use of the adjective *praepes*, which is usually applied to birds and literally means 'straight-flying' or 'swift-flying', but comes to mean 'well-favoured, auspicious' through its association with augury.

8.3 *Mera Miracula*

squalebant et habitu aspectuque taetro erant), serves a similar purpose. The suggestion seems to be that by the second century CE, marvels now truly belong to the Greek past. The undertone in this passage is clear: marvellous material is dangerous, alluring and potentially destructive. There is even perhaps a sense that the overindulgence in *mirabilia*, this concentration on wonder, has led to the decay of Greek culture itself. Are the squalid *uolumina* metonymic stand-ins here for Greek cultural power? Is an unhealthy interest in marvels to blame for the Greeks' cultural decay, at least from a Roman point of view?

At the same time, there is a strong sense in this passage that the marvellous Greek material is inherently ambivalent and double-edged: tawdry and cheap, as reflected in the physical condition and price of the books (*mira atque insperata uilitate libros plurimos aere pauco emo*), yet simultaneously authoritative and attractive, worthy of Gellius' enthusiasm as he rushes avidly forth to buy the rolls in bulk. After all, these writers are of no small authority (*non paruae auctoritatis*), as he himself admits. Indeed, each named author was well-known in antiquity for either ethnographic accounts of far-off places, travel narratives or historical writing which contained, at least in part, descriptions of natural and man-made wonders. The first writer mentioned by Gellius, Aristeas of Proconnesus, is a particularly ancient and authoritative figure: a semi-mythical epic poet, supposedly dating to the seventh century BCE, he was famous in antiquity both for his supposed shamanic ability to leave his body and travel to distant lands, and for the composition of an epic poem called the *Arimaspea*. This poem told of Aristeas' journey to the land of the Scythians and Issedones in the far north and described the things which he learned on his travels about the one-eyed Arimaspeans and Hyperboreans who inhabited the very furthest northern edges of the earth.[15] The most detailed and famous account of Aristeas' abilities and poem is found in another later account of a distant land, the Scythian *logos* in book four of Herodotus' *Histories* (4.13–16). But it was not the content of the *Arimaspea* alone

---

[15] See Bolton (1962) 119–41 for a discussion of Aristeas' life, and pp. 74–118 for a discussion of the potential form and content of the *Arimaspea*.

Epilogue: *Thaumata Polla*

which was considered to be marvellous in later periods. Aristeas himself also later appears as a marvel at the beginning of Apollonius Paradoxographus' marvel-collection.[16] The work of the other authors mentioned is also commonly cited in later paradoxographical collections. Isigonus of Nicaea, a paradoxographer of the first century BCE or first century CE, wrote a work entitled *Unbelievable Things* (Ἄπιστα), which had at least two books and seems to have contained marvels relating to the natural world (particularly wondrous bodies of water): this text was itself drawn upon and excerpted by later paradoxographers in their own marvel collections.[17] The doctor and historian Ctesias (late fifth century–early fourth century BCE) is the writer mentioned by Gellius who is best known to us in the modern world: his historical and ethnographic accounts of eastern lands, *Persica* and *Indica*, provided material for later paradoxographers as well.[18] Callimachus' pupil Philostephanus of Cyrene (third century BCE), as mentioned in Chapter 3, is known to have produced verse epigrams on paradoxographical themes which were cited in later marvel-collections.[19] The two other authors mentioned by Gellius are both known for writing histories about Alexander the Great which probably contained ethnographic marvels relating to the lands he visited on campaign: Hegesias of Magnesia (third century BCE) and Onesicritus of Astypalaea (c. 380–300 BCE), a man who we know actually accompanied Alexander on his eastern travels.

As well as provoking paradoxical feelings of attraction and repulsion, these book rolls stuffed with marvels also seem to call forth a peculiarly paradoxographical response in the author of the *Noctes* himself, as he plunges into these thaumatic Greek texts of the past and avidly seizes any appealing or relevant *mirabilia*

---

[16] See entry 2 in Apollonius Paradoxographus' *Marvellous Investigations* (= *PGR* 120–3).
[17] See *PGR* 146–8 for fragments and testimonia relating to Isigonus.
[18] For example, the Hellenistic paradoxographical collection of Antigonus of Carystus (see *PGR* 31–109 for the text of this marvel-collection) contains many marvels which ultimately derive from Ctesias' work: see e.g. entries 15b, 145, 150, 165–6; cf. entries 17 and 20 in Apollonius Paradoxographus' marvel-collection (see *PGR* 128–31). On the relation of Ctesias' work to Hellenistic paradoxography, see Nichols (2018) 3–16.
[19] See *PGR* 21–3 for testimonia and fragments relating to Philostephanus' paradoxographical output. On Hellenistic verse paradoxography see Chapter 3, Section 1.

8.3 *Mera Miracula*

needed to adorn his own work. Gellius is careful to present himself as the ultimate connoisseur of marvels, a perfect paradoxographer exercising necessary Roman discernment to neuter the potentially dangerous and distracting power of the Greek *thaumata* he has stumbled across. He knows precisely how to properly prune and cull this material (*in legendo carpsi exinde*); he knows which marvels need to be noted down (*notaui mirabilia*); he knows how and where and when to scatter and arrange marvels in his own writings (*eaque his commentariis aspersi*). In fact, the description of his method here recalls the earlier discussion of his wider methodology in the preface of the *Noctes*. There Gellius tells us that unlike many previous writers of miscellanistic collections, 'especially Greek ones' (*maxime Graeci*), who after eagerly reading many varied accounts ... indiscriminately swept things together, aiming at sheer quantity alone' (*sine cura discriminis solam copiam sectati conuerrebant*, *NA* pr. 11), he himself excerpts and reports only a few choice things (*modica ex his eaque sola accepi*) which might either lead others towards a further 'desire for learning' (*eruditionis cupidinem*) or 'save men from an undoubtedly shameful and uncultivated ignorance of important matters and words' (*homines ... a turpi certe agrestique rerum atque uerborum imperitia uindicarent*, *NA* pr. 12). This idea that Gellius' arts of excerption are able to rescue his readers from the spectre of shameful ignorance is repeated once again in the anecdote about his encounter with marvellous Greek texts at Brundisium when the reader is assured that the author's judicious sprinkling of choice Greek marvels in the Latin *Noctes* will ensure that none of his readers will ever run the risk of being considered 'completely uncultivated and ἀνήκοος (ignorant)'.

At the opening of this anecdote Gellius thus presents himself as the ideal mediating lens through which marvellous Greek *thaumata*, shorn of any particularly unappealing, unbelievable or uneducative aspects through a careful process of selection, filtration and refinement, might be enjoyed by the curious and cultivated Roman reader. In fact, the very setting of the anecdote hints at the significance of issues of cultural mediation which the appearance of marvellous Greek texts will go on to raise, since Brundisium, as the main Italian port through which Greece was

Epilogue: *Thaumata Polla*

accessed in antiquity, is a natural setting for an encounter which mediates between the two cultures of Greece and Rome. Even the throwaway reference to Quintus Ennius – an undoubtedly learned but seemingly redundant detail at first glance – is relevant to the ideas of cultural mediation and translation which Gellius raises through his encounter with Greek *thaumata* in this passage, since just as Ennius famously brought hexameter epic from Greece to Rome, Gellius too will transfigure a Greek mode of writing into its appropriate Roman form. In this sense, then, Brundisium really is an 'auspicious' place, as the Ennian epithet which Gellius uses to describe the port suggests, since this seemingly chance encounter with Greek marvels has the potential to both elevate the author of the *Noctes Atticae* to the head of the Latin miscellanistic tradition and position him as a new sort of Ennian heir: 'As Ennius translated Greek hexameters into Latin epic, I will transform distracting Greek *thaumata* into useful and refined Latin *mirabilia*', Gellius almost seems to say to us in this passage.[20]

But is Gellius' claim to innovation true? Had native Latin writers really resisted the lure of the Greek marvellous before Gellius came along to put them straight? The answers to these questions become clearer as we continue through the passage and discover which specific Greek *thaumata* have been selected and recorded for the edification of Roman readers over the course of Gellius' two nights of reading. Gellius begins (9.4.6) with material about strange and wonderful distant peoples, such as the Scythian cannibals called Anthropophagoi, the Arimaspians with one eye in the middle of their foreheads and another unnamed far-northern people whose feet are turned backwards. After mentioning two other strange peoples – men from Albania whose hair turns white in childhood and who can see better in the night than the day, and the Sauromatae, who are accustomed to eating only once every two days – Gellius suddenly casually mentions another writer's

---

[20] Brundisium is of course already an extremely resonant location in Latin literature, which helps to explain why Gellius refers to it as *portu illo inclito* at the opening of 9.4 (see Lindermann (2006) 122). The most famous extant examples of the port's importance in the Latin literary tradition are probably its place as the supposed location of Pacuvius' birth and Virgil's death (see Gowers (2012) 212–13), and as the end point of Horace's journey with Maecenas in the final line of *Sat.* 1.5 (*Brundisium longae finis chartaeque uiaeque est*, 104).

8.3 *Mera Miracula*

name in a way that might make us suddenly stop and wonder (9.4.7):

id etiam in isdem libris scriptum offendimus, quod postea in libro quoque Plinii Secundi *naturalis historiae* septimo legi, esse quasdam in terra Africa hominum familias uoce atque lingua effascinantium.

Furthermore, in those same books I came upon this account, which afterwards I also read in the seventh book of Pliny's *Natural History*, that in the land of Africa there are certain bands of men who perform enchantments with their voices and tongues.

Seeing as Gellius has already taken such pains to insist that the type of marvellous material contained within the Greek book rolls he stumbled across at Brundisium has been 'almost completely unexplored by Latin writers' (*scriptoribus fere nostris intemptata*, 9.4.5), it seems strange that he should here mention that Pliny the Elder, a fellow Latin writer, had also already shown a similar interest in precisely the same Greek *thaumata*. But what is even stranger is the fact that every marvel Gellius has so far mentioned in this passage, including those listed above, is also found in the seventh book of Pliny's *Natural History*, reported in precisely the same order.[21] In fact, the most likely scenario seems to be that Gellius has not stumbled across any Greek books in Brundisium at all, but has excerpted all of this material from a single book of Pliny.[22] In Gellius' world, despite his protestations, marvels are firmly Roman already.[23]

---

[21] See Plin. *HN* 7.9–26. On Gellius' dependence on Pliny at *NA* 9.4, see Holford-Strevens (1988) 30–1, 50–1, Gunderson (2009) 185, Keulen (2009) 200–1 and Howley (2018) 114–20, 123–34. On Gellius' contested relationship with Pliny in general, see Holford-Strevens (1988) 121–2, Keulen (2004) 238–41, Gunderson (2009) 181–5 and Howley (2018) 112–56. On Pliny's pronounced interest in *mirabilia* and wonder in the *HN* see Beagon (1992) 8–11, (2005) 17–24, (2007) 19–40 and (2011) 80–6, Conte (1994) 85–6, Carey (2003) 84–101, Murphy (2004) 18–22, Naas (2004) 253–64 and (2011) 57–70, Woolf (2011) 81–5.

[22] See Zetzel (1981) 59 and Holford-Strevens (1982) 65–8 on the seemingly fictional nature of the anecdote at *NA* 9.4.

[23] In fact, Roman interest in collecting marvellous material goes back at least to Varro and Cicero: the former is said (at Macrob. *Sat.* 3.15.8) to have written a book entitled *Gallus de admirandis*; the latter supposedly wrote a book of marvels entitled *Admiranda*, which is cited twice in Plin. *HN* 31.12 (*Cicero in admirandis posuit*) and 31.51 (*quod admirandis suis inseruit M. Cicero*). Pliny also made great use of the work on marvels by his contemporary Mucianus in the *HN*: see Ash (2007) 1–17 on the contents and purpose of his work.

Epilogue: *Thaumata Polla*

In the end, Gellius' attempt to distance Roman culture from marvellous modes of Greek writing does not stand up to much scrutiny at all. But the way in which he characterises the wonders and the feeling of wonder as distinctively Greek in this account certainly suggests that the writing of marvels is something of a contested practice by this period. This is surely partly because, by the time Gellius is writing the *Noctes*, the already-rich textual tradition of wonder has made marvel-writing into an extremely contested mode which almost by definition raises questions of fictionality and belief. After all, is it really ever possible to trust the authority of previous writers fully when it comes to 'unheard of things, unbelievable things' (*res inauditae, incredulae*, 9.4)? Perhaps it is no wonder then that by second century CE it is not only the content of the material Gellius describes which is beyond belief but even his marvellous description of an autoptic encounter with the marvel-writing of the past.

One of the most obvious reasons why Gellius' attitude towards *mirabilia* is so ambivalent in the *Noctes* is the fact that, at certain moments, his own work seems to come perilously close to assuming the paradoxographical form of marvel-writing. This risk is clearest a few books later in the *Noctes*, when entextualised marvels make a further appearance in another Gellian autobiographical anecdote. This narrative relates to the composition of the *Noctes* itself (14.6.1–3):

> homo nobis familiaris, in litterarum cultu non ignobilis magnamque aetatis partem in libris uersatus, 'adiutum' inquit 'ornatumque uolo ire *Noctes* tuas' et simul dat mihi librum grandi uolumine doctrinae omnigenus, ut ipse dicebat, praescatentem, quem sibi elaboratum esse ait ex multis et uariis et remotis lectionibus, ut ex eo sumerem, quantum liberet rerum memoria dignarum. accipio cupidus et libens, tamquam si copiae cornum nactus essem, et recondo me penitus, ut sine arbitris legam. atque ibi scripta erant, pro Iuppiter, mera miracula: quo nomine fuerit, qui primus 'grammaticus' appellatus est; et quot fuerint Pythagorae nobiles, quot Hippocratae; et cuiusmodi fuisse Homerus dicat in Vlixis domo λαύρην; et quam ob causam Telemachus cubans iunctim sibi cubantem Pisistratum non manu adtigerit, sed pedis ictu excitarit; et Euryclia Telemachum quo genere claustri incluserit; et quapropter idem poeta rosam non norit, oleum ex rosa norit.

> A friend of mine, not unknown on the literary scene and well-versed with it for the majority of his life, said to me: 'I'd like to help you polish up your *Nights*',

8.3 *Mera Miracula*

straightaway presenting me with a book roll of massive bulk, bubbling over, as he himself put it, with knowledge of every sort. He said that he had put it together from wide and varied and recondite reading, and that I should borrow from it as much as I thought worthy of recording. I received the book greedily and gladly, as though I'd obtained the horn of plenty, and hid myself away so that I could read it without witnesses. But – by Jupiter! – the things that were written in it were pure marvels! The name of the first man who was called a 'grammarian'; how many famous men were named Pythagoras, and how many were named Hippocrates; what sort of thing Homer meant when he talked about the λαυρή (narrow passage) in Odysseus' house;[24] the reason why Telemachus, while lying down, woke up Pisistratus, who was lying next to him, by striking him with his foot rather than touching him with his hand;[25] with what kind of bolt Eurycleia shut Telemachus in;[26] and for what reason the same poet has no knowledge of roses, but does know about rose oil.[27]

Gellius' list of 'pure marvels' (*mera miracula*) does not end here. He continues in a similar vein (14.6.3–4): the massive book roll also contained the names of the companions of Odysseus whom Scylla snatched away and tore apart, as well as meditations on a much-debated topic of Homeric geography, the question of whether Odysseus sailed around the 'inner' (i.e. the Mediterranean) or 'outer' sea (i.e. the Atlantic) during his wanderings. The book roll even includes examples of Homeric verses which are isopsephic (i.e. consecutive lines which, when each letter in the line is assigned a numeric value, add up to the same total), Homeric acrostics spelling out the names of characters, and lines in which each word is a syllable longer than the preceding word.[28] Other sorts of intractable peculiarities relating to the Homeric texts are not excluded: for example, Menelaus' description in the *Odyssey* of his encounter with astonishingly fertile Libyan ewes during his wanderings after the Trojan War is transformed into a zoological question about the ability of livestock to breed three times within a year, while the precise ordering of the multiple layers of Achilles' famous shield in the *Iliad* becomes yet another problem to be discussed.[29]

---

[24] *Od.* 22.128, 22.137.
[25] *Od.* 15.44–5.
[26] *Od.* 1.441–2.
[27] *Il.* 23.186.
[28] On such phenomena in the Homeric poems and ancient responses to them see Hilton (2011) and (2013).
[29] See *Od.* 4.86 on Libya's sheep: τρὶς γὰρ τίκτει μῆλα τελεσφόρον εἰς ἐνιαυτόν (for three times the sheep give birth in the course of a full year). This claim of hyper-fertility really

Epilogue: *Thaumata Polla*

There are two things which immediately strike us about the *miracula* that Gellius lists here. Almost all of these 'marvels' are typical questions of ancient literary scholarship, and all relate to Greek figures or texts; most, in fact, relate to the Homeric poems. In the Homeric scholia, and in other extant testimonia of ancient debates in Homeric scholarship, we find evidence that many of the issues which Gellius here mentions were actually discussed in ancient scholarship on the Homeric text. For example, the seemingly irrelevant question of why Telemachus prods Pisistratus awake with his foot rather than his hand really does seem to have exercised Alexandrian critics. In the remaining scholia on *Odyssey* 15.45 it is suggested that certain critics may have considered the line to be spurious because it does not seem fitting for Telemachus to use such a forceful action, even if the expression 'roused with his foot' (λὰξ ποδὶ κινήσας) is also found in the *Iliad* (10.158) when Nestor kicks the sleeping Diomedes awake – an action which the scholiast argues is fitting because old age renders Nestor unable to bend down and touch Diomedes with his hand; for Telemachus, however, there is no such excuse.[30] The other questions mentioned by Gellius also attracted comment among Homeric scholars and commentators to a greater or lesser degree. This ranged from clarification of the meaning of specific unusual words and comment on stylistic aspects of the text, to infamous full-blown critical debates between famous Homeric scholars, such as Aristarchus and Crates' argument about the geographical

---

did cause ancient critics to raise their eyebrows: see e.g. Σ ad. *Od.* 4.86. The wondrous hyper-fertility of Libya is something other writers comment upon in antiquity: see e.g. Hdt 4.199 on the three harvest seasons of Cyrene, a phenomenon which he declares 'worthy of wonder' (ἀξίας θώματος). The ordering of the layers of Achilles' shield was another cause of comment and dispute in ancient Homeric scholarship: the problem centred on *Il.* 20.267–72, which tells us that Aeneas' spear passed through two layers of bronze before stopping in the third layer, made of gold, and leaving two layers of tin untouched. The question is how or why the spear would be stopped by the (outer?) layer of gold while managing to penetrate the harder or more internal bronze layers. Aristotle raises this as a Homeric question at *Poet.* 1461a31–5 but provides no answer. Later Hellenistic Homeric scholars were equally troubled by such a seeming incongruity: Aristarchus perhaps athetised the lines as a result (see Σ ad. *Il.* 20.269–72). For the responses of modern critics to this problem see Edwards (1991) 323.

[30] See Σ ad. *Od.* 15.45; the issue is also mentioned at Σ ad. *Il.* 10.158. The scholiast's reasoning concerning Nestor's old age is obviously nonsensical given his continued vigour in Iliadic battle. See also further discussion of the Odyssean passage at Hoekstra (1989) 233–4.

8.3 *Mera Miracula*

location, and by extension the historical accuracy, of Odysseus' wanderings.[31]

How does Gellius respond to this book overflowing with Greek literary scholarship? Given that by this point in the *Noctes* his persona as an eager yet discriminating literary scholar is already well-developed, we might expect him to approve of his friend's learned book. But the previous designation of the book's contents as 'pure marvels' (*mera miracula*) turns out to have been a hint at Gellius' forthcoming negative reaction (14.6.5):

haec atque item alia multa istiusmodi scripta in eo libro fuerunt. quem cum statim properans redderem, 'ὄναιό σου,' inquam 'doctissime uirorum, ταύτης τῆς πολυμαθίας et librum hunc opulentissimum recipe nil prosus ad nostras paupertinas litteras congruentem'.

These things and many other things of the same kind were written in that book. And rushing to return it to him immediately I said: 'May you profit from this display of wide knowledge, most learned man! But take back this most extravagant book: it has nothing at all in common with my poor writings'.

Gellius' response makes clear that his description of the book's contents as 'pure marvels' was far from a positive one. But this reaction also carries a hint of irony. After all, the *Noctes* is full of discussions similar to the ones which Gellius disdains in this instance. There is, however, one important difference between the discussions in the marvel-filled book belonging to the learned literary friend and the *Noctes* itself: Gellius' literary discussions almost invariably relate to Latin rather than Greek texts.[32]

---

[31] For discussions of the specific Homeric words and problems mentioned by Gellius see e.g. Σ ad. *Od.* 22.128, which defines the word λαυρή as a 'narrow passage'; Σ ad. *Od.* 1.441–2 for traces of a long discussion of the meaning of each word which relates to fastening the door shut at *Od.* 1.441–2; Σ ad. *Il.* 23.186 on Homer's mention of rose oil. Traces of this famous debate between Aristarchus and Crates concerning the location of Odysseus' wanderings survive in later ancient texts: book one of Strabo's *Geography* is particularly important in this regard. On later discussions and debates concerning Odysseus' wanderings see e.g. Porter (1992) 67–114, Romm (1992) 186–90, Buonajuto (1996) 1–8 and Lightfoot (2019b) 671–97.

[32] See e.g. Gellius' discussions of textual issues/issues of interpretation/anecdotes about Virgil: *NA* 1.21, 2.6, 2.16, 5.8, 6.20, 7.6, 8.5, 9.9, 9.10, 10.16, 13.27, 16.6, 17.10. Gellius very rarely weighs in on issues relating to Homer or the Homeric text. He does so most explicitly at 3.11, where he criticises Accius for arguing that Hesiod was older than Homer. The emphasis here, however, is on proving Accius wrong, rather than genuinely inquiring about the relative dates of Homer and Hesiod.

Epilogue: *Thaumata Polla*

We see once again that for Gellius, wonder and the marvellous have become terms which represent complex responses to the type of textual material in which his own literary output is grounded. On the one hand, he is clearly trying to distance his own miscellanistic text from the style and content of other contemporary works, though it is also clear that his own writing is in many ways very similar. Even typical questions of textual scholarship can now be labelled as 'marvels' of a sort in the *Noctes*; it is striking that in this chapter we see the same combination of eager desire and enthusiasm at the opportunity to experience a new text as Gellius takes the book from his friend 'greedily and gladly' (*cupidus et libens*), and then eventual disgust and rejection felt towards these textual marvels, just as the marvel-filled Greek texts which he supposedly found in Brundisium are first consumed 'greedily' (*auide*, 9.4.2), before a seemingly inevitable sense of 'disgust' (*taedium*, 9.4.12) grips Gellius once he has noted down the *thaumata* contained within the Greek book rolls.[33] By the time Gellius writes the *Noctes*, wonder has become a way of thinking about how texts relate to other texts, and about the idea of the text itself as a kind of marvel.

This study has suggested that it is in the Hellenistic paradoxographical collection that wonder can first explicitly be seen as an important prism through which to view the means by which relationships between literary texts, and the effects of these relationships, are constructed. As Gellius' *Noctes Atticae* suggests, these relationships become only more complicated once they are transfigured and transformed within the traditions of Latin literature and scholarship. It is no accident that Gellius in his own work configures the marvellous as an intensely Greek textual experience, even when other Roman writers like Pliny are the sources of the information he is specifically labelling as wondrous and purely Hellenic. The Greekness of the concept of wonder in Latin texts is an issue that remains to be explored. This book has shown that some of the most familiar texts from the Archaic to early

---

[33] See also *NA* 10.12.1–6, where a similar sense of 'disgust' (*pertaesum est*) overcomes Gellius when he records some *mirabilia* which Pliny the Elder attributed to the Greek philosopher Democritus. On Gellius' attitude towards Pliny and *mirabilia* at *NA* 10.12 see e.g. Gunderson (2009) 183–4 and Howley (2018) 135–42.

8.3 *Mera Miracula*

Hellenistic period provide new perspectives on Greek culture itself when viewed through the lens of wonder. The new perspectives on Greek and Roman culture that can be reached by assessing the impact of the Greek marvellous on Rome – and vice versa – remain to be examined.

BIBLIOGRAPHY

Acosta-Hughes, B. and Stephens, S. A. (2012) *Callimachus in Context: From Plato to the Augustan Poets*. Cambridge.

Allan, W. (1999–2000) 'Euripides and the Sophists: Society and the Theatre of War'. *ICS* 24–5: 145–56.

Allison, J. W. (1997) *Word and Concept in Thucydides*. Atlanta, GA.

Alonso Troncoso, V. (2013) 'The Diadochi and the Zoology of Kingship: The Elephants', in Alonso Troncoso, V. and Anson, E. M. (eds.), *After Alexander: The Time of the Diadochi (323–281 BC)*. Oxford: 254–70.

Amati, M. F. (2010) 'Meton's Star-City: Geometry and Utopia in Aristophanes' *Birds*'. *CJ* 105: 213–27.

Angelucci, M. (2014) 'Water and Paradoxography: Polemon's Work Περὶ τῶν ἐν Σικελίᾳ θαυμαζομένων ποταμῶν'. *OTerr* 12: 9–25.

Annas, J. (1981) *An Introduction to Plato's Republic*. Oxford.

Annas, J. (2011) 'Changing from Within: Plato's Later Political Thinking'. The Corbett Lecture, University of Cambridge, November 2011. [Unpublished lecture, online]. Available at: www.u.arizona.edu/~jannas/Forthcoming/corbett.pdf [Accessed Sept. 2020].

Armstrong, D. (2004) 'Horace's *Epistles* I and Philodemus', in Armstrong, D. (ed.), *Vergil, Philodemus, and the Augustans*. Austin: 267–98.

Arrowsmith, W. (1973) 'Aristophanes' *Birds*: The Fantasy Politics of Eros'. *Arion* 1: 119–67.

Ash, R. (2007) 'The Wonderful World of Mucianus', in Bispham, E. and Rowe, G. (eds.), *'Vita vigilia est': Essays in Honour of Barbara Levick*. London: 1–17.

Asper, M. (2005) 'Group Laughter and Comic Affirmation: Aristophanes' *Birds* and the Political Function of Old Comedy'. *Hyperboreus* 11: 5–30.

Austin, C. and Bastianini, G. (2002) *Posidippi Pellaei quae supersunt omnia*. Milan.

Austin, C. and Olson, S. D. (2004) *Aristophanes: Thesmophoriazusae*. Oxford.

Avery H. C. (1973) 'Themes in Thucydides' Account of the Sicilian Expedition'. *Hermes* 101: 1–13.

Balme, D. M. (1972) *Aristotle: De partibus animalium I and De generatione animalium I*. Oxford.

Baragwanath, E. (2012) 'The Wonder of Freedom: Xenophon on Slavery', in Hobden, F. and Tuplin, C. J. (eds.), *Xenophon: Ethical Principles and Historical Enquiry*. Leiden: 631–63.

Bibliography

Barrett, W. S. (1964) *Hippolytos*. Oxford.
Barth, H. (1968) 'Zur Bewertung und Auswahl des Stoffes durch Herodot'. *Klio* 50: 93–110.
Bartoňková, D. (1999) 'Il prosimetrum nella Paradossografia Greca'. *Sborník prací Filozofické fakulty brněnské university* 3–4: 63–7.
Beacham, R. (2013) 'Heron of Alexandria's "Toy Theatre" Automaton: Reality, Allusion and Illusion', in Reilly, K. (ed.), *Theatre, Performance and Analogue Technology: Historical Interfaces and Intermedialities*. Basingstoke: 15–39.
Beagon, M. (1992) *Roman Nature: The Thought of Pliny the Elder*. Oxford.
Beagon, M. (2005) *The Elder Pliny on the Human Animal: Natural History Book 7*. Oxford.
Beagon, M. (2007) 'Situating Nature's Wonders in Pliny's *Natural History*', in Bispham, E. and Rowe, G. (eds.), *'Vita vigilia est': Essays in Honour of Barbara Levick*. London: 19–40.
Beagon, M. (2011) 'The Curious Eye of the Elder Pliny', in Gibson, R. K. and Morello, R. (eds.), *Pliny the Elder: Themes and Contexts*. Leiden: 71–88.
Becker A. S. (1992) 'Reading Poetry Through a Distant Lens: Ecphrasis, Ancient Greek Rhetoricians, and the Pseudo-Hesiodic Shield of Heracles'. *AJP* 113: 5–24.
Becker, A. S. (1995) *The Shield of Achilles and the Poetics of Ekphrasis*. Lanham, MD.
Beekes, R. S. P. (2010) *Etymological Dictionary of Greek*. Leiden.
Belfiore, E. S. (1992) 'Aristotle and Iphigenia', in Rorty, A. O. (ed.), *Essays on Aristotle's Poetics*. Princeton: 359–77.
Bernabé, A. (2012) 'The Sixth Definition (*Sophist* 226a–231 c): Transposition of Religious Language', in Bossi, B. and Robinson, T. M. (eds.), *Plato's Sophist Revisited*. Berlin and Boston: 41–56.
Berrey, M. (2017) *Hellenistic Science at Court*. Berlin.
Berryman, S. A. (2003) 'Ancient Automata and Mechanical Explanation'. *Phronesis* 48.4: 344–69.
Berryman, S. A. (2009) *The Mechanical Hypothesis in Ancient Greek Natural Philosophy*. Cambridge.
Bianchi, O and Thévenaz, O. (2004) *Conceptions et représentations de l'extraordinaire dans le monde antique*. Bern.
Bing, P. (1995) 'Ergänzungsspiel in the Epigrams of Callimachus'. *A&A* 41: 115–31.
Bing, P. (2003) 'The Unruly Tongue: Philitas of Cos as Scholar and Poet'. *CP* 98.4: 330–48.
Bing, P. (2005) 'The Politics and Poetics of Geography in the Milan Posidippus Section One: On Stones (AB 1–20)', in Gutzwiller, K. J. (ed.), *The New Posidippus: A Hellenistic Poetry Book*. Oxford: 119–40.
Bishop, T. (1996) *Shakespeare and the Theatre of Wonder*. Cambridge.
Bobrick, E. (1991) 'Iphigeneia Revisited: *Thesmophoriazusae* 1160–1225'. *Arethusa* 24: 67–76.

Bibliography

Bolton, J. D. P. (1962) *Aristeas of Proconnesus*. Oxford.
Bowe, G. S. (2017) '*Thaumata* in Aristotle's *Metaphysics* A'. *Acta Classica* 60: 50–72.
Bowen, A. J. (1998) *Xenophon: Symposium*. Warminster.
Bowie, A. M. (1993) *Aristophanes: Myth, Ritual, and Comedy*. Cambridge.
Broadie, S. (2012) 'A Science of First Principles *Metaphysics* A 2', in Steel, C. and Primavesi, O. (eds.), *Aristotle's Metaphysics Alpha: Symposium Aristotelicum*. Oxford: 43–66.
Bruno, V. J. (1977) *Form and Colour in Greek Painting: A Study of the Colour Harmonies and Shading Techniques Used by the Major Painters of Ancient Greece*. New York.
Brunschwig, J. (2003) 'Revisiting Plato's Cave', in Cleary, J. J. and Gurtler, G. M. (eds.), *Proceedings of the Boston Area Colloquium in Ancient Philosophy 19*. Leiden: 145–77.
Budelmann, F. (2019) 'Dare to Believe: Wonder, Trust and the Limitations of Human Cognition in Euripides' *Iphigenia in Tauris*', in Braund, D., Hall, E. and Wyles, R. (eds.), *Ancient Theatre and Performance Culture Around the Black Sea*. Cambridge: 289–304.
Bundy, E. L. (1986) *Studia Pindarica*. Berkeley.
Buonajuto, A. (1996) 'L'ἐξωκεανισμός dei viaggi di Odisseo in Cratete e negli Alessandrini'. *A&R* 41: 1–8.
Burkert, W. (1983) *Homo Necans: The Anthropology of Ancient Greek Sacrificial Ritual and Myth*. Translated by Peter Bing. Berkeley.
Burnett, A. P. (1971) *Catastrophe Survived: Euripides' Plays of Mixed Reversal*. Oxford.
Burnyeat, M. F. (1999) 'Culture and Society in Plato's *Republic*'. *Tanner Lectures on Human Values* 20: 215–324.
Burstein, S. M. (1989) *Agatharchides of Cnidus: On the Erythraean Sea*. London.
Calame, C. (1996) *Thésée et l'imaginaire athénien: légende et culte en Grèce antique*. Lausanne.
Cambiano, G. (1994) 'Automaton'. *StudStor* 35: 613–33.
Cambiano, G. (2012) 'The Desire to Know *Metaphysics* A 1', in Steel, C. and Primavesi, O. (eds.), *Aristotle's Metaphysics Alpha: Symposium Aristotelicum*. Oxford: 1–42.
Cambitoglou, A. and Turner, M. (eds.) (2008) *Corpus Vasorum Antiquorum: Australia [Fasc. 1]. The Nicholson Museum, The University of Sydney: The Red Figure Pottery of Apulia*. Sydney.
Campbell, M. B. (1999) *Wonder and Science: Imagining Worlds in Early Modern Europe*. Ithaca, NY.
Cappelletto, C. (2011) 'The Puppet's Paradox: An Organic Prosthesis'. *RES: Anthropology and Aesthetics* 59/60: 325–36.
Carey, S. (2003) *Pliny's Catalogue of Culture: Art and Empire in the Natural History*. Oxford.

Bibliography

Casadesús Bordoy, F. (2012) 'Why Is it So Difficult to Catch a Sophist? Pl. *Sph.* 218d3 and 261a5', in Bossi, B. and Robinson, T. M. (eds.), *Plato's Sophist Revisited*. Berlin and Boston: 15–27.
Càssola, F. (1975) *Inni omerici*. Milan.
Casson, L. (1993) 'Ptolemy II and the Hunting of African Elephants'. *TAPA* 123: 247–60.
Cave, T. (1988) *Recognitions: A Study in Poetics*. Oxford.
Clarke, K. (2018) *Shaping the Geography of Empire: Man and Nature in Herodotus' Histories*. Oxford.
Clay, D. (1992) 'Plato's First Words'. *YCS* 29: 113–29.
Clay J. S. (2006) *The Politics of Olympus: Form and Meaning in the Major Homeric Hymns*. 2nd ed. London.
Coleridge, S. T. (1817) *Biographia Literaria*. London.
Collard, C. and Cropp, M. (2008) *Euripides, Fragments: Aegeus-Meleager*. Cambridge, MA.
Conacher, D. J. (1998) *Euripides and the Sophists: Some Dramatic Treatments of Philosophical Ideas*. London.
Conte, G. B. (1994) *Genres and Readers*. Baltimore.
Cornford, F. M. (1907) *Thucydides Mythistoricus*. London.
Cozzoli, A.-T. (2011) 'The Poet as a Child', in Acosta-Hughes, B., Lehnus, L. and Stephens, S. A. (eds.), *Brill's Companion to Callimachus*. Leiden: 407–28.
Cropp, M. J. (1997) 'Notes on Euripides, *Iphigenia in Tauris*'. *ICS* 22: 25–41.
Cropp, M. J. (2000) *Euripides: Iphigenia in Tauris*. Warminster.
Csapo, E. (2003) 'The Dolphins of Dionysus', in Csapo, E. and Miller, M. C. (eds.), *Poetry, Theory, Praxis: The Social Life of Myth, Word and Image in Ancient Greece. Essays in Honour of William J. Slater*. Oxford: 69–98.
Csapo, E. and Miler, M. C. (2007) 'General Introduction', in Csapo, E. and Miller, M. C. (eds.), *The Origins of Theater in Ancient Greece and Beyond: From Ritual to Drama*. Cambridge: 1–38.
Cunningham, V. (2007) 'Why Ekphrasis?' *CP* 102: 57–71.
Cursaru, G. (2012) 'Les sandales d'Hermès III: enquête sur les traces des σάνδαλα dans l'*Hymne homérique à Hermès*'. *Mouseion* 12: 17–50.
D'Alessio, G. (2013) '"The Name of the Dithyramb": Diachronic and Diatopic Variations', in Kowalzig, B. and Wilson, P. (eds.), *Dithyramb in Context*. Oxford: 113–32.
Danek, G. (2001) 'Das Staunen des Chores: Götter und Menschen im *Ion* des Euripides'. *WS* 114: 47–58.
D'Angour, A. (2011) *The Greeks and the New: Novelty in Ancient Greek Imagination and Experience*. Cambridge.
Danzig, G. (2013) 'Plato's *Charmides* as a Political Act: Apologetics and the Promotion of Ideology'. *GRBS* 53.3: 486–519.
Danzig, G. (2014) 'The Use and Abuse of Critias: Conflicting Portraits in Plato and Xenophon'. *CQ* 64: 507–24.

Bibliography

Daston, L. and Park, K. (1998) *Wonders and the Order of Nature, 1150–1750*. New York.

Davies, M. (1998) 'Euripides' *Electra*: The Recognition Scene Again'. *CQ* 48: 389–403.

Dearden, C. W. (1995) 'Pots, Tumblers and Phlyax Vases', in Griffiths, A. (ed.), *Stage Directions: Essays in Ancient Drama in Honour of E. W. Handley*. London: 81–6.

De Sanctis, D. (2016) 'The Meeting Scenes in the *Incipit* of Plato's Dialogue', in Cornelli, G. (ed.), *Plato's Styles and Characters: Between Literature and Philosophy*. Berlin: 119–35.

Detienne, M. (1994) *The Gardens of Adonis: Spices in Greek Mythology*. Princeton.

Dettori, E. (2000) *Filita grammatico: testimonianze e frammenti*. Rome.

Dickie, M. W. (2001a) 'Mimes, Thaumaturgy, and the Theatre'. *CQ* 51: 599–603.

Dickie, M. W. (2001b) *Magic and Magicians in the Greco-Roman World*. London.

Diels, H. and Kranz, W. (1951–2) *Die Fragmente der Vorsokratiker*. 3 vols. 6th ed. Berlin.

Diggle, J. (1981a) *Euripides: Fabulae, II*. Oxford.

Diggle, J. (1981b) *Studies on the Text of Euripides: Supplices, Electra, Heracles, Troades, Iphigenia in Tauris, Ion*. Oxford.

Dobrov, G. W. (1997) 'Language, Fiction, and Utopia', in Dobrov, G. W. (ed.), *The City as Comedy: Society and Representation in Athenian Drama*. Chapel Hill, NC: 95–132.

Dorandi, T. (1999) *Antigone de Caryste: Fragments*. Paris.

Dorandi, T. (2005) 'Accessioni a Antigono di Caristo'. *SCO* 51: 119–33.

Dunbar, N. (1995) *Aristophanes: Birds*. Oxford.

Dunn, F. M. (2017) 'Euripides and His Intellectual Context', in McClure, L. K. (ed.), *A Companion to Euripides*. Chichester: 447–67.

Edgar, C. C. (1925) *Zenon Papyri: Catalogue général des antiquités égyptiennes du Musée du Caire*, Vol. 1: *(Cat. 79)*. Cairo.

Edwards, M. (1991) *The Iliad: A Commentary*, Vol. 5. Cambridge.

Elsner, J. (2014) 'Lithic Poetics: Posidippus and His Stones'. *Ramus* 43.2: 152–72.

Erskine, A. (1995) 'Culture and Power in Ptolemaic Egypt: The Museum and Library of Alexandria'. *G&R* 42: 38–48.

Evans, R. J. W. and Marr, A. (eds.) (2006) *Curiosity and Wonder from the Renaissance to the Enlightenment*. Aldershot.

Fantuzzi, M. and Hunter, R. L. (2004) *Tradition and Innovation in Hellenistic Poetry*. Cambridge.

Faraone, C. A. (1987) 'Hephaestus the Magician and Near Eastern Parallels for Alcinous' Watchdogs'. *GRBS* 28: 257–80.

Bibliography

Faulkner, A. (2011) 'The Collection of the *Homeric Hymns*: From the Seventh to the Third Centuries BC', in Faulkner, A. (ed.), *The Homeric Hymns: Interpretative Essays*. Oxford: 175–205.
Fearn, D. (2007) *Bacchylides: Politics, Performance, Poetic Tradition*. Oxford.
Fearn, D. (2017) *Pindar's Eyes: Visual and Material Culture in Epinician Poetry*. Oxford.
Fisher, R. K. (1995) 'The Concept of Miracle in Homer'. *Antichthon* 29: 1–14.
Flashar, H. (1972) *Aristoteles: Mirabilia*. Berlin.
Flores, S. O. (2018) 'The Development of Critias in Plato's Dialogues'. *CP* 113: 162–88.
Folch, M. (2013) 'Unideal Genres and the Ideal City: Comedy, Threnody, and the Making of Citizens in Plato's *Laws*', in Peponi, A.-E. (ed.), *Performance and Culture in Plato's Laws*. Cambridge: 339–67.
Folch, M. (2015) *The City and the Stage: Performance, Genre, and Gender in Plato's Laws*. Oxford.
Ford, A. L. (1992) *Homer: The Poetry of the Past*. Ithaca, NY.
Ford, A. L. (2002) *The Origins of Criticism: Literary Culture and Poetic Theory in Classical Greece*. Princeton.
Fornara, C.W. (1971) 'Evidence for the Date of Herodotus' Publication'. *JHS* 91: 25–34.
Fraser P. M. (1972a) *Ptolemaic Alexandria*, Vol. 1. Oxford.
Fraser P. M. (1972b) *Ptolemaic Alexandria*, Vol. 2. Oxford.
Frede, D. (2010) 'Puppets on Strings: Moral Psychology in *Laws* Books 1 and 2', in Bobonich, C. (ed.), *Plato's Laws: A Critical Guide*. Cambridge: 108–26.
Gabba, E. (1981) 'True and False History in Classical Antiquity'. *JRS* 71: 50–62.
Gallagher, C. and Greenblatt, S. (2000) *Practicing New Historicism*. Chicago.
Gerolemou, M. (2018) *Recognizing Miracles in Antiquity and Beyond*. Berlin and Boston.
Giannini A. (1963) 'Studi sulla paradossografia greca, I: Da Omero a Caliimaco, motivi e forme del meraviglioso'. *RIL* XCVII: 247–66.
Giannini, A. (1964) 'Studi sulla paradossografia greca, II: Da Callimaco all'età imperial: la letteratura paradossografica'. *Acme* 17: 99–140.
Giannini, A. (1966) *Paradoxographorum Graecorum reliquiae*. Milan.
Gibert, J. C. (2019) *Euripides: Ion*. Cambridge.
Gilhuly, K. (2009) *The Feminine Matrix of Sex and Gender in Classical Athens*. Cambridge.
Gilula, D. (1981) 'Who's Afraid of Rope-Walkers and Gladiators? (Terence, *Hec.* 1–57)'. *Athenaeum* 59: 29–37.
Gilula, D. (2002) 'Entertainment at Xenophon's *Symposium*'. *Athenaeum* 90.1: 207–13.
Giraud, M. H. (1987) 'Les Oiseaux dans l'*Ion* d'Euripide'. *RPh* 61: 83–94.
Gocer, A. (1999) 'The Puppet Theater in Plato's Parable of the Cave'. *CJ* 95.2: 119–29.
Goldberg, S. M. (2013) *Terence: Hecyra*. Cambridge.

Bibliography

Gonzalez, F. J. (2003) 'How to Read a Platonic Prologue: *Lysis* 203A–207D', in Michelini, A. N. (ed.) *Plato as Author: The Rhetoric of Philosophy.* Leiden.

González, J. M. (2013) *The Epic Rhapsode and His Craft: Homeric Performance in a Diachronic Perspective.* Washington, DC.

Gotthelf, A. (2012) *Teleology, First Principles, and Scientific Method in Aristotle's Biology.* Oxford.

Gould, J. (1989) *Herodotus.* London.

Gow, A. S. F. (1954) 'Asclepiades and Posidippus: Notes and Queries'. *CR* 68: 195–200.

Gow, A. S. F. and Page, D. L. (1965) *The Greek Anthology: Hellenistic Epigrams,* Vol. 2. Cambridge.

Gowers, E. (2012) *Horace: Satires Book 1.* Cambridge.

Gray, V. J. (2001) 'Herodotus' Literary and Historical Method: Arion's Story (1.23–24)'. *AJP* 122: 11–28.

Green P. (1970) *Armada from Athens.* New York.

Greenblatt, S. (1990) 'Resonance and Wonder'. *Bulletin of the American Academy of Arts and Sciences* 43.4: 11–34.

Greenblatt, S. (1991) *Marvelous Possessions: The Wonder of the New World.* Oxford.

Grenfell, B. P. and Hunt, A. S. (1899) *The Oxyrhynchus Papyri,* Vol. 2. London.

Griffiths, E. M. (2017) '*Ion:* An Edible Fairy Tale?', in McClure, L. K. (ed.), *A Companion to Euripides.* Chichester: 228–42.

Gunderson, E. (2009) *Nox Philologiae: Aulus Gellius and the Fantasy of the Roman Library.* Madison, WI.

Gutzwiller K. J. (1986) 'The Plant Decoration on Theocritus' Ivy-Cup'. *AJP* 107: 253–5.

Gutzwiller, K. J. (2002) 'Art's Echo: The Tradition of Hellenistic Ecphrastic Epigram', in Harder, M. A., Regtuit, R. F. and Wakker, G. C. (eds.), *Hellenistic Epigrams.* Groningen: 85–112.

Gutzwiller, K. J. (2007) *A Guide to Hellenistic Literature.* Oxford.

Habinek, T. N. (1990) 'Sacrifice, Society, and Vergil's Ox-Born Bees', in Griffith, M. and Mastronarde, D. J. (eds.), *Cabinet of the Muses: Essays on Classical and Comparative Literature in Honor of Thomas G. Rosenmeyer.* Atlanta: 209–23.

Hall, E. (1987) 'The Geography of Euripides' *Iphigenia among the Taurians*'. *AJP* 108: 427–33.

Hall, E. (1989) 'The Archer Scene in Aristophanes' *Thesmophoriazusae*'. *Philologus* 133: 38–54.

Hall, E. (2012) *Adventures with Iphigenia in Tauris: A Cultural History of Euripides' Black Sea Tragedy.* Oxford.

Hall, E. (2020) 'Aristophanes' Birds as Satire on Athenian Opportunists in Thrace', in Rosen, R. M. and Foley, H. P. (eds.), *Aristophanes and Politics: New Studies.* Leiden: 187–213.

Halliwell S. (1986) *Aristotle's Poetics.* London.

Bibliography

Halliwell, S. (1987) *The Poetics of Aristotle*. London.
Halliwell, S. (2011) *Between Ecstasy and Truth: Interpretations of Greek Poetics from Homer to Longinus*. Oxford.
Hansen, W. (1996) *Phlegon of Tralles' Book of Marvels*. Exeter.
Harb, L. (2020) *Arabic Poetics: Aesthetic Experience in Classical Arabic Literature*. Cambridge.
Harder, M. A. (2012) *Callimachus: Aetia, Vols. 1 and 2*. Oxford.
Hardie, P. R. (2009) *Paradox and the Marvellous in Augustan Literature and Culture*. Oxford.
Harte, V. (2007) 'Language in the Cave', in Scott, D. (ed.), *Maieusis: Essays on Ancient Philosophy in Honour of Myles Burnyeat*. Oxford: 195–215.
Hartigan, K. (1991) *Ambiguity and Self Deception: The Apollo and Artemis Plays of Euripides*. Frankfurt am Main.
Hartog F. (1980) *Le miroir d'Hérodote: essai sur la représentation de l'autre*. Paris.
Hartog, F. (1988) *The Mirror of Herodotus: The Representation of the Other in the Writing of History*. Berkeley.
Hauben H. (1984–6) 'Onagres et hémionagres en Transjordanie au IIIe s. av. J. C. À propos d'une lettre de Toubias'. *AncSoc* 15–17: 89–111.
Hedreen, G. (2011) '*Bild*, Mythos, and Ritual: Choral Dance in Theseus's Cretan Adventure on the François Vase'. *Hesperia* 80: 491–510.
Hedreen, G. (2013) 'The Semantics of Processional Dithyramb: Pindar's *Second Dithyramb* and Archaic Athenian Vase-Painting', in Kowalzig, B. and Wilson, P. (eds.), *Dithyramb in Context*. Oxford: 171–97.
Heiden, B. (1998) 'The Simile of the Fugitive Homicide, *Iliad* 24.480–84: Analogy, Foiling and Allusion'. *AJP* 119: 1–10.
Herington J. (1985) *Poetry into Drama: Early Tragedy and the Greek Poetic Tradition*. Berkeley.
Hersey, G. L. (2009) *Falling in Love with Statues: Artificial Humans from Pygmalion to the Present*. Chicago.
Hilton, J. L. (2011) 'On Isopsephic Lines in Homer and Apollonius of Rhodes'. *CJ* 106.4: 385–94.
Hilton, J. L. (2013) 'The Hunt for Acrostics by Some Ancient Readers of Homer'. *Hermes* 141.1: 88–95.
Hoekstra, A. (1989) 'Books XIII–XVI', in Heubeck A. and Hoekstra, A. (eds.), *A Commentary on Homer's Odyssey, II: Books IX–XVI*. Oxford.
Hoffer, S. E. (1996) 'Violence, Culture, and the Workings of Ideology in Euripides' *Ion*'. *ClAnt* 15: 289–318.
Holford-Strevens, L. (1982) 'Fact and Fiction in Aulus Gellius'. *LCM* VII: 65–68.
Holford-Strevens, L. (1988) *Aulus Gellius: An Antonine Scholar and His Achievement*. London.
Hornblower, S. (2002) *The Greek World, 479–323 BC*. 3rd ed. London.

Bibliography

Hornblower, S. (2004) *Thucydides and Pindar: Historical Narrative and the World of Epinikian Poetry.* Oxford

Hornblower, S. (2008) *A Commentary on Thucydides*, Vol. 3: *Books 5.25–8.109.* Oxford.

Howie J. G. (1983) 'The Revision of Myth in Pindar *Olympian* 1: The Death and Revival of Pelops (25–27, 36–66)', reprinted in Howie J. G. (2012) *Exemplum and Myth, Criticism and Creation: Papers on Early Greek Literature.* Prenton: 161–90.

Howley, J. A. (2018) *Aulus Gellius and Roman Reading Culture: Text, Presence, and Imperial Knowledge in the Noctes Atticae.* Cambridge.

Hubbard, T. K. (1997) 'Utopianism and the Sophistic City in Aristophanes', in Dobrov, G. W. (ed.), *The City as Comedy: Society and Representation in Athenian Drama.* Chapel Hill, NC: 23–50.

Hubbell H. M. (1935) 'Ptolemy's Zoo'. *CJ* 31: 68–76.

Hughes, A. (2008) 'Αἱ Διονυσιάζουσαι: Women in Greek Theatre'. *BICS* 51: 1–27.

Hunter, R. L. (1992) 'Callimachus and Heraclitus'. *MD* 28: 113–23.

Hunter, R. L. (1999) *Theocritus: A Selection.* Cambridge.

Hunter V. (1986) 'Thucydides, Gorgias, and Mass Psychology'. *Hermes* 114: 412–29.

Hunzinger, C. (1993) 'L'étonnement et l'émerveillement chez Homère: les mots de la famille de *thauma*'. *Revue des Etudes Grecques* 106: 17–9.

Hunzinger, C. (1995). 'La notion de θῶμα chez Hérodote'. *Ktèma* 20: 47–70.

Hunzinger, C. (2015) 'Wonder', in Destrée, P. and Murray, P. (eds.), *A Companion to Ancient Aesthetics.* Chichester: 422–37.

Hunzinger, C. (2018) 'Perceiving *Thauma* in Archaic Greek Epic', in Gerolemou, M. (ed.), *Recognizing Miracles in Antiquity and Beyond.* Berlin and Boston: 259–73.

Huss, B. (1997) 'In Xenophontis Symposium obseruatiunculae criticae'. *ICS* 22: 43–50.

Huss, B. (1999) *Xenophons Symposion: ein Kommentar.* Stuttgart.

Hutchinson G. O. (1988) *Hellenistic Poetry.* Oxford.

Jacob, C. (1983) 'De l'art de compiler à la fabrication du merveilleux. Sur la paradoxographie grecque'. *LALIES* 2: 121–40.

Jacob, C. (2000) 'Athenaeus the Librarian', in Braund, D. C. and Wilkins, J. (eds.), *Athenaeus and His World: Reading Greek Culture in the Roman Empire.* Exeter: 85–110.

Jacob, C. (2013a) 'Fragments of a History of Ancient Libraries', in König, J., Oikonomopoulou, K. and Woolf, G. (eds.), *Ancient Libraries.* Cambridge: 57–81.

Jacob, C. (2013b) *The Web of Athenaeus.* Washington, DC.

Jacoby, F. (1913) 'Herodotos'. *RE Suppl.* 2: 205–520.

Johnson, W. (1998) 'Dramatic Frame and Philosophic Idea in Plato'. *AJP* 119.4: 577–98.

Bibliography

Johnstone, S. (2014) 'A New History of Libraries and Books in the Hellenistic Period'. *ClAnt* 33: 347–93.

Joho, T. (2017) 'The Revival of the Funeral Oration and the Plague in Thucydides Books 6–7'. *GRBS* 57.1: 16–48.

Jones, C. P. (1991) 'Dinner Theater', in Slater, W. J. (ed.), *Dining in a Classical Context*. Ann Arbor: 185–98.

Jordan, B. (2000) 'The Sicilian Expedition Was a Potemkin Fleet'. *CQ* 50: 63–79.

Jordan, D. R. (2006) 'Patterns and Laughter in Euripides' *Helen*'. *Symbolae Osloenses* 81: 6–28.

Jouanna, J. (1992) 'Le statut du thauma chez les médecins de la Collection hippocratique', in Thivel, A. (ed.), *Le miracle grec*. Paris: 223–36.

Kahn, L. (1978) *Hermès passe ou les ambiguïtés de la communication*. Paris.

Kaklamanou, E. and Pavlou, M. (2016) 'Reading the Proemium of Plato's *Theaetetus*: Euclides in Action'. *GRBS* 56: 410–37.

Kallet, L. (2001) *Money and the Corrosion of Power in Thucydides: The Sicilian Expedition and Its Aftermath*. Berkeley.

Kannicht, R. (2004) *Tragicorum Graecorum Fragmenta, Vol. 5.1: Euripides*. Göttingen.

Karasmanis, V. (1988) 'Plato's *Republic*: The Line and the Cave'. *Apeiron* 21: 147–71.

Kareem, S. T. (2014) *Eighteenth-Century Fiction and the Reinvention of Wonder*. Oxford.

Karttunen, K. (2002) 'The Ethnography of the Fringes', in Bakker, E. J., de Jong, I. J. F. and van Wees, H. (eds.), *Brill's Companion to Herodotus*. Leiden: 457–74.

Kazantzidis, G. (2019) 'Introduction: Medicine and Paradoxography in Dialogue', in Kazantzidis, G. (ed.), *Medicine and Paradoxography in the Ancient World*. Berlin and Boston: 1–40.

Kennedy, G. A. (1991) *Aristotle On Rhetoric: A Theory of Civic Discourse*. Oxford.

Kenny, N. (1998) *Curiosity in Early Modern Europe: Word Histories*. Wiesbaden.

Kenny, N. (2004) *The Uses of Curiosity in Early Modern France and Germany*. Oxford.

Kenny, N. (2006) 'The Metaphorical Collecting of Curiosities in Early Modern France and Germany', in Evans, R. J. W. and Marr, A. (eds.), *Curiosity and Wonder from the Renaissance to the Enlightenment*. Aldershot: 43–62.

Keulen, W. (2004) 'Gellius, Apuleius, and Satire on the Intellectual', in Holford-Strevens, L. and Vardi, A. (eds.), *The Worlds of Aulus Gellius*. Oxford: 224–44.

Keulen, W. (2009) *Gellius the Satirist: Roman Cultural Authority in Attic Nights*. Leiden.

Keuls, E. (1978) *Plato and Greek Painting*. Leiden.

Bibliography

Kitchell, K. F. (1989) 'The Origin of Vergil's Myth of the Bugonia', in Sutton, R. F. (ed.), *Daidalikon: Studies in Memory of Raymond V. Schoder*. Wauconda: 193–206.

Klimek-Winter, R. (1993) *Andromedatragödien: Sophokles, Euripides, Livius Andronikos, Ennius, Accius*. Stuttgart.

Klotz, F. and Oikonomopoulou, K. (2011) 'Introduction', in Klotz, F. and Oikonomopoulou, K. (eds.), *The Philosopher's Banquet: Plutarch's Table Talk in the Intellectual Culture of the Roman Empire*. Oxford: 1–31.

König, J. (2007) 'Fragmentation and Coherence in Plutarch's *Sympotic Questions*', in König, J. and Whitmarsh, T. (eds.), *Ordering Knowledge in the Roman Empire*. Cambridge: 43–68.

König, J. and Whitmarsh, T. (eds.) (2007) *Ordering Knowledge in the Roman Empire*. Cambridge.

Konstan, D. (1997) 'The Greek Polis and Its Negations: Versions of Utopia in Aristophanes' *Birds*', in Dobrov, G. W. (ed.), *The City as Comedy: Society and Representation in Athenian Drama*. Chapel Hill, NC: 3–22.

Kosak, J. C. (2006) 'The Wall in Aristophanes' *Birds*', in Rosen, R. M and Sluiter, I. (eds.), *City, Countryside, and the Spatial Organization of Value in Classical Antiquity*. Leiden: 173–80.

Kosak, J. C (2017) '*Iphigenia in Tauris*', in McClure, L. K. (ed.), *A Companion to Euripides*. Chichester: 214–27.

Kowalzig, B. (2013) 'Dancing Dolphins: Dithyramb and Society in the Archaic Period', in Kowalzig, B. and Wilson, P. (eds.), *Dithyramb in Context*. Oxford: 31–58.

Krevans, N. (2004) 'Callimachus and the Pedestrian Muse', in Harder, M. A., Regtuit, R. F., Wakker, G. C. (eds.), *Callimachus II*. Groningen: 173–84.

Krevans, N. (2005) 'The Editor's Toolbox: Strategies for Selection and Presentation in the Milan Epigram Papyrus', in Gutzwiller, K. J. (ed.), *The New Posidippus: A Hellenistic Poetry Book*. Oxford: 81–96.

Krevans, N. (2011) 'Callimachus' Philology', in Acosta-Hughes, B., Lehnus, L. and Stephens, S. A. (eds.), *Brill's Companion to Callimachus*. Leiden: 118–33.

Kroll, W. (1935) 'Θαυματοποιοί'. *RE* Suppl. VI: 1278–82.

Kurke, L. (2012) 'The Value of Chorality in Ancient Greece', in Papadopoulos, J. K. and Urton, G. (eds.), *The Construction of Value in the Ancient World*. Los Angeles: 218–35.

Kurke, L. (2013) 'Imagining Chorality: Wonder, Plato's Puppets, and Moving Statues', in Peponi, A.-E. (ed.), *Performance and Culture in Plato's Laws*. Cambridge: 123–70.

Kyriakou, P. (2006) *A Commentary on Euripides' Iphigenia in Tauris*. Berlin.

Kyselý, R. (2010) 'Breed Character or Pathology? Cattle with Loose Horns from the Eneolithic Site of Hostivice–Litovice (Czech Republic)'. *Journal of Archaeological Science* 37: 1241–46.

Bibliography

Lada-Richards, I. (2004) 'Authorial Voice and Theatrical Self-Definition in Terence and Beyond: The *Hecyra* Prologues in Ancient and Modern Contexts'. *G&R* 51.1: 55–82.
Lada-Richards, I. (2007) *Silent Eloquence: Lucian and Pantomime Dancing*. London.
Laks, A. and Most, G. W. (eds) (2016) *Early Greek Philosophy*. 9 vols. Cambridge, MA.
Lämmle, R. (2013) *Poetik des Satyrspiels*. Heidelberg.
Lämmle, R. (2019) 'Precarious *Choreia* in Satyr Play'. *BICS* 62.2: 29–48.
Lather, A. (2017) 'The Sound of Music: The Semantics of Noise in Early Greek Hexameter'. *Greek and Roman Musical Studies* 5: 127–46.
Lebrère, M. (2015) 'L'artialisation des sons de la nature dans les sanctuaires à automates d'Alexandrie, du IIIe s. av. J.-C. au Ier s. apr. J.-C.'. *Pallas* 98: 31–53.
Lee, K. (1997) *Euripides: Ion*. Warminster.
Leigh, M. (2013) *From Polypragmon to Curiosus: Ancient Concepts of Curious and Meddlesome Behaviour*. Oxford.
Lemon, L. T. and Reis, M. J. (1965) *Russian Formalist Criticism: Four Essays*. Lincoln, NE.
Lennox, J. G. (2001) *Aristotle: On the Parts of Animals*. Oxford.
Lightfoot, J. (2019a) 'Galen's Language of Wonder: *Thauma*, Medicine and Philosophy in *On Prognosis* and *On Affected Parts*', in Kazantzidis, G. (ed.), *Medicine and Paradoxography in the Ancient World*. Berlin and Boston: 163–82.
Lightfoot, J. (2019b) 'Textual Wanderings: Homeric Scholarship and the Written Landscape of Strabo's *Geography*'. *AJP* 140.4: 671–97.
Lightfoot, J. L. (2002) 'Nothing to Do with the τεχνῖται of Dionysus?', in Easterling, P. E. and Hall, E. (eds.), *Greek and Roman Actors: Aspects of an Ancient Profession*. Cambridge: 209–24.
Lightfoot, J. L. (2009) *Hellenistic Collection: Philitas, Alexander of Aetolia, Hermesianax, Euphorion, Parthenius*. Cambridge, MA.
Lindermann, J.-O. (2006) *Aulus Gellius Noctes Atticae, Buch 9: Kommentar*. Berlin.
Llewelyn, J. (1988) 'On the Saying that Philosophy Begins in *Thaumazein*', in Benjamin, A. (ed.), *Post-Structuralist Classics*. London: 173–91.
Lloyd-Jones, H. (1996) *Sophocles: Fragments*. Cambridge, MA.
Lloyd-Jones, H. and Parsons, P. (1983) *Supplementum Hellenisticum*. Berlin.
Lonsdale, S. H. (1993) *Dance and Ritual Play in Greek Religion*. Baltimore.
Loraux, N. (1986) *The Invention of Athens: The Funeral Oration in the Classical City*. Cambridge, MA.
Loraux N. (1990) 'Kreousa the Autochthon: A Study of Euripides' *Ion*', in Winkler, J. J. and Zeitlin, F. I. (eds.), *Nothing to Do with Dionysos? Athenian Drama in Its Social Context*. Princeton: 168–206.
Lucas, D. W. (1968) *Aristotle: Poetics*. Oxford.

Bibliography

Luz, C. (2010) *Technopaignia, Formspiele in der griechischen Dichtung*. Leiden.
Maass, E. (1892) *Commentariorum in Aratum reliquiae*. Berlin.
Macleod C. W. (1982) *Iliad: Book XXIV*. Cambridge.
Macleod C. W. (1983) *Collected Essays*. Oxford.
Manakidou, F. P. (2012) 'Philitas, Theocritus, and Thorny Plants: A Reconsideration of Their Relationship'. *Prometheus* 1: 107–27.
Marshall, C. W. (2000) 'Female Performers on Stage? (*PhV* 96 [*RVP* 2/33])'. *Text and Presentation* 21: 13–25.
Marshall, C. W. (2003) 'Sophocles' *Nauplius* and Heron of Alexandria's Mechanical Theatre', in Sommerstein, A. H. (ed.), *Shards from Kolonos: Studies in Sophoclean Fragments*. Bari: 261–79.
Marshall, C. W. (2009) 'Sophocles' *Chryses* and the Date of *Iphigenia in Tauris*', in Cousland, J. R. C. and Hume, J. R. (eds.), *The Play of Texts and Fragments: Essays in Honour of Martin Cropp*. Leiden: 141–56.
Marshall, C. W. (2014) *The Structure and Performance of Euripides' Helen*. Cambridge.
Martin, G. (2018) *Euripides, Ion*. Berlin and Boston.
Martin, J. (1974) *Scholia in Aratum Vetera*. Stuttgart.
Martin, R. P. (2005) 'Pulp Epic: The *Catalogue* and the *Shield*', in Hunter, R. L. (ed.), *The Hesiodic Catalogue of Women: Constructions and Reconstructions*. Cambridge: 153–75.
Mayer, R. (1994) *Horace: Epistles, Book I*. Cambridge.
McAvoy, M. (1996) 'Carnal Knowledge in the *Charmides*'. *Apeiron* 29: 63–103.
McCabe, M. M. (2007) 'Looking Inside Charmides' Cloak: Seeing Others and Oneself in Plato's *Charmides*', in Scott, D. (ed.), *Maieusis: Essays on Ancient Philosophy in Honour of Myles Burnyeat*. Oxford: 1–19.
McCarter, S. A. (2015) *Horace between Freedom and Slavery: The First Book of Epistles*. Madison, WI.
McCoy, M. B. (2008) *Plato on the Rhetoric of Philosophers and Sophists*. Cambridge.
McCoy, M. B. (2009) 'Alcidamas, Isocrates, and Plato on Speech, Writing, and Philosophical Rhetoric'. *AncPhil* 29: 45–66.
McPhee, B. D. (2017) 'Apollo, Dionysus, and the Multivalent Birds of Euripides' *Ion*'. *CW* 110.4: 475–89.
Mette, H. J. (1960) '"Schauen" und "Staunen"'. *Glotta* 39: 49–71.
Meyer, D. (2007) 'The Act of Reading and the Act of Writing in Hellenistic Epigram', in Bing, P. and Bruss, J. S. (eds.), *Brill's Companion to Hellenistic Epigram*. Leiden: 187–210.
Meyer, S. S. (2015) *Plato Laws 1 and 2*. Oxford.
Milanezi, S. (2004) 'À l'ombre des acteurs: les amuseurs à l'époque classique', in Hugoniot, C., Hurlet F. and Milanezi, S. (eds.), *Le statut de l'acteur dans l'Antiquité grecque et romaine*. Tours: 183–209.
Monoson, S. S. (2012) 'Dionysius I and Sicilian Theatrical Traditions in Plato's *Republic*: Representing Continuities Between Democracy and Tyranny', in

Bibliography

Bosher, K. (ed.), *Theater Outside Athens: Drama in Greek Sicily and South Italy*. Cambridge: 156–72.
Moore, K. (2014) 'Plato's Puppets of the Gods: Representing the Magical, the Mystical and the Metaphysical'. *Arion* 22.2: 37–72.
Moran, R. (1996) 'Artifice and Persuasion: The Work of Metaphor in the *Rhetoric*', in Rorty, A. O. (ed.), *Essays on Aristotle's Rhetoric*. Berkeley: 385–98.
Morgan, K. A. (2012) 'A Prolegomenon to Performance in the West', in Bosher, K. (ed.), *Theater Outside Athens: Drama in Greek Sicily and South Italy*. Cambridge: 35–55.
Morgan, L. (1999) *Patterns of Redemption in Virgil's Georgics*. Cambridge.
Morgan, T. J. (2011) 'The Miscellany and Plutarch', in Klotz, F. and Oikonomopoulou, K. (eds.), *The Philosopher's Banquet: Plutarch's Table Talk in the Intellectual Culture of the Roman Empire*. Oxford: 49–73.
Morris S. P. (1992) *Daidalos and the Origins of Greek Art*. Princeton.
Moulton C. (1981) *Aristophanic Poetry*. Göttingen.
Muir, J. V. (2001) *Alcidamas: The Works and Fragments*. London.
Munson, R. V. (2001) *Telling Wonders: Ethnographic and Political Discourse in the Work of Herodotus*. Ann Arbor.
Murphy, S. (1995) 'Heron of Alexandria's *On Automaton-Making*'. *HTechn* 17: 1–44.
Murphy, T. M. (2004) *Pliny the Elder's Natural History: The Empire in the Encyclopedia*. Oxford.
Musso, O. (1976) 'Sulla struttura del cod. *Pal. gr.* 398 e deduzioni storico-letterarie'. *Prometheus* 2: 1–10.
Musso O. (1977) *Michele Psello: Nozioni paradossali*. Naples.
Musso, O. (1985) *[Antigonus Carystius]: Rerum mirabilium collectio*. Naples.
Nails, D. (2002) *The People of Plato: A Prosopography of Plato and Other Socratics*. Indianapolis.
Naas, V. (2004) '*Opera mirabilia in terris* et *Romae operum miracula* dans l'*Histoire naturelle* de Pline l'Ancien', in Bianchi, O and Thévenaz, O. (eds.), *Conceptions et représentations de l'extraordinaire dans le monde antique*. Bern: 253–64.
Naas, V. (2011) 'Imperialism, *Mirabilia* and Knowledge: Some Paradoxes in the *Naturalis Historia*', in Gibson, R. K. and Morello, R. (eds.), *Pliny the Elder: Themes and Contexts*. Leiden: 57–70.
Neer, R. T. (2010) *The Emergence of the Classical Style in Greek Sculpture*. Chicago.
Neer, R. T. and Kurke, L. (2019) *Pindar, Song, and Space: Towards a Lyric Archaeology*. Baltimore.
Nenci G. (1957/8) 'La concezione del miracoloso nei poemi omerici'. *AAT* XCII: 275–311.

Bibliography

Nesselrath, H-G. (2014) 'Ancient Comedy and Historiography: Aristophanes Meets Herodotus', in Olson, S. D. (ed.), *Ancient Comedy and Reception: Essays in Honor of Jeffrey Henderson*. Berlin and Boston: 51–61.

Nichols, A. (2018) 'Ctesias' *Indica* and the Origins of Paradoxography', in Gerolemou, M. (ed.), *Recognizing Miracles in Antiquity and Beyond*. Berlin and Boston: 3–16.

Nightingale, A. W. (2002) 'Distant Views: "Realistic" and "Fantastic" Mimesis in Plato', in Annas, J. and Rowe, C. (eds.), *New Perspectives on Plato, Modern and Ancient*. Cambridge, MA: 227–48.

Nightingale, A. W. (2004) *Spectacles of Truth in Classical Greek Philosophy: Theoria in Its Cultural Context*. Cambridge.

ní Mheallaigh, K. (2014) *Reading Fiction with Lucian: Fakes, Freaks and Hyperreality*. Cambridge.

O'Brien, M. J. (1988) 'Pelopid History and the Plot of *Iphigenia in Tauris*'. *CQ* 38: 98–115.

Olsen, S. (2017) 'The Fantastic Phaeacians: Dance and Disruption in the *Odyssey*'. *ClAnt* 36: 1–32.

Olson, S. D. and Sens, A. (1999) *Matro of Pitane and the Tradition of Epic Parody in the Fourth Century BCE: Text, Translation, and Commentary*. Atlanta, GA.

O'Rourke, F. (2006) 'Aristotle and the Metaphysics of Metaphor'. *Proceedings of the Boston Area Colloquium of Ancient Philosophy* 21.1: 155–90.

O'Sullivan, N. (1992) *Alcidamas, Aristophanes and the Beginnings of Greek Stylistic Theory*. Stuttgart.

Packman Z. M. (1991) 'The Incredible and the Incredulous: The Vocabulary of Disbelief in Herodotus, Thucydides, and Xenophon'. *Hermes* 119: 399–414.

Padel, R. (1974) 'Imagery of the Elsewhere: Two Choral Odes of Euripides'. *CQ* 24: 227–41.

Page, D. L. (1981) *Further Greek Epigrams*. Cambridge.

Pajón Leyra, I. (2011) *Entre ciencia y maravilla: el género literario de la paradoxografía griega*. Zaragoza.

Pajón Leyra, I. (2014) 'Little Horror Stories in an Oxyrhynchus Papyrus: A Re-edition and Commentary of *P. Oxy.* II 218'. *APF* 60: 304–30.

Pajón Leyra, I. and Sánchez Muñoz, L. (2015) 'The Magnetic Stone of Posidippus' Poem Nr. 17: The Earliest Description of Magnetic Polarity in Hellenistic Egypt'. *ZPE* 195: 30–7.

Parker, H. N. (1996) 'Plautus vs. Terence: Audience and Popularity Re-examined'. *AJP* 117.4: 585–617.

Parker, L. P. E. (1997) *The Songs of Aristophanes*. Oxford.

Parker, L. P. E. (2016) *Euripides: Iphigenia in Tauris*. Oxford.

Passmore, O. (2018) 'Thaumastic Acoustics: Typhoeus and "Ty-phonics" in Pindar, *Pythian* 1.26 and Hesiod, *Theogony* 834'. *Mnemosyne* 71.5: 733–49.

Pavlou, M. (2012) 'Bacchylides 17: Singing and Usurping the Paean'. *GRBS* 52.4: 510–39.

Bibliography

Pelling, C. B. R. (1997) 'East Is East and West Is West – Or Are They? National Stereotypes in Herodotus'. *Histos* 1: 51–66.

Pelling, C. B. R (2000a) 'Fun with Fragments: Athenaeus and the Historians', in Braund, D. and Wilkins, J. (eds.), *Athenaeus and His World: Reading Greek Culture in the Roman Empire*. Exeter: 171–90.

Pelling, C. B. R (2000b) *Literary Texts and the Greek Historian*. London.

Pelling, C. B. R. (2016) 'Herodotus' Persian Stories: Narrative Shape and Historical Interpretation'. *Syllecta Classica* 27: 65–92.

Peponi, A.-E. (2009) 'Χορεία and Aesthetics in the *Homeric Hymn to Apollo*: The Performance of the Delian Maidens (Lines 156–64)'. *ClAnt* 28: 39–70.

Pfeiffer, R. (1949) *Callimachus, Vol. 1: Fragmenta*. Oxford.

Pfeiffer, R. (1968) *History of Classical Scholarship from the Beginnings to the End of the Hellenistic Age*. Oxford.

Platnauer M. (1938) *Iphigenia in Tauris*. Oxford

Platt, P. G. (1997) *Reason Diminished: Shakespeare and the Marvelous*. Lincoln.

Platt, V. (2011) *Facing the Gods: Epiphany and Representation in Graeco-Roman Art, Literature, and Religion*. Cambridge.

Porter, J. I. (1992) 'Hermeneutic Lines and Circles: Aristarchus and Crates on the Exegesis of Homer', in Lamberton, R. and Keaney, J. J. (eds.), *Homer's Ancient Readers: The Hermeneutics of Greek Epic's Earliest Exegetes*. Princeton: 67–114.

Poulakos, J. and Crick, N. (2012) 'There is Beauty Here, Too: Aristotle's Rhetoric for Science'. *Ph&Rh* 45.3: 295–311.

Power, T. (2010) *The Culture of Kitharôidia*. Cambridge, MA.

Power, T. (2011) 'Cyberchorus: Pindar's Κηληδόνες and the Aura of the Artificial', in Athanassaki, L. and Bowie, E. (eds.), *Archaic and Classical Choral Song: Performance, Politics and Dissemination*. Berlin: 67–113.

Prier R. A. (1989) *Thauma Idesthai: The Phenomenology of Sight and Appearance in Archaic Greek*. Tallahassee.

Priestley, J. (2014) *Herodotus and Hellenistic Culture: Literary Studies in the Reception of the Histories*. Oxford.

Prioux, É. (2009) 'On the Oddities and Wonders of Italy: When Poets Look Westward', in Harder, M. A., Regtuit, R. F. and Wakker, G. (eds.), *Nature and Science in Hellenistic Poetry*. Leuven: 121–48.

Pulitani, G., Caldana, I., Busato, R., Schiavon, F., Conti, G., Rampazzo, E. and Vidale, M. (2017) 'Performances of (and on) Greek Potter's Wheels: An Experimental Project'. *Eidola* 14: 35–56.

Race, W. H. (1988) *Classical Genres and English Poetry*. London.

Radt, S. (1999) *Tragicorum Graecorum Fragmenta*, Vol. 4: *Sophocles*. Göttingen.

Redfield J. (1985) 'Herodotus the Tourist'. *CP* 90: 97–118.

Reece, A. S. (1998) 'Drama, Narrative, and Socratic *Eros* in Plato's *Charmides*'. *Interpretation* 26: 65–76.

Bibliography

Reeve, C. D. R. (2006) 'A Study in Violets: Alcibiades in the *Symposium*', in Lesher, J. H., Nails, D. and Sheffield, F. C. C. (eds.), *Plato's Symposium: Issues in Interpretation and Reception*. Cambridge, MA: 124–46.

Reinhardt, K. (1960) *Tradition und Geist: Gesammelte Essays zur Dichtung*. Göttingen.

Rice E. E. (1983) *The Grand Procession of Ptolemy Philadelphus*. Oxford.

Richardson, N. J. (1993) *The Iliad: A Commentary*, Vol. 6. Cambridge.

Richardson, N. J. (2010) *Three Homeric Hymns: To Apollo, Hermes and Aphrodite*. Cambridge.

Robert, L. (1929) 'Epigraphica VIII: au théâtre de Delphes'. *REG* 42.198: 427–38.

Roby, C. (2016) *Technical Ekphrasis in Greek and Roman Science and Literature: The Written Machine between Alexandria and Rome*. Cambridge.

Rocco, A. (1954) *Corpus Vasorum Antiquorum, Italia 24: Napoli, Museo Nazionale 3*. Rome.

Rogkotis, Z. (2006) 'Thucydides and Herodotus: Aspects of Their Intertextual Relationship', in Rengakos, A. and Tsakmakis, A. (eds.), *Brill's Companion to Thucydides*. Leiden: 57–86.

Romm J. S. (1992) *The Edges of the Earth in Ancient Thought: Geography, Exploration, and Fiction*. Princeton.

Ronca, I. (1992) '*Semper Aliquid Novi Africam Adferre*: Philological Afterthoughts on the Plinian Reception of a Pre-Aristotelian Saying'. *Akroterion* 37: 146–58.

Rood, T. (1998) *Thucydides: Narrative and Explanation*. Oxford.

Rood, T. (1999) 'Thucydides' Persian Wars', in Kraus, C. S. (ed.), *The Limits of Historiography: Genre and Narrative in Ancient Historical Texts*. Leiden: 141–68.

Rood, T. (2006) 'Herodotus and Foreign Lands', in Dewald, C. and Marincola, J. (eds.), *The Cambridge Companion to Herodotus*. Cambridge: 290–305.

Rothwell, K. S. (2007) *Nature, Culture, and the Origins of Greek Comedy: A Study of Animal Choruses*. Cambridge.

Rouveret, A. (1989) *Histoire et imaginaire de la peinture ancienne (Ve siècle av. J. C.–Ier siècle ap. J. C.)*. Rome.

Rudd, N. (1993) 'Horace as a Moralist', in Rudd, N. (ed.), *Horace 2000: A Celebration – Essays for the Bimillennium*. Ann Arbor: 64–88.

Rudebusch, G. (2002) 'Dramatic Prefiguration in Plato's *Republic*'. *Ph&Lit* 26: 75–83.

Rusten, J. (2013) 'The Mirror of Aristophanes: The Winged Ethnographers of *Birds* (1470–93, 1553–64, 1694–1705)', in Bakola, E., Prauscello, L. and Telò, M. (eds.), *Greek Comedy and the Discourse of Genres*. Cambridge: 298–315.

Rutherford, R. B. (1982) 'Tragic Form and Feeling in the *Iliad*'. *JHS* 102: 145–60.

Sandbach, F. H. (1982) 'How Terence's *Hecyra* Failed'. *CQ* 32.1: 134–5.

Bibliography

Sansone, D. (1975) 'The Sacrifice-Motif in Euripides' *IT*'. *TAPA* 105: 283–95.
Sbardella, L. (2000) *Filita: testimonianze e frammenti poetici*. Rome.
Scanlon, T. F. (1994) 'Echoes of Herodotus in Thucydides: Self-Sufficiency, Admiration, and Law'. *Historia* 43: 143–76.
Schaeffer, D. (1999) 'Wisdom and Wonder in *Metaphysics* A: 1–2'. *The Review of Metaphysics* 52.3: 641–56.
Schäfer, A. (1997) *Unterhaltung beim griechischen Symposion: Darbietungen, Spiele und Wettkämpfe von homerischer bis in spätklassische Zeit*. Mainz.
Schepens, G. and Delcroix, K. (1996) 'Ancient Paradoxography: Origin, Evolution, Production and Reception', in Pecere, O. and Stramaglia, A. (eds.), *La letteratura di consumo nel mondo greco-latino*. Cassino: 373–460.
Schmid, W. and Stählin, O. (1920–4) *Geschichte der griechischen Literatur*. Munich.
Schofield, M. (2007) 'Metaspeleology', in Scott, D. (ed.), *Maieusis: Essays on Ancient Philosophy in Honour of Myles Burnyeat*. Oxford: 216–31.
Schofield, M. (2016) 'Plato's Marionette'. *Rhizomata* 4.2: 128–53.
Scodel, R. (1996) 'Δόμων ἄγαλμα: Virgin Sacrifice and Aesthetic Object'. *TAPA* 126: 111–28.
Scullard H. H. (1974) *The Elephant in the Greek and Roman World*. Ithaca, NY.
Segvic, H. (2006) 'Homer in Plato's *Protagoras*'. *CP* 101: 247–62.
Shannon-Henderson, K. E. (2020) 'Constructing a New Imperial Paradoxography: Phlegon of Tralles and His Sources', in König, A., Langlands, R. and Uden, J. (eds.), *Literature and Culture in the Roman Empire, 96–235: Cross-Cultural Interactions*. Cambridge: 159–78.
Shelmerdine, S. C. (1981) *The Homeric Hymn to Hermes: A Commentary (1–114) with Introduction*. PhD thesis, University of Michigan at Ann Arbor.
Shershow, S. C. (1995) *Puppets and 'Popular' Culture*. Ithaca, NY.
Shklovsky, V. (1916) 'Art as Technique', translated in Lemon, L. T. and Reis, M. J. (eds.) (1965) *Russian Formalist Criticism: Four Essays*. Lincoln: 3–24.
Slater, N. W (1997) 'Performing the City in *Birds*', in Dobrov, G. W. (ed.), *The City as Comedy: Society and Representation in Athenian Drama*. Chapel Hill, NC: 75–94.
Slater, N. W. (2000) 'Religion and Identity in Pacuvius's *Chryses*', in Manuwald, G. (ed.), *Identität und Alterität in der frührömischen Tragödie*. Würzburg: 315–23.
Slater, W. J. (2004) 'Where Are the Actors?', in Hugoniot, C., Hurlet, F. and Milanezi, S. (eds.), *Le statut de l'acteur dans l'Antiquité grecque et romaine*. Tours: 143–60.
Smith, D. G. (2004) 'Thucydides' Ignorant Athenians and the Drama of the Sicilian Expedition'. *SyllClass* 15: 33–70.
Smith, M. (2004) 'Elusive Stones: Reading Posidippus' λιθικά through Technical Writing on Stones', in Acosta-Hughes, B., Kosmetatou, E. and

Bibliography

Baumbach, M. (eds.), *Labored in Papyrus Leaves: Perspectives on an Epigram Collection Attributed to Posidippus (P.Mil.Vogl. VIII 309)*. Cambridge, MA: 105–17.

Smith, S. D. (2014) *Man and Animal in Severan Rome: The Literary Imagination of Claudius Aelianus*. Cambridge.

Smith, A. H. and Pryce, F. N. (eds.) (1926) *Corpus Vasorum Antiquorum: Great Britain. British Museum 2*. London.

Snell, B. (1953) *The Discovery of Mind: The Greek Origins of European Thought*. Oxford.

Sommerstein, A. (1987) *Aristophanes: Birds*. Warminster.

Sommerstein, A. H. (1994) *Aristophanes: Thesmophoriazusae*. Warminster.

Spanoudakis, K. (2002) *Philitas of Cos*. Leiden.

Spivey, N. J. (1997) 'Bionic Statues', in Powell, A. (ed.), *The Greek World*. London: 442–59.

Squire, M. (2013) 'Ekphrasis at the Forge and the Forging of Ekphrasis: The "Shield of Achilles" in Graeco-Roman Word and Image'. *Word and Image* 29: 157–91.

Steiner, D. T. (1994) *The Tyrant's Writ: Myths and Images of Writing in Ancient Greece*. Princeton.

Steiner, D. T. (2001) *Images in Mind: Statues in Archaic and Classical Greek Literature and Thought*. Princeton.

Steiner, D. T. (2011) 'Dancing with the Stars: *Choreia* in the Third Stasimon of Euripides' *Helen*'. *CP* 106.4: 299–323.

Stephanis, I. E. (1988) *Dionysiakoi Technitai: Symboles stên prosôpographia tou theatrou kai tês mousikês tôn archaiôn Hellênôn*. Heraklion.

Stern, J. (2008) 'Paradoxographus Vaticanus', in Heilen, S. (ed.), *In Pursuit of Wissenschaft: Festschrift für William M. Calder III zum 75. Geburtstag*. Hildesheim: 437–66.

Stewart A. (1990) *Greek Sculpture: An Exploration*. New Haven.

Stramaglia, A. (2006) 'The Textual Transmission of Ancient Fantastic Fiction: Some Case Studies', in Hömke, N. and Baumbach, M. (eds.), *Fremde Wirklichkeiten: literarische Phantastik und antike Literatur*. Heidelburg: 289–310.

Sutton, D. F. (1984) *The Lost Sophocles*. Lanham, MD.

Swift, L. A. (2009) 'The Symbolism of Space in Euripidean Choral Fantasy (*Hipp.* 732–75, *Med.* 824–65, *Bacch.* 370–433)'. *CQ* 59: 364–82.

Swiggers, P. (1984) 'Cognitive Aspects of Aristotle's Theory of Metaphor'. *Glotta* 62: 40–5.

Taylor, M. C. (2010) *Thucydides, Pericles, and the Idea of Athens in the Peloponnesian War*. Cambridge.

Thalmann, W. G. (1993) 'Euripides and Aeschylus: The Case of the *Hekabe*'. *ClAnt* 12: 126–59.

Thein, K. (2014) 'Aristotle on Why Study Lower Animals: (*De partibus animalium*, I,5, 644b22–645a36)'. *Eirene* 50: 208–29.

Bibliography

Thomas, O. R. H. (2015) 'Sophocles, Seduction and Shrivelling: *Ichneutai* Fr. 316 Radt 65.1'. *CQ* 65.1: 364–5.

Thomas, O. R. H. (2020) *The Homeric Hymn to Hermes*. Cambridge.

Thomas, R. (2000) *Herodotus in Context: Ethnography, Science, and the Art of Persuasion*. Cambridge.

Tipton, J. A. (2014) *Philosophical Biology in Aristotle's* Parts of Animals. Heidelberg.

Todorov, T. (1970) *Introduction à la littérature fantastique*. Paris.

Torrance, I. (2011) 'In the Footprints of Aeschylus: Recognition, Allusion, and Metapoetics in Euripides. *AJP* 132: 177–204.

Torrance, I. (2013) *Metapoetry in Euripides*. Oxford.

Trendall A. D. (1952) 'Paestan Pottery: A Revision and a Supplement'. *PBSR* 10: 1–53.

Trendall, A. D. (1967a) *The Red-Figured Vases of Lucania, Campania and Sicily*, Vol. 1. Oxford.

Trendall, A. D. (1967b) *The Red-Figured Vases of Lucania, Campania and Sicily*, Vol. 2. Oxford.

Trendall A. D. (1967c) *Phlyax Vases*. 2nd ed. London.

Trendall, A. D. (1987) *The Red-Figured Vases of Paestum*. London.

Trivigno, F. V. (2011) 'Philosophy and the Ordinary: On the Setting of Plato's *Lysis*'. *GRBS* 51.1: 61–85.

Tschemplik, A. (1993) 'Framing the Question of Knowledge: Beginning Plato's *Theaetetus*', in Press, G. A. (ed), *Plato's Dialogues: New Studies and Interpretations*. Lanham: 169–78.

Turkeltaub, D. (2003) *The Gods' Radiance Manifest: An Examination of the Narrative Pattern Underlying the Homeric Divine Epiphany Scenes*. PhD thesis, Cornell University, Ithaca, NY.

Tybjerg, K. (2003) 'Wonder-Making and Philosophical Wonder in Hero of Alexandria'. *SHPS* 34.3: 443–66.

Vanotti, G. (2007) *Aristotele: Racconti meravigliosi*. Milan.

Vardi, A. (2004) 'Genre, Conventions, and Cultural Programme in Gellius' *Noctes Atticae*', in Holford-Strevens, L. and Vardi, A. (eds.), *The Worlds of Aulus Gellius*. Oxford 159–86.

Vergados, A. (2007) 'The *Homeric Hymn to Hermes* 51 and Antigonus of Carystus'. *CQ* 57.2: 737–42.

Vergados, A. (2011) 'The *Homeric Hymn to Hermes*: Humour and Epiphany', in Faulkner, A. (ed.), *The Homeric Hymns: Interpretative Essays*. Oxford: 82–104.

Vergados, A. (2013) *The Homeric Hymn to Hermes: Introduction, Text and Commentary*. Berlin.

Vernant J. P. (1983) *Myth and Thought among the Greeks*. London.

Vickers, M. J. (1999) *Ancient Greek Pottery*. Oxford.

Voutiras, E. (2000) 'La cadavre et le serpent, ou l'héroïsation manquée de Cléomène de Sparte', in Pirenne-Delforge, V. and Suárez de la Torre, E.

Bibliography

(eds.), *Héros et héroïnes dans les mythes et les cultes grecs*. Liège: 377–94.

Warmington, E. H. (1936) *Remains of Old Latin II: Livius Andronicus, Naevius, Pacuvius, Accius*. Cambridge, MA.

Warren, J. (2014) *The Pleasures of Reason in Plato, Aristotle, and the Hellenistic Hedonists*. Cambridge.

Welser, C. S. (2009) 'Two Didactic Strategies at the End of Herodotus' *Histories* (9.108–122)'. *ClAnt* 28: 359–85.

Wenskus, O. (2000) 'Paradoxographoi', in *Der Neue Pauly 9*. Stuttgart: 309–12.

West, M. L. (2003) *Homeric Hymns, Homeric Apocrypha, Lives of Homer*. Cambridge, MA.

Westermann, A. (1839) *Paradoxographoi: Scriptores rerum mirabilium Graeci*. Braunschweig.

White, S. A. (1992) 'Aristotle's Favorite Tragedies', in Rorty, A. O. (ed.), *Essays on Aristotle's Poetics*. Princeton: 221–40.

Whitman, C. H. (1974) *Euripides and the Full Circle of Myth*. Cambridge, MA.

von Wilamowitz-Moellendorff, U. (1881) *Antigonos von Karystos*. Berlin.

von Wilamowitz-Moellendorff, U. (1883) 'Die beiden Elektren'. *Hermes* 18: 214–63.

Wilberding, J. (2004) 'Prisoners and Puppeteers in the Cave'. *OSAPh* 27: 117–39.

Wilkins, J. (2000) 'Dialogue and Comedy: The Structure of the *Deipnosophistae*', in Braund, D. C. and Wilkins, J. (eds.), *Athenaeus and His World: Reading Greek Culture in the Roman Empire*. Exeter: 23–37.

Wilson, P. J. (2003) 'The Sound of Conflict: Kritias and the Culture of μουσική in Athens', in Dougherty, C. and Kurke, L. (eds.), *The Cultures within Ancient Greek Culture: Contact, Conflict, Collaboration*. Cambridge: 181–206.

Winnington-Ingram R. P. (1969) 'Euripides: *Poiêtês Sophos*'. *Arethusa* 2: 127–42.

Wohl, V. (2004) 'Dirty Dancing: Xenophon's *Symposium*', in Murray, P. and Wilson, P. J. (eds.), *Music and the Muses: The Culture of Mousike in the Classical Athenian City*. Oxford: 337–63.

Wolff, C. (1992) 'Euripides' *Iphigenia among the Taurians*: Aetiology, Ritual, and Myth'. *ClAnt* 11: 308–34.

Woolf, G. (2011) *Tales of the Barbarians: Ethnography and Empire in the Roman West*. Chichester.

Woolf, G. (2013) 'Introduction: Approaching the Ancient Library', in König, J., Oikonomopoulou, K. and Woolf, G. (eds.), *Ancient Libraries*. Cambridge: 1–20.

Wright, M. (2005) *Euripides' Escape-Tragedies: A Study of Helen, Andromeda, and Iphigenia Among the Taurians*. Oxford.

Wright, M. (2006) '*Cyclops* and the Euripidean Tetralogy'. *PCPhS* 52: 23–48.

Young, D. C. (1968) *Three Odes of Pindar: A Literary Study of Pythian 11, Pythian 3 and Olympian 7*. Leiden.

Bibliography

Zacharia, K. (2003) *Converging Truths: Euripides' Ion and the Athenian Quest for Self-Definition*. Leiden.

Zanker, G. (2004) *Modes of Viewing in Hellenistic Poetry and Art*. Madison, WI.

Zeitlin, F. I. (1989) 'Mysteries of Identity and Designs of the Self in Euripides'. *Ion*'. *PCPhS* 35: 144–97.

Zeitlin, F. I. (1990) 'Thebes: Theater of Self and Society in Athenian Drama', in Winkler, J. J. and Zeitlin, F. I. (eds.), *Nothing to Do with Dionysos? Athenian Drama in Its Social Context*. Princeton: 130–67.

Zeitlin, F. I. (2011) 'Sacrifices Holy and Unholy in Euripides' *Iphigenia in Tauris*', in Prescendi, F. and Volokhine, Y. (eds.), *Dans le laboratoire de l'historien de religions: mélanges offerts à Philippe Borgeaud*. Geneva: 459–66.

Zeitlin, F. I. (2012) 'A Study in Form: Three Recognition Scenes in the Three Electra Plays'. *Lexis* 30: 361–78.

Zetzel, J. E. G. (1981) *Latin Textual Criticism in Antiquity*. New York.

Ziegler, K. (1949) 'Paradoxographoi'. *RE* 18.3: 1137–66.

SUBJECT INDEX

aesthetic response, 2, 11, 18, 98
aetiology
    and *thauma*, 70–1, 83, 97, 101, 105
agalma, 18, 20–1, 27
Agatharchides of Cnidus, 50, 53
Alcidamas, 29–30
Alexandria, 47, 51, 53, 56
anagnorisis. See recognition
animate/inanimate, 19, 20, 29, 34, 36, 88, 89, 193, 194, 203, 204, 209
Antigonus of Carystus, 42–5, 47–9, 54–7, 81–2, 83–8
    and authorial comment in the *Collection of Marvellous Investigations*, 73
    use of source texts, 72–8
Apollonius Paradoxographus, 49, 218
Archelaus the Egyptian/of Chersonesus, 42, 43, 54–7
Aristeas of Proconnesus, 217–18
Aristophanes, 142–58
Aristotle
    biological works, 69–70, 72–8, 85
    influence on Shklovsky's conception of defamiliarisation, 10, 141
    on language and *thauma*, 138–42
    on learning and wonder, 139–41
    on metaphor, 139–41
    on myth and *thauma*, 118
    on philosophy and *thauma*, 1, 69, 118
    on pleasure and wonder, 10, 139–41
    on the wonder of the natural world, 70, 84
    on tragedy and wonder, 117–18, 127–8
Athens, 132, 152, 156, 158, 160
    as *thauma*, 15, 141, 143, 149, 161–6
automata, 202–5, 208–14
autopsy, 47, 61, 129, 147, 163, 164, 222

belief/disbelief, 14, 58, 74, 104, 110, 118, 125–7, 128–32, 147–9

Callimachus, 50
    and wonder in the *Aitia*, 70–1
    as paradoxographer, 47–9
Callixeinus of Rhodes, 54
causes, 38, 69, 72, 73, 78, 79, 209
choreia, 13, 91, 98–100, 101
Critias, 26–8, 31
Ctesias of Cnidus, 48, 218
curiosity, 4, 26, 58, 69, 109, 118

dance, 13, 34, 89, 106, 177
deception, 26, 93, 119, 142, 172, 181, 188, 190, 192, 194
defamiliarisation, 9–10, 14, 72, 138–42, 155, 158, 159, 173, 196, 199
Democritus, 207–8

edges of the earth, 12, 59–65, 111, 123, 133, 143–4, 148, 149–52, 155
    and *thauma* in Herodotus, 59–65
ekphrasis, 12, 32–41, 133–4, 203
ekplexis, 3–5, 14, 30, 160, 172, 187
Epicureanism, 205
epigram, 38–41, 43, 54–7
    and *Ergänzungsspiel*, 78
    and paradoxography, 56, 57, 78–9
epiphany, 13, 19, 20, 37, 83, 95, 97, 98, 101–6, 108, 112–15, 212–13
epitaphioi logoi, 162–6
eros, 15, 19, 22, 31, 167
eschatiai. See edges of the earth
ethnography, 12, 15, 58–68, 149, 158, 160
    Aristophanic para-ethnography, 142, 145–9, 154–8
Euripides, 109–12, 119–37, 150–3
    and myth, 111, 122, 123–7, 130
    distant settings in, 110, 121–3, 130, 150–3
    'escape-plays', 110–11, 119–20, 151
    recognition scenes in, 110–11, 127, 136

Subject Index

familiar/unfamiliar, 109, 112, 132, 134, 137, 138, 140, 145, 161–2, 167
Formalism, 7, 9, 141

Gellius, 215–27
gods, 2, 13, 20–1, 33, 88–106, 112–15, 124–6, 155, 176, 181, 202, 204–5, 208–10, 211–13
Gorgias, 4, 158
Greenblatt, Stephen, 6–9

Hartog, François, 8
Hegesias of Magnesia, 218
Hephaestus
   crafting of wondrous objects, 3, 32, 33, 34, 36, 204–5
Hero of Alexandria, 208–14
Herodotus, 8–9, 12, 58–68, 119, 122, 144–9, 160, 217
   escalating sense of wonder in the *Histories*, 59, 60–1, 62, 64
   influence on paradoxography, 58–68
   on *thauma* and the edges of the earth, 59–65
   on wonder and wonders in the *Histories*, 58–68, 102–6
   reputation as a liar, 119
Hesiodic *Scutum*, 35–6
Homer, 31–5, 98–9, 108, 112–17, 163–4, 204–5, 224–5
Homeric Hymn to Apollo, 99–100
Homeric Hymn to Hermes, 82, 88–98, 100–1
Horace, 205–6

imperialism, 14, 15, 120, 142, 158–60, 161, 163, 167, 171
Isigonus of Nicaea, 218

kleos, 33–4, 163

learning, 109, 139–41
libraries, 46, 52, 53

mechanics, 210–14
metaphor, 139–41, 149, 156, 158
mimesis, 15, 37, 118, 132, 139–41, 173, 187–92, 193, 194, 200, 209, 214
mirabilia, 216–22, 224–6

miscellanistic texts, 40, 45, 68, 87, 215, 219, 226
music, 13, 81, 82, 96–8, 102–6, 177
Myrsilus of Methymna, 49
myth, 111, 117, 122, 123–7, 130, 132, 164

near/far, 69, 109, 111, 115–16, 121, 132–3, 142, 143, 161–2, 166–73, 186, 188, 191–2
Neer, Richard, 6, 17, 105
New Historicism, 6–9
nil admirari, 205–8
Nymphodorus, 50

Onesicritus of Astypalaea, 218

Paradoxographus Florentinus, 50
Paradoxographus Palatinus, 50, 85
Paradoxographus Vaticanus, 50
paradoxography, 10, 12, 16, 40, 42–57, 65–79, 81–8, 215–18
   and ethnography, 58–68
   arrangement and ordering of paradoxographical collections, 45, 46, 47, 60, 65–8, 73
   content of paradoxographical collections, 47–51
   defamiliarising effects in paradoxographical collections, 72
   purpose of paradoxographical collections, 51–2, 77–9
   similarities to epigram form, 57, 78–9
   titles of paradoxographical collections, 46–7
   verse paradoxography, 56
Peripatetics, 12, 40, 43, 49, 85, 200
   influence of Peripatetic writing on paradoxography, 68–78
perspective, 133, 173, 175, 187–92
Philitas of Cos, 85–8
Philo of Byzantium, 210, 213
philosophy
   thauma as the beginning of, 1, 26, 69–70, 78, 109, 118, 198
Philostephanus of Cyrene, 50, 218
Phlegon of Tralleis, 50
Pindar, 1, 125–7, 168, 199
pity, 108, 109, 112, 115, 117

Subject Index

Plato, 18–31, 174, 182–4, 192–8, 200–5
  Cave Allegory, 15, 174, 192–8, 201, 203, 205
  on philosophy and *thauma*, 1, 26, 109, 174
  on *thauma* and perspective, 133, 187–92
  on the dangers of *thauma*, 12, 26, 30–1, 109, 174, 178, 180, 192–8, 205
pleasure, 10, 29, 78, 139, 178–80, 192, 195
Pliny the Elder, 220–2
Polemon of Ilium, 50
Posidippus of Pella, 38–41, 78
Ps. Aristotle, *On Marvellous Things Heard*, 49, 66–7
Ptolemies
  collection of natural *thaumata*, 53–4
  court of, 55
puppets, 177, 192, 201–4
Pythagoras, 207

realism, 3, 34–5, 37, 214
recognition, 14, 69, 97, 108–11, 115–19, 127–32, 133, 136, 140, 205
refamiliarisation, 10, 159, 173, 196
rhetoric, 15, 138–42, 157–8, 167, 172–3
Rome, 180, 207, 215–27

semata, 13, 93–8
Shield of Achilles, 3, 33–5, 36, 163, 223
Shklovsky, Viktor, 9–10, 141
Sicily, 161
  Athenian expedition against, 15, 120, 158–62, 166–73

silence, 4, 29, 81
skiagraphia, 188–9
song, 92–3, 106
sophists, 4, 182–4, 189–92
Sophocles, 90–1, 122, 127, 144, 213
spectacle, 12, 91, 154, 168, 170, 177, 178, 180, 181, 186, 193, 195, 201, 206, 209
stasis, 3–5, 192, 197, 201
statues, 18, 20, 21, 26, 193
Stoicism, 205–8
symposium, 89, 92, 176, 181–7

textuality, 12, 16, 18, 28–30, 36–41, 45, 53, 57, 68, 79, 87, 215, 222–7
thauma idesthai, 3, 32, 33, 35, 204
thaumatopoiia, 16, 175–87, 191–8, 201, 203, 209
thaumatourgia, 16, 175–87, 209
theatre, 127, 132, 177–80, 206, 213–14
Theocritus, 36–8
Theophrastus of Eresus, 38, 85
Thucydides, 158–73

utopia, 13, 142, 153

vision, 3, 11, 12, 31–3, 58, 103, 113, 189, 195–6, 200
visual artworks, 17, 19, 29, 32–40, 194

Wunderkammer, 16

Xenophon, 181–7

INDEX LOCORUM

AELIAN
De natura animalium
2.7: 56 n.31
2.20: 77 n.58
7.5: 56 n.31
16.39: 54 n.27
17.45: 77 n.58

AESCHYLUS
Choephori
164–245: 110

AGATHARCHIDES OF CNIDUS
On the Erythraean Sea
fr. 1 Burstein: 53

ALCIDAMAS
On Sophists
27: 29
28: 30

ANTIGONUS OF CARYSTUS
Collection of Marvellous Investigations
1–6: 81
7–8: 80, 82, 84
15b: 218 n.18
18: 43
19: 43, 55–6, 87
21: 63 n. 43
26–115: 72–3
43: 64 n.65
60: 43, 73
73: 74–6
74: 74, 76–7
75: 43, 74, 77–8
88: 44
89: 42
90: 44
129–73: 48
129: 47 n.8, 48
145: 218 n.18
150: 218 n.18
164–6: 48–9
165–6: 218 n.18

APOLLONIUS PARADOXOGRAPHUS
Marvellous Investigations
2: 218 n.16
17: 218 n.18
20: 218 n.18

ARISTOPHANES
Birds
3: 143
9: 143
65: 143
68: 143
144–5: 143
145–8: 144
165: 144
275: 144
363: 159
416: 147
492–8: 156 n.30
550–2: 145
639: 159
712: 156 n.30
1125–9: 145–6
1130–41: 146–7
1164–7: 148
1199–224: 148
1337–71: 153
1372–409: 153
1410–69: 153
1470–81: 149
1470–93: 154–6
1482–93: 149
1553–64: 149, 156–7
1694–705: 149, 157–8

253

Index Locorum

ARISTOPHANES (cont.)
Frogs
  52–3: 119–20
  1309–12: 153
Thesmophoriazusae
  1060–1: 120 n.20
Wasps
  421: 158 n.33

ARISTOTLE
De generatione animalium
  734b9–14: 211 n.9
  746b8: 143 n.9
De motu animalium
  701b1–17: 211 n.9
De partibus animalium
  644b: 139 n.3
  644b29–645a17: 140 n.5
  644b-665a: 186 n.19
  645a15-17: 69–70, 84
  655a12–16: 77 n.57
  675a4: 76 n.56
Historia animalium
  507a34–6: 75
  507b34: 75
  508b10–12: 75–6
  516b9–11: 76
  517a20–3: 77
  517a28–9: 77
  517a29–30: 77
  536a: 90 n.18
  538b12: 85 n.6
  544b32: 85 n.6
  545a22: 85 n.6
  556b28–557a3: 44
  557b6–8: 44
  581a17: 85 n.6
  581b6: 85 n.6
  606b19: 143 n.9
  616a6–12: 64 n.45
Metaphysics
  982b12–15: 1, 140 n.5
  982b12–21: 69, 118, 186 n.19
  983a12–14: 211 n.9
Poetics
  1448b4–17: 139–40
  1452a4: 118 n.16
  1452a5–11: 128 n.33
  1452a32–b7: 127 n.32
  1454a2–4: 117 n.15
  1454a3–7: 127 n.32
  1455a16–18: 117–18 n.15
  1455a16–19: 128 n.33
  1455a16–21: 127 n.32
  1459a7: 140 n.4
  1461a31–5: 224 n.29
Rhetoric
  1371a31–b8: 139
  1404b8–14: 10, 138–9, 141
  1405a8–9: 139
  1410b10–13: 140
  1412a11–13: 140
  1460a 141 n.5
Topica
  126b17–24: 4 n.6

[ARISTOTLE]
On Marvellous Things Heard
  4: 67 n.48
  7: 67 n.48
  8: 67 n.48
  9–12: 66–8
  13: 67 n.48
  14: 67 n.48
  165: 63 n.43

ATHENAEUS
Deipnosophistae
  19e: 177
  129d: 182 n.14
  158e: 110 n.2
  197c–203b: 54
  221b: 56 n.31
  320a: 85 n.7
  409c: 43 n.2, 56 n.30, 56 n.31
  457a: 90 n.17
  561a: 110 n.2

BACCHYLIDES
  17.123: 105 n.,*48*

CALLIMACHUS
Aitia
  fr. 43–43a Harder: 71
  fr. 43b1–4 Harder: 71
Collection of Marvels from Every Land Arranged According to Places
  frs. 407–11 Pf.: 47–9

Index Locorum

CICERO
De finibus
   5.29.87: 207–8
Tusculan Disputations
   3.30: 206–7

DEMOCRITUS
   D295 LM = 68 B216 DK: 208 n.6
   D322 LM = 68 B215 DK: 208 n.6

DIODORUS SICULUS
   3.18.4: 53 n.26
   3.35.7: 77 n.58
   3.36–7: 53
   12.53.3: 4 n.7

DIOGENES LAERTIUS
   2.17: 56 n.30
   5.2.43: 85 n.7

ENNIUS
Annales
   457: 216 n.14

Etymologicum Magnum
   443.37–48: 3 n.5

EURIPIDES
Andromeda
   fr. 145 *TrGF* Kannicht: 111 n.5
Electra
   508–84: 110
Hecuba
   560: 19 n.4
Helen
   549: 4
   1108–10: 153
   1478–9: 153 n.25
   1479–82: 153 n.25
   1491–4: 153 n.25
Hippolytus
   715–31: 150
   732–4: 150
   736–7: 150
   746–7: 151
Ion
   24: 132 n.36
   158–9: 135
   162: 135
   171: 135
   184–218: 133
   190–200: 133–4
   247–8: 135
   251: 132 n.36
   262–3: 135 n.39
   384–5: 132 n.36
   585–6: 132–3, 188 n.22
   645: 132 n.36
   1141–5: 134
   1202–6: 135–6
   1278: 132 n.36
Iphigenia among the Taurians
   1–9: 121–2
   30: 121
   380–91: 124–5
   388: 125
   636–901: 127
   759–87: 128
   793–7: 128–9, 130
   798–826: 128
   806–9: 129
   811: 129
   822–6: 129–30
   838–40: 130
   900–1: 131
   1089–105: 151–2
   1089–152: 151
   1095: 152
   1138–42: 152–3
   1317–24: 131
   1321: 131 n.35

GELLIUS
Noctes Atticae
   pr. 11: 219
   pr. 12: 219
   1.21: 225 n.32
   2.6: 225 n.32
   2.16: 225 n.32
   3.11: 225 n.32
   5.8: 225 n.32
   6.20: 225 n.32
   7.6: 216 n.14, 225 n.32
   8.5: 225 n.32
   9.4.1–5: 215–22
   9.4.2: 226
   9.4.6: 220
   9.4.7: 221

Index Locorum

GELLIUS (cont.)
  9.4.12: 226
  9.9: 225 n.32
  9.10: 225 n.32
  10.12.1–6: 226
  10.12.8–10: 211 n.9
  10.16: 225 n.32
  13.27: 225 n.32
  14.6.1–3: 222–5
  14.6.3–4: 223
  14.6.5: 225
  16.6: 225 n.32
  17.10: 225 n.32

GORGIAS
  Palamedes
    4: 4

HERO OF ALEXANDRIA
  Peri Automatopoietikes
    1.1: 211
    1.7: 211
    3.1–19.5: 212
    4.1: 212 n.11
    4.2: 212 n.12
    20.1–5: 213
    21.1: 214
    22.1: 214
    22.3–4: 214
    22.5: 214
    22.6: 214
  Pneumatica
    1.proem.12–17: 211
    1.12: 213
    1.17: 213
    1.38: 213
    2.21: 213
    2.3: 213

HERODOTUS
  Histories
    1.1: 119
    1.23–4: 102–5
    1.178–9: 145–6
    2.35: 62
    2.75: 61–2
    3.98–105: 60
    3.102: 60
    3.106: 59–60, 65
    3.107: 60–1
    3.108: 62
    3.109: 62
    3.110: 63
    3.111: 63–4
    3.112: 64
    3.113: 64–5
    3.114: 65
    3.115: 151 n.23
    3.116: 65
    4.13–16: 217
    4.103: 122
    4.199: 224 n.29

HESIOD
  Theogony
    500: 134
    834: 32 n.27
  Works and Days
    365: 88–9

[HESIOD]
  Scutum
    140: 35
    160: 35
    165: 35
    218: 35
    232–3: 35
    244: 35
    314–20: 35–6

HOMER
  Iliad
    5.724–5: 32
    10.158: 224
    10.439–40: 32
    15.286: 95 n.26
    15.290: 95 n.26
    18.82–4: 32
    18.83: 3
    18.372–7: 32, 204
    18.417–18: 204
    18.462–7: 33
    18.467: 36, 163 n.40
    18.494–6: 34
    18.539: 34
    18.548–9: 3 n.3, 34–5
    20.267–72: 224 n.29
    20.344: 95 n.26

Index Locorum

23.186: 223 n.27
23.222: 116
24.352–467: 114
24.471–87: 107
24.477: 113
24.479: 112
24.480–1: 112
24.483: 113, 114 n.9
24.483–4: 112
24.486: 114, 116
24.507: 116
24.629–32: 115
Odyssey
  1.381–2: 32 n.27
  1.441–2: 223 n.26, 225 n.31
  4.43–4: 32
  4.86: 223 n,29
  4.638–9: 32 n.27
  7.142–5: 113 n.7
  7.203: 156
  8.261–5: 98–9
  10.326: 3 n.4
  11.13–15: 155
  11.15–19: 155
  15.44–5: 223 n.25
  14.45: 224
  18.410–11: 32 n.27
  19.36: 95 n.26
  19.40: 95 n.26
  20.268–9: 32 n.27
  22.128: 223 n.24
  22.137: 223 n.24

HOMERIC HYMN TO APHRODITE
  84–5: 97 n.33

HOMERIC HYMN TO APOLLO
  134–9: 97 n.33
  149–64: 99–100
  414–15: 97 n.33

HOMERIC HYMN TO DIONYSUS
  34: 37, 97 n.33
  38–41: 37
  50: 97 n.33

HOMERIC HYMN TO HERMES
  3–12: 92 n.21
  28: 89

30–8: 88–9
38: 90
40: 90
42: 90
51: 80
52: 90
52–9: 92
79–81: 93–4
80: 93
86: 94
55: 94
218–25: 94–5
342–3: 95
439–46: 96–7
440: 93
455: 97
475–8: 89 n.14

HORACE
  Epistles
    1.6.1–8: 205–6
  Satires
    1.5.104: 220 n.20

HYGINUS
  Fabulae
    120–1: 123 n.25

MACROBIUS
  Saturnalia
    3.15.8: 47 n.5, 221 n.23

MATRO OF PITANE
  Attic Dinner Party
    fr. 1.121 Olson-Sens: 182 n.14

OPPIAN
  Cynegetica
    2.90–5: 77 n.58

PARADOXOGRAPHUS PALATINUS
  20: 84–5

PHILITAS OF COS
  fr. 18 Sb.: 80

PINDAR
  Olympian 1
    1.28: 1, 119, 199

PINDAR (cont.)
    1.28–9: 125–6
    1.30–5: 126
    1.36–40: 126
    1.36–53: 125 n.30
  Pythian 1
    1.26: 32 n.27
  Pythian 3
    3.20: 168
    3.22: 168

PLATO
  Charmides
    153a: 23 n.14
    154b–d: 17, 19–21
    154d: 21–2
    154e: 22
    155a: 28 n.19
    155c–d: 22
    159b: 27
    160e: 27
    161b: 27
    162b: 27 n.18
    162c–d: 27
  Euthydemus
    271c: 186 n.20
    276d: 5, 186 n.20
    283a–b: 186 n.20
    286b–c: 186 n.20
    288a–b: 186 n.20
    294a: 186 n.20
    294e: 186 n.20
    295a: 186 n.20
  Hippias Major
    282c: 182
    282d: 183
    282e: 183
  Ion
    535b: 183
    535b–e: 183 n.15
    535d–e: 183–4
  Laches
    181b: 24
  Laws
    644d–e: 201–2
    645a: 202
    658a: 178–9
    658b–c: 179
    658d: 179–80

    739a: 201
  Menexenus
    235a–b: 165
  Meno
    80a–b: 197 n.35
  Phaedrus
    252d: 20 n.8
    274b–278e: 28
    275d: 29 n.20
  Republic
    514a–b: 174–5, 192–8
    514c–515a: 193
    515a: 196–7
    532b–c: 198
    598a–d: 191 n.25
    602c–d: 188–9
  Sophist
    234b–c: 189–91
    235a–b: 191–2
  Symposium
    215b: 21 n.8, 197 n.35
    215d: 21 n.8, 197 n.35
    216c: 21 n.8, 197 n.35
    216d: 197 n.35
    216e–217a: 21 n.8
    217a: 197 n.35
    219c: 197 n.35
    220a–b: 24 n.15, 197 n.35
    220c: 24 n.15, 197 n.35
    221a–c: 24
    221c: 197 n.35
    222a: 21 n.8
  Theaetetus
    142b: 23
    143e–144b: 24–5
    154c: 25
    155c: 25–6
    155d: 1, 26, 198
  Timaeus
    20e: 28 n.19

PLINY THE ELDER
  Natural History
    7.9–26: 221
    8.77: 56 n.31
    8.218: 56 n.31
    11.125: 77 n.58
    31.12: 47 n.5, 221 n.23
    31.51: 47 n.5, 221 n.23

Index Locorum

PLUTARCH
Lycurgus
    19.2: 178
Moralia
    44b: 207

POLYBIUS
Histories
    12.13.9: 211 n.9

POSIDIPPUS OF PELLA
Lithika
    13 AB: 39–40
    15 AB: 39–40
    17 AB: 39–40

SCHOLIA TO HOMER
Iliad
    3.126–7: 34 n.29
    10.158: 224 n.30
    20.269–72: 224 n.29
    23.186: 225 n.31
Odyssey
    1.441–2: 225 n.31
    4.86: 224 n.29
    15.45: 224 n.30
    22.128: 225 n.31

SENECA THE YOUNGER
Epistulae
    8.5: 207

SOPHOCLES
Chryses
    frs. 726–9 *TrGF* Radt: 122
Ichneutai
    229–30: 91 n.20
    249–50: 91
    278: 91
    299–300: 91
Tyro
    fr. 654 *TrGF* Radt: 144

STRABO
Geography
    1.3.16: 207
    1.3.21: 208
    14.2.19: 86
    16.4.5–7: 53 n.26
    17.1.5: 53 n.26
    17.1.14: 43 n.2

TERENCE
Hecyra
    2–3: 180
    4–5: 180
    34: 180

THEOCRITUS
Idylls
    1.29–31: 37
    1.56: 36

THEOGNIS
    1229–30: 90 n.17

THEOPHRASTUS
Characters
    6.4: 179 n.9
    27.7: 179 n.9

THUCYDIDES
History
    1.10.2–3: 164
    2.39.4: 163 n.39
    2.41.1: 163
    2.41.3–4: 162–4, 171
    3.104: 84 n.2
    6.1.1: 161
    6.11.4: 166–7
    6.12.2: 169
    6.13.1: 167
    6.16.2: 169
    6.16.3: 169
    6.20.3: 170
    6.24.1: 167
    6.24.2: 167
    6.24.3: 167–8
    6.30–1: 170
    6.31.1: 170
    6.31.4: 170
    6.31.6: 170
    6.46.4: 172 n.50
    7.55.2: 171
    7.56.2: 171
    7.63.3: 171, 172 n.49
    7.70.6: 172
    7.71.7: 172

Index Locorum

TZETZES
Chiliades
   2.35.154: 46

VARRO
De re rustica
   2.3.5: 56 n.31
   3.2.4: 56 n.31
   3.12.4–5: 56 n.31
   3.16.4: 56 n.30, 56 n.31

VIRGIL
Georgics
   4.281–314: 87 n.12
   4.538–58: 87 n.12

VITRUVIUS
De architectura
   8 pr.1: 110 n.2

XENOPHON
Symposium
   2.1: 181–2
   7.2: 184
   7.3–4: 185–7

ZENON PAPYRI
   I 59075: 54 n.27

Lightning Source UK Ltd.
Milton Keynes UK
UKHW020519060921
390052UK00009B/88